W9-API-593

The Great Fashion Designers

The Great Fashion Designers

From Chanel to McQueen, the names that made fashion history

Brenda Polan and Roger Tredre

BLOOMSBURY VISUAL ARTS
LONDON • NEW YORK • OXFORD • NEW DELHI • SYDNEY

BLOOMSBURY VISUAL ARTS
Bloomsbury Publishing Plc
50 Bedford Square, London, WC1B 3DP, UK
1385 Broadway, New York, NY 10018, USA

BLOOMSBURY, BLOOMSBURY VISUAL ARTS and the Diana logo are trademarks of Bloomsbury Publishing Plc

First published in Great Britain by Berg in 2009
This edition published by Bloomsbury Visual Arts 2020

Copyright © Brenda Polan and Roger Tredre, 2020

Brenda Polan and Roger Tredre have asserted their right under the Copyright, Designs and
Patents Act, 1988, to be identified as Authors of this work.

For legal purposes the Acknowledgements on p. vii constitute an extension of this copyright page.

Cover design: Adriana Brioso
Cover image © Dominique Charriau/WireImage

All rights reserved. No part of this publication may be reproduced or transmitted in any form or by
any means, electronic or mechanical, including photocopying, recording, or any information storage
or retrieval system, without prior permission in writing from the publishers.

Bloomsbury Publishing Plc does not have any control over, or responsibility for, any third-party websites
referred to or in this book. All internet addresses given in this book were correct at the time of going to
press. The author and publisher regret any inconvenience caused if addresses have changed or sites
have ceased to exist, but can accept no responsibility for any such changes.

A catalogue record for this book is available from the British Library.

A catalog record for this book is available from the Library of Congress.

ISBN: PB: 978-1-3500-9160-3
ePDF: 978-1-3500-9161-0
eBook: 978-1-3500-9163-4

Typeset by Deanta Global Publishing Services, Chennai, India
Printed and bound in India

To find out more about our authors and books visit www.bloomsbury.com and sign up for our newsletters.

Contents

Acknowledgements vii

Preface viii

Introduction x

Part One Early days 1

Introduction 2

1   Charles Frederick Worth 5

2   Callot Soeurs 11

3   Jeanne Paquin 17

4   Paul Poiret 23

5   Mariano Fortuny 29

Part Two 1910s–1930s 35

Introduction 36

6   Jeanne Lanvin 39

7   Gabrielle 'Coco' Chanel 45

8   Jean Patou 51

9   Madeleine Vionnet 57

10   Elsa Schiaparelli 63

11   Mainbocher 69

12   Adrian 75

13   Salvatore Ferragamo 81

14   Madame Alix Grès 87

Part Three 1940s–1950s 93

Introduction 94

15   Cristóbal Balenciaga 97

16   Christian Dior 103

17   Charles James 111

18   Claire McCardell 117

19   Hubert de Givenchy 123

20   Norman Norell 129

21   Pierre Cardin 135

22   Mary Quant 143

23   Rudi Gernreich 149

Part Four 1960s–1970s 155

Introduction 156

24   Yves Saint Laurent 159

25   André Courrèges 167

26   Valentino Garavani 175

27   Karl Lagerfeld 181

28   Halston 189

29   Kenzo 195

30   Ralph Lauren 201

31   Issey Miyake 207

32   Geoffrey Beene 213

33   Calvin Klein 219

34   Giorgio Armani 225

Part Five 1980s 231

Introduction 232

35   Rei Kawakubo 235

36   Yohji Yamamoto 243

37   Vivienne Westwood 249

38   Paul Smith 255

39   Azzedine Alaïa 261

40   Gianni Versace 267

41   Jean Paul Gaultier 273

42   Dolce & Gabbana 279

43   John Galliano 287

44   Donna Karan 293

Part Six 1990s 299

Introduction 300

45   Miuccia Prada 303

46   Martin Margiela 309

47   Marc Jacobs 315

48   Tom Ford 321

49   Alexander McQueen 327

50   Nicolas Ghesquière 333

Part Seven 2000s–2010s 339

Introduction 340

51   Raf Simons 345

52   Hedi Slimane 351

53   Phoebe Philo 357

54   Alessandro Michele 363

55   Demna Gvasalia 369

Bibliography 374

Acknowledgements

The authors gratefully wish to acknowledge the academics and fellow journalists who have been quoted and referenced in this book and the many who may not figure here but have, over the years, provided a basis of knowledge and insight upon which our own expertise is built. The history and culture of dress has become a well-explored field, but, in researching and writing this book, which is intended to inspire further study, we have concluded that, when it comes to fashion, among all the picture books, there are still plenty of gaps on the shelves, gaps that should be filled with real thought and analysis. There are many fascinating books, works of research and scholarship on the great fashion designers and their often equally interesting peers just begging for an author.

Very special thanks to Faith Marsland and Georgia Kennedy at Bloomsbury, and to the exceptional Benedetta Melini for her efficient, meticulous and enthusiastic research for this second edition. Having worked on the first edition with the celebrated fashion show photographer Christopher Moore, for this edition the authors were delighted to collaborate with Niall McInerney, a master of the Nikon FM2, whose archive forms the core of the Bloomsbury Fashion Archive. We acknowledge with gratitude additional research funding support from Central Saint Martins, University of the Arts London, for image research.

Brenda Polan would like to thank the many editors who have employed her to write about fashion, particularly Dame Liz Forgan who, as *The Guardian*'s women's editor, glanced across a crowded features room and plucked her off the late subbing shift and on to the front row at Yves Saint Laurent. She dedicates this book to her siblings, Anthony and Sonia, and to her travelling companion, Colin.

Roger Tredre would like to thank his former colleagues at *The Independent,* in particular Sarah Mower, Lisa Armstrong, Tamsin Blanchard and Marion Hume, and at *The Observer* and *WGSN*. Over fifteen years, he appreciated the support and encouragement of the late Louise Wilson at Central Saint Martins and, more recently, of Fabio Piras, Hywel Davies, Adam Murray and the ultimate roomie, David Kappo. A big thanks to the 200-plus MA students he has been fortunate to teach. Many thanks also to Oriole Cullen at the Victoria & Albert Museum for suggesting the inclusion of Callot Soeurs; to the brilliant Professor Caroline Evans for incisive notes on the Introduction; to Charlotte Brachtendorf, Reva Ochuba, Katharine Zarrella, Cecilia Alba Luè, Serena Buccoliero and Isabella Coraça Da Gama Vajano who all made helpful suggestions or provided research support. He dedicates this book to his parents and to his family – Jennifer, Olivia and Nicholas.

Preface

There are fifty-five designers in this book. Are they really the greatest designers of all time? Your call! Our selection was achieved only through much debate, sometimes learned and courteous, sometimes outrageous and fine wine-fuelled. We acknowledge the impossibility of achieving consensus for such a list. Creating a list of the all-time greats of fashion design is a wonderful parlour game that we hope all our readers can enjoy playing. Our choices reflect our careers and our personal interests, although not too much (we hope) our British nationality. And, yes, we wish we could have included Lucile, Jacques Fath, Edward Molyneux, Walter Albini, Pierre Balmain, Bill Gibb, Ossie Clark, Helmut Lang, Dries Van Noten, Stephen Jones, Michael Kors, Alexander Wang, Stella McCartney, Virgil Abloh and many more.

We began on this project modestly enough by simply planning to bring together in book form our collected interviews with designers over the years, published mostly in British newspapers and magazines. It was a comprehensive list, we thought, dating right back to Brenda Polan's interview with André Courrèges in August 1979 for *The Guardian*. They ranged from the detailed and in-depth (four interviews with John Galliano over a period of four months leading up to his spring/summer 1991 show in Paris) to the on the fly and brief (twenty minutes with Tom Ford backstage after a YSL menswear show in January 2001). In total, we have interviewed nineteen of the designers in this book (and many more who are not).

In his witty and insightful book *The Glass of Fashion*, Cecil Beaton wrote: 'Dressmakers … are apt to hate their *genus* and seldom meet one another, for jealousy, envy and rivalry consume them. With few exceptions they are a tiresome, unreliable brood. Almost all inarticulate, they have never invented their own vocabulary, and their abuse of the French words *chic* and *élégant* have almost robbed these adjectives of their significance.' Although we regretfully note that some designers do indeed live down to Beaton's critique, we found the names we've spoken to over the years were often articulate – particularly if you caught them away from the frenzy of the show season.

But our plan to turn our collected interviews into a book was abandoned after thoroughly rereading them. Although these interviews provide valuable insights into designers' thought processes and work methods, they are moments in time. Many of them read to us as outdated. The designers had moved on, and so had we. How much better, we thought, to write essays that summed up these designers' careers, drawing on our personal insights into their work and all those valuable transcripts gathered over the years. We also read widely, including the available books and academic literature and the wealth of interviews in newspapers and magazines (mostly in Britain and America) by our journalistic colleagues. We have endeavoured to cite all our sources accurately: if we have overlooked any reference, we will rectify it in future editions of this book.

The book evolved into a broader project as we debated the suitable subjects for inclusion. As we both segued in our respective careers during the early Noughties from the arena of journalism to the world of teaching at University of the Arts London, our interests broadened and deepened. Exploring the career of Karl Lagerfeld naturally led us to revisit the career of Chanel; likewise Nicolas Ghesquière and Demna Gvasalia prompted a rediscovery of Balenciaga.

We have endeavoured to produce the book we wish we had in our hands when we were feeling our way into fashion: a comprehensive introduction to the most important designers, with guidance for further reading, written in an accessible but authoritative style. The personalities of the designers are as interesting to us as their designs – the two often intertwine, most notably in the career and life of Chanel. Our book complete, we marvel at the constant capacity of fashion to renew itself and stay fresh. And we hope that you, the reader, enjoy sharing this with us.

Introduction

In 2001 the American fashion trade newspaper *Women's Wear Daily* (*WWD*) marked its ninetieth anniversary by asking fifty-three leading designers to list the three most important designers of the past ninety years. The results were fascinating, not perhaps for the runaway 'winners' (Coco Chanel with thirty-four votes and Yves Saint Laurent with twenty-nine), but for the other names cited and the explanations offered. Giorgio Armani cited Jean Paul Gaultier among his top three ('for his ability to make fashion ironic'). Nicolas Ghesquière included Issey Miyake ('he gave the Japanese concept of deconstruction a European femininity and sensibility'). More unpredictable names, who are also featured in this book, included Adrian and Rudi Gernreich. The ever-prolific Karl Lagerfeld, who received three citations himself, sent a five-page fax dividing the twentieth century into three distinct periods: 1905–1939 (Poiret, Vionnet and Chanel); 1945–1960 (Dior, Balenciaga and Chanel); and 1960–1970 (Courrèges, Saint Laurent, Vionnet, Chanel and Balenciaga).

The very earliest couturiers received barely a look-in, perhaps reflecting the short-term memory of fashion (although Alexander McQueen voted for Charles Frederick Worth). The constant interaction between craft and commerce was highlighted, and designers were quick to applaud fellow designers who were skilled at business and marketing as much as creativity. Influence was paramount. 'Who has the biggest influence?' declared Karl Lagerfeld. 'It's unimportant who is the most gifted.'

One means of determining influence is to ask the question: who is the most copied? Designers have had an equivocal attitude towards this issue from the very early days of couture, on the one hand threatening legal action against copyists, and on the other hand happy to sell models to upmarket stores for copying. Few have been as relaxed about the issue as Coco Chanel – or American designer Norman Norell, who provided working sketches of his 1960 culotte suit to the trade free of charge to ensure that his design would be copied properly. These days, designers often work directly with their biggest copyists, the fast fashion chain stores, in effect copying themselves by creating low-priced collections in short- or long-term retail linkups.

For the *WWD* survey, the designers were also asked to name the three most important designers since 1980: Karl Lagerfeld won the most votes, followed closely by Giorgio Armani, Rei Kawakubo, Jean Paul Gaultier and Tom Ford. Lagerfeld noted Chanel, Gucci and Prada but put fashion designers firmly in their place by referencing Nike, Levi's and Adidas. 'They are fashion for today, too, and worn by more people than the fashion of the fashion world we talk about.' Marc Jacobs brought the designers down to earth by recalling the celebrated comment from fellow American designer

Bill Blass that the words 'dress' and 'important' should never be mentioned in the same sentence. 'I'm going to paraphrase,' said Jacobs. 'The words "designer" and "important" should never be mentioned in the same sentence.'

This second edition takes into account the rapid changes of recent years, with the luxury fashion sector evolving into a hugely successful global industry. The sector remains dominated by European and American companies although scholars now rightly challenge the assumption that fashion is a purely European invention. This belief, originating with the German sociologist Georg Simmel in 1904, led conventional thinking for more than a century. Recently Carlo Belfanti has pointed out that China, India and Japan all at times had fashion systems similar to the Western model. While debating this point is beyond the scope of this book, we would point out that while the industry may be Eurocentric, its great designers are not always so and an even broader diversity of talent is likely to be a theme of the rest of the twenty-first century. A high proportion of current design graduates are Chinese or Korean, and a high proportion of the 'young designer' prizewinners are too. Many have the potential to make an impact.

For global success, they may well need to hook up with the juggernauts of international luxury in Europe such as LVMH and Kering. The modern fashion system remains tightly controlled by these Western companies – and the rest of the world has by and large heavily invested in their Western narrative. Magazines such as *Vogue* have helped to package the message and spread the word. It's a captivating sell: as Giorgio Riello and Peter McNeil note, European fashion history's allure is reinforced by dramatic and absorbing stories and narratives, many of which feature in this book. But it is clearly an unequal playing field: the established Western fashion houses hold the trump cards.

Recent years have also seen a wave of interest in the question of cultural appropriation. Fashion has appropriation at its very (romantic) heart and calls it inspiration, as Lou Taylor has pointed out. Coco Chanel herself was the ultimate *bricoleur*, believing it was her role to steal all the ideas she could. From Paul Poiret to John Galliano, Western designers have plundered the Asia-Pacific region and, in truth, scarcely an indigenous culture in the world has been left untapped. Designers, who are enchanted by the beauty and the history of clothing from other cultures, will continue to plunder, although perhaps with greater sensitivity.

The very word 'fashion' has also been questioned. Lou Taylor, writing in the journal *Fashion Theory*, suggests that 'dress' is more inclusive than fashion. Dress, she argues, is the means by which we express and negotiate identity. The creative pioneers who have steered the course of high-end fashion – the pioneers who are the focus of this book – understand this point intrinsically, although not all of them have influenced and affected the broader market for dress.

The last section in this book points the way forward for fashion, exploring the careers of the names who have dominated during the second decade of the twenty-first century. From Phoebe Philo, a woman designing for women, to Demna Gvasalia, a designer who plays the new marketing codes of fashion like a maestro, our choices will provoke debate. Our final choices of Gvasalia and Alessandro Michele followed a day-long seminar with MA Fashion Communication students at Central Saint Martins in November 2018, with a vote taken.

Over the past two decades, the meaning of the term 'designer' in relation to fashion has invited a wide variety of interpretations. From business moguls to celebrities to genuine creative geniuses, anyone can claim designer status. The industry was dominated by couturiers until the 1960s when the ready-to-wear *styliste* and *créateur* came to the fore. In more recent years, the broader interpretation of designer has made it challenging to define true greatness – many designers are only as good as the team behind them. Is the product manager a designer? Can the famous personality behind a celebrity brand be considered a designer? And where (as Joanne Entwistle has pointed out) is fashion truly 'made' – on the drawing board, by the fashion buyer, or by modern-day social media influencers and the stylists of upscale magazines? The debate intensified in May 2019 with the launch of Fenty, a new luxury label fronted by Barbadian music star Rihanna and backed by LVMH. For the purposes of this book, we have accepted an all-embracing interpretation of the word, covering skill sets ranging from pure design to brand management and marketing to pure business. In the final analysis, though, it is the *influence* of each individual designer that has driven our selection. Echoing Karl Lagerfeld's point to *WWD*, talent is not enough.

We have acknowledged the significance of commercial achievements in compiling our list. The success of British designer Paul Smith is as an Englishman creating an international fashion brand without the backing of a major luxury group. It gives him a unique status, surpassed only by Burberry. Success is founded, he says, on being '90 per cent businessman and 10 per cent designer'.

It may become even harder in the future to identify the skill sets of a designer. New technology makes design by computer a doddle. Even the once time-consuming process of research can be shrunk in an instant to a few hours on the internet. Not all designers have been proficient in all aspects of design, as Dean L. Merceron points out in his biography of Jeanne Lanvin. For years, Paul Smith referred to himself as a 'getter-togetherer of fashion' rather than as a designer. Jean Patou once famously said: 'I wouldn't know how to design. I couldn't even if I wanted to, for I can't draw, and a pair of scissors in my hands becomes a dangerous weapon.'

The skills needed to be a fashion designer are certainly changing; there is less emphasis on technical prowess and more on an instinct for trends. In future, more consumers are likely to design their own clothing and order items directly from the manufacturer. Since the early 2010s, traditional retail has been challenged by the energy of the internet, with e-commerce and social media driving both marketing and sales. Many shops will change to become places where customers pick up pre-purchased clothing, although we are confident there will always be a need for a physical environment where consumers can browse and admire clothes close-up.

As we noted in the first edition of this book, designers are increasingly interpreters of other people's visions, playing a more mercenary role. Back in 2009, we highlighted Karl Lagerfeld at Chanel and Fendi, John Galliano at Dior and Nicolas Ghesquière at Balenciaga. Designers have moved around to an even more remarkable degree in the ten years since. The pace is frenetic, the results sometimes spectacular, often uneven. From the fashion media's perspective, it's all rather exciting. For the purist with an eye on history, it's alarming – heritage often thrust aside, even deliberately trashed, in favour of the lucrative shock of the new.

Many great designers have had a business head, many have had entrepreneurial partners, but all have been servants of commerce. Fashion is an applied art and designers cannot toil in a garret and wait for posterity to acknowledge them. All have understood the need to please a customer while expressing a creative response to the world around them. An observant reporter for *The New York Times,* writing back in 1913, said of Jeanne Paquin: 'She maintains the attitude of an artist, but we know she is the most commercial artist alive.'

Another important point to make is that the development of fashion – just as the development of history itself – is not a story of constant progress towards modernity and rationality. Fashion (perhaps like history too) has an intrinsic pendulum nature. As the work of the fifty-five designers in this book shows, it sways backwards as much as forwards, as much enamoured of its own rich history as of a brave new world. The pursuit of excellence is common to both strands, however. Couture is no longer at the heart of the modern fashion system, although its support for age-old craft through the ateliers remains heroic and important. However, this book does not lament a lost world. We share the view of Nicolas Ghesquière: 'I don't think couture fits our world. … Anyway, I have the luxury of using the couture techniques in my ready-to-wear.'

We have skewed our selection towards the second half of the twentieth century and the early twenty-first century, reflecting our interests and the perceived interests of our readers. The fashion world has a notoriously short memory. As curator Harold Koda has written, 'The high fashion system with its seasonal advocacy of the new and an associated obsolescence of preceding styles, perhaps inevitably dismisses, if not obliterates, its own history.' How important is the fashion designer today? Harold Koda says designers rarely dictate. 'Now you can have so many designers that each one becomes a barometer of a different aspect of our consciousness of the world.'

The designer's job today remains challenging. Miuccia Prada reflected on changing times in an interview with Ingrid Sischy in 2006: 'In general, designers of past decades had to deal with a small community of rich bourgeois people in France, in Italy, in America, or in England. … And so, to do clothes for these people in a way was much easier, because it was very simple. Now, in a way we have to dress people of different culture, different nationalities, different religions, different worlds.'

This book is ostensibly about clothes that only the wealthy can afford. The authors' aim is not to defend price tags on Vetements hoodies selling for $1,000-plus. Luxury fashion houses have always understood how restricting supply drives the allure of luxury and sustains high prices. A focus on the excesses of high-end fashion turns rapidly into a debate about the idiosyncrasies of our consumer-driven society and about capitalism itself – an important debate for a planet with finite resources, but beyond the scope of this book.

In business terms, the designer clothes themselves have often been a loss-leader, with bags, shoes and fragrances making the real profits. But high-end fashion has made a significant contribution to the European, and global, cultural conversation. Some reject this as a move towards an enervating cultural homogeneity but high-end fashion undeniably asks relevant questions too. Consider Raf Simons' commentaries on modern America during his time at Calvin Klein between 2016 and 2018, or Demna Gvasalia's challenging remixes at Balenciaga. High-end design ideas *do* influence the broader market. Like all creative endeavour, great design can tell us something about the world around us, enriching the mind and lifting the spirits.

Historical academic research these days often prefers to play down the roles of prominent individuals, exploring the broader socio-economic context. There is an alternative history that explores the contribution of *les petites mains,* the (mostly) women who toiled in the ateliers to bring the designers' creations to life. They emerge as the unexpected stars of *Dior et moi*, the documentary film about Raf Simons' first couture collection for Dior, released in 2014. Research at Central Saint Martins in London aims to deconstruct the myth of the designer as sole creative genius by exploring the role of the pattern cutter.

For *les petites mains*, the fashion world has rarely been glamorous. The word *atelier* should not be used to disguise the fact that the big couture businesses of the early decades of the twentieth century were essentially factories: in 1901, *Femina* magazine described the house of Redfern as 'a veritable factory of elegance'. Only a small handful of enlightened employers, most notably Madeleine Vionnet, showed compassion to their workforce. Chanel, by contrast, was monstrous.

All that said, we believe the personal stories of the great names of fashion bring alive the industry with a special vibrancy. Through the achievements of these designers, we see fashion at its most inspirational. The British journalist Claudia Croft, writing in *The Sunday Times* in February 2009, noted that 'one of fashion's great strengths is its ability to make us dream. As much as it reflects the times, it also provides respite from them.' We, of course, agree. Fashion is a sociocultural indicator and it is a business, but it is also (to quote John Galliano) a journey into escapism, fun and fantasy. Join us on that journey.

Part One

Early days

Introduction

In the nineteenth century, fashion was a game of social status reserved for high-society women and theatre stars of independent means. Trends trickled down, but not very far and not very fast: the sheer cost of clothing ensured that. Women's fashion was spectacularly restrictive. The corset squeezed the rib cage while the crinoline and full-length hemlines restricted movement. Individuality was frowned upon: the role of a woman in genteel society was essentially conformist, focusing on children and social life.

Until the emergence of Englishman *Charles Frederick Worth* in Paris in the late 1850s, a customer would buy fabrics separately, and then take them to a dressmaker to be made up. Worth brought these activities together and created the model for the fashion house that dominated throughout the twentieth century and into the early twenty-first. Although his dresses reflected the restrictive ethos of their time, his achievement as the founder of the modern fashion system remains undiminished.

The late nineteenth century saw the first stirrings of women's emancipation. British tailors Charles Poynter at Redfern and Henry Creed, who both flourished with shops in Paris, had introduced tailoring to women's fashion. But Pre-Raphaelite artists and the Aesthetes promoted a new kind of dressing, drawing on ancient Greek models that followed the natural silhouette. Most of their ideas remained theoretical, but the guidelines were in place for change. Arthur Lasenby Liberty founded his London store Liberty & Co. in 1875, championing Art Nouveau in the 1890s and finding inspiration from Asia. Women were also beginning to find a place for themselves in the business of fashion. *Jeanne Paquin* founded her couture house in Paris in the 1890s, while Marie Callot Gerber and her sisters established the house of *Callot Soeurs*.

Paris was booming creatively at the dawn of the twentieth century. The 1900 Exposition Universelle in Paris presented the very best of French design to the world, including women's fashion. Right from the start, couture acknowledged the dual nature of its creative and industrial identities. In 1911, the Chambre Syndicale de la Couture Parisienne was founded, defining only the houses listed on its calendar as 'haute couture'.

At the very beginning of the century, the core fashion message from Paris showed few signs of moving forward. The S silhouette, which thrust a woman's breasts forward and her *derrière* backward, was the fashionable look of the period. *Mariano Fortuny*'s loose Delphos Dress, created in 1907 and worn by the dancer Isadora Duncan, hinted at a radical shift in direction, but it was *Paul Poiret* who had the biggest impact, promoting a natural silhouette, loosening the constricted waist and doing away with the more severe versions of the corset. His emergence came as the brassiere received a mention in *Vogue* for the first time.

Both Worth and Poiret believed their expertise gave them the right – and duty – to dictate to their customers. A woman must be guided in her desire for a new fashion, they thought. But couturières such as Jeanne Paquin and Callot Soeurs were more inclined to listen to their customers. The first decade of the twentieth century concluded with Paul Poiret at his peak, inspired by Orientalism, which drew influence from all points east.

1

Charles Frederick Worth (1825–1895)

Worth created the modern couture system that remained dominant until the rise of ready-to-wear in the 1960s.

Charles Frederick Worth, an Englishman from the quiet county of Lincolnshire, was the first couturier of modern times. His one rival to that title, Rose Bertin, milliner and dressmaker to Marie Antoinette, was from a different era, the late eighteenth century. The story of how an Englishman rose from unpromising roots to international renown is one of the most extraordinary episodes in the history of fashion. Before Charles Frederick Worth, only women were dressmakers; men were tailors or haberdashers. Before Worth, a customer would purchase fabrics separately and then take them to a dressmaker to be made up. Before Worth, clothes-makers were not society figures. Worth focused on fit and construction, the qualities that are at the core of haute couture. He was, said his biographer Diana de Marly, 'like an engineer or an architect for whom the soundness of the construction was the fundamental consideration'.

For four decades, Worth was the dominant force in Western fashion, developing many of the fundamental components of the modern fashion system. These ranged from the creation of a collection in advance of the season, to the development of styles that typically endured for around five years, and the creation of the fashion label (stamped, at the house of Worth, in gold on silk Petersham ribbon). Charles Frederick Worth's apprenticeship in London and Paris was long and hard, but when the breakthrough came with a coveted order for a dress from Empress Eugénie of France, his career was made virtually overnight. To appreciate fully his achievements, it is helpful to understand the mindset of high society in nineteenth-century Europe. The concept of a man fitting clothes to a woman's body was not merely unusual; it was considered immoral, indeed thoroughly shocking. The English, who did not have a word to match couturier, reported that Worth was a 'man-milliner' running a house that was, so the rumours ran, more of a bordello.

Image 1.1 *Charles Frederick Worth, 1870. Photo: Hulton Archive via Getty Images.*

Worth also set the tone for the couturier as dictator, rapidly acquiring much of the arrogance of the French court he served, with prices to match. 'Those ladies are wisest who leave the choice to us,' he told an interviewer. According to his son, Jean-Philippe, 'in time he came to have no awe of anything … and to recognise only two higher in authority than himself – God and the Emperor.' He also had an innate appreciation of the insecurities and competitiveness of the ladies of high society. Speaking to the journalist F. Adolphus, Worth once said: 'Women dress, of course, for two reasons: for the pleasure of making themselves smart, and for the still greater joy of snuffing out the others.'

He was born in 1825 in Bourne, Lincolnshire, one of five children. Disaster hit the family eleven years later when his father, William, a solicitor, went bankrupt and left his family to fend for themselves. His impoverished mother was left with little choice but to find an apprenticeship for her son, who worked at a printer's shop. The young boy, however, hated the work and persuaded his mother to allow him to move to London to gain employment at Swan & Edgar, a haberdashers located in the recently constructed Regent Street. This was effectively Worth's home through his teenage years; legend has it that he even slept beneath the counter. The opportunity to work with textiles gave Worth an outstanding grounding for the future. Perhaps equally important were his frequent visits to the new National Gallery, within walking distance of both Swan & Edgar and Lewis & Allenby, the royal silk mercers, to which he moved in 1845. Society fashion drew heavily and freely on the costumes of past centuries, particularly for balls and masquerades. Thus, Worth's encyclopaedic knowledge of costume history, garnered from observation of portraits in the National Gallery, stood him in good stead.

At the age of just twenty, Worth arrived in Paris in 1845, determined to make his way in the capital of fashion. He lived on the breadline for more than a year, making money where he could and picking up French along the way. It took him two years to land a job at Gagelin in the rue de Richelieu selling fabrics and another eleven years before he was in a position to set up his own business. Worth's breakthrough innovation went unnoticed at the time: he persuaded his employers at Gagelin to allow him to open a dressmaking department. Never before had textiles and dressmaking been brought together under the same roof – and never before had a man been a dressmaker. Gagelin entered dresses to the Great Exhibition in the Crystal Palace in 1851, the year Worth also married the Gagelin in-house model Marie. In 1855, Paris hosted its own international event, the Exposition Universelle, where Worth's court train, unusually suspended from the shoulders rather than the waist, won a first-class medal. Three years later, Worth joined forces with Otto Bobergh, a young Swede with similar skills to Worth, to open Worth et Bobergh at 7 rue de la Paix.

Paris had been in political and social upheaval during Worth's early years in the French capital. But the creation of the Second Napoleonic Empire in 1852 under Napoleon III, son of Napoleon I's brother Louis, unleashed a period of imperial extravagance that put Paris at the heart of the European social scene. Empress Eugénie required a new dress for every occasion, as did the guests at imperial balls, masquerades and country visits. A veritable gold mine awaited Worth, although breaking through the barriers of court convention to secure the first royal order required all Worth's skills of salesmanship, acquired on the shop floor over the years in London and Paris. The story goes that Empress Eugénie did not like the first gown Worth made for her in 1860, rejecting the heavy brocade from Lyon as looking like 'curtain material'. Napoleon entered the room at that precise moment, whereupon Worth explained that support for the silk makers of Lyon, a city with a republican tradition, might be very advantageous to the emperor. Remarkably, this Machiavellian switch of sales patter paid off – Worth was on his way.

Empress Eugénie's patronage opened the flood-gates for Worth. If the empress wore Worth, then so did most of her ladies-in-waiting and guests. For one ball alone, Worth might be called on to make up to 1,000 dresses. *The House of Worth: Portrait of an Archive* (2014), a scholarly book by Amy de la Haye and Valerie Mendes, provides outstanding insights into this rarefied world, explaining the myriad classifications of balls. The house's ability to respond to such a volume of orders was boosted by recent advances in technology, specifically the development of the Singer sewing machine for long seams. Worth also industrialised the process, creating standard patterns that could be used as the basis for apparently new designs. Countless variations were developed around similar dresses, often refreshed through trimmings alone. In colour terms, Worth was more restricted: white was the required colour for court dress, with silver playing the decorative role. For masquerades, the parties where the court collectively let its hair down, Worth was freer, often drawing inspiration from the eighteenth century and creating fantastical costumes that delighted his clients.

Worth's approach to design was to find simple solutions to the challenges thrown up by nineteenth-century propriety and society values. He was not afraid to innovate, using his wife Marie to test the market with some of his more daring designs. She was outstanding at presenting a dress to best effect, making her a forerunner of the modern fashion model. Princess von Metternich was another important ally for much of his career, not least because of her social connections. For Empress Eugénie's walk by the seaside, he created ankle-length skirts, a breakthrough after thirty years of ground-length hemlines. Likewise, he made the unwieldy crinoline more practical by pushing the volume round to the back rather than to the sides, enabling the wearer to walk through a doorway without having to turn sideways. Another innovation was the gored skirt with panels that are wide at the hemline and narrow at the top, a smoother option to gathering. Worth achieved such dominance as an arbiter of style that he could achieve remarkable changes in fashion in short order, such as replacing the bonnet with the hat as the favoured form of headwear or removing the crinoline altogether, a step he took finally in 1868.

By this date, Worth himself was a considerably wealthy man with a country house outside Paris at Suresnes, which he expanded and transformed into a chateau over the years. In Paris, he had more than 1,000 seamstresses working for his house. He created dresses for royal courts throughout Europe besides that of Napoleon III in Paris and also designed for the theatre and the opera. His clients would be expected to make an appointment at rue de la Paix and stride backward and forward in his creations while he observed from a sofa. Over the years, Worth came to consider himself as much more than a dressmaker – he became an artist and began to dress as such, wearing a velvet beret and a

Image 1.2 *Worth and Bobergh silk ensemble, 1862–1865. Brooklyn Museum Costume Collection at The Metropolitan Museum of Art, Gift of the Brooklyn Museum, 2009; Designated Purchase Fund, 1987.*

Image 1.3 *Empress Eugénie, photographed by Olympe Aguado de las Marismas, 1860. Gilman Collection, Museum Purchase, 2005.*

silk scarf round his throat and consorting and collaborating with artists such as Winterhalter. The adoption of aesthetic dress by Pre-Raphaelite artists in England struck a chord with him. Aesthetic style with its looser dresses and rejection of corsets was a reaction against the swift-changing whims of fashion in favour of more natural lines and less restrictive clothing.

The glories of the 1860s ended abruptly for Worth in 1870 when Napoleon III was overthrown by the Prussians at the Battle of Sedan. By January of the following year the Prussians were in Paris, Napoleon III and Empress Eugénie were in exile in England, and even Princess von Metternich left shortly afterwards. Worth vowed to carry on the business, now without Bobergh. Such was his fame that business continued to pour in, although with a new clientele, including Americans and other international visitors to Paris. In 1874, Worth brought his sons into the business, with Jean-Philippe helping with design and his older brother Gaston focusing on business. In fashion terms, he continued to innovate, slimming down the skirt and creating the Princess line, a one-piece dress with a fitted waist but no waistseam. In the 1880s, he reintroduced the bustle with the launch of the crinolette. Even in the final years of his life, he was experimenting with seamless dresses and bias cuts.

After his death in 1895, his son Jean-Philippe followed confidently in the footsteps of his father, emerging as a couturier of assurance in his own right, creating the trousseau and wedding dress for Consuelo Vanderbilt's marriage to the Duke of Marlborough, the most feted society wedding of the 1890s.

His brother Gaston ran the business and financial side of the house. Opulence, rather than innovation, was Jean-Philippe's key attribute. As Diana de Marly put it: 'He could not conceive of a dress that was without splendour.' Stepping down in 1910, Jean-Philippe was succeeded by Gaston's sons Jacques and Jean-Charles, the latter another couturier of note who responded confidently to the fashion trends of the 1920s (the Victoria & Albert Museum archive in London includes fifty-four exceptional behind-the-scenes photographs of the House of Worth in 1927). Jacques and Roger, a fourth generation of Worths, carried the Paris house into the 1940s, although it finally sold out to its London branch in 1946. As a fashion house, the business ground to a halt in 1954 when a perfume company bought the name.

Charles Frederick Worth created the modern couture system that remained dominant until the rise of ready-to-wear in the 1960s. Among his many innovations were the sale of toiles and patterns and the use of models. More importantly, he took dressmaking to a higher plane through the rigorous focus on fit and construction, a tradition that was carried on by Worth's sons after his death. When he died of pneumonia in 1895, his funeral service drew 2,000 mourners. His widow, Marie, received telegrams of condolence from all the courts of Europe. But although the pioneer was dead, the new world of haute couture was only just beginning.

Further reading: Diana de Marly's biography, *Worth: Father of Haute Couture* (1980), is an excellent introduction to the couturier's work and life. *The House of Worth: Portrait of a Fashion Archive* (2014) by Amy de la Haye and Valerie Mendes is an outstanding work of scholarship.

Image 1.4 *Tea gown, Charles Frederick Worth, ca 1900. Photo: Chicago History Museum via Getty Images.*

2

Callot Soeurs (1895–1937)

Callot Soeurs had a genius at turning the exotic into the new for discerning customers.

Callot Soeurs, a Parisian fashion business run by three sisters, began as a specialist in lace, developing into a fully fledged house renowned for the quality of its work and precise details. Although the house closed its doors in 1937 and is little known today, in its prime it was one of the greatest of all couture businesses, rated by French novelist Marcel Proust as one of the four greatest in his novel, *A la Recherche du Temps Perdu* (Remembrance of Things Past), alongside Paquin, Doucet and Chéruit.

A complete reappraisal of the house is long overdue, but even a brief exploration of its work suggests that Callot Soeurs deserves greater prominence in any consideration of early-twentieth-century fashion. Making an important contribution to its rehabilitation, Camille Janbon researched Callot Soeurs for a Courtauld Institute of Art master's thesis in 1999. She highlighted the achievement of three sisters operating as couturières in an era when a business run by women for women was a novel concept treated with suspicion or open disapproval. It is clear the dominance of women at their couture house fed into the clothes that were created, typically combining comfort with elegance. The Callots were quick to abandon the corset in their designs. Putting a modern spin on their achievements, Janbon concludes the house was, in essence, 'a very feminist structure which promoted women and femininity but always in a discreet way'.

That said, as with all their competitors, they made clothes for a rich elite class of women, initially in Paris and increasingly in America. In their heyday, a day dress was priced at around 2,500 French francs, compared with a ready-made dress price of less than 300 francs. They were supreme exponents of the orientalist style, producing dresses that drew inspiration from the regions of the world known for much of the twentieth century to Westerners as the Near East and Far East. These dresses were spectacularly embroidered and coloured and dubbed *robes phéniciennes* for no very obvious reason. Dresses of embroidered satin featured panels with a cornucopia of motifs from all points east. During the 1920s, their cubist-influenced dresses continued to draw on Oriental motifs and colours. Overshadowed historically by more extrovert personalities, such as Paul Poiret, the sisters were also

Image 2.1 *Mlle Marie-Louise Herrouette in robe du soir, Callot Soeurs, 1909. Photo: Reutlinger/Mansell/ The LIFE Picture Collection via Getty Images.*

considerable innovators. Callot Soeurs was the first couture house to show evening dresses made from gold and silver lamé, a fabric composed of metal threads. They also pioneered the combination of lace blouses with tailored suits and developed rubberised gabardine for sportswear.

In the beginning there were four sisters: Josephine, the youngest, committed suicide in 1897. Of the remaining three, Marie Callot Gerber was the design talent, a striking figure with red hennaed hair and a confident manner that impressed all who met her. The other sisters were Marthe, later Madame Bertrand, and Regine, later Madame Chantrell, who had a reputation for being domineering and conservative in attitude. Gerber was hugely admired by no less an authority than Vionnet, who worked as her toile maker for six years and rated her higher than Poiret. Madame Gerber, she recalled years later, 'was a great lady totally occupied with a profession that consists of adorning women … not constructing a costume'. In perhaps the most celebrated comment on the influence of Callot Soeurs, Vionnet added: 'Without the example of the Callot Soeurs, I would have continued to make Fords. It is because of them that I have been able to make Rolls Royces.'

The Callot sisters were from a family steeped in textiles. Their father, Jean-Baptiste, was a painter and antiques dealer, and their mother, Eugenie, was a lacemaker from a lacemaking family. In 1879, Jean-Baptiste set up his daughters in a small shop in Place de la Trinité. Marie Gerber worked as première in the atelier of Raudnitz & Cie for most of the 1880s, learning her craft. The family shop became celebrated for its quality lingerie and above all for its lace, often antique lace from the eighteenth century reconstituted for modern tastes. The Callot sisters were fashion's supreme exponents of lace, even though the novelist Marcel Proust thought they used a little too much of it. Marie Gerber acknowledged the development of machine-made lace as 'a triumph of imitation and also an adieu to the past'.

In 1895, the couture house of Callot Soeurs was formally founded on the rue Taitbout and developed steadily. In the early days, the sisters played to their strengths, using antique laces and ribbons for lingerie and blouses, and then offering period gowns in the style of Louis XV in floral silks adorned with lace ruffles. Few couture houses had a better appreciation of the skills of the textile producers of Lyon, France's historic textiles centre. Business grew apace: by the time of the Exposition Universelle in 1900, they had 200 employees and sales of 2 million French francs. This event was a magnificent promotional event for all twenty couture houses involved, as one million visitors were exposed to their work. Few took as much advantage as the Callots, who doubled sales and tripled their workforce in the year after the exhibition. The S silhouette, created by a corset that propelled the bust forward and the hips backward, dominated the looks at the Exposition Universelle, but change was in the air. When Poiret abandoned the corset in 1903, the Callots were with him every step of the way. And when Poiret embraced Orientalism, the Callots were once again singing the same tune. Gerber found inspiration through her friendship with Edmond de Goncourt, a renowned collector of Japanese art. Orientalism, particularly influenced by Japan, had been bubbling under the surface in Paris since the late 1880s, although it was the Exposition Universelle of 1900 that brought it to the fore. Gerber, who always focused closely on sleeve construction, developed a particular fascination for the kimono sleeve.

If Gerber had shared the ebullient personality, not to mention the gender, of Paul Poiret, perhaps her achievements would have been more widely recognised. Fashion historian Caroline Rennolds Milbank highlights Gerber's genius at turning the exotic into the new for her discerning customers. 'No one was more skilled at combing history and the far corners of the world and translating these foreign motifs into contemporary Parisian terms.' In her history of haute couture, fashion historian Diana de Marly preferred to highlight Gerber's heavily decorated gowns, overhung with networks of beads or tiers of lace. But many of the Callot dresses preserved in modern museum collections reveal a delightful lightness of touch and make it clear that Gerber was an innovative designer who reflected the trends of the period while making them her own. Richard Martin of the Metropolitan Museum of Art in New York revealed himself to be a fan in his catalogue for an haute couture exhibition in 1995: 'It is hard to describe Callot Soeurs as either conservative or radical, so thoroughly combined and compatible are the traits of each pole.'

The atelier was a hushed environment; work was carried out with rigour and precise attention to detail. Gerber herself was not a dressmaker in the conventional sense. She was interested in construction, developing her ideas by draping fabric on a line model in muslin, then leaving it to her toile maker (Vionnet from 1901 to 1906) to execute her designs. 'Carried by her creative genius, she did not burden herself with the practical side of things,' said Vionnet. The Callots did, however, face up to the growing challenge of copying or, more seriously, counterfeiting. Fake designer labels were often

Image 2.2 *Callot Soeurs evening dress, 1921. Photo: Chicago History Museum via Getty Images.*

sewn into garments in America, highlighted in an article written for *Ladies' Home Journal* in 1913 by Samuel Hopkins Adams and subtitled 'How American Women Are Being Fooled by a Country-Wide Swindle'. In response, Callot Soeurs published in *Women's Wear* a list of American companies that had made authorised purchases from them in Paris. By the following year Gerber, now fully aware of the originality of her designs, took to registering many of them at the Depot Legal – the records are now housed in the collection of the Musée de la Mode et du Textile in Paris.

By 1917, Callot Soeurs had added branches in London and Buenos Aires as business continued to flourish. The house's work had been popular since its early days with Parisian actresses, including Cécile Sorel, Jeanne Graiser and Eve Lavallière, but Callot Soeurs also built a substantial following in America, where their day dresses were well received at the Universal Exhibition in San Francisco in 1915. During the First World War, this support was critical: American buyers would descend on Paris in July and place orders for between 300 and 800 pieces. The house's greatest supporter in America was Rita de Acosta Lydig. This New York society lady of Spanish heritage had married an ageing millionaire from whom she was divorced within four years, leaving her with money and time aplenty. Camille Janbon points out that Callot Soeurs' relationship to this flamboyant character was similar to that of a nineteenth-century dressmaker, allowing the rich client to make the demands. This was good business sense because, as Janbon says, 'she never ordered one single dress but a dozen at a time with variations in the materials and forms'.

Rita de Acosta Lydig became renowned for her individualistic style, was painted in Callot dresses by the artist Giovanni Boldini, and remained an unwavering enthusiast for the house until her death in 1925. In 1919, Callot Soeurs moved location to 9–11 avenue Matignon, but even bigger change followed in 1920 with the sudden death of Marthe, Madame Bertrand, and the decision of Regine, Madame Chantrell, to retire (she had been widowed early and chose to devote her attention to her son's education). Gerber continued to run the house singlehandedly for a further seven years, displaying a sureness of touch and ability to move with the times. A day suit in white ottoman silk and lace at the Musée de la Mode et du Textile is a striking statement in black and white, and a sumptuous but simple driving coat in soft leather trimmed with astrakhan was among the designs registered at the Depot Legal in 1925.

Despite the best efforts of Chanel, Orientalism continued to influence fashion well into the 1920s. The celebrated Exposition des Arts Décoratifs in Paris in 1925 saw Callot Soeurs imbibing dark lacquer influences from East Asia. A beautiful piece from 1926 by Gerber features Chinese shawl motifs on a dress with an asymmetric hem, rising at the front to well above the knees. Callot Soeurs, as Camille Janbon notes, responded to Orientalism with a deftness of touch that might be contrasted favourably with Poiret's approach. The woman always came first for Gerber. 'The dress is everything which should be part of the woman,' she said. 'Not the woman part of the dress.' Callot Soeurs reflected other art movements of the 1920s, including cubism, in a still preserved dress that mixes lace and embroidery in a collage effect. 'The dresses of Marie Gerber were true masterpieces,' reflected Vionnet, ever supportive of her former employer.

On the death of Gerber in 1927, an obituary in *Le Figaro* commented: 'One of the most beautiful figures of the Parisian luxury business has now disappeared.' Her sons Pierre and Jacques were left in charge. Jacques had focused more on the development of fragrance for Callot Soeurs, launching La Fille du Roi de Chine in 1923 (there was no king of China, but the continuing allure of Orientalism made this name sound suitably seductive). Callot continued to sell to a loyal clientele who felt alienated by the unforgiving straight lines of much of 1920s style. As with many other businesses, the economic crash of 1929 had a heavy impact, and the business was finally absorbed by Calvet in 1937. Gerber's granddaughter published a memoir in 1978, but this did little to revive the reputation of Callot Soeurs until costume museums began to display their work in the 1990s.

Further reading: There is no full-length monograph on Callot Soeurs, although 'Callot Soeurs', an unpublished MA thesis by Camille Janbon at the Courtauld Institute of Art (1999), is informative. Diana de Marly's *The History of Haute Couture 1850–1950* (1980) sets the context authoritatively.

Image 2.3 *Callot Soeurs afternoon dress, circa 1917. Photo: Chicago History Museum via Getty Images.*

3

Jeanne Paquin (1869–1936)

Paquin saw fashion as part of the broader cultural picture.

Jeanne Paquin was the queen of haute couture for nearly thirty years. She was the first major female couturier, running one of the biggest couture houses of the early twentieth century, employing 2,700 employees at its height. She was also one of the pioneers of the modern fashion business, building her label as an international enterprise – and becoming the first Parisian name to open stores in cities such as London, New York, Madrid and Buenos Aires. Why, then, is so little known about Jeanne Paquin compared with Poiret or Worth? Fashion historian Jan Reeder speculated that she has been largely overlooked simply because she was a woman, lumped in with the myriad of other female Parisian dressmakers who emerged during the Belle Époque period, sandwiched between two men, Charles Frederick Worth and Paul Poiret, who have received much greater attention from historians.

Unlike Poiret, Paquin did not believe in dictating to her customers. Paquin's viewpoint was that designers should reflect and respond to the subtle changes in style initiated by 'women in the street', as she put it. Paquin modified the most adventurous of new trends to make them wearable to her customers. Poiret's controversial hobble skirts, for example, were also produced by Paquin, but, as historian Valerie Steele has highlighted, Paquin's versions had ingenious hidden pleats to make them more practical. 'This tendency towards moderation has probably made her seem less significant in the eyes of history,' suggests Steele. An unpublished paper by Laetitia Elting (The Courtauld Institute, 1999) makes a strong case for Paquin as a true innovator. In 1912, she produced a collection of coats and skirts for sports, travel and shopping, creating *tailleurs* (tailored suits) that were both practical and stylish. That same year she opened a sportswear department in her London shop for golf, motoring and shooting clothing. Paquin, it could be argued, predated many of Chanel's achievements in the 1920s. A report in *Health & Home* magazine in October 1912 praised Paquin's 'simple yet smart gowns, which are the very thing for golfing or motoring and yet will not disgrace their wearer should she elect to lunch at a fashionable restaurant in the meantime'.

Image 3.1 *Jeanne Paquin, 1912. Photo: ullstein bild/ullstein bild via Getty Images.*

As the fashion historian Diana de Marly has noted, when Paquin made an innovation, it was for very practical reasons. In 1913, she produced a dress that was a blend of tailoring and drapery, formal enough for daytime but soft enough for informal evening occasions. It was the first day-into-evening dress. Her tailoring tended to be less severe than that of English tailoring specialists, with a touch of softness and femininity. Paquin herself often wore dark blue serge suits decorated with black chiffon. Despite her moderation as a designer, Madame Paquin, as she was always known, was no shrinking violet. Interviews with her in the newspapers of the day built a picture of a passionate, highly articulate and confident woman. She could also write well and penned lyrical pieces on fashion and culture. She saw fashion as part of the broader cultural picture and encouraged collaboration and cross-fertilisation between designers and artists, theatre designers and architects (contrasting with couture houses such as Redfern, Worth and Doucet, which all rejected the collaborative approach).

Jeanne Marie Charlotte Beckers was born in 1869, the daughter of a physician. In the manner of the time, she was sent out to work while still a young teenager and learned her craft very rapidly, rising through the ranks at Maison Rouff to become première, in charge of the atelier. In 1891 she married Isidore-René Jacob, also known as Paquin, an ebullient businessman who owned Paquin Lalanne, a couture house that had grown out of a menswear shop, Paquin Frères, back in the 1840s. They quickly renamed the business just Paquin and set about building the company with impressive energy and verve at 3 rue de la Paix. The success of Charles Frederick Worth, the first modern couturier, which had been continued by his son Jean-Philippe Worth, had overshadowed female dressmakers in Paris. With the arrival of Paquin, the dressmakers began to have their say. Paquin was the first woman to achieve the status of couturière. While the house of Worth bestowed dignity on its customers, the house of Paquin brought lashings of glamour.

As a confident and sociable woman, now with the inestimable advantage of a wealthy husband, Jeanne Paquin was well placed to make an impact. Designer Maggy Rouff later recalled: 'I can still hear the crystal voice of Madame Paquin [saying that fashion] must constantly renew itself, without weakness or fear, even with audacity.'

Paquin loved colour. She initially embraced the pastel tones that were popular in the early 1900s. Later, she developed her signature red – and often focused on colour as a starting point for her designs. She gave new life to black, associated with mourning and gravitas through most of the nineteenth century, but used by Paquin as a foil for her richer colours. Her dresses reflected the Orientalist fashions of the early 1900s, but there was superbly realised tailoring too, including wool decorated with inserts of crochet lace. She also had a strong eye for contrasting details, such as using fur trims on silk or chiffon rather than wool, raising the ordinary into something extraordinary.

Paquin focused on design while her husband nurtured the clients. They ranged from royalty (the Queens of Spain, Portugal and Belgium were all customers) to celebrated courtesans such as La Belle Otero and Liane de Pougy. Indeed, the house was happy to dress everyone who could afford the opulent dresses and fur-trimmed coats. The couple showed an astute touch to their marketing and kept their prices at a more modest level than their competitors. The main events of the social calendar were clearly communicated to the vendeuses at the beginning of every year. An in-house stage was created to serve as an aid for dresses for theatre customers. A Paris guidebook of 1906 praised their open-door policy: 'From the first this clever and ornamental young couple followed a new system. No haughty seclusion, no barred doors, at the Maison Paquin.'

By the standards of the time, they were also enlightened in their attitude towards their employees, purchasing a villa in Le Touquet that employees could use for relaxation. When the world of Paris couture was threatened by a strike in 1917, Paquin expressed sympathy for the strikers, a viewpoint that displeased many of her fellow couturiers. Isidore and Jeanne had shrewd business instincts, taking the bold decision to open a London store in 1896. It was here that the young Madeleine Vionnet worked. Stores followed in Madrid and Buenos Aires, plus a furrier on Fifth Avenue, New York, named Paquin-Joire, run with her half-brother Henri Joire. In 1900, she was appointed organiser of the fashion section of the Exposition Universelle, which raised more than a few eyebrows among her rivals. She confidently created a mannequin of herself for the display. By 1907, Paquin was a flourishing business, with customers delighted by the couturière's new Japanese kimono-sleeved coats. But then tragedy struck: Isidore Paquin fell sick and died at the age of forty-five. Some 2,000 people attended the funeral. Jeanne was a widow at thirty-eight.

After Isidore's death, the business became Jeanne's life more than ever. Henceforth, she dressed mostly in black and white, again predating Chanel. The Prix Isidore Paquin was created in her husband's memory to recognise gifted young artists. In 1908, she revived the Directoire look and introduced tailoring for the first time, a turning point that made Paquin into a full fashion house, including couture, lingerie, furs and accessories (Jeanne Lanvin went on to take this process further, turning Lanvin into arguably the first lifestyle brand). Between 1910 and 1915, Paquin participated in a number of international exhibitions that were important marketing platforms. The Paquin pavilion, decorated as a Greek temple, was a huge hit at an exhibition in Turin in 1911, and Paquin introduced an entrance fee in an attempt to control the visitor numbers. The same year Paquin's love for art was given full flower with the creation of an album of designs for accessories, fans and clothes illustrated by artists Paul Iribe, Georges Lepape and Georges Barbier. Paquin was also swept up in the excitement over the arrival of the Ballets Russes in Paris and made up costumes designed by Leon Bakst and Paul Iribe. As historian Nancy Troy has made clear, beneath Paquin's genuine enthusiasm for the arts, she was well aware of the commercial advantages of such associations and was also aware of the complex balancing act that was required to appeal both to the avant-garde and to more traditionally minded customers. An astute reporter for *The New York Times*, writing in 1913, commented: 'She maintains the attitude of an artist, but we know she is the most commercial artist alive.'

Paquin was also tough-minded, proving just as ready to protect her designs as her rival Paul Poiret. In 1906, she took legal action against two magazines for publishing photographs of new models before

Image 3.2 *Workers Leaving the Maison Paquin, 1912. Photo: Fine Art Images/Heritage Images via Getty Images.*

they were displayed. She also won a long-running action against the Beer couture house for copying and was awarded 8,000 francs in damages. Yet another legal case, against a Paris-based tailoring house, launched in 1911, resulted in victory seven years later. Paquin was nothing if not dogged. The period leading up to the First World War was golden for Paquin, who became the first woman dressmaker to be awarded the Légion d'Honneur. That was in 1913, a year in which shareholders in the company received a 211 per cent return on their investment. 'I am glad that the government has acknowledged my work quite irrespective of sex,' she said. 'That is as far as my feminism goes. I only want justice, that work in any particular branch in which a woman excels shall be recognised.'

The tango dress of 1913 was one of her most celebrated designs, created for dancing the tango, a craze which was sweeping Paris. A typical Paquin design, it comprised a tunic and double skirt, including a chiffon underskirt, and made generous use of pleats and godets to ensure freedom of movement. In Paquin's hands, women did not need to fear ridicule – fashion was never allowed to triumph over function. The tango dresses featured in a tango fashion show at the Palace Theatre in London. *The Daily Express* newspaper, impressed by the public interest in the event, wrote that 'these new fashion shows were rivalling in popularity the ordinary theatre play.' The outbreak of war encouraged Paquin to develop new markets, including America, where the Paquin-Joire shop had thrived since opening in 1912. In 1914, four of Paquin's best mannequins toured America for three weeks with her sister-in-law, Madame Joire, to drum up publicity. The so-called *croisade de l'élégance* visited New York, Boston, Philadelphia, Pittsburgh, Chicago and New York, charging three dollars a ticket, later raised to five dollars, and crowds were still turned away. This successful marketing ploy had been first initiated by Poiret, but Paquin was no less successful. The models' coloured wigs drew particular comment for their modern spirit.

Paquin's status was recognised in 1917 when she was appointed president of the Chambre Syndicale, which represented the couturiers of Paris, a post she held until 1919. By then, she had retired as house designer in favour of Madeleine Wallis, whose particular skill was in furs, which became the signature of Paquin. She finally retired altogether in the early 1930s and died in 1936. The house lasted twenty years after her death, continuing to make her celebrated fur-trimmed coats. In 1953, it acquired the French business of Worth, its old rival, before both were forced to recognise their time was past, closing in 1956.

Further reading: Although there is little on Paquin in English, Dominique Sirop wrote her biography, *Paquin* (1989), in French. An unpublished paper by Laetitia Elting, 'Revealing the Accomplishments of Madame Paquin, the Very Queen of Dressmakers' (1999), is at the Courtauld Institute in London. *The Mechanical Smile: Modernism and the First Fashion Shows in France* (2013), by Caroline Evans, is an outstandingly researched book, with many references to Paquin.

Image 3.3 *Paquin dress, 1910. Photo: Chicago History Museum via Getty Images.*

4

Paul Poiret (1879–1944)

Poiret was the precursor for much of the contemporary fashion world.

To describe Paul Poiret as a fashion designer may be to do him an injustice. Consider the achievements of the year 1911, his annus mirabilis, when he created the Rosine house of perfume, the Martine school of decorative arts (with accompanying shop), the Colin paper and packaging workshop, and a fabric printing factory in collaboration with the artist Raoul Dufy. That same year also saw his publication of *Les choses de Paul Poiret vues par Georges Lepape*, a book of exquisite fashion drawings that did much to fuel the revival of fashion illustration. All this, combined with his achievements as a couturier, made Paul Poiret a central figure in the artistic and creative development of Paris in the early twentieth century. In the 1910s, he was known in America as the King of Fashion, while in Paris he was Le Magnifique. To cap it all, he was also an outstanding cook.

As a couturier, his list of accomplishments was spectacular, led by his championing of a revival of the neoclassical style of 1790s France – high-waisted flowing clothes that followed the fluid, natural lines of the body. This revival swept away in a few short years most of the nineteenth-century styles that squeezed, exaggerated or disguised the body. Paradoxically, Poiret was also responsible for the hobble skirt, cut so tight that the wearer could barely walk, an innovation that aroused ridicule while fuelling the oxygen of publicity for the designer. More positively, his enthusiasm for Orientalism, drawing on influences from India to China and Japan, infused fashion and interior design with a burst of strong, dynamic colours, even before the Ballets Russes and Bakst had reached Paris. He paved the way for the style known as Art Deco, making a spectacular contribution both in terms of fashion and interior decoration to the Exposition des Arts Décoratifs in 1925, the event that gave the movement its name.

Poiret was a true Parisian, born in 1879 near Les Halles, to parents who owned a wool cloth shop. As a young child, he was an avid art gallery visitor, entranced by colours in particular. He was also a lover of the theatre, sketching the costumes of the actresses at the Comédie-Française. Forced by his father to become an apprentice to an umbrella maker, he preferred to spend every spare moment developing his sketching

Image 4.1 *Poiret at a fitting, 1925. Photo: Lipnitzki/Roger Viollet via Getty Images.*

abilities. The breakthrough came in 1898 when the couturier Jacques Doucet offered him a job as a junior assistant. His first piece, a red wool cape, received orders from 400 customers. Poiret went on to design for two star actresses of the period, Gabrielle Réjane and Sarah Bernhardt, but was sacked by Doucet after a falling-out with Bernhardt. Following a brief and unhappy period of military service, he went to work at the house of Worth, where he created a coat cut like a kimono that famously upset its potential client, Russian Princess Bariatinsky, but was a precursor of his Orientalist style. Once again, however, he lost his job.

In 1903, with money from his mother, he opened his own house at 5 rue Auber. Encouraged by the magnanimous Jacques Doucet and championed by the actress Gabrielle Réjane, Poiret swiftly began to make waves. His muse was Denise, the daughter of a Normandy textile manufacturer. They were married in 1905. In those early days as a couturier, his enemy was the corset. As he put it himself, 'It was in the name of Liberty that I brought about my first revolution, by deliberately laying siege to the corset.'

Poiret always designed on live models, working from the shoulders, initially creating a series of surprisingly plain gowns that skimmed the outlines of the figure. By 1906, he had banished the corset, replaced by the girdle and the brassiere, which he can lay claim to have invented. Among the other designers of the period who also dropped the corset were Lucile and Madeleine Vionnet, but Poiret, a brilliant self-publicist, stole most of the credit. Unlike Vionnet, he tended to work on the straight grain rather than on the bias. As Metropolitan Museum of Art Costume Institute curators Harold Koda and Andrew Bolton have pointed out, the new natural silhouette marked a fundamental shift of emphasis in fashion away from the skills of tailoring to those based on the skills of draping, inspired by a mixture of sources, including the Greek chiton, the Japanese kimono and the North African caftan. 'Poiret's process of design through draping is the source of fashion's modern forms,' conclude Koda and Bolton.

Between 1906 and 1911, Poiret revived a high-waisted line, referencing both the Directoire period of the 1790s and the ancient Greeks. He mischievously provoked outrage by appearing at the Longchamp racetrack, accompanied by three young women wearing dresses with the sides slit from the knees showing off coloured stockings. He received even more precious media coverage in London by showing his collection at a tea party organised by Margot Asquith, wife of the prime minister. Poiret was by then a considerable celebrity in his own right, with the élan of a theatre impresario and a swaggering, confident personality that swept all before him. In 1909, he moved his premises to an eighteenth-century mansion on avenue d'Antin and created a veritable fashion empire, kept in check financially only by the conscientiousness of bookkeeper Emile Rousseau. Nor were his customers spared from his dominant, sometimes aggressive personality: Poiret, in his own eyes, could do no wrong. The cardboard sign outside his office read: 'Danger!!! Before knocking ask yourself three times – Is it absolutely necessary to disturb HIM?'

His glory years saw Poiret move far beyond fashion, developing links with a series of artists, most notably Paul Iribe (who produced a catalogue of illustrations for him in 1908) and Raoul Dufy, who became a lifelong friend. Poiret's catalogues prompted the creation by magazine editor Lucien Vogel of *Gazette du Bon Ton*, which was essential reading for the fashion set in Paris from 1912 to 1925. Poiret's love of the theatre was reflected in a series of extravagant parties, the most notable being his 'The Thousand and Second Night' or 'Persian Celebration' in June 1911, where his three hundred guests dressed in Oriental costume and his wife, Denise, was locked in a golden cage and released like a bird. Erté became an assistant designer for Poiret in 1913, working with him on his theatrical designs. Poiret's costumes for Mata Hari in a play, *Le Minaret*, were a sensation, featuring a tunic-crinoline shaped like a lampshade, which Erté said was 'inspired by the transparent veils of the Hindu miniatures and by the pleated kilts of Greek folk costumes'.

Poiret foreshadowed the magpie tendencies of designers in the latter decades of the twentieth century through his happy plundering of styles from all points east of Paris. From harem pantaloons to kimono coats to Indian turbans, the couturier found inspiration in everything. His colour explosion brought orange, green, red and purple to the fore as never before, marking a break with the understated pastels of the Art Nouveau period. For a while, Poiret was the most celebrated couturier of the age, particularly famed for his coats, capes and cloaks, notable for their sheer lavish use of fabric, often with fur trimmings. By 1913, his love of bold colours and extravagant prints reflected the work of the Wiener Werkstatte, an influential decorative arts company in Vienna. Poiret did much to popularise the design ideas coming out of Austria and Germany (which led to some criticism from French patriots during the First World War).

Poiret always had entrepreneurial instincts and was bursting with ideas for making money. In 1913, he was the first couturier to embark on the conquest of America, touring department stores. Poiret was also the first couturier to give lectures, attracting huge audiences in the United States and across Europe. Despite his overbearing personality, he always insisted that the couturier's role was not to be a dictator but to be a servant blessed with extreme sensitivity, able to detect the precise moment when a woman's enthusiasm for a fashion was beginning to wane. His American tour was a triumph, but Poiret returned in a state of shock at the widespread copying of his designs. This led him to push for the creation in 1914 of Le Syndicat de Défense de la Grande Couture Française, of which he was the first president. Two years later, he tried a different strategy, producing reduced-price copies of his own dresses, advertised in *Vogue* in 1916 and also promoted in America. In her ground-breaking research, American academic Nancy Troy has shown the contradictions in the way Poiret presented himself as an artist not only to sell to wealthy clients but also to promote the mass production of his designs. The First World War put a stop to grand plans for expansion in America, and any last pretence at financial discipline evaporated after the war. Likewise, after the horrors of four years of war, Poiret's love of theatrical extravagance struck a false note, contrasting with Chanel's functional style and the garçonne look. Although Poiret continued to produce many outstanding collections, his heyday had passed, and a period of slow, sometimes painful decline followed.

Behind the extravagant personality, Poiret was a devoted father to his three children (Rosine, Martine and Colin, who all gave their names to the spurt of initiatives in 1911; he was devastated by

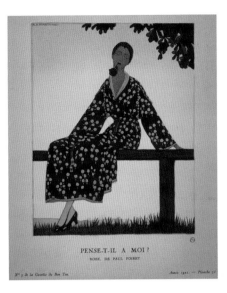

Image 4.2 *Advertising image from* La Gazette du Bon Ton, *1921. Photo: Fotosearch via Getty Images.*

the early death of Rosine from otitis). He divorced from his wife and muse, Denise, in 1928, telling the governess, 'Make sure to tell Madame to take anything she wishes.' In the 1920s, Poiret continued to have no lack of admirers and opportunities. The sadness was that his creative energies were matched by a reckless attitude to money that resulted in years of penury and near ruin despite the constant efforts of friends and admirers to help him out. By 1929, his extravagance led to the closure of his house, and the final years of his life were a depressing downward spiral, exacerbated by the advent of Parkinson's disease. In 1937, a proposal raised at the Chambre Syndicale de la Haute Couture to grant Poiret a pension was vetoed by Jacques Worth.

However, the later years of his life were not empty and showed that Poiret was still a forward-thinking innovator. In 1927, he wrote a far-sighted article for *The Forum* magazine, predicting the future dominance of synthetics and plastics. In another ground-breaking move in the twilight years of his career, he designed for both Printemps and Liberty of London in the 1930s. Poiret's status was fully recognised in 2007 through a lavish exhibition, *Poiret: King of Fashion*, at the Metropolitan Museum of Art in New York, prompted by a treasure trove of clothing from the collection of his wife, Denise, that came up for auction in Paris in 2005: the Met acquired more than twenty pieces. In particular, a pair of 1920s nightdresses, inspired by classical Greek style and worn by Denise, confirm the lightness of his touch and the importance of his influence. But his more extravagant costumes also struck a chord. By the late 1920s, as fashion historian Caroline Rennolds Milbank put it: 'Poiret's global exoticism would not seem modern again until the beginning of the twenty-first century, when the haute couture had found new resonance as one of the most dramatic of arts.'

Fashion historian Diana de Marly called Poiret 'a liberator' (hobble skirts aside): his lean line marking the death knell of the restricted waist, his narrow styles reducing the need for layers of petticoats. Thanks to Poiret, clothes for women began the shift from burdensome impediment to lightweight and more practical adornment. For Met curators Harold Koda and Andrew Bolton, Poiret 'effectively established the canon of modern dress and developed the blueprint of the modern fashion industry'. Poiret was indeed the precursor for much of the contemporary fashion world. Fashion historians are fortunate to have plenty of insights into his design philosophy from the couturier himself, thanks to his many lectures, magazine interviews and a late autobiography. Never mind that his message is sometimes as contradictory as those awkward hobble skirts. At his best, he stripped away the absurdities of late-nineteenth-century European fashion and ushered in a new age for his customers, urging women to, in his own words, 'simply wear what becomes you'.

Further reading: Paul Poiret summarised his own career in *My First Fifty Years* (trans., 1931). Biographers include Yvonne Deslandres, *Poiret* (1987); Alice Mackrell, *Paul Poiret* (1990); and Palmer White, *Poiret* (1973). Nancy Troy's *Couture Culture: A Study in Modern Art and Culture* (2003) highlights the commercial acumen of the couturier. Harold Koda and Andrew Bolton's *Poiret* (2007), the catalogue to the *Poiret: King of Fashion* exhibition at the Metropolitan Museum of Art, includes an illuminating reappraisal of his achievements.

Image 4.3 *From* Les Choses de Paul Poiret, *by Georges Lepape, 1911. Photo: Photo12/UIG via Getty Images.*

5

Mariano Fortuny (1871–1949)

Fortuny's ability to thrive outside the fashion system of Paris makes him a very special case.

Not without reason was Mariano Fortuny known as a latter-day Renaissance man. The Spaniard's span of interests was too broad for one-word descriptions. He was as much artist and inventor as designer: over three decades he registered more than twenty inventions in Paris. His great contribution to fashion, summed up in one dress, the Delphos, was to free the body from the restrictions of fashionable nineteenth-century dress. Created as early as 1907, the Delphos was a long, simply cut, pleated silk dress that hung loosely from the shoulders and could be scrunched up into a ball for travelling. In an age when most women were tightly corseted and fitted, it represented a liberation, summed up best in photos from the period of the celebrated dancer Isadora Duncan in lithe, free-flowing garments. Fortuny recognised the importance of the Delphos, patenting one of the designs (with batwing sleeves) in Paris in 1909. Fortuny brought the worlds of art and fashion close together, as did his contemporary Sonia Delaunay. The interrelationship between art and fashion has been a theme in popular culture ever since, explored in the modern-day era by a host of designers, most recently led by Raf Simons.

Mariano Fortuny y Madrazo was born in Granada, Spain, in 1871 into a family full of artists and blessed with plenty of money. His father, Mariano, a distinguished painter, had married Cecilia de Madrazo, also from a family of artists. From 1872, they lived in Rome, where his father had a studio, and Paris. Mariano's father died of malaria in 1874 at the age of only thirty-six, a loss that grieved the son throughout his life (he edited a book on his father as late as 1933). Besides the skills of a painter, Mariano inherited from his father a taste for collecting antiques and objets d'art from exotic places, particularly the Arab world. The family collection included a treasure trove of textiles, often displayed as wall hangings.

After his father's death, the family moved to Paris, where Fortuny began painting at the age of seven. He absorbed the work of the Old Masters, such as Rubens, learning the importance of colour

Image 5.1 *Mrs William Wetmore in Fortuny gown,* Vogue, *1935. Photo: Lusha Nelson/Condé Nast via Getty Images.*

that stood him in good stead in the future. The young Fortuny was plagued with asthma and hay fever in Paris, brought on by an allergic reaction to horses. So, in 1889, his mother moved with him and his sister, Maria Luisa, to horse-free Venice and the Palazzo Martinengo on the Grand Canal. Venice remained his base for the rest of his life. He attended night classes at the Accademia in Venice to improve his drawing and continued to copy the Old Masters, including Tintoretto and other great Venetian artists. Further inspiration came from a visit in 1892 to Bayreuth, home of opera composer Richard Wagner. The grand all-embracing vision of Wagner inspired Fortuny, who immersed himself in the world of theatre for many years, developing new lighting systems. Fortuny was as much technician as artist. All art forms had merit in his vision, and everything could be harnessed by the artist.

In 1897, Fortuny met a young Frenchwoman, Henriette Negrin, in Paris. Despite his mother's lifelong disapproval (Henriette was a divorcee), Fortuny adored her for the rest of his life as wife, lover, companion and muse. She moved to Venice in 1902, by which time Fortuny had relocated to his own home, the Palazzo Pesaro Orfei. This splendid thirteenth-century palazzo, built on a truly Wagnerian scale, was the perfect stage for Fortuny to develop his ideas and inventions and display his antiques collection (today, it is a museum, Palazzo Fortuny). A vast salon-studio was at the heart of the palazzo, though the private rooms were relatively small and simple. Here, Fortuny was able to play the host. A tall man with piercing blue eyes, he wore lightweight suits in dark blue serge with a white silk cravat and cut a dash in Venice, where a new generation of artists had been emerging since the 1880s. There was a sizeable foreign colony, attracted by this most romantic of cities. He got to know Italy's leading literary star, Gabriele D'Annunzio, whom he met for the first time in 1894.

However, any attempt to locate Fortuny within the context of artistic movements of the time is tricky because the man himself largely ignored the work of his contemporaries and rarely stepped outside Venice. His biographer, Guillermo de Osma, situated him most convincingly within the Aesthetic Movement, whose exponents thought clothing had become a prison. The Aesthete painters looked back for inspiration to classical Greece and the Middle Ages (the dress of that period was particularly admired by the Pre-Raphaelites). But these clothes were only featured in their paintings and never realised, with the single exception of some toga satin dresses produced by Liberty's of London, inspired by the work of Sir Lawrence Alma-Tadema.

Fortuny's move into the world of textiles and fashion is thought to have begun in 1906 by experimenting with the printing of textiles at his palazzo. Some sketches for a play, *Francesca da Rimini*, were turned into costumes, receiving a lukewarm response. More promising were costumes for a ballet in Paris in the same year featuring his distinctive silk veils printed with geometric designs inspired by Cycladic art. These became known as Knossos scarves, which was a touch misleading because they were rectangular pieces of silk that could be used in all sorts of ways, as much clothing as accessory. They remained a feature of his work for more than fifteen years. 'From these simple scarves, which showed him how to fuse form and fabric, Fortuny developed his entire production of dresses,' wrote his biographer Guillermo de Osma.

The Knossos scarf was most impressively worn over the celebrated Delphos Dress. Fortuny's patent registration described it thus: 'Its design is so shaped and arranged that it can be worn and adjusted with ease and comfort.' To this day, there is some mystery over how Fortuny created the pleating on the dress. The folds are irregular and were probably developed by applying heat while the material was wet. With the exception of hand-blown glass beads from Murano, everything was made by hand at the palazzo. To counter the stretchiness of the pleats, Fortuny sewed cords strung with beads along the sides of his dresses.

Fortuny began with silk, usually bought raw and in off-white and imported direct from China and Japan; later he added velvet, imported from Lyons. Both silk and velvet were used in countless variations. He experimented enthusiastically with printing, using wood blocks initially, then introducing hand-painting and developing his own high-quality stencils made of silk. He created his own colours, exploring ingredients from many sources and countries. Kennedy Fraser, writing in *The New Yorker* in 1981, commented: 'The colors that Fortuny created are still rare and luscious after the passage of decades: blushing peach and apricot, purple grape and candlelit claret, blue of fountains and of peacocks' tails.'

Fortuny was never recognised as a creator of fashion by the couturiers in Paris. In the early years, his dresses were worn only at home, considered far too louche for formal outdoors wear. He stood outside the rigidly controlled couture system and chose instead to develop his own sales and marketing operation. This included a ground-floor shop at the palazzo and a small network of shops and sales

Image 5.2 *Fortuny in his studio, with an assistant, 1890s. Photo: Mondadori Portfolio via Getty Images.*

agents across Europe. Two of the literary giants of the period did their best to create an aura around Fortuny's work. Marcel Proust refers to Fortuny no less than sixteen times in his novel *A la Recherche du Temps Perdu*. Gabriele D'Annunzio referenced Fortuny beautifully for one of his fictional heroines, the Marchesa Casati Stampa: 'She was enveloped in one of those very long scarves of Oriental Gauze that the alchemist Mariano Fortuny plunges into the mysterious dyes of his vats and withdraws tinted with strange dreams, and with his thousand hand-printing blocks marks new generations for stars, planets, animals.'

In 1909, the arrival of Diaghilev's Ballets Russes in Paris marked the increasing dominance of Aesthete modes of dress; the costumes by Bakst were clearly inspired by Fortuny. Bakst had seen Isadora Duncan perform in a Fortuny dress on a tour of Russia back in 1906. Bakst reinterpreted her dress with loose, liberating costumes for at least three ballets in 1911 and 1912. This tribute turned out to be of great benefit to Fortuny, for it popularised his designs and boosted his order book to such an extent that he eventually opened a shop in Paris in 1920 at 67 rue Pierre Charron, not far from Paul Poiret. The ornate interior of the palazzo was meticulously recreated. It seems likely that Poiret himself was influenced by the work of Fortuny; a green silk chiffon tunic made by Fortuny was sold in Poiret's shop as early as 1908. Other names who drew on the work of Fortuny included Maria Monaci Gallenga in Rome and Madame Babani in Paris.

By the early 1920s, fashion had moved on from the influence of the classical period, but Fortuny's emphasis on clothing the natural form chimed with the mood of the times. As Fraser Kennedy has noted, before the First World War, Fortuny's clothes essentially carried on the tradition of idealistic and artistic female dress begun with the Aesthetes and Pre-Raphaelites. 'After the war, they seemed liberated, even slightly naughty, and totally modern attire for wear to cocktail parties in the Jazz Age.' That said, Fortuny continued to stand aside from the fashion industry. At the celebrated Art Deco exhibition of 1925 in Paris, Fortuny did not even show in the fashion pavilion.

The decade proved a period of spectacular success for the designer, fuelled by the opening of a factory for cotton textile production on the island of Giudecca near Venice, using long-staple Egyptian cotton spun in England. More significant in the long term than the opening of the Paris shop was the addition of a stockist in New York from 1923. The Brick Shop ordered Fortuny's cotton fabrics, which became popular interior furnishings for the elite of Manhattan. The silk and velvet dresses, meanwhile, achieved a classic status that reflected their classical inspiration. Looking back on the decade, Lady Bonham-Carter commented: 'I think everyone I knew had a Fortuny dress. … We all wore them, especially the "gels" with good figures. They clung a bit, you see, and they weren't quite so perfect on lumpy figures.'

The Great Depression of 1929 marked the beginning of hard times for Fortuny. He found crucial support from American interior decorator Elsie McNeill, later the Countess Elsie Lee Gozzi, who bought the rights to sell Fortuny in 1927 and opened a shop at 509 Madison Avenue. In quick succession, Fortuny endured the death of his mother in 1932 and the receivership of his Giudecca factory in 1933. Somehow, he found the funds to buy the factory out of receivership himself. His sister Maria Luisa died in 1936, a troubled year in his homeland, with the Spanish Civil War under way. Elsie Lee continued to market Fortuny effectively in America, financing the rebuilding of the Giudecca factory. However, the advent of the Second World War forced its closure again. When it reopened after the war, it was on a much-reduced scale. Fortuny's final years, until his death in 1949, saw his wealth significantly diminished.

During the 1950s, Fortuny's work was virtually forgotten, although from the 1960s and 1970s museums began to acquire his dresses and the word spread among costume collectors. The real explosion of interest in Fortuny dates from the 1980s, when the house of Fortuny was also acquired by the Riad family (the current creative director is Mickey Riad; it designs fabrics, furniture and lighting). These days, Fortuny's status in the roll call of great designers is assured. His ability to thrive outside the fashion system of Paris makes him a very special case. Customers treasured their Fortuny dresses and returned time and time again, developing an emotional attachment to the clothes. Throughout his career, Fortuny worked with a handful of simple ideas and shapes developed in many different variations. It is famously hard to date his dresses because the themes did not evolve in a logical sequence, instead mutating according to his own interest. His biographer, Guillermo de Osma, wrote: 'Fortuny invented fashion outside fashion, fashion that does not change, fashion as art.'

Further reading: Guillermo de Osma's biography, *Fortuny* (1984, updated edition), did much to remind the modern era of Fortuny's talents. *Peacock and Vine: Fortuny and Morris in Life and at Work* (2016), by novelist AS Byatt, evocatively explores connections between the designer and William Morris.

Part Two

1910s–1930s

Image 5.3 *Delphos Fortuny dress, 1948. Photo: Chicago History Museum via Getty Images.*

Image 6.1 *Lanvin, dinner dress, from* Les Modes, *1909. Photo: Henri Manuel/Mansell/The LIFE Picture Collection via Getty Images.*

6

Jeanne Lanvin (1867–1946)

Lanvin ran her business like a modern designer: the Lanvin story is a case study in brand management.

The founder of the oldest surviving couture house in near-continuous existence, Jeanne Lanvin was established as one of the most commercially successful couturières in Paris by the 1920s. Until recently, she has been neglected by fashion historians: her romantic, nostalgic approach to design was considered backward looking, contrasting with the resolutely modern styles of Gabrielle Chanel or Jean Patou. Renewed interest in Lanvin was boosted partly by the success of Central Saint Martins-trained designer Alber Elbaz, from Israel, at the helm of the design studio from 2001 to 2015, but more fundamentally by the research of fashion historians such as Nancy Troy, who treats commercial achievements with the same seriousness as creative influence (and, indeed, explores the interlinkage between the two). And, although Jeanne Lanvin does not fall easily within the conventional narrative of the development of modern fashion design, her success raises important questions about the very nature of that narrative, highlighting the nostalgic and retrospective characteristics of much of the greatest fashion.

What is not in doubt is that Jeanne Lanvin made exquisitely beautiful clothes that celebrated traditional concepts of femininity. Her finest designs were her *robes de style*, full-skirted evening dresses typically in silk taffeta that looked back to the eighteenth century and were a reaction to the garçonne look of the 1920s. Renowned as a sensitive colourist, she created her own Lanvin blue and through her dye-works developed a palette of harmony and exceptional delicacy. Lanvin was a pragmatic designer who responded to the varied needs of a woman's wardrobe and delivered time after time what her customers sought most. Furthermore, she created modern children's fashion, designing clothes specifically for her daughter, Marguerite. But her influence on fashion history has less to do with pure design and more to do with the evolution of the concept of a designer as it is known today. She ran her business like a modern designer: the Lanvin story is a case study in brand management and development that still has lessons for today's designer brands. She researched like a modern designer, scanning museums, art galleries, history books and any resource that might provide inspiration.

Lanvin was also a lifestyle designer, creating a sophisticated fashion house that covered a broad array of products, invariably brilliantly marketed. The achievement is all the more remarkable because the couturière was a retiring, taciturn woman, reluctant to meet her clients. This reticence should not, however, be confused with a lack of confidence. She had an iron will and a strong belief in her own abilities, based on a long apprenticeship and thorough immersion in her craft.

Born in 1867, Jeanne-Marie Lanvin was the eldest of ten children fathered by Constantin Bernard Lanvin, a staunchly middle-class journalist. In the manner of the times, she was in employment from the age of thirteen, initially as a dressmaker's errand girl. She was careful with her money from an early age: one story recounts how, when asked to deliver parcels and given the fare for taking a bus, she chose to run behind the bus and save the money. She worked for most of her teen years as an apprentice milliner at Madame Felix in the rue du Faubourg Saint-Honoré, followed by a spell at Talbot, a dressmaker, where she learned about fabrics, before setting up her own hat workshop at the age of just eighteen, initially in the rue du Marché Saint-Honoré. Saving money from a three-month stint working for a Barcelona-based dressmaker, Madame Maria-Berta Valenti, Lanvin opened her own millinery shop in 1890 at 16 rue Boissy d'Anglas.

In 1895, Lanvin married the Italian nobleman Henri Emile-Georges di Pietro, their initial encounter predictably occurring at the Longchamp racetrack, one of the primary locations for the fashion-aware to strut and court in late nineteenth-century Paris. Although the marriage lasted only eight years, it did result in the birth of a daughter, Marguerite Marie-Blanche, in 1897, who was dressed more beautifully than perhaps any child in history by her adoring mother. In 1907, four years after her divorce, Lanvin married again, this time to Xavier Melet, a journalist like her father, who later became French consul in Manchester, England. This marriage was businesslike, rather than romantic, with Melet playing the role of loyal husband. It meant that Lanvin was no longer a single mother, which then had a status of some social shame.

Focusing initially on millinery, Lanvin's business grew organically, each achievement leading logically to the next. Clients' admiration for her dresses for Marguerite encouraged her to open a children's department by 1908. A year later, it made sense to extend this to women's clothing too, creating empire-waist chemise frocks in Fauvist colours and showing an assured use of black and white. She also emphasised her ambition by swiftly joining the Syndicat de la Couture. The First World War proved little more than an interlude in the development of the young fashion house; by the end of 1918 Lanvin had secured the entire building at 33 rue du Faubourg Saint-Honoré, comprising nine workshops, including two for embroidery – an innovation as this highly skilled work was usually passed on to outsiders, who had both motivation and opportunity to plagiarise. Keeping embroidery in-house did not solve the problem of copying, although it did prove over time to be a shrewd business move. Lanvin's exquisite beadwork was at the heart of the fashion house's reputation in the 1920s and beyond.

Lanvin visited America as early as 1915, so she was well aware of the opportunities across the Atlantic for her house to grow. Her instinct for business was finely tuned, developing steadily through the 1920s but always closely monitored with a strong personal touch that gave Lanvin the stamp of heartfelt authenticity. By the 1920s, Lanvin was a wealthy woman, commissioning Armand-Albert Rateau to design her shops at 15 and 22 rue du Faubourg Saint-Honoré as well as her town house at rue Barbet-de-Jouy and her villa at Vésinet. Rateau became a friend, designing the spherical bottle of Lanvin's celebrated Arpège fragrance in 1927 and managing her Lanvin-Sport business. With Rateau, she created Art Deco-inspired decorative objects for the home. Her bedroom, boudoir and bathroom, commissioned from Rateau, are now installed at the Musée des Arts Décoratifs in Paris. Her daughter, Marguerite Marie-Blanche, was a true muse to her, always immaculately dressed in clothes that were both beautiful and practical. Previously, children from society families used to wear watered-down versions of adult clothing, but by 1921 Lanvin's influence on children's fashion was noted by *Vogue* – 'loose and simple clothes … easy to put on and take off again'. Through the 1920s, Lanvin attracted many actresses, including Mary Pickford, the American silent screen star, and Yvonne Printemps, for whom she designed costumes. A stage set was created in her atelier for fittings for costumes. The year 1923 saw Lanvin create costumes for seventeen shows.

In 1924, Lanvin's daughter married the Comte Jean de Polignac, and she shortened her name to Marie-Blanche. This event was more than personal: it took Jeanne Lanvin and her family into a new social circle, elevating her status with knock-on benefits for the business. The Polignac family became important customers, adding social cachet to the company. A year later, Lanvin herself was made Chevalier de la Légion d'Honneur in recognition of her achievements. While Chanel and Patou stole

Image 6.2 *Lanvin, evening gown,* Vogue, *1935. Photo: Christian Berard/Condé Nast via Getty Images.*

the headlines, Lanvin simply went on expanding, with clothes that were beautiful and renowned for their exceptionally intricate seaming, beading and embroidery. Her career might, indeed, be hailed as the ultimate celebration of the work of *les petites mains,* the French name for the hard-working women who laboured in the couture workshops of Paris.

Lanvin had a number of signature touches, including a penchant for ribbons flowing at the hip, spiralling ruffles and taffeta applied to tulle for a floaty romantic effect. Flowers, ribbons and sunbursts were repetitive motifs that she adored. Over the years, she built up a memory bank of motifs, including the daisy (or marguerite) that was her daughter's keep-sake, a series of three-part Japanese *mons* (family crests) and symbols that reflected her Catholic faith. 'A design inevitably reflects the artistic motifs stored in one's memory,' she said, 'drawing on those which are the most alive, new and fertile all at the same time.' Her *robes de style* were produced throughout the 1920s, in defiance of the rise of the flapper or garçonne, and right up to the late 1930s, when wartime austerity frowned on such lavish use of fabric. Artist Paul Iribe sketched Lanvin and her daughter in *robes de styles* (the sketch was actually based on a 1907 photograph), a sweet image that was refined by Armand-Albert Rateau to become the Lanvin signature, reproduced on labels.

Lanvin herself was already well into her fifties when the 1920s dawned. Thus, she was not strictly a contemporary of Chanel. Decades later, Karl Lagerfeld said: 'Her image was not as strong as that of Chanel because she was a nice old lady and not a fashion plate.' Looking at it from another perspective, it might also be instructive to compare Jeanne Lanvin's achievement in building a business founded on her own financial means and unrelenting hard work with Chanel's opportunism as mistress to a succession of wealthy lovers who certainly smoothed her path to fortune. As biographer Dean Merceron puts it, which of them is the greater exemplar for the modern woman? Although Chanel was the ultimate modernist, obsessed with function, Lanvin did not believe in creating clothes that were too practical. 'Modern clothes need a certain romantic feel,' she argued, reflecting her teenage years in Belle Époque Paris. Couturières, she said, 'should take care not to become too everyday and practical'. Speaking to *Vogue* in 1934, she said: 'I act on impulse and believe in instinct. My dresses aren't premeditated. I am carried away by feeling and technical knowledge helps me make my clothes become a reality.'

Her business strategy was, by contrast, thoroughly practical, exploring every opportunity that presented itself. Shops were created for home decor, menswear, furs and lingerie – a true retail empire. Thinking ahead, Lanvin invested in a company-owned dye factory in Nanterre as early as 1923, responding to the demand for her colours. Silver was often combined with black, or with an array of colours that included soft pinks, greens and blues. Above all, there was the Lanvin blue, a pretty lavender blue. These colours were researched intensively: Lanvin blue was most likely inspired by the blues in Fra Angelico frescoes, and other colours reflected her favourite artists, such as Édouard Vuillard, Pierre-Auguste Renoir and Odilon Redon (all of whom she collected). Lanvin was an avid collector throughout her life, assembling a remarkable array of paintings, sculptures, fabrics, exotic clothes and libraries, catalogued and recorded with the meticulous precision that was her hallmark. Much of her collection was auctioned in Paris in September 2006, highlighting the diversity and richness of her interests, particularly her fascination with Japonism. Novelist Elizabeth Barille writes: 'She was like a bee, tasting everything in order to make her exceptionally delicious honey.'

The outbreak of the Second World War also marked the declining years of Lanvin herself, by then in her seventies. The continuity sustained at the house of Lanvin is one of its greatest achievements. After her death in 1946, the company was run by family members for several decades, going through a number of different owners (including L'Oréal) before turning private in 2001 under investment group Harmonie, headed by a Taiwanese media businesswoman. The sensitive, intuitive designer Alber Elbaz, who acknowledged the inspiration he garnered from the Lanvin archive, gave a new creative impetus to the house, but another change of ownership and his departure in 2015 marked a new period of turbulence with designers coming and going. An exhibition at the Palais Galiera, Paris, in 2015 was judged a magnificent retrospective of Jeanne Lanvin's achievements.

Further reading: Jeanne Lanvin's career is well illustrated and documented in Dean L. Merceron's *Lanvin* (2007). An introduction by Harold Koda analyses in detail why Lanvin has been overlooked by fashion historians. Elizabeth Barille's *Lanvin* (1997) is a concise introduction to her work. *Lanvin*, the catalogue to the exhibition at the Palais Galiera, is available only in French.

Image 6.3 *Jeanne Lanvin at a fitting, 1930s. Photo: Laure Albin-Guillot/Roger Viollet via Getty Images.*

7

Gabrielle 'Coco' Chanel (1883–1971)

Chanel had an exceptional ability to sense change in the air.

The most celebrated fashion designer in history, Gabrielle ('Coco') Chanel continues to be treated with reverence nearly fifty years after her death. No designer can match her for influence on the modern women's wardrobe. No designer, with the exception of Karl Lagerfeld, inheritor of her mantle at the house of Chanel, has thrived for so long. Her Parisian fashion house was launched as early as 1915, reached remarkable heights in the 1920s and 1930s and blossomed once again in the 1950s and 1960s.

Mademoiselle, as she was always called by her employees, took concepts from sportswear and men's clothing and turned them into practical, effortlessly elegant clothes for women, launching her revolution at a time when women's fashion was so overwrought that many wealthy women could not dress themselves without assistance. Her early contemporaries recognised her achievements through gritted teeth. For Paul Poiret, Chanel's clothes were 'miserabilisme de luxe'. While he explored bright colours and great swathes of fabric, Chanel pared down her design message time and time again. Call it functional chic; she was synonymous with the concept that 'less is more'. She did not sketch, preferring to work directly on a model's body, with sessions often lasting many hours with no break. Photographer Cecil Beaton, lunching with her in the twilight of her career in 1965, recalls the way she moulded the napkins in the restaurant. He was captivated by this small woman with hard black eyes who spoke in a torrent of words. Publisher and journalist John Fairchild watched Chanel at the age of eighty cut an armhole on a live model, drawing blood.

To her artist connections, she was often extravagantly generous. In the atelier and with her employees, she was tough, demanding and ruthless – qualities that won her few friends and made her increasingly isolated in later life. Money, and the making of money, certainly transfixed her, giving her

Image 7.1 *Coco Chanel at home, 1929. Photo: Sasha via Getty Images.*

the independence she cherished so much. 'She possessed the wily foxiness of a country horse trader,' her lawyer Robert Chaillet said.

But there was something more to Chanel. She had an exceptional ability to sense change in the air, an attribute common to the handful of designers who were influential throughout their careers. 'Fashion is something in the air,' she said. 'You feel it coming, you smell it.'

Her life story is as remarkable as her talents as a designer. She was born Gabrielle Chanel, the illegitimate daughter of market traders, in a poor-house hospice in Saumur in 1883. Her mother died when she was only twelve, so the young Gabrielle spent much of her childhood in an orphanage near Brive-la-Gaillarde. At the age of eighteen she was accepted as a charity student at a convent boarding school in Moulins and attracted attention for her striking looks, particularly her elegant long neck and deep black eyes. Local trader Henri Desboutin hired her as a shop assistant in his lingerie and hosiery shop. Chanel sang for a while at a local music hall, La Rotonde, where she gained the name Coco, after a lost dog in a popular song of the time. She was boosted in her early career by the support of a succession of wealthy and well-connected lovers; these connections also permitted her to rise far beyond the social status usually associated with dressmakers or couturiers. Her first lover, Etienne Balsan, owned an estate in Royallieu, where she lived for several years: he subsidised her first solo business selling hats from his apartment on boulevard Malesherbes. There then followed a passionate liaison with Captain Arthur Capel, known as Boy, an English playboy and polo player. He financed her first project in the rue Cambon, the Paris street that has become synonymous with her name. A small hat shop opened in 1910, followed by a boutique in the seaside resort of Deauville in 1913, selling knit separates and dresses. Biographers agree that Boy was the big love of her life; his death in a car crash in 1919 was a devastating blow.

Her rise to fame was rapid and based on applying her own pared-down personal style to her business. That style was founded on knits and flannels, materials generally considered only appropriate for sports clothing. In later life, she liked to say her fortune was built on an old jersey jumper borrowed from Boy that she had customised by snipping through the front to create a cardigan. She borrowed ideas heavily from men's clothing, ransacking her lovers' wardrobes for inspiration, dressing her adolescent-boy physique in clothes that had been endlessly reworked to achieve the perfect fit. In her personal life, men brought her both great happiness and sadness. But in her professional life, there was no contest: magazine editor Alexander Liberman believed she learned all her sense of elegance from men.

By 1915, she had opened a fashion house in Biarritz, subsidised by Boy. A year later, she produced her first full collection, unveiled in Biarritz to immediate and widespread acclaim. It included her take on a men's sweater, with the neckline cut lower and a ribbon through the buttonholes, paired with a pleated skirt. Also included was a khaki jersey skirt suit with a jacket shape like a male army jacket. It should be remembered that this was wartime, when practical dressing was de rigueur. A year after the First World War ended, Chanel officially registered as a couturière and set up at 31 rue Cambon, where the house of Chanel is still located today. Together with Jean Patou, whose contribution has been underestimated, she brought simplicity and practicality to fashion in the 1920s. She blew away the ostentation of Belle Époque fashion, producing accessible clothes that continued to borrow heavily from the working man's wardrobe. The youthful energy and vigour of Chanel's clothes chimed with the open-air sports-obsessed mood of the times.

In the early 1920s, she was the arch exponent of the garçonne or flapper look, the boyish style that dominated the decade. Her women wore sweaters, short pleated skirts with dropped waistlines and cloche hats. Boni de Castellane, a Parisian dandy, said: 'Women no longer exist. All that's left are the boys created by Chanel.' The little black dress, a reaction to Paul Poiret's Orientalist colours and derived from the chemise dress, was a signature piece. Previously, black was for mourning clothes only; Chanel made it chic. Black and white, for her, created a 'perfect harmony'. In 1926, American *Vogue* made a celebrated comparison with the Ford motor car: 'Here is Ford signed Chanel – the frock that all the world will wear.' After the shock of Boy's death in 1919, Chanel dallied briefly with the Grand Duke Dmitri of Russia, picking up a penchant for all things Russian, including oversized pieces of jewellery, that fed into her collections. Perhaps more important was her friendship (and on-off romance) with Misia Sert, a well-connected society hostess with a fiery temperament to match Chanel's own mercurial personality. Sert had friends scattered throughout the art world, such as Cocteau, Picasso, Diaghilev and Stravinsky. The quick-witted Chanel adapted quickly to this milieu, and the two women enjoyed a long-lasting love-hate friendship.

Her love life continued to flourish, culminating in an intense relationship with the Duke of Westminster, known to his friends as Bendor, the richest man in Britain. She admired his British tweeds, which she

Image 7.2 *Chanel tweed suit,* Vogue, *1962. Photo: Horst P. Horst/Condé Nast via Getty Images.*

turned into coats for her customers, trimmed with fur for a luxurious and softer look. She even created flared trousers inspired by the sailors' bell-bottoms on Bendor's yacht. Meanwhile, he widened her social circle to include dignitaries on both sides of the channel, most notably Winston Churchill. All the riches of the world were now hers to enjoy; nothing and no one was beyond her orbit. The orphan girl had come a long way. But the Duke chose to marry elsewhere in 1930, leaving Chanel alone again. Her solution was to plough herself into her work. During the 1930s, the house of Chanel achieved new heights, with a team of some 4,000 employees and production of up to 28,000 dresses a year. A brief flirtation with Hollywood aside, Chanel was based in Paris, where she slept at her suite in the Ritz hotel and received guests in her apartment in the rue Cambon. A fierce rivalry with Elsa Schiaparelli, both personal and professional, gave a competitive edge to her work. Yet another lover, the illustrator and designer Paul Iribe, held out hope of marriage once again. However, after four years together, he died of a heart attack in 1935, collapsing right before her at their holiday home in Roquebrune in the south of France.

The advent of war with Germany in 1939 created hardship for all the Paris couturiers. Chanel's business solution was to close the couture house but to keep open the boutique, selling only her celebrated Chanel No. 5 scent and accessories. Her personal solution – finding a German lover, Hans Gunther von Dincklage, who was both a diplomat and a spy – proved an unmitigated disaster. As biographer Rhonda K. Garelick makes clear, Chanel was attracted by Nazi authoritarianism and had anti-semitic views. She even tried to use her Nazi relationships to wrest her fragrance business away from the Wertheimers, the Jewish family that owned the rights to her scent and had escaped to America. When the war ended, Chanel was arrested, accused of treachery and forced into exile in Switzerland. For years, with her personal reputation in tatters, she mooched around Lausanne with occasional visits to Paris. Not until 1954, at the age of seventy, did she astonish the Paris fashion world by announcing her comeback.

Dwindling sales of Chanel No. 5 prompted the Wertheimers to make an extraordinary offer to Chanel. She would sell the house of Chanel to them, while they in return would pay all her bills for the rest of her life. With the deal sewn up, Chanel set about recapturing the magic of her pre-war house. The first show, staged on 5 February 1954 and attended by an adolescent Karl Lagerfeld, was not an instant success. The collection was like a 'time warp', recalled one junior American *Vogue* editor. But Bettina Ballard, then editor of French *Vogue*, felt differently. Her eye was caught by a navy blue wool-jersey suit that, she felt, summed up Chanel's style. The jacket had square shoulders and was lightly padded with patch pockets and sleeves that unbuttoned to reveal white cuffs. The Chanel suit remains one of the great creations of modern fashion. The armhole was crucial, always small and high, constantly reshaped by Chanel herself to create a close fit. This emphasised the slenderness and fragility of the wearer's shoulders and neck. Another internal detail, a gold chain sewn into the hems of the jacket, ensured that the jacket hung straight and did not ride up. The essential accessories included a hat, flesh-coloured stockings and two-toned sling-back shoes. As for jewellery, Chanel did not stint, from her trademark strings of pearls to her enjoyment in mixing both fake and real, which appears particularly modern from a twenty-first-century perspective.

Within three collections, Chanel had made a spectacular comeback. The girl who came from nowhere now made the suit that every young high-society woman chose to wear. The suit was copied relentlessly in America and Europe, bringing Chanel style to a generation of women who could not afford couture prices. In her later years, Chanel became a French icon. She surrounded herself with her cabinet of young models and a close-knit circle of trusted friends and servants. Many of the celebrated Chanel maxims emerged from the 1960s, such as: 'A woman's education consists of two lessons: never to leave the house without stockings, never to go out without a hat.'

It is doubtful that the young Chanel, who broke through so many traditions back in the 1920s, would have had much time for such stipulations. But the old Chanel had come full circle, now locked in her own legend. Since her death in 1971, at the age of eighty-eight, that legend has remained intact, while the house of Chanel, led creatively by Karl Lagerfeld from 1983 to 2019 (followed by Virginie Viard and Eric Pfrunder), has continued to flourish. Her status as an outsider may hold the key to her success. As Katell Le Bourhis, director of the Musée des Arts de la Mode et du Textile, in Paris, put it: 'She had no references, no education, no upbringing, so she was free to invent her own rules of dress.'

Further reading: There is a wealth of writing on Chanel, from Edmonde Charles-Roux's early biography, *Chanel* (1976), to Alice Mackrell's *Coco Chanel* (1992) and *Mademoiselle: Coco Chanel and the Pulse of History* (2014) by Rhonda K. Garelick. Harold Koda and Andrew Bolton's *Chanel* (2005), the catalogue to the Chanel exhibition at the Metropolitan Museum of Art in New York, has some illuminating essays. *The Allure of Chanel*, by Paul Morand (translated by Euan Cameron in 2008), is also of interest.

Image 7.3 *Coco Chanel, 1936. Photo: Lipnitzki/Roger Viollet via Getty Images.*

8

Jean Patou (1880–1936)

A Patou design was so beautifully cut that you lived in it until it wore out.

Often overshadowed in his lifetime and beyond by his arch-rival Coco Chanel, French designer Jean Patou was equally influential during his heyday, which can be precisely traced from the end of the First World War in 1918 through to the Great Crash of 1929. Perhaps, like Chanel, he might have made a glorious comeback, but he died relatively young and impoverished by his great vice – gambling.

Of all his many achievements, his development of sportswear for women is perhaps the most significant. In 1921, he dressed the tennis player Suzanne Lenglen at Wimbledon in a straight white sleeveless cardigan and a short white silk pleated skirt, creating an instant sensation. This boyish, sporty look – known as the garçonne – was a dominant image of women's fashion for much of the decade, reflecting an era when women were enjoying freedom as never before, including the freedom to exercise, sunbathe and show off their legs. The extent of this influence may have been exaggerated, recent research suggests. Certainly, as with so much sportswear, many of the clothes were in reality bought by women who did not participate in sport and were more interested in showing off their Patou monogrammed cardigan sweaters to their envious friends. Patou knew this well enough, ensuring that his swimsuits, launched in the mid-1920s, included practical styles in shrink-resistant fabrics for real bathers *and* styles more suited for social display on the beach.

He never married but had, it appears, countless affairs and liaisons, living the life of a playboy. His perceptive biographer, Meredith Etherington-Smith, points out that Patou's boyish women contrasted curiously with his own voracious heterosexual appetites. 'Perhaps it was simply because Patou was not deeply involved with one woman that he was able to view women objectively, yet with a sympathy that enabled him, with an obvious sensitivity, to create clothes that combined the new spirit of freedom and yet appealed to men.' If there was a muse, it was his sister, Madeleine Patou, in the early post-war years, although Lenglen and other sportswomen and actresses also came to fulfil that role. Madeleine's

Image 8.1 *Jean Patou on board, 1925. Photo: APIC via Getty Images.*

10

Elsa Schiaparelli (1890–1973)

Even now, her best work is startlingly, thrillingly modern.

Art met fashion head-on in the form of Elsa Schiaparelli, an Italian designer who came to fashion late and proved a breath of fresh air in a world often caught up in its own high seriousness. She was a surrealist by instinct, with a playful ability to change the predictable into the unpredictable. To the surrealists, one might also add the Italian futurists, whose verve, speed and joie de vivre excited the young Schiaparelli. All this energy was encapsulated in the intense pink – shocking pink – that became her hallmark. 'Bright, impossible, impudent, becoming, life-giving, like all the light and the birds and the fish in the world put together … a shocking colour,' she said with suitable hyperbole in an autobiography that shares some surreal characteristics of her design work.

Even now, her best work is startlingly, thrillingly modern. Choose from the crossword-puzzle sweaters and zippered dresses, the knitted hats and costume jewellery, the culottes and jumpsuits, the experimentation with new synthetic fabrics, and, above all, the bold way with colours. Her celebrated tear dress, made from a fabric designed by Salvador Dali, created the illusion of material that had been ripped: to modern eyes, it looks thoroughly Punk in spirit. Ignorance was bliss for this untrained fashion designer. Rules were there to break, and Schiaparelli enjoyed upsetting the bourgeoisie. 'Madame Schiaparelli trampled down everything that was commonplace,' said Yves Saint Laurent, who dressed her and adored her. She was, said biographer Palmer White, 'a gifted bull in a china shop'. Meanwhile, her arch-rival, Chanel, derided her as 'that Italian who's making clothes'.

Schiaparelli was from a conventional enough background, born in Rome in 1890, the daughter of Celestino, a Piedmontese intellectual who was in charge of Rome's historic Lincei Library. Her mother, Maria Luisa, was from an aristocratic family in Naples. She spent her childhood in Rome's Palazzo Corsini, surrounded by art and history, growing up with a surfeit of potential inspiration about her. A sensitive, shy young girl, she initially experimented with poetry and published her first book at the age of twenty. The passionate subject matter shocked her father, who promptly dispatched

Image 10.1 *Schiaparelli dress,* Vogue, *1947. Photo: Horst P. Horst/Condé Nast via Getty Images.*

as its products, including an enormous stuffed bear dyed shocking pink by Salvador Dali with drawers inserted in its stomach. By now, she had 600 employees producing 10,000 pieces a year, promoted through two major and two minor collections a year.

Her willingness to experiment with fabric is the less-appreciated story of her career. Schiaparelli worked with rayon and nylon, paper and Cellophane, even rubber and latex. In 1934, she created glass-look tunics that were fashioned from a synthetic called Rhodophane. Even more conventional fabrics were used in unconventional ways. Tweeds were introduced to evening wear, a waterproof taffeta was explored for raincoats, and cotton was passed off as linen. After her retirement, she was quick to appreciate the emerging influence of denim. Every detail required rethinking by Schiaparelli, who derided the mundane. Her buttons, for instance, were legendary. 'The most incredible things were used,' she recalled later in life. 'Animals and feathers, caricatures and paperweights, chains, locks, clips and lollipops. Some were of wood and others of plastic, but not one looked like what a button was supposed to look like.'

Although Schiaparelli breezed through the challenges of the Great Depression, the same could not be said of the Second World War. She hung on in Paris for a while, producing a series of underrated but inspired collections that made the best of the shortage of materials and responded to the mood of the times for functional, practical clothes. Her most recent biographer, Meryle Secrest, reveals that Schiaparelli was treading a fine line (at the very least) in occupied France with friends who were Vichy officials. In May 1941, on the advice of the American consul, she left Paris and spent most of the war in America, where she worked as a fund-raiser and nurse, but was kept under surveillance by the FBI.

With the end of the war, Schiaparelli hoped to pick up where she had left off, but Christian Dior's New Look swept most of the pre-war designers away. The hint of collaboration with France's Vichy government also hung over her. Furthermore, Schiaparelli's weaknesses – a tendency to overstate, a reliance on gimmicks – were exposed. Surrealism, the force that inspired her best work, had peaked. A series of collections in the 1940s were politely but not enthusiastically received. The spirit of innovation was still there, such as her Constellation travel coat and bag for the new generation of air travellers, but her timing was off. Post-war women wanted escapism and a return to traditional femininity.

Only in America, a country that Schiaparelli had come to know well during prolonged residences in the early 1920s and early 1940s, did she appear to retain the same magical touch. In 1949 she opened a branch of her company at 530 Seventh Avenue, New York City, to mass produce suits, dresses and coats. Her 'shortie' jackets, Pyramid line of coats and shocking pink lingerie were all well received. Back home in France, the business continued to bleed financially into the early 1950s. Despite this, she went on creating collections until 1954, with the continued success of her perfumes, most notably Shocking, carrying the financial burden. In retirement, she led an active peripatetic life, enjoying her home in Tunisia, until a series of strokes confined her to her home at 22 rue de

Berri, Paris. Schiaparelli never married again after the disaster of her first marriage. Although she had affairs, she deliberately avoided serious attachments. Aged eighty-three, she died in her sleep in 1973.

As an employer, Schiaparelli was demanding and sparing with compliments. That said, she paid well and inspired fierce loyalty among her staff. She also formed long-lasting professional liaisons that served her well, championing the embroidery house of Lesage and exploring new synthetic fabrics with Charles Colcombet. As for artists, there were few who did not know or collaborate with Schiaparelli, the results varying from a Salvador Dali lobster on an evening dress to a spirited Jean Cocteau sketch transformed into a Lesage embroidery. Such a symbiosis between art and fashion gives her a unique place in twentieth-century fashion history. American curator Richard Martin called her 'a visionary [who] touched clothing with the capacity to be art'.

Schiaparelli was often frustrated by the transience of fashion. 'Dress designing … is to me not a profession but an art,' she wrote in her autobiography. 'I found it was a most difficult and unsatisfying art, because as soon as the dress is born it has already become a thing of the past.' Schiaparelli concluded her autobiography, published in 1954, with her 'Twelve Commandments for Women'. Commandment number five said: 'Ninety per cent [of women] are afraid of being conspicuous, and of what people will say. So they buy a gray suit. They should dare to be different.' It was a philosophy that she followed herself with the utmost devotion.

Further reading: Elsa Schiaparelli: A Biography (2014) by American biographer Meryle Secrest is an entertaining summary of her life. Palmer White also produced a lively biography, *Elsa Schiaparelli: Empress of Paris Fashion* (1986). Schiaparelli's autobiography is fun, as the title, *Shocking Life* (1954), suggests. Dilys Blum produced a very well-researched catalogue, *Shocking! The Art and Fashion of Schiaparelli* (2003), for the exhibition she authoritatively curated at the Philadelphia Museum of Art. Richard Martin's *Fashion and Surrealism* (1987) is an overview with many Schiaparelli references.

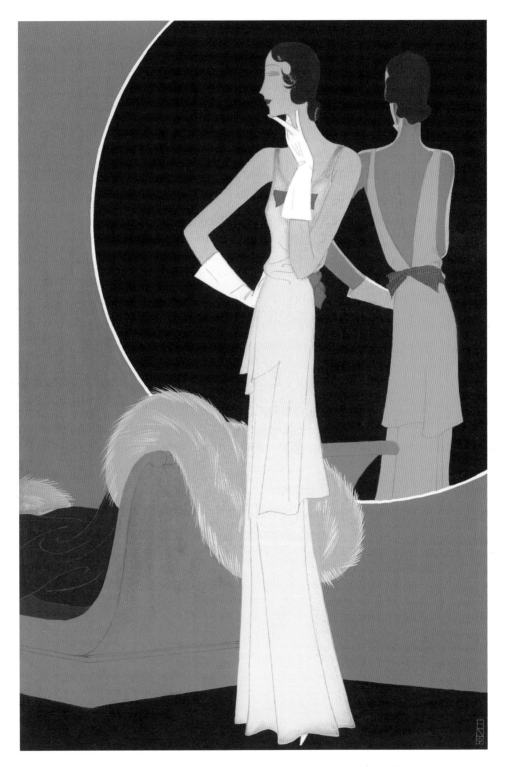

Image 11.1 *Mainbocher dress,* Vogue, *1931. Photo: Eduardo Garcia Benito/Condé Nast via Getty Images.*

11

Mainbocher (1890–1976)

Mainbocher favoured simplicity over complication, decrying exaggeration in fashion.

The long life of American couturier Mainbocher spanned a remarkable period in the history of fashion, from the frothy confections of the Belle Époque to the ready-to-wear explosion of the 1960s and 1970s. In one sense, as a proud couturier who shunned the mass-market companies of New York's Seventh Avenue, he looked back to an era that became history during his lifetime. In another sense, the purity and refined severity of his finest creations suggest a designer who looked forward to the minimalism of the 1990s. Late in his career, when he was in his seventies, Mainbocher showed he could still lead the way with a series of pared-down dresses, including a bias-cut white crepe dinner dress, lauded and photographed by *Harper's Bazaar*. More broadly, as the first American couturier in Paris, he was an important symbol of the rising self-confidence of the American fashion industry.

If his achievement has been underappreciated, this may be connected to his reluctance to play the media game. He shunned interviews and was perceived as an aloof recluse in his later years – 'the great loner', according to *Time* magazine in 1963. The irony was that Mainbocher was himself a distinguished fashion journalist during the 1920s. Nostalgia for that period in his career did not extend to offering the hand of friendship to his former colleagues. *Vogue* editor Bettina Ballard speculated that this was all a ploy: 'He had a way of making *Vogue* feel guilty about something most of the time; so he could name his own terms when he let us take anything.' Always elegantly dressed and suave, he was a small and broad man with a serious manner and an old-world sense of decorum.

'I am', he said, 'the Rolls-Royce of the fashion trade.' The critic Dale McConathy called him 'one of the last of the great snobs – an eighteenth-century French cardinal who somehow got himself born on the West Side of Chicago'.

Countering this was his strong emotional connection with his Midwestern roots. Writer and friend Janet Flanner noted in 1940 that 'though Bocher takes pride in serving Lanson '21 champagne with dessert, he still thinks homemade banana ice cream is the ideal note on which to end a dinner party.' Mainbocher adored the women in the paintings of John Singer Sargent, admiring their individualism and sense of style. He saw a connection between the outer and the inner selves, telling *Vogue* in 1964, 'I have never known a really chic woman whose appearance was not, in large part, an outward reflection of her inner self'. Orientalist references were never part of his repertoire – he was no fan of Paul Poiret, describing his clothes as 'expensive expressions of clothing that is more of a costume than a dress'.

He was proud to be descended from French Huguenot pioneers who arrived in America in the 1640s. Main Rousseau Bocher (he contracted his name in 1929) was born in 1890 in Chicago, growing up on Monroe Street in a close-knit family with a sister, Lillian. Music was his great joy as a young man, particularly the opera, to which he remained addicted for the rest of his life. He was also skilled at drawing, which drew him to study art. The death of his father when he was in his first year at the University of Chicago forced Mainbocher to grow up quickly. In 1909, he attended the Art Students League in New York and took his portfolio around magazines looking for illustration work. But his real goal was to go to Europe, which had an exalted status in the mind of the young man, as it did for many young Americans.

Persuading his mother to sell their house in Chicago, Mainbocher set off in 1911 for Europe, where, he said later, he was 'born again'. He studied art in Munich and travelled regularly to Paris, breathing in the music and culture of the Old World. The rococo period was a particular delight to him, a frothiness of style that as a couturier he chose to set against restrained shapes. The outbreak of war in 1914 sent him and his family heading back to America, where he made his first steps in the fashion industry, creating a dress for a friend for a charity fashion show and earning money from fashion drawings for a wholesale clothing manufacturer. By 1917, he was back in France, serving as a sergeant major in the American Expeditionary Force Intelligence Corps. In post-war Paris, Mainbocher determined to focus on music, studying voice and opera. But it was his sideline job as a sketcher for the Paris office of *Harper's Bazaar* that came to dominate, not least when Mainbocher lost his voice shortly before going on stage to sing (it took him three years to recover). His accomplished drawings and elegant writing, founded on a precise eye for detail and an innate sense of style, were highly prized attributes in the relatively new profession of fashion journalism. After three years at *Harper's Bazaar*, Mainbocher switched to *Vogue*, where he was both Paris editor and then editor of French *Vogue* over a seven-year period lasting until 1929. He was best known during these years for his discovery and encouragement of the photographer Baron Hoyningen-Huene and the illustrator Carl Erickson, known as Eric.

Many fashion journalists have attempted to make the switch to design. None has succeeded as triumphantly as Mainbocher. It was an abrupt decision, he later claimed. 'It was nothing that crept up on me. … It was an immediate and very agreeable explosion. It came from the unconscious. The whole idea was born and in twenty-four hours became absolutely upright'. He bought some mannequins from the Galeries Lafayette and positioned them in the library of his Left Bank apartment. Through cutting, pinning and fitting, he taught himself the principles of couture. He also swiftly showed all the skills of the natural-born marketer, contracting his name, most likely in emulation of Augustabernard, a couturier he greatly admired. His sumptuous salon at 12 avenue George V was filled with mirrored mantelpieces,

Nymphenburg china and flowers. An aura of exclusivity was established from the beginning, although Mainbocher preferred to serve his guests iced water rather than champagne. He imposed a caution – a guarantee of purchase, priced at the cost of the cheapest dress – on all those clients who attended his show. Only a handful of magazines and newspapers, including *Vogue, Harper's Bazaar* and *The New York Times*, were allowed to cover his collections. If featured, Mainbocher dresses had to appear on facing pages, he insisted. Although he disparaged the power of the fashion magazines, their favourable coverage in the early days created a momentum that swiftly enabled him to build a successful business.

He was influenced by the refined and deceptively simple designs of Augustabernard, who was forced into retirement in 1934 by financial problems. A more celebrated influence was Madame Vionnet, whose use of the bias cut and skill with draping were closely studied by Mainbocher. Fabric, twisted and run through his hands, was the prompt for his designs, which were then sketched by an assistant. Less was more, superfluous details were ruthlessly eliminated. These frocks were so pared down they became known as 'don't dress frocks' by the press. Mainbocher's business grew rapidly on the back of four collections a year and a formidable client list, including Elsie De Wolfe, Lady Mendl, considered the best-dressed woman in the world. Besides the social elite, Mainbocher was also favoured by the *demi-mondaines*, the mistresses who were openly flaunted in 1930s' Paris. At its peak, the house employed 350 people and had sales of 100 million francs a year. His most celebrated client, the Duchess of Windsor, was, like him, an American living in Europe. For her wedding, Mainbocher designed a blue silk crepe dress with a wide inset corselet and fitted jacket – the most talked about and copied couture dress in European history, at least until the wedding of Diana, Princess of Wales. For

Image 11.2 *Mainbocher, 1938. Photo: ullstein bild via Getty Images.*

Image 11.3 *Mainbocher gown, modelled by Mary Jane Russell,* Vogue, *1949. Photo: Horst P. Horst/ Condé Nast via Getty Images.*

the Duchess, he created a special blue, Wallis blue – the colour of her eyes. The wedding dress, which is now in the Metropolitan Museum collection in New York, has since faded to grey. One fashion writer, Ernestine Carter, writing in 1980, described it as 'one of the least happy of his inspirations and, unfortunately, one of the most copied'.

In 1939, the imminent threat of war spelt the end of Mainbocher's Paris period. His final collection, featuring nipped-in waists and corselets, was ill-timed but demonstrated his couturier's vision and anticipated Christian Dior's New Look by some eight years. Shortly afterwards, Mainbocher shut up shop in Paris and sailed for New York, together with his mother and sister. Profiled enthusiastically by *The New Yorker* in early 1940, Mainbocher quickly settled back into his native country. 'He has spent twenty years of his life in Europe with Europeans, but his Illinois identity has remained intact,' concluded *The New Yorker*. Thanks to a contract with the Warner Brothers Corset Company, he had the funds to reopen his house near Fifth Avenue at 6 East 57th Street, replicating the atmosphere of the salon in the Avenue George V and swiftly picking up where he had left off in Paris. The client list swelled again, including iconic society ladies such as Gloria Vanderbilt Cooper, Barbara Paley and Ceezee Guest.

In 1942, Mainbocher volunteered to design uniforms for the WAVES (Women Accepted for Volunteer Emergency Service), creating a much-admired blue and white tailored jacket with a slightly flared six-gore skirt. The cachet of wearing a Mainbocher uniform even enticed some women to join the WAVES. 'I can detach the insignia after the war, and get at least three or four years' good wear out of it,' one recruit said. This specific comment would have appealed to Mainbocher: he loved the idea that his clients could reuse his designs time and time again. He also admired clients who were individualists and perfectionists, prepared to endure his famously long fittings without complaint. At the top of his list of achievements were his black evening dresses, typically short and versatile. He designed simple dresses with tie-ons, such as lace or brocade aprons or overskirts, creating a radical transformation. Belts were frequently used for simple effect. Also much admired and copied were his beaded cashmere sweaters, perfect for an evening look that mixed formal and informal in one. Furthermore, Mainbocher enjoyed experimenting with fabrics, such as batiste, voile, organdy, and pique, creating surprising juxtapositions, such as a lumber jacket in lamé or an evening dress in gingham. The versatility of his work chimed with the mood (and the regulations) of America during the early 1940s, when the country was at war. Repetition was a core theme of his repertoire. Drawing on his musical experience, Mainbocher described his design development as similar to classical musical development, where themes are restated and revisited. Critic Dale McConarthy wrote, 'For Mainbocher, there was nothing new in fashion. He possessed an extreme self-consciousness about his work that caused him to return again and again to his sources. … He often repeated himself and glorified in the women who wore his dresses for twenty or thirty years and returned to have them copied.'

In America, Mainbocher maintained his status as a couturier and steered clear of Seventh Avenue and the ready-to-wear industry. He never licensed his name, although a fragrance called White Garden was released in 1948. While his costumes for Broadway brought his work to a larger audience, most notably for Mary Martin in *One Touch of Venus* in 1943, he showed no interest in reaching a broader market. Until her retirement in 1956, Carmel Snow, editor of *Harper's Bazaar*, was a champion of his work. In the early 1960s, Mainbocher was still a favourite of America's best-connected women, who adored his boxy suits worn with sleeveless blouses, his four-seam sheath dresses and, as always, his bias-cut evening wear that looked back to the 1930s and forward to the 1970s. He favoured simplicity over complication, decrying exaggeration in fashion (he had a particular loathing for Schiaparelli in the 1930s). 'I dislike fashions that go off in your hands like fire-crackers,' he said. Fashion editor Bettina Ballard described him as 'a sort of magic fashion mountain to climb for the woman who is sure enough of her money, her success, or her social position to wear his understated clothes'. But as the ready-to-wear sector developed through the 1960s, Mainbocher became increasingly irrelevant to the onward march of fashion. By the time of his retirement in 1971, the years of his greatest triumphs were but distant memories.

Further reading: The definitive account of Mainbocher's life up to his return to America is 'Pioneer' (13 January 1940), an article by Janet Flanner published in *The New Yorker*. Mainbocher is also profiled by Dale McConathy in *American Fashion* (1975), edited by Sarah Tomerlin Lee. *Making Mainbocher: The First American Couturier* (2016), by curator Petra Slinkard, is the book of the exhibition at the Chicago History Museum.

12

Adrian (1903–1959)

Adrian created no look or style that changed the course of fashion, but he was an influencer for millions of women.

He was known simply as Adrian, enjoying a rise to success that was meteoric by any standards. He was the American costume designer who dressed Greta Garbo, Joan Crawford and a galaxy of Hollywood stars in the 1920s and 1930s, then switched to launch his own ready-to-wear fashion house in the 1940s. As chief costume designer at MGM during the golden years of Hollywood, designing costumes for more than 260 films, he had a spectacular influence on a generation of American women and was copied relentlessly by the manufacturers of Seventh Avenue. Elsa Schiaparelli noted: 'What Hollywood designs today, you will be wearing tomorrow.'

Designing for films far ahead of their release put particular pressure on Adrian to think into the future. In 1938, he explained: 'With modern fashions, I get entirely away from current trends, for screen fashions must, of necessity, be designed so that they will be, dramatically, months ahead when they will be seen on the screen by the world at large.'

For all his talents, his inclusion in a roll call of designer greats would probably have been questioned by his contemporary American fashion editors. In her memoirs published in 1954, *Vogue* editor Edna Woolman Chase gave him merely one, somewhat patronising, reference: 'There was a time when, in all conscience, I had to be severe with him about his designing.' The failure to appreciate fully Adrian's important role in fashion history might be partly ascribed to a collective sneer at his origins in costume design and the vulgarity of his more fantastical designs for the Hollywood stars. Then there was the issue of his location on the West Coast, always second best for American fashion, which was (and is) driven by New York's Seventh Avenue. Finally, his greatest work was achieved during a period when the American fashion industry was still in thrall to the fashion houses of Paris: the concept of an American designer was somewhat novel.

Image 12.1 *Joan Crawford in* Letty Lynton, *1932. Photo: George Hurrell/John Kobal Foundation via Getty Images.*

By the end of his life, the influence of Paris was less omnipotent, for which Adrian deserves some credit. This was the designer who faced up to Christian Dior in a much publicised public debate over Dior's New Look. That he would lose the debate was never in doubt, but he had struck a new defiant attitude for American fashion designers. Other design talents have emerged from Hollywood, including Bonnie Cashin and Irene of California. But Adrian, in the words of fashion historian Caroline Rennolds Milbank, proved that 'America could have its own style and that it didn't have to evolve from sportswear but could emanate from Hollywood, bypassing Paris altogether.'

Adrian arguably created no look or style that changed the course of fashion, but he was an influencer for millions of women, both in America and beyond. In 1930, eight million Americans were going to the cinema each week. By 1938, *Vogue* acknowledged that Hollywood 'is certainly the most perfect visual medium of fashion propaganda that ever existed'. An outstanding example of Adrian's influence was the impact of a long dress in white organdy with extravagant ruffled sleeves, designed for the actress Joan Crawford in the film *Letty Lynton* (1932) and widely copied on Seventh Avenue. The film studio even encouraged copying by leaking details of the dress before the film had been released: Macy's was reported to have sold 50,000 copies, which was probably an exaggeration, but not by much. Adrian himself did not believe American women should try to dress in his more fanciful Hollywood creations. 'The average woman should limit herself to the costumes worn by the heroines of light comedies … in moderate-sized towns.' By switching from costume design to ready-to-wear in the 1940s, Adrian made explicit the connection between Hollywood and the American fashion industry that continues to this day. He was also a superb publicist and spokesman for his own brand, always immaculately dressed and ready with a quote.

His family background was ideal for a designer. He was born Adrian Adolph Greenburg in 1903 in Naugatuck, Connecticut, the son of milliners Gilbert and Helena Greenburg. Taught sewing by a Swedish nanny, he displayed exceptional early talent as a draughtsman, encouraged by his uncle Max Greenberg, a scenic designer. A place at Parsons School of Fine and Applied Art in New York beckoned by 1921, where teachers quickly agreed that his undoubted talents might be more challenged and developed in the Paris branch of Parsons. Changing his name to Adrian, he arrived in Paris in 1922 and stayed a mere four months – time enough to create a costume for a friend at the prestigious Bal Du Grand Prix and secure an invitation from Irving Berlin to design costumes for his New York revue.

That commission took Adrian back to America in double-quick time. Although Adrian's contribution to the revue turned out to be much smaller than he had hoped, it was not long before other theatre folk were taking notice of the confident young man. Natacha Rambova, the flamboyant wife of Rudolph Valentino, gave Adrian his first major break, inviting him to Hollywood to work on a Valentino film. He bought himself a white suit and a black cape lined in red satin and prepared to take the West Coast by storm. At the tender age of twenty-four, he found himself designing costumes for Cecil B. DeMille's *The King of Kings*, a biblical epic on which no expense was spared. Adrian had arrived.

The popular new costume designer was blessed with exceptional confidence in his own abilities and a talent for charming people that made him a social hit in Hollywood. He was swiftly headhunted by Louis B. Mayer, the autocratic but perceptive boss of MGM. His first movie for Mayer was *A Woman of Affairs*, starring Greta Garbo. Right from the start, Adrian caught the eye of Seventh Avenue, too: Garbo's slouch hat and belted trench coat made the pages of American trade newspaper *Women's Wear Daily*. During Adrian's twelve-year stint working for MGM, Hollywood emerged as an important influence on American women's style, arguably as influential as the fashion houses of Paris.

Adrian's output was extraordinary, regularly amounting to fifty or more sketches in a day. The work pace was relentless, particularly for the period epics, such as *Marie Antoinette*, which required some 4,000 costumes, including thirty-four for leading lady Norma Shearer. He designed virtually everything Joan Crawford wore both on and off the screen, including her signature square-shouldered suits, from 1929 until 1943. Rather like a method actor, Adrian spent time thinking his way into the period of each movie, determined to capture the essence of the era before creating his costumes. His way of working was punctilious and disciplined, aiming to fit his actresses early in the morning before they were tired out by shooting. No expense was spared, no director's fantasy left unfulfilled, from the spectacular coronation robe worn by his favourite actress, Greta Garbo, in *Queen Christina* to

Image 12.2 *Janet Gaynor, actress, wife of Adrian, 1935. Photo: Hulton Archive via Getty Images.*

Image 12.3 *Adrian, circa 1930. Photo: General Photographic Agency via Getty Images.*

the bugle-beaded negligee with twenty-two inch ostrich-frond cuffs worn by Jean Harlow in *Dinner at Eight*. His futuristic costumes for Garbo in *Mata Hari* drew particular attention; perhaps only an actress of her stature could have carried them off. By contrast, he also designed Judy Garland's blue and white gingham pinafore and sequinned red shoes in *The Wizard of Oz*.

Hollywood studios worked directly with retailers for tie-in deals. At Macy's in New York, a Cinema Shop was opened where imitations of the clothes worn by actresses could be bought. For example, suits, coats and hostess gowns inspired by the film *Queen Christina* were offered for sale in 1933. Academic Anne Massey notes that sewing and knitting patterns were also created to imitate the fashions of the big screen. She points out that 'Hollywood cinema played a crucial role in creating and disseminating a streamlined *moderne* style that made a massive impact internationally.'

Adrian's lifestyle was comfortable and lavish, buoyed by a salary of $1,000 a week. He hosted lunch parties and oversaw an antiques shop on Sunset Strip. He also bought a ranch shack in the desert at Palm Springs, which he used as a retreat for painting and for visits by favoured friends who could handle the rudimentary facilities. Marriage to Fox star Janet Gaynor completed the picture of a designer who lived life to the full. A colourful paisley print smock he designed for her pregnancy caught the attention of the media, and Seventh Avenue's copyists were not far behind.

The good times did not last. As MGM and other studios sought to impose cost controls in the late 1930s, the nothing-spared atmosphere was replaced by a more cautious attitude to film production. Garbo's last film, *Two-Faced Woman*, was also Adrian's last at MGM. Depressed by the new mood, one afternoon Adrian tore up his sketches and walked out. His next move, long nurtured and discussed with Woody Feurt, a friend with fashion industry experience, was to launch Adrian Ltd in Beverly Hills. The beginnings were not promising, with the rest of the world at war, and America, after the Japanese attack on Pearl Harbour, poised to play its role, too. Struggling with the logistical and financial challenges of launching a fashion house, Adrian was obliged to show his first collection on the patio of his home. For a second collection, shown in August 1942, Adrian decided to pull out all the stops. The result was a storming success, with orders flooding in to the fledgling house. His broad-shouldered suits were applauded, and a black dress went on to become a long-term bestseller.

Adrian realised that the war, which had forced most Paris fashion houses to close their export operations, presented an opportunity for American designers. Together with the publicist Eleanor Lambert, he urged his fellow designers to take advantage. Material, particularly wool fabric, was in short supply, forcing designers to use all their ingenuity to keep the look fresh. Adrian responded to the L-85 regulations, introduced to restrict the use of materials for the fashion industry during wartime, by narrowing sleeves and introducing self-piping ties on jacket fronts to replace buttons. He mixed materials to conserve the finest for the key pieces. His broad-shouldered tailored silhouette was the wartime favourite, establishing Adrian as a household name – despite little support from the East Coast-edited fashion magazines. In 1944, he won a prestigious Coty Award.

Adrian's skill with fabric was exceptional. Pola Stout's striped and geometric woven fabrics were a favourite for jackets, skirts and dresses. He enjoyed cutting the fabric into panels and resewing them in patches on jackets. He also combined similar fabrics in one look to dramatic effect. His suits often comprised long collarless jackets with a single closure at the waist worn with a straight skirt with a kick pleat. His evening dresses, perfectly draped, reflected his experience in creating show-stopping dresses for the MGM stars. His cocktail dresses and ball gowns sometimes tipped too far towards his roots in costume design, certainly way too far for the tastes of the arbiters of style at *Vogue* and *Harper's Bazaar*. Fashion historian Caroline Rennolds Milbank considered him at his best when working within the restrictions of a theme, such as for a Greek collection with columnar white dresses or for a Gothic collection with jersey dresses and trailing medieval themes. The link with the disciplines of his Hollywood career was self-evident.

After the war, Christian Dior's New Look, with its return to full skirts and restricted waists, caught a new mood. Adrian's response was to clash with Dior in a broadcast debate and to stick to his broad-shouldered look. 'I do not like padded hips,' he told *Life* magazine. 'To try and make women pad their hips in this day and age is a little like selling armour to a man.' Determined not to lose momentum, he showed his collection for the first time in New York in 1948 at the store of Gunther-Jaeckel, prompting a buying frenzy from public and store buyers alike. What ultimately stopped Adrian was not the changing tides of fashion – uncomfortable though they were for the designer – but ill health. In early 1952, he suffered a heart attack and, after some soul-searching with his business partner Woody Feurt, decided to close the business. Thereafter, he spent much of his time with his wife and family in Brazil, where he designed a jungle hideaway. Tempted by friends back into designing costumes (for a stage musical, this time) in 1958, he was poised to re-enter the world of work again, only to suffer a second and fatal heart attack in September 1959.

Further reading: Christian Esquevin's *Adrian: Silver Screen to Custom Label* (2008) is a long overdue summary of the designer's career. In *American Fashion* (1975), edited by Sarah Tomerlin Lee, Robert Riley contributes a section on Adrian. *Creating the Illusion: A Fashionable History of Hollywood Costume Designers* (2015) by Jay Jorgensen and Donald L. Scoggins is full of interesting information and photos of the Hollywood stars.

13

Salvatore Ferragamo (1898–1960)

*Ferragamo was a determined and driven individual, sure from his childhood
of what he was destined to do.*

In the history of dress, shoes have never been accorded quite the consequence they deserve. In the drama that is fashion, shoes are quite literally accessories, supporting characters, there to facilitate the action, way down the cast list. It is true that in the first decade of the twenty-first century they elbowed their way centre stage but that was probably more the result of marketing than a real shift in our perceptions. Yet, when it comes to defining gender, class and erotic intent, shoes have, through most of history, packed a bigger punch than mere clothes. Nothing else people wear has been quite so thoroughly and repetitively fetishised. Even so, fashion and its contemporary commentators have tended to overlook shoemakers, regarding them as artisans rather than artists or designers.

Many shoemakers have been great designers and innovators, but the first to break through those barriers of anonymity was Salvatore Ferragamo, an Italian born in respectable poverty in Bonito, near Naples, the eleventh of fourteen children, who left behind a dynasty that became a luxury goods empire. He wrote in his autobiography that he did not so much learn how to make shoes as 'remember', as if in an earlier life or many earlier lives he had already been a shoemaker. 'I was born to be a shoemaker,' he wrote. 'I know it; I have always known it. As I look back now on the long lesson of my life I can see quite clearly how strong, how remorseless, how unrelenting is the passion within me that has driven me on and on, along a path strewn with so many hardships. Many are the times when I wondered why I was not as other men … content with the things they possessed, hankering not after the fruits of tomorrow. Yet I could not swerve from my predestined path, no matter what the cost. It was against Nature, it was against God.'

His explanation of his unlearned skill was mystical: 'But from whence does my knowledge come? It is not inherited. In later years I searched the records of my ancestors through 400 years. There was no shoemaker among them. I found many humble property owners, I found a poet, I even found an

Image 13.1 *Ferragamo fitting a shoe, 1950. Photo: Time & Life Pictures via Getty Images.*

alchemist; but no shoemakers, not one. Nor have I had to learn in the accepted sense. From my first day with shoes – yes, even with the little white shoes I made for my sisters – I have remembered all about shoemaking. I have remembered: that is the only way to describe it. I have only to sit down and think, and the memory comes to me out of the days – it can only be this – when in some previous existence upon this earth, I was a shoemaker.'

A lifelong experimenter with materials and structure, Ferragamo invented wedges, the rounded toe, Roman sandals, the invisible nylon shoe, the crystal-soled shoe, sculpted heels, the 'gloved' arch, shell soles and the stiletto heel (he called it the 'spike'). The political and economic exigencies of his century forced his ingenuity beyond even his fertile inclination, and he developed ways to use the unlikeliest materials in shoes of seductive beauty: crystal and Cellophane, fish skin, feathers, crocheted silk, satin, embroidery and mosaics of gem-cut crystals and Venetian glass beads, mirror glass, pearls, diamonds and diamond dust, raffia and cork, wood and rubber, Bakelite and nylon thread, felt and all manner of animal skin, including antelope, kangaroo and lizard.

He was a determined and driven individual, sure from his childhood of what he was destined to do. His parents were poor farmers, and two of his brothers trained to be tailors but, in village society, the cobbler was 'the lowest of all the classes' and for their son to become apprenticed to him was beneath his family's dignity. 'It would bring the family into disrepute,' he recalled. It was only after he had played truant from several other apprenticeships and then, without training, sat up all night making his little sisters' First Communion shoes from canvas and cardboard (his parents were too poor to buy any for them) that they finally relented. Long before he was ten years old he had learned everything the village shoemaker could teach him. That year his father died and, in 1909 when he was eleven, Salvatore left home to go to Naples to attempt to learn more advanced skills. Moving from shoemaker to shoemaker, spending a day here, three there, he absorbed knowledge, before borrowing money from his mother's brother, a priest, and setting up as a shoemaker in his home village of Bonito. He was a prodigy, not only in terms of skill and talent but also in his precocious business acumen. Rapidly he developed a good business making shoes for the local gentry. In 1912, he was enticed to America to join his older brothers and sisters, all of whom had emigrated as they became old enough. At fourteen he made the long sea journey alone, pausing only briefly on the East Coast to dismiss the shoe factory where his brother-in-law worked and head out West to join his brothers in Santa Barbara, where they opened a shoe-repair shop and Salvatore began his meteoric career as shoemaker to the stars – first on set and then in their private lives.

He was only twenty-four when he followed the fledgling movie business to Hollywood and took out an enormous $35,000 bank loan to open his Hollywood Boot Shop on the corner of Hollywood and Las Palmas Boulevards. Next to the shop was his workshop, and he developed a small manufacturing operation as well as employing ever-increasing numbers of outworkers. Gradually he developed links with factories across the country, selling wholesale to stores throughout America while his own shop focused on retail. He was commissioned by Cecil B. DeMille to put shoes on the feet of the actors and hordes of extras in *The Ten Commandments* and *The King of Kings* and also shod D. W. Griffith's *Way Down East* and *The White Rose* as well as James Cruze's *The Covered Wagon*.

He would research archaic costumes in the library, but there was little recorded so, once more, he 'remembered' it – very successfully. He also studied anatomy at the University of Southern California at Los Angeles. Although his creativity and inventiveness in terms of style and materials were boundless, his real quest was comfort, the secret of which he discovered through his study of anatomy. The weight of the body is borne by the arch of the foot, he learned; that is what needs supporting while the ball of the foot and the heel (the areas most shoemakers prefer to support) should float free so that the bones and muscles can move as nature intended. As a consequence, any dancer who had worn a pair of Ferragamo's shoes refused to wear any other. All Hollywood's leading ladies wore Ferragamo, from Mary Pickford to Ava Gardner, from Jean Harlow to Marilyn Monroe, from Katharine Hepburn to Audrey Hepburn.

When the machine production did not measure up to his high standards, Ferragamo decided to move back to Italy where he believed he could employ enough skilled artisans to make his shoes by hand. His return to his native land in 1927 was initially a disaster and, owing to greedy backers in America, deceitful debtors and perfidious creditors plus recalcitrant Italian shoemakers, ended in bankruptcy. Ferragamo paid all his debts, real and fictional, over the next few years, rebuilt his business and acquired the Palazzo Feroni-Spini in Florence and the Villa Il Palagio at Fiesole, on the hillside overlooking the city.

Image 13.2 *Ferragamo shoes, 1953. Photo: Corbis Historical via Getty Images.*

Then the larger world handed him another reversal of fortune. In 1935, Italy's fascist dictator, Benito Mussolini, invaded Ethiopia, and in 1936, the League of Nations imposed sanctions on Italy, killing Ferragamo's export trade and cutting off his sources of raw materials. Ferragamo was forced to new heights of resourcefulness. Fiddling with the Cellophane wrapper from a chocolate while seeking a substitute for the fine kidskins that could be painted silver or gold for evening shoes, he came up with a fine rolled transparent Cellophane tube enclosing a gold or silver thread. It was strong, and it was glamorous. The second invention forced upon him by necessity at this time was the 'wedgie'. He could obtain only low-grade steel at this time, and the shanks on his shoes were continuously snapping. After much thought he tried filling in the space between the heel and the ball of the foot, sculpting Sardinian cork. He then persuaded the most fashionable duchess in Florence to wear the wedge to church – and the queues formed on Monday morning.

By 1939, Ferragamo was shoemaker to most of the royalty of Europe as well as that of Hollywood. At one point, he recalled, four queens were being fitted simultaneously in his Rome salon – the queens of Yugoslavia, Greece, Spain and the Belgians. Queen Elena of Italy was a devoted customer, and he also made boots and shoes for Mussolini, thereby curing his corns and calluses, and for the dictator's wife and mistress as well as Hitler's mistress, Eva Braun. 'How was it possible', he demanded in his autobiography, 'for a bankrupt in 1933 to own within five and a half years a great palace and a beautiful villa and, above all, to number among his clients the greatest names in the world?'

His answer was that his unique fitting system permitted 'Nature' to effect a cure of the 'crippled feet' of his clients. His theory was that many ills, from bad temper and obesity to insanity, could be traced to ill-fitting shoes. Throughout his career, the style of the shoes, although an endless source of joy to him, was never as important as the structure and fit. He wrote: 'Normally I do not institute new fashions. There are a number of dress and shoe designers who struggle to be different for the sake of being different, meaning that they want to impose a startling new fashion line upon the woman, but if designers must wait for their customers to become conscious of new styles who, then, determines fashion? The answer is: new fashion begins in the mind of the designer. He must not stifle all his ideas merely because the world is not yet ready for them. I have no season.'

The war that broke out in 1939 meant the collapse of business as his workers were called up into the army and trade ceased. The forty-one-year-old Ferragamo took advantage of a period of relative inactivity to find a wife. Wanda Miletti, the daughter of the doctor and mayor of Bonito, was twenty-three years younger than him, but it was love at first sight for both. Their six children were all to work in the family business. In 1947, on a trip to the United States to accept a Neiman-Marcus plaque for 'distinguished services to fashion', he shared the voyage with Christian Dior (of whom he had never heard). The two designers were astonished to discover that Ferragamo's shoes complemented Dior's clothes perfectly – both had instinctively been working in the same materials, colours and mood. 'I had for many years,' he reflected, 'believed that the fashion trend is not the exclusive prerogative of one designer but is "in the air" – a sort of manifestation of the world will, if I may put it like that – with the result that two men, working 400 miles apart, unknown to each other and with widely different means of inspiration (I draw my creations from my memory, while Dior prefers to find his inspiration from practical items like paintings and drawings) can arrive at similar conclusions at the same period in time.'

Salvatore Ferragamo died in 1960 at the relatively youthful age of sixty-two. Wanda Ferragamo led the company for twenty years, gradually handing over various functions to her six children. She died in 2018 at the age of ninety-six. The company, still family controlled, is today a highly successful luxury goods brand with a ready-to-wear collection. British shoe designer Paul Andrew was appointed creative director in 2017.

Further reading: Salvatore Ferragamo's autobiography, *Shoemaker of Dreams* (1957), is still an essential read. For a good historical perspective, see Stefania Ricci's *Salvatore Ferragamo: Evolving Legend 1928–2008* (2008). For an understanding of the whole field, see Giorgio Riello and Peter McNeil's *Shoes: A History from Sandals to Sneakers* (2006).

Image 13.3 *Ferragamo's 'invisible shoe', 1947. Photo: Alfred Eisenstaedt/The LIFE Picture Collection via Getty Images.*

14

Madame Alix Grès (1903–1993)

Grès was, along with Chanel, the most important post-war couturière.

Revivals of classical dress have tended to be countercultural, a critique of a corrupt, oppressive or over-luxurious regime and an expression of a desire to return to the pure ideals of Hellenic Greece or the Rome of the Republic. Significantly, the style only became mainstream in the late eighteenth century, the time of revolutions and the setting up of new political orders, of the British Regency and the French Directoire. The original clothes of antiquity were not really cut and stitched but made up of simple rectangles of fabric hung and draped around the body and secured with pins, brooches and belts. The Greek chiton or tunic was partially sewn together, but the *peplos* was folded, pinned and girdled. The *himation* was a loose wrap worn like a cloak or a poncho. Roman men dressed in a tunic and toga (the wrap-like garment), and Roman women wore a long tunic or *stola* with an overwrap called a *palla*. These were essentially simple clothes without much bulk, depending for richness on expensive dyes, embroidery and decoration. However, when the sculptors, the great and enduring memorialisers of both cultures, got hold of them, they became something else. To generalise, in Greece they became ethereal, often erotic elements of the artist's composition, balancing, obscuring, revealing, emphasising human beauty; in Rome they became grandiose, plastic and imposing, insisting on their space – in short, what we have learned to call monumental (because in many eras no monument was complete without a togaed grave-faced statue).

Greece and Rome declined and died but the statues, idealised and elaborated, remained, an inspiration to artists, philosophers, politicians and dressmakers alike. Along with Paul Poiret, Mariano Fortuny and Madeleine Vionnet, Alix Grès, who had longed to train as a sculptor, loved the simplicity and purity of draped fabric softly clinging and floating around the body, unconstrained by the artificiality of corsets and padding. In 1981, Barbara Burman Baines wrote that her style was best summed up in a photograph taken in 1937 by Man Ray for *Harper's Bazaar*: 'A model in a long, white

Image 14.1 *Mrs Leo d'Erlanger, gown by Grès,* Vogue, *1936. Photo: Horst P. Horst/Condé Nast via Getty Images.*

halter-neck dress, seemingly made of nothing but multifarious pleats, leans dreamily by an antique statue of winged victory attired in a long tunic of fluid folds'.

The year before, in 1936, the same magazine had written, 'Alix stands for the body Rampant, for the rounded, feminine sculptural form beneath the dress.' In academic Valerie Steele's judgement, Grès was, along with Chanel, the most important post-war couturière. Their approaches were very different. Chanel was focused on dressing women for modern life, on 'sexual politics and social signals', as Anne Hollander put it. Grès simply wanted to create beauty using 'fabric as a fundamental artistic substance'. Grès's clothes, added Hollander, were solutions to abstract problems, with beauty the overriding standard. Like a sculptor, she worked directly with her material, leaving no sketches or pattern pieces to posterity. Biographer Patricia Mears noted how Grès draped and manipulated fabric with great speed and dexterity. Sometimes, these dresses draped directly on to a mannequin used more than twenty metres of fabric. 'In her neoclassicism,' wrote Harold Koda, 'Grès conformed to the antique notion of uninterrupted lengths of cloth, stitched but not cut into shape. From her earliest work, Grès introduced windows on to the body with cut-outs that bared the back and midriff.'

Alix Grès was born Germaine Emilie Krebs in Paris in 1903. The secretive couturière hated her name and used two professional aliases during her career. The first, Alix Barton, was probably taken from an early employer, Julie or Juliette Barton, but Grès was content to let journalists assume it was her maiden name. However she did reveal that her family was bourgeois, her father an 'industrialist', and that one of her grandmothers was Italian and one of her grandfathers was German. She first wanted to be a dancer and then a sculptor, both of which ambitions were discouraged by her family.

Dressmaking was her default choice in that it would allow her to be creative while earning her independence. She entered her profession on the eve of an economic depression that adversely affected the business of all Paris's couturiers. The Wall Street Crash came in 1929 and Grès joined the couture house of Premet in 1930 for a three-month apprenticeship in sketching and cutting. As with much of Grès's life, the next stage is unclear. Mears quotes several conflicting versions, which include making toiles freelance, working for Julie Barton and opening a shop, adding that what seems clear is that she set up her own maison de couture, named Alix, in 1934. (One version told by Grès to Cathy Horyn of *The New York Times* was that Julie Barton renamed her own business after her more talented assistant.)

Alix Barton received much admiring press attention in the 1930s, her work featuring in magazines as often as that of Chanel, Schiaparelli, Mainbocher and Vionnet. One profile in *Harper's Bazaar* in 1938 commented, 'She is not yet thirty and she looks far more like a nun than a dressmaker.' It is noteworthy, perhaps, that Grès had already started to lie about her age. She was also a commercial success, especially in America, and attracted the attention of the bohemian elite in Paris. In 1935, Jean Cocteau and Jean Giraudoux commissioned her to design the costumes for their play, *La Guerre de Troie n'aura pas lieu* (The Trojan War Will Not Take Place). The costumes, 'whiffs of navy blue chiffon', received good press.

Image 14.2 *Alix Barton, the future Alix Grès, 1933. Photo: Lipnitzky/Roger Viollet via Getty Images.*

Image 14.3 *Gown, Madame Grès,* Vogue, *1952. Photo: Frances McLaughlin-Gill/Condé Nast via Getty Images.*

During the 1930s Grès did not restrict herself to Attic draperies. She also experimented with ethnic styles such as the sari or Chinese tunic, described by Mears as 'loose interpretations of "exotic" prototypes. Garments such as the Serpent of the Nile and the Dutch-inspired Lowlands ensembles were as fanciful as their names.' In the 1950s, however, she was more successful with her development of garment construction derived from traditional shapes such as the kaftan, poncho, serape and kimono.

In 1937 Alix married a Russian painter, Serge Anatolievitch Czerefkow, converting to the Russian Orthodox faith to do so. Czerefkow signed his paintings with a partial anagram of his first name, Grès, and his new wife appropriated it, becoming Alix Grès. Although their daughter, Anne, was born in 1939, Czerefkow chose to live a separate life, returning to his home in Tahiti and a string of affairs with Polynesian concubines. Alix brought up her daughter with the help of 'Muni', Anne's godmother, a former model and actress who shared Alix Grès's life for more than forty years.

When the Nazis arrived in Paris in the spring of 1940, Grès fled, settling in a small village near the Spanish border. In exile, she worked on cobbled-together mannequins made from hay, tin and wood and, because she could not visit a hairdresser, she took to covering her long hair with a turban. This was to become a signature look. Mears has pieced together what happened next. She returned to Paris in the same year to sell her 50 per cent of the business to her partner and former employer, Julie Barton. In 1942 Lucien Lelong, head of the Chambre Syndicale de la Couture Parisienne, persuaded

Grès to use the money to open a new house, Grès, on the rue de la Paix. The Nazi authorities closed the house in 1944 because of her infringement of fabric restrictions. She said later, 'I was doing the opposite of everything I was supposed to do.'

She was given permission to reopen in time to launch a legendary poke-in-the-eye collection in the *tricolore* of the French flag, red, white and blue just before the liberation of Paris. The two years that followed were tough: two harsh winters, rationing of essential goods and shortages of everything else. The only thing that thrived was the black market. In October 1944, just weeks after the liberation of Paris, *Le Figaro* published a communiqué from the Chambre Syndicale: 'Prepared during a period of incredible material difficulties, these new fashion shows offering a reduced number of models are the result of a tremendous collective effort, and demonstrate the desire of Parisian fashion houses to lead the way to a rapid recovery of the national economy.'

The couturiers dressed miniature mannequins for an international touring exhibition titled Le Théâtre de la Mode. The dolls were posed on stages designed by Christian Bérard, Jean Cocteau and Boris Kochno. For a secondary touring exhibition, the Gratitude Train, specifically created for America and concerned with historical outfits, 'Madame Grès created a gown with a high waist and draped bodice à la Grecque, from a design by Leroy, couturier to Empress Josephine, ca. 1808.' After the years of utilitarian clothes and fabric restrictions, Madame was back in business.

But it quickly became clear that the emphasis of Parisian couture had shifted. Although the private clients were still important, it was the sale of toiles to ready-to-wear manufacturers, especially those in America, and the granting of licences that would refuel the industry and boost France's economy. In the wake of Christian Dior's New Look, Grès adjusted her style, nipping waists, rounding shoulders, making longer, fuller skirts. She even introduced an interior corset made for her by Alice Cadolle, which allowed her to create strapless Grecian dresses that were a great success in the 1950s. Although the New Look was partially intended to promote the greater consumption of fabric, Grès's natural propensity to use it by the tens of metres was hardly appropriate for mass manufacture. She could not, however, compromise her artistic integrity.

Throughout the 1960s and 1970s Grès was to reinterpret the high-waisted neoclassical gown again and again, but she also developed more geometric shapes in stiffer, heavier fabrics that were less sensuously seductive but more imposing. What these had in common with the Grecian dresses was the way in which they proceeded from a three-dimensional sense of the body. Her fashion sense remained acute through the 1960s, when she designed op-art dresses and flower-power gowns for rich hippies, and the 1970s, when she was able to exploit fashion's nostalgia for the 1930s with updated versions of her own best pieces.

In 1979 she did relent on her refusal to create a ready-to-wear collection, but it lasted only two seasons. Two years earlier she had told Marian McEvoy of *Women's Wear Daily*, 'Couture always gives the ideas to prêt-à-porter. The prêt-à-porter designers are always influenced by the couturiers. I feel that prêt-à-porter has indeed given the woman in the street a better, neater appearance, but couture is the creative key. It is a grand work – it is truth – couture brings something to the world.'

Grès continued to design couture clothes of great beauty that kept pace with fashion and modern concerns (she developed less formal daywear and youthful leisurewear), but failing to make a go of her ready-to-wear line was only one of her mistakes. She was, says Mears, too influenced by Muni and by an employee named Mufthah, whose decisions embroiled her in legal actions that lasted years. Gradually, the press coverage grew less and less as the perception of her significance waned.

Grès did, however, become active in the politics of the industry, succeeding Lucien Lelong as president of the Chambre Syndicale in 1972. In 1983 she sold a controlling interest in her house, which eventually became wholly owned by the Japanese company Yagi Tsusho. Alix Grès retired after presenting her spring 1988 collection. She settled in her second home in Saint Paul de Vence with her daughter, Anne, who later moved her mother to an inexpensive nursing home in the Var, where she died in 1993, penniless. Anne hid her mother's death for more than a year. Mears concluded that the daughter, described as immature, simply wanted her famous mother all to herself at last.

In 1998 Hubert de Givenchy, who had befriended Grès in her declining years, acquired Alix Grès's personal collection: 'Three hundred dresses,' he wrote in the introduction to *The Givenchy Style* in 1998, 'beautiful enough to go mad over.'

Further reading: Richard Martin and Harold Koda's book, *Madame Grès*, for the Metropolitan Museum exhibition in 1994 seems dated, but its enthusiasm is justified and re-awoke interest in the designer. Patricia Mears's *Madame Grès: Sphinx of Fashion* (2007) is the definitive read. *Madame Grès: Sculptural Fashion* (2012) by Olivier Saillard is the thoughtful book of an exhibition he curated at the Musée Bourdelle. 'Madame Grès: Couturier at Work' (2014) by Paola di Trocchio in *Fashion Theory* is a review of the exhibition.

Part Three

1940s–1950s

Image 14.4 *Silk jersey dress, Madame Grès, 1959. Photo: Chicago History Museum via Getty Images.*

Introduction

This period in fashion can be looked upon as elitism's last hurrah. At its start, couture was dominant, spawning myriad watered-down copies; at its end, mass-produced ready-to-wear, specifically designed for the young, drove innovation, with a new breed of art-school trained designers poised to make a mark. The Second World War naturally imposed stagnation – materials and labour were needed for other, more pressing purposes; clothing was rationed; and fashion, for most people, became an irrelevant frivolity.

In France, however, frivolity became an act of defiance, and Paris couture, so important not just in terms of exports but also as a symbol of French identity, fought hard to stay alive and functioning. Before the fall of France in 1940, the couturiers who had been called into the army were given two weeks' leave to design and make their collections before returning to the front. At the spring collections the Americans placed a huge number of orders. With the occupation of Paris, its couturiers could no longer export to most of their usual markets: many moved to Vichy France; Charles Creed moved back to London; Mainbocher and *Charles James* abandoned Europe entirely to return to New York; and others, led by Lucien Lelong, chairman of the Chambre Syndicale de la Couture Parisienne, began a long struggle against the Nazis' efforts to relocate the industry to Berlin or Vienna.

The couturiers of London and New York now eclipsed those of Paris. The Incorporated Society of London Fashion Designers (ISLFD) was led by Edward Molyneux and included Norman Hartnell, Elspeth Champcommunal at Worth, Digby Morton, Peter Russell, Bianca Mosca, Victor Stiebel and Hardy Amies – who doubled as a Secret Service agent. In compliance with the Utility Clothing Scheme introduced by the British government in 1942, the ISLFD created austerity couture, clothes that were functional, warm and skimpy. In America, couture was led by Hollywood designers Adrian and Omar Kiam, as well as *Charles James. Norman Norell* showed his first collection in 1940, and *Claire McCardell* seized her moment, removing shoulder pads and redirecting fashion towards comfort and ease of movement, becoming the most celebrated exponent of the first truly American style of dress, the mass-manufactured genre of designer sportswear. In her wake, *Rudi Gernreich* further developed the deconstructed, athletic, natural body shape that epitomised the relaxed, outdoors lifestyle of his adopted California.

At the end of the war the French government made it a priority to re-establish the country's pre-eminence in fashion. Coco Chanel, in disgrace because of her liaison with a German officer, was in exile in Switzerland, but *Balenciaga,* Grès, Schiaparelli, Lelong, Fath and Balmain were back in Paris. However, it was *Christian Dior* who made modernity redundant when, in 1947, he introduced the New Look based on Belle Époque styles. The significance of his Corolle Line has been extensively re-examined by twenty-first-century academics, either from a feminist perspective or as part of an exploration of the extent to which the nostalgic ultra-femininity of the New Look was a response to the traumas of war. Alexandra Palmer has identified within French culture as a whole a stratagem of collective forgetting of the humiliations and treacheries of the Nazi Occupation. She also suggests that the referencing of the dress of some of the greatest periods of French history – the eighteenth century and the Second Empire as well as the Belle Époque – was a riposte to the peasant-maiden styles produced in wartime Vichy France in shameful imitation of Hitler's dirndl-wearing Aryan mädchens. Traditional, urban feminine elegance erased the memory of the fascist rural operetta chorus line.

Certainly, the New Look and its celebration of the hourglass-shaped female body accurately captured the mood of men and women in the aftermath of a devastating war. The men returning from the battlefront had witnessed things many could never bear to speak about. They needed the comfort of conventional relationships, they needed their jobs back from the women who had been enlisted to replace them – and they needed children to replace the depleted populations.

The post-war years were tough for all of Europe and for the countries in Asia and Africa that had been ravaged by the conflict; many economies languished into the 1950s. In the 1940s, the United States was the first to switch from war-footing production to healthy consumerism, and its home-grown design talent thrived. It was, however, undeservedly disregarded and treated as a parochial, naive and copycat country cousin by European industry for some decades. The Iron Curtain countries of Eastern Europe and Mao's China suppressed their entrepreneurs and creatives, using uniform clothing as a crude but potent symbol of a threadbare equality. Thus, high-end fashion remained centred in Western Europe and in France in particular.

As the 1960s dawned, the baby-boom generation benefited from growing economies in which there were jobs for all, particularly in a burgeoning media and a democratised fashion industry. The ultra-femininity of their mothers' clothes was replaced by an ethos based on the simplicity of children's and men's clothes. Couture, with its high-priced, labour-intensive clothes, was under threat from a ready-to-wear, factory-produced culture that wanted something new and cheap every Saturday. The youthquake movement spawned the miniskirt, which sprang from the mods on the streets of London to the imaginations of *Mary Quant* in London and *Pierre Cardin* and *André Courrèges* in Paris. Couturiers such as Chanel, Schiaparelli and *Hubert de Givenchy* scurried to keep up, introducing boutique lines and moving into prêt-à-porter. The scene was set for a massive paradigm shift.

Image 15.1 *Toulouse-Lautrec collection, Balenciaga, 1951. Photo: The LIFE Picture Collection via Getty Images.*

15

Cristóbal Balenciaga (1895–1972)

His method, a subtle progression over his three decades of dominating couture, was a gradual refinement.

Balenciaga is the designer's designer, the most frequently credited by other designers as inspirational, the man even Chanel grudgingly admired (the only male couturier thus honoured) and Christian Dior graciously acknowledged as his master. This serious, shy and retiring Spaniard was a technical genius, the architect of cloth, conjuring flattering, dramatic shapes. He was also the most remarkable of far-sighted innovators, capable of sensing shifts in society's mood. His pre-war collections prefigured Dior's post-war New Look, and after the war he resisted Dior's retrospective fantasy and worked towards a crisp, pure-lined modernity. Cecil Beaton, who in 1954 referred to Balenciaga as 'the greatest dressmaker of today', wrote: 'If Dior is the Watteau of dressmaking – full of nuances, chic, delicate and timely – then Balenciaga is fashion's Picasso. For like that painter, underneath all his experiments with the modern, Balenciaga has a deep respect for tradition and a pure classic line. All artists who, apart from their unique personal gift, are also mediums transmitting the message of the art of the past, inevitably are timely as well as timeless.'

Colin McDowell, in *McDowell's Directory of Twentieth Century Fashion*, called Balenciaga 'unquestionably the greatest designer of the twentieth century'. François Baudot wrote in awestruck hyperbole: 'You may have thought you were looking at a Zurbarán, a Velazquez or a Goya, but it was always Balenciaga. Discouraging imitators, he created his aloof garments in an atmosphere of secrecy and calm for a small and elite number of wealthy beauties who saw him as a cult figure.' As his self-appointed acolyte and lifelong friend, Hubert de Givenchy recalled in 2006, 'Balenciaga was like his clothes, perfection. He is still my god.'

Cristóbal Balenciaga Eisaguirre was born in 1895 in Guetaria, a small Basque fishing village. His father, the captain of a pleasure boat, died while Cristóbal was still a child, and his mother, Martina Eisaguirre, supported her three children by working as a seamstress, an activity for which her younger son developed a passion. The story goes that this untypical boy was forward enough to admire the

Drécoll *tailleur* worn to church by an ageing local aristocrat, the Marquesa de Casa Torres. Her interest piqued, the Marquesa discovered that the thirteen-year-old's ambition was to be a couturier. She gave him a length of expensive fabric and the Drécoll suit to copy. Balenciaga described how petrified and yet how elated he was. He found the courage to cut into the cloth and, whatever the quality of the resulting outfit, the Marquesa was gracious enough to wear it. She became his first patron, arranging his apprenticeship with a tailor in San Sebastián.

In 1919 Balenciaga opened his own atelier, Eisa, in the town which was becoming the favoured resort of the Spanish royal family and its court. He established a Madrid branch in 1932 and one in Barcelona in 1938, employing members of his extended family to run them. His workroom staff were trained to high standards of traditional craftsmanship, and he visited Paris regularly as a buyer, attending shows and buying toiles, which he then translated for his own customers. Lesley Ellis Miller emphasises one other background factor that contributed to Balenciaga's unique and uniquely rigorous approach to fashion. 'His appreciation of art was similarly formed. In all parts of Spain, painting and sculpture are accessible to everyone in the churches and in the streets – as well as in art galleries and museums. Immense baroque churches dwarf the tiniest villages, and their interiors often contain elaborate chapels and overpowering altarpieces.'

Balenciaga was a devout man, and the church and its grandly modelled spaces, monumental images, sculpted draperies and lavishly painted, richly caparisoned saints would have lodged themselves securely in his receptive visual imagination – a semiotic language to be used in his search for an imposing beauty infused with dignity and meaning.

His colour sense was simultaneously subtle (his range of greys, browns and blacks was a focus of press wonder) and bold, in their depth and richness often reminiscent of late Renaissance or Baroque religious paintings. He would hazard unusual colour combinations that worked in a most spectacular way: ginger and bottle green, greige and granite, black and brown, honey beige on black.

Balenciaga moved to Paris in 1937, establishing a couture business on avenue George V with two partners, one with Basque connections. Some commentators have suggested that he was escaping the dangers and uncertainties of the Spanish Civil War (both Madrid and Barcelona were under siege from 1935, and San Sebastián fell to Franco's forces in 1936), but it is likely that Balenciaga intuited the economic stagnation and isolation – and consequent poverty – that would follow a Franco victory. He tried London first but could not get a work permit, then took the advice of Madge Garland, the fashion journalist and later educator, that he would be better received in Paris.

He was by no means in exile – he was able to run his business in Spain from 1940 on – but, as he told Prudence Glynn of *The Times* in an interview conducted in 1971 after his retirement, 'Paris used to have a special ambience for fashion because it contained hundreds of dedicated craftsmen making buttons and flowers and feathers and all the trimmings of luxe which could be found nowhere else.'

He stayed open through the war, supporting Lucien Lelong, head of the Chambre Syndicale de la Couture Parisienne, when the Nazis attempted to move the French couture industry to Berlin or

Image 15.2 *Cristóbal Balenciaga, 1927. Photo: Lip News Service/Roger Viollet via Getty Images.*

Image 15.3 *Balenciaga,* Vogue, *1942. Photo: Horst P Horst/Condé Nast via Getty Images.*

Vienna, standing up to 'six enormous Germans' with the suggestion that '[Hitler] might just as well take all the bulls to Berlin and try to train bullfighters there.' Although his circle of friends included the artists Braque, Chagall, Picasso, Miro and Palazuelo, he did not collect their work. Bettina Ballard, editor of *Vogue*, described his preferred decor as 'simple, almost austere', the atmosphere of the couture house as 'convent-like'. Photographs of his Spanish country home in Igueldo show the dark carvings of traditional Spanish furnishings and religious antiquities.

After the war, the French government concentrated on reviving the couture, levying a tax on all exports so that the Chambre Syndicale de la Couture Parisienne and its members could afford to mount the shows that would bring back the customers from around the world. Its reasons were only partially economic; Paris was couture and couture was Paris. The restoration of couture was essential for the restoration of a humiliated nation's self-respect. In the absence of Chanel, whose wartime collaboration with the enemy meant a necessary self-banishment to Switzerland, it soon became clear that two giants would bestride fashion's next decade, Christian Dior and Cristóbal Balenciaga. They were very different giants.

As Claire Wilcox wrote in 2007, 'Dior, an intuitive man, developed an extraordinary sensitivity to the climate of the day. Although shy and nervous of his own innovations, he moved quickly. … The fanfare with which his first collection was met on February 12, 1947, set the designer on an upward spiralling path upon which innovation was vital in order to maintain media interest.' Part of that innovation was commercial – the necessity for ready-to-wear collections and licences. 'Balenciaga, in contrast,' wrote Wilcox, 'was resistant to the idea of producing luxury ready-to-wear on the grounds that only haute couture, to which he was totally dedicated, could meet his own exacting standards. He was a traditional man who built his work gradually, developing his ideas over two or three years.'

gowns at a Red Cross benefit evening for the opening of Arden's new store. He opened another house under his own name on Madison Avenue and, in 1947, made a brief, triumphant return to Paris to show his collection there, his lush gowns completely in step with Dior's New Look. 'His eye for colour', wrote Annette Bissonette who curated an exhibition of James's work at Kent State University in 2007,

> resulted in unexpected combinations, in which pumpkin and mauve coexisted, linings added drama, and layers of tulle in many colours produced mysterious results. His ability to drape cloth, at times directly on a person, was at the heart of some of his most important work. Yet his legacy in the twenty-first century lies overwhelmingly in his ability to cut the cloth to produce abstract and complex shapes brought to life through experimentation and imagination.

James was evangelical about his work and the necessity for rigorous perfectionism. He designed academic courses for the Pratt Institute on dress design, calling one 'The Calculus of Fashion' to reflect fashion's state of constant change, appropriating from the early-nineteenth-century writer Johann Wolfgang van Goethe the term 'meta-morphology' to describe the phenomenon.

Despite the turmoil in his business life and despite the way he treated his clients (Gerber Klein memorably describes him as 'a perfect blend of beautiful manners and dreadful behaviour'), he retained some very important ones. Among them were Austine (Mrs William Randolph) Hearst, Mrs Harrison Whitney, Dominique de Menil and Anne, Countess of Rosse, as well as the wives of two rival designers, Mrs Lucien Lelong and Adrian's wife, Janet Gaynor, and influential women in publishing, such as Clare Boothe Luce, Mrs Condé Nast, Elsa Peretti, Carmel Snow and Diana Vreeland – and those two feuding couturières, Elsa Schiaparelli and Coco Chanel. You can almost hear the chuckle as Milbank points out that Schiaparelli got a bill but Chanel did not. Richard Martin wrote, 'He offended some of his most loyal clients, who longed for the designer's dresses and paid dearly for them, not only in money but in tolerating insults and abuse.' One of James's best customers was the beautiful, magenta-haired Standard Oil heiress, Millicent Rogers, whose extravagance, according to Cecil Beaton, outstripped that of all the other 'poor little rich girls'. For long periods, Rogers patronised Charles James exclusively and in 1949 she presented a panoply of James's clothes to the Brooklyn Museum following a 1948 exhibition based on her collection, titled 'A Decade of Design for Mrs Millicent H. Rogers'.

It is upon these clothes that much of James's rescued reputation rests and why costume historians know so much about how he achieved the structure of his gowns. He named many of his designs – Petal, Swan, Tulip, Butterfly, Four-Leaf Clover, Tree – in a system that had more to do with an abstract shape, a curve or a plane, summoned at some remove by the object than anything representational. His most famous dress was probably La Sirène, where soft silk is wrapped, draped and gathered round a slender, rigid inner sheath. He, however, regarded the Four-Leaf Clover gown of 1953 as the culmination of his career.

The grand gowns James conjured were imagined in great rooms with high ceilings and classical decoration. In 1948, for a photograph entitled 'The James Encyclopaedia', Cecil Beaton, who shared his background, grouped nine of them in just such a salon, its decor pale cream carved panelling in the Second Empire style. The ladies, their bare shoulders and elegant, vulnerable necks glowing in the soft, pinkish light, their vast skirts jostling for space, are taking coffee while they wait for the gentlemen, still around the dining table passing the port and smoking. It is a pre-war world to which the nostalgic yearned to return and the socially upwardly mobile longed to enter. It may have appealed to Beaton, but Annette Bissonette wrote, 'Like those he inspired, such as Christian Dior … he generated garments that, although visually intoxicating, returned women to an era of discomfort and subjugation. His talents were nonetheless widely sought and his custom work for clients and collaboration with manufacturers led to new silhouettes that had enormous impact on the fashion industry.'

In 1955 James, who was known to be homosexual and rumoured to go dancing in his own frocks, astonished everyone by marrying the wealthy Nancy Lee Gregory, with whom he had two children. This is echoed in *Phantom Thread* in the character of Alma, a waitress seduced and married by Woodcock. In 1956 James started to design children's wear, but by 1958 he found himself bankrupt once again. The marriage failed in 1961, and by 1964 James had moved into the Chelsea Hotel where he established a small studio. He attracted few clients; his reputation for falling out, failing to deliver and reneging on deals was, by now, poisonous. He did, however, make the acquaintance of the illustrator, Antonio Lopez, who, over the next few years, made it his private project to draw the best of James's designs. In 1975 he held a solo exhibition at the Everson Museum of Art in Syracuse. New York. Three years later Charles James died of pneumonia, a victim of self-neglect. In 1980, the Brooklyn Museum mounted a second larger retrospective.

Further reading: The biography *Charles James: Portrait of an Unreasonable Man* (2017) by Michèle Gerber Klein is beautifully written and rich in detail. Richard Martin's *Charles James*, part of the Fashion Memoir series, is a good analytical account of James's career and character, and Caroline Rennolds Milbank's account in *Couture: The Great Fashion Designers* (1985) places James in context. Timothy A. Long's *Charles James: Designer in Detail* is a brilliantly illustrated analysis of garments in various museum collections.

18

Claire McCardell (1905–1958)

She produced instant classics that were to form the basis of American designer sportswear.

Impatient for a modern style of dress that reflected in both practical and conceptual ways the way women wanted to live and dress in the twentieth century, Claire McCardell invented it. Her ideas have so influenced and pervaded contemporary fashion that in 1990 *Life* magazine named her one of the 100 most important Americans of the twentieth century. Four years later, Bernadine Morris of *The New York Times* referred to her as 'this country's finest designer'. A quintessentially American designer often compared to Frank Lloyd Wright, Raymond Loewy and Martha Graham, Claire McCardell had a democratic approach to fashion that gave style to everyday clothing and led the way towards shaking off the long-distance French dominance of American fashion – Richard Martin even characterised it as a 'thraldom to Parisian design'.

In her book, *What Shall I Wear?*, published in 1956, McCardell looked back on her early days in the 1920s on Seventh Avenue. 'I did what everybody else did,' she wrote, 'copied Paris.' In particular she copied Molyneux, Maggy Rouff and Alix (not yet known as Madame Grès) and took apart the dresses of Alix and Vionnet to discover their structure – a structure she simplified for the mass-manufacturing techniques with which she worked. But her instincts could never be satisfied by second-hand inspiration. McCardell was a questioner of basic precepts, a revolutionary. 'Clothes,' she told one interviewer, 'ought to be useful and comfortable. I've always wondered why women's clothes had to be delicate – why they couldn't be practical and sturdy as well as feminine.' She co-opted easy styles and hard-wearing fabrics from all kinds of work wear and children's wear and made them smart: suits in denim, big-pocketed shirts in ticking or cotton calico, loose dresses and jumpsuits in gingham, madras check and flannel. Her guiding principles were clean-lined, utilitarian design that satisfied the modernist dictum that form should follow function, that a product should be fit for its purpose, and that one should have respect for the fabric.

Image 18.1 *Claire McCardell evening shirt and skirt, 1955. Photo: Frances McLoughlin-Gill/Condé Nast Collection via Getty Images.*

She produced instant classics that were to form the basis of the fashion genre known as American designer sportswear and within which she had many successors. Richard Martin wrote:

Significantly, they re-thought fashion from its very roots, not simply paring away some of the accretions of traditional prettiness but founding a new standard for a practical, modern style more in accord with the lives of the women of their era. Furthermore the chief impetus came from women designers, not from men. The sportswear tradition in America includes male manufacturers and a few early-generation pioneers such as Sydney Wragge and later John Weitz, but the driving force of fashion's fresh invention resides with the women who answered women's needs.

It is a long roll call: among these women were Elizabeth Hawes, Anne Fogarty, Muriel King, Emily Wilkens, Tina Leser, Frances Sider, Carolyn Schnurer, Jo Copeland, Bonnie Cashin, Ceil Chapman, Louella Ballerino, Vera Maxwell, Mollie Parnis, Clare Potter, Nettie Rosenstein, Pauline Trigère and Valentina. In the 1930s and 1940s, American women made their way into the workplace in ever-greater numbers, enjoyed an active social life often based on a sporting activity – golf, tennis, cycling, swimming – and demanded affordable, mass-produced clothes to look good in at all these times. These were the designers who, also living that life, answered their needs. Of them all, McCardell was the most creative, the leader in what was really a paradigm shift in fashion.

Claire McCardell was born in 1905 in Frederick, Maryland. She was the first child of Adrian Leroy McCardell, a state senator and president of the Frederick County National Bank, and Eleanore Clingan McCardell, daughter of a Confederate officer from Jackson, Mississippi. Three brothers followed, Adrian, Robert and John. Claire's first exposure to fashion was through her Southern belle mother who subscribed to all the American and European fashion periodicals. A school friend remembered five-year-old Claire cutting out pictures from the magazines and, with her scissors, remaking them, grafting a bodice from one on to the skirt of another, changing a neckline, editing out some sleeves. This was the point at which, McCardell remembered half a century later, 'my eyes began their training'. She would also, of course, dress up in her mother's clothes and reflected as an adult, 'It wasn't me in the clothes, or just wearing them that interested me – it was the clothes in relation to me – how *changed* I felt once in them.'

Perhaps her most powerful influence was Annie Koogle, the family dressmaker who was a skilled adapter of *Vogue* patterns, often draping and fitting on the body. From her, McCardell learned to understand clothing's relationship to the body and its construction. A sporting girl, she was soon taking apart and remaking her clothing and that of her brothers in not always successful attempts to make herself more comfortable clothes for an active life. However, this intimate knowledge of men's clothing was to shape her approach to designing for women. She found men's wear infinitely more rational than contemporary women's clothing and was to filch for women generous side pockets in trousers, deeper armholes in jackets, sturdy topstitching borrowed from Levi's jeans, and practical, washable fabrics like cotton shirting.

Image 18.2 *Claire McCardell, 1940. Photo: Serge Balkin/Condé Nast Collection via Getty Images.*

Image 18.3 *Claire McCardell swimsuit, 1945. Photo: Serge Balkin/Condé Nast Collection via Getty Images.*

In 1923, with graduation from Frederick High School approaching, McCardell announced her intention to study fashion illustration and costume design in New York. Her father would not hear of it, and she spent the next two years studying home economics at Hood College, a liberal arts college conveniently close to the McCardell home. She dropped out towards the end of her second year and, with the support of her mother, convinced her father to let her go to New York to study at the School of Fine and Applied Arts that would, in time, become the Parsons School of Design. In her foundation year she shared a room with two other students at the Three Arts Club. To her delight, the wealthy members would sell the students in residence their cast-off Paris originals for a few dollars. She bought as many as she could afford and took them apart to discover their construction before remaking them. This was a practice she continued in her second year when she finally got to study fashion design and construction in Paris, arriving there in the autumn of 1926. Madeleine Vionnet, whose training as a lingerie designer gave her an intimate understanding of the sensuous possibilities of cloth on the female body, was a particularly strong influence on McCardell, who began at an early stage to explore several of her techniques including the bias cut and the sashes used for wrapping and tying. From Vionnet, McCardell said she learned 'the way clothes worked, the way they felt'.

Back in America, McCardell graduated in the spring of 1928 and had a few false starts, including some modelling engagements and a short stint designing knitwear, which ended when she was fired after eight months for making clothes 'to please herself'. Yohannan and Nolf point out that this very tendency was to be the basis of her success and her status as a major fashion innovator. In 1965, *Time* magazine quoted her saying she had designed things she needed for herself, and 'it just turns out that other people need them too.'

priced at $2. This was such a success that the family moved to Indianapolis when Norman was five. He was a thin little boy with a hot temper, he later recalled. At the age of nineteen, fashion design was his chosen subject of study, but there was no such course so he studied illustration in New York at Parsons, a school with which he retained a lifelong connection. He also chose to contract his name, ditching the workaday Levinson in favour of Norell. He explained: 'Nor for Norman, L for Levinson, with another L added for looks.'

Norell took his first steps as a designer in 1922 in the field of costume design, working at the Astoria Studio of Paramount Pictures. The stars for whom he designed included Gloria Swanson in *Zaza* and Rudolph Valentino in *The Sainted Devil*. The studio closed shortly afterwards and Norell worked on some Broadway musicals before joining Charles Armour, a dress manufacturer, who sent him to Europe for the first time. The defining moment of his career came in 1928, when he joined Hattie Carnegie. A fierce perfectionist, Carnegie was brilliant in her own way, although the process was unoriginal – visiting the couturiers in Paris, buying pieces, pulling them apart back in New York to understand how they were designed, and turning them into more affordable clothes for their American clients. This was the way the American fashion industry worked, founded on the creative insecurity of the American industry and the dominance, often laced with arrogance, of the Paris-based couturiers. The regular visits to Paris were an extraordinary training ground for Norell, an opportunity to understand the secrets of the great European couturiers and develop a profound technical knowledge of the process of creating great fashion. Over twelve years, he developed his skills and his eye, benefiting from the formidable tutelage of Carnegie. He put it simply: 'I learned everything I knew from her.'

Carnegie never allowed Norell to take any credit. He worked for more than a decade in 'complete anonymity', as one Vogue editor put it. A shy and gentle man, he did not appear to be put out by this: the clash with Carnegie that led to his departure in 1940 was creative rather than ambition driven. They had a row over a dress worn by Gertrude Lawrence in *Lady in the Dark* on Broadway (he thought it perfect; she wanted it toned down). His decision to go solo came at a moment when the American fashion industry was poised to come of age, cut off from the influences of Paris during wartime and ready to make its own mark. Anthony Traina, a manufacturer best known for larger sizes, contacted him. 'He offered me a larger salary if my name were not used,' recalled Norell. 'A smaller amount if it were.' Thus Traina-Norell was created. From the beginning, it was conceived as a full collection rather than a series of pieces, which tended to be the way on Seventh Avenue. The principles of the Paris couture, founded on precision of fit, were now applied to ready-to-wear. Norell was therefore an important bridge between couture and ready-to-wear. Bettina Ballard, an influential editor at *Vogue* with a razor-sharp eye, recalled in her autobiography: 'I loved Norman's clothes. They had the same single-mindedness as Balenciaga's or Chanel's, and the same fanatical attention to quality. ... I bought as many as I could afford.'

He drew inspiration from the 1920s, a favourite decade for him, including silk jersey dresses and long wool evening dresses in his first collection. Norell had a sure sense of timing, a key ingredient of any designer's success. A full-length sweater dress, also shown in 1941, was another star piece. His friend, the fashion editor Bernadine Morris, wrote later: 'What Norman Norell had accomplished in that first collection was to give American fashion – producers and wearers alike – a freedom from dependence on foreign sources of inspiration. The American industry felt it could set its own directions, its own styles.' Norell went on to play a dominant role in American fashion for three decades. As early as 1943, his achievement was recognised with the first Coty American Fashion Critics Award, recognising the quality of his chemise dresses, sequined cocktail dresses and fur-lined coats. An invitation to a Norell show was a prized ticket: the collection was shown at 9 p.m. (with a black-tie dress code) right through until 1969, when the time was shifted to 5 p.m.

No doubt drawing on his twelve years of visiting Paris, Norell had an instinctive feel for trends and very rarely got it wrong. In 1942, he introduced the no-waistline chemise or shirt dress, not seen since the 1920s, which became a staple of his collections. When he was once asked to sum up his major contribution to fashion, Norell chose to focus on a detail: simple, high round necklines. 'I hated necklines. I always thought they made women look older. So I started making simple Peter Pan collars or no collars at all. Just a plain round neckline, no crap on it. … I do think it changed the look of clothes.' Another recurring theme was nautical, inspired by a childhood sailor suit he had worn and introduced as early as 1933 at Hattie Carnegie. Indeed, many of his ideas, according to Bernadine Morris, had their origin in the styles he bought in Paris for Carnegie in the 1930s. The influence of menswear, recalling his own father's roots in menswear retailing, also percolated through his work, such as in the creation of a sleeveless jacket over a bowed blouse and slim wool skirt.

Norell's own personal style was neat and precise. He believed day wear should be simple with the razzmatazz saved for evening, an attitude that is still at the heart of the New York way of dressing. During the 1950s, however, he adapted to changing tastes, creating shirtwaist dresses with full skirts in silk and lace and mixing tweed jackets with satin collars with satin ball gowns. Norell's sequined dresses were much-admired, dubbed mermaid dresses for their slithery, sensual appeal. In 1960, Anthony Traina was obliged through ill health to step down, allowing Norell to take over the business entirely, with some financial backing. Traina-Norell became Norman Norell, and he created an immediate sensation with a culotte-skirted wool flannel day suit in his very first solo collection. Eventually, he bought out his backers too, buoyed by the success of a fragrance launched with Revlon. Norell was copied, naturally. But this time the flow was back across the Atlantic: Paris-based companies picked up many of his designs, such as his culotte suit and his gored ice-skating skirt. With great magnanimity, Norell produced working sketches of the culotte suit free of charge for the trade with the intention of ensuring that his design would be copied properly – an extraordinary gesture that won him huge goodwill on Seventh Avenue and beyond.

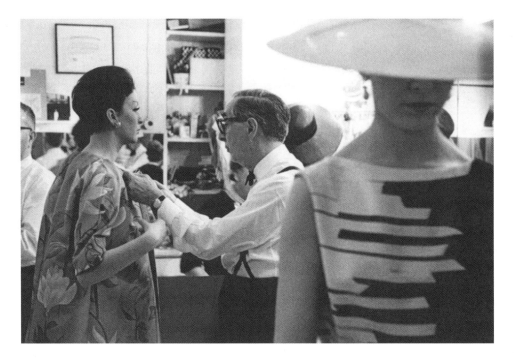

Image 20.2 *Norell at work, 1963. Photo: Bert Stern/Condé Nast via Getty Images.*

Through the 1960s, Norell remained a vibrant force in American fashion, often ahead of the pack. He designed the first evening jumpsuit in 1961, created trouser suits for 1963, and set the pace again by bringing back belts in 1966, heralding the return of emphasis on the waistline. He made news too, sending back his Coty Hall of Fame award in 1963 in protest at an award for the provocative Rudi Gernreich. There were mistakes: his culottes of 1960 were judged too early for the market. American trade newspaper *Women's Wear Daily*, then entering its golden age under the dynamic editorship of John Fairchild, also chose to give him the cold shoulder for a period. But by then Norell had attained the status of eminence grise. As the founder and first president of the Council of Fashion Designers of America, he can rightly be acclaimed as the father of the country's fashion industry. Sadly, the Metropolitan Museum's retrospective of 1972 was never seen by Norell. He suffered a stroke only a day before the opening and died ten days later. The house continued for a further five years with designer Gustave Tassell. In 2004, Patrick Michael Hughes, a lecturer at Parsons, attempted to revive the label.

Norell always downplayed his approach to design. He could make it sound very easy, but this was founded on decades of study and reflection. 'I believe in thinking out what the next logical and natural trend in fashion will be,' he said in 1952. 'Once I have decided, the rest is easy. I simply take the most straightforward approach to it, without any extra, fancy trimmings. I don't like over-designed anything.'

Further reading: The most recent survey of his career, *Norell: Master of American Fashion* (2018), by designer Jeffrey Banks, is a detailed and thorough work of affectionate tribute. Bernadine Morris, who was fashion editor of *The New York Times* and a friend of Norell, summarised his career in *American Fashion: The Life and Lines of Adrian, Mainbocher, McCardell, Norell, and Trigére* (1975), edited by Sarah Tomerlin Lee.

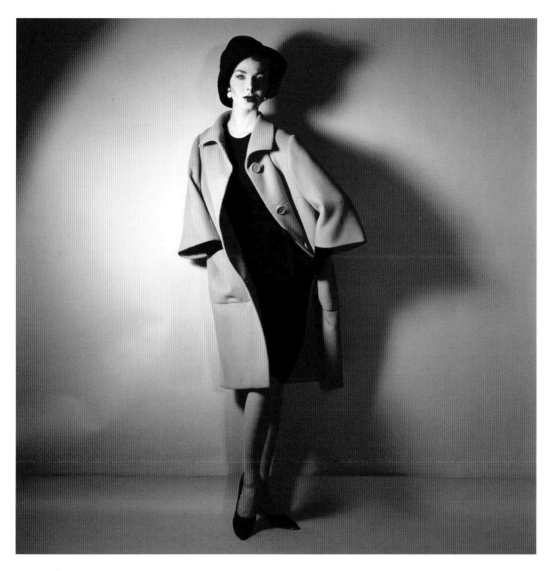

Image 20.3 *Norman Norell coat, 1961. Photo: Horst P. Horst/Condé Nast via Getty Images.*

Image 21.1 *Dresses by Pierre Cardin, 1968. Photo: Bill Ray/Life Magazine/The LIFE Picture Collection via Getty Images.*

21

Pierre Cardin (1922–)

Cardin was one of the epoch-defining designers of the 1960s.

Asked in 2006 to define himself in one word, Pierre Cardin replied, 'as a sculptor.' Although coming from a fashion designer that might sound hubristic, there is justice in his claim. His style – which we call futuristic because so much of it seems inspired by 1950s modernism, by the romance of the space race and by images from sci-fi pulp magazines – was in fact the consequence of applying a bold abstractionism to the human body. Three-dimensional, plastic, his designs have always had a sculptural quality, a clean profile, occasionally a sense of monumentality and a hierarchical presence.

Most importantly, they broke dramatically with tradition in their design and in their target market. In the 1950s, Cardin already understood that, together, American scientific optimism and London's vital youth culture with its globe-conquering music and inventive fashion scene were the forces powering society into the world of tomorrow – and the world of tomorrow is where Cardin always wanted to be. He famously tried on Neil Armstrong's moon-visiting spacesuit and designed functioning spacesuits. He gave his models space helmets and moon boots to wear. And he gave the world the bubble dress, the cocoon coat, the trapezoidal cut, enormous circular collars and sharp-edged asymmetric cuts that, along with materials like vinyl, Perspex and mouldable 'Cardine', proclaimed themselves the high-tech future. Long before he became the first designer to identify China as an emerging market, his design handwriting owed something to Chinese theatre and traditional dress in its love of geometry, illusion and drama. Ernestine Carter of *The Sunday Times* wrote in 1974, 'He is an explosion of talent, a fountain of ideas, which he tosses out like confetti, always an innovator but, except in his menswear, rarely an influence.'

The adjective most frequently applied to this designer, mega-entrepreneur and French academician, however, is egotistical. The clothes – witty, insouciant, and very sexy – deceive you into expecting a sense of humour. One might hope that the designer who, to celebrate his Chinese coup, gave his men's suits flicked-up 'pagoda' shoulders would surely be a giggle to meet, but in person any levity is hard to find. In an interview, he does not wait for the questions but leads with the assertion that his is the biggest fashion name of all time, circling back to that statement repeatedly to make sure one hasn't

Before, the middle-aged had always tried to give the young what they thought the young needed; the youth revolution came as a terrible shock because the middle-aged hadn't noticed the new economic freedom and didn't know what had hit them. They were stuck deep in old attitudes; a woman was daddy's daughter until she became someone's wife. In the mid-1950s, women started, without analysing it, to grab a time when they were their own person by moving out from under daddy's roof and sharing a usually overcrowded, usually scruffy flat with other girls.

The mini was part of that. The mini said: 'Look at me'. It was very exuberant, pure glee. Looking back, it was the beginning of the women's movement. Clothes always say it first, you know, then comes the effect. All those retro fashions of the 1970s betrayed the nervousness that was to come.

In her autobiography, Quant wrote, 'Fashion is the product of a thousand and one different things. It is a whole host of elusive ideas, influences, cross-currents and economic factors captured into a shape and dominated by two things … impact on others, fun for oneself. It is unpredictable, indefinable. It is successful only when a woman gets a kick out of what she is wearing; when she feels marvellous and looks marvellous.'

As Amy de la Haye wrote in 1996, 'Bazaar caused a fashion revolution. Its short production runs of youthful ready-to-wear clothes were a far cry from the established formula for formal, structured and highly accessorised styles. In comparison to haute couture pieces, Mary Quant's clothes were considered cheap. Rejecting the conventional categories of day and evening wear and seasonal collections, she produced new designs all year round.'

The short skirts of 1955 still covered the knee – as they still did in a photograph of Bazaar's window taken in 1961 (and it was not until 1966 that *Time* magazine noticed that something quite significant was happening and ran its cover story on Swinging London). 'Nevertheless,' said Quant in a radio interview with Colin McDowell in 2009, for his BBC Radio 4 essay, *The Shock of the Knee*, 'from the beginning bowler-hatted types would knock on the window and shake their umbrellas at us to admonish us.' Asked if she was perhaps deliberately provoking that sort of person, she agreed that indeed she was. Felicity Green, fashion editor of *The Daily Mirror* in the 1960s, was challenged by her chairman, Hugh Cudlipp, for supporting Quant with regular exposure on her pages. She refused to mend her ways and was told, 'I probably ought to fire you.'

The second Bazaar opened in 1957 in Knightsbridge, and in 1962 Quant accepted a contract to produce four collections a year for JC Penney, the American store group. She expanded the range of the fabrics she used, including nylon, PVC, men's suitings and rugby-shirt jersey. Her innovations included the skinny-rib sweater and hot pants, with many of her designs based on a playful subversion of classic garments: the Norfolk jacket, knickerbockers, tab-collared shirts and Liberty bodices. In 1961, she launched her first wholesale collection, followed two years later by Ginger Group, a lower-priced line. By the mid-1960s, she was designing underwear, swimwear, night attire, stockings and tights, rainwear, furs, sewing patterns for Butterick and a hugely successful range of cosmetics beloved for its witty nomenclature (courtesy of Alexander). In 1965, she took her collection on a whistle-stop tour of the United States. With thirty outfits and her own models, she showed in twelve cities in fourteen days. Sporting miniskirts and Vidal Sassoon's five-point geometric haircuts just like Quant's own, the models ran and danced down the catwalk. It was the epitome of Swinging London, taking America by storm. In 1966, the company adopted the abstract daisy as its logo and Mary was awarded the OBE. Her son, Orlando, was born in 1970.

The Quant triumvirate embraced the concept of lifestyle brand in the early 1970s and over the following decades Quant's name was attached to stationery, spectacle frames and sunglasses, household furnishings and carpets, wine and toys. In 1981, she relaunched a new fashion range and a shoe collection. Mary Quant remained a genuine fashion innovator well into the 1990s on the back of the lifestyle retailing boom. Her market had grown up with her and she was able to anticipate its demands. As well as her autobiography, *Quant by Quant*, she wrote several books on beauty and cosmetics.

Mary Quant has been multiply honoured by the British Fashion Council and by various universities. Alexander Plunket Greene died in 1990, and Mary Quant herself stepped down as director of Mary Quant Ltd. in 2000 while remaining a consultant for the myriad products she pioneered over her long career. She was made a Dame in 2015 and was the subject of two London exhibitions in 2019: *Swinging London: A Lifestyle Revolution – Terence Conran/Mary Quant* at the Fashion and Textile Museum; and a retrospective exhibition, *Mary Quant*, at the Victoria & Albert Museum. Her son advised on the latter.

Further reading: Mary Quant's autobiography (1965), *Quant by Quant*, is a must-read. Amy de la Haye's *The Cutting Edge: 50 Years of British Fashion* (1996) and Christopher Breward, David Gilbert and Jenny Lister's *Swinging Sixties: Fashion in London and Beyond 1955–1970* (2006) provide good background. *Mary Quant* (2019) by Jenny Lister, the companion book to the V&A exhibition, contains much new material.

Image 22.4 *Eyelet mini dress, Mary Quant,* Vogue *1968. Photo: Art Kane/Condé Nast via Getty Images.*

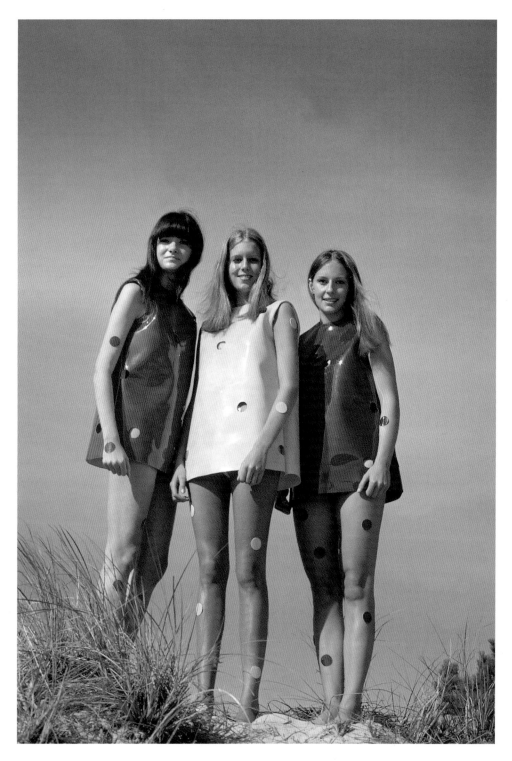

Image 23.1 *Rudi Gernreich plastic mini-dresses, 1967. Photo: William Connors/Condé Nast via Getty Images.*

23

Rudi Gernreich (1922–1985)

He believed the couturiers of Paris produced clothes that constricted and trussed up women. Gernreich's mission was to set them free.

Rudi Gernreich was a blast of fresh air in the fashion world of the 1950s and summed up the youthful, irreverent spirit of the 1960s. His flair for self-publicity was matched by an enthusiasm, bordering on obsession, with being ahead of his contemporaries. That mix makes him a controversial figure in the history of fashion, but the global media furore over the creation of a topless swimsuit in 1964 has obscured this Californian designer's more significant achievements. As his long-term muse and friend Peggy Moffitt put it, 'I have always felt that Rudi's great talent was overlooked because of the headlines.'

In fact, Gernreich showed some reluctance to unveil his topless swimsuit, despite having predicted its emergence in 1962. He acknowledged that it was ahead of its time and had no plans to put it into production, until influential fashion editor Diana Vreeland urged him to do so. He was also haunted by the fear that Emilio Pucci, his rival on the other side of the Atlantic as a torchbearer for youth-driven innovation, might beat him to it. Moffitt, who modelled the suit in a celebrated photograph only published by trade newspaper *Women's Wear Daily* at the time, thought it was an unwise move in retrospect. 'Rudi did the suit as a social statement,' she said in 1985. The suit, she emphasised, was about freedom and was not intended to be judged too literally. Gernreich's much more significant contribution to the evolution of fashion was taking forward the pioneering spirit of Claire McCardell's sportswear for a new generation, producing clothes that were unconstructed, unrestricting and, he always felt, liberating. He believed the couturiers of Paris produced clothes that constricted and trussed up women. Gernreich's mission was to set them free. With the creation of the so-called no-bra bra in 1965, made from soft transparent nylon with neither padding nor boning, he did just that.

He was born in 1922 in Vienna, Austria, a world away from the California that became his home as an adult. His father, Siegmund Gernreich, a hosiery manufacturer, committed suicide in 1930 when Gernreich was just eight, so he grew up under the watchful eye of his mother and his aunt, who ran a dress shop that he later described as a 'sanctuary' from the austere world of interwar Vienna. Here, he could sketch to his heart's content and learn about clothes in a welcoming environment. Austrian influences popped up in his professional career years later in America: checkerboard trousers, memorably worn by Lauren Bacall in a shoot for *Life* in 1953, recall the geometrics of the Bauhaus movement. In 1938 the Austrian Anschluss with Adolf Hitler's Germany sparked a Jewish exodus from Vienna, and Gernreich and his mother were among those who chose California as their destination. Bizarrely, his first job in America was working in a mortuary. 'I do smile sometimes when people tell me my clothes are so body-conscious I must have studied anatomy,' recalled Gernreich. 'You bet I studied anatomy!'

More conventionally, he also studied art at Los Angeles City College. He then worked briefly in the publicity department at RKO Studios before becoming enthused about the world of dance and joining Lester Horton's West Coast troupe, inspired by the work of choreographer Martha Graham. His dance study was supplemented by freelance fabric design work for Hoffman California Fabrics in the mid-1940s. In 1950 he recognised that dance was not his future and left Lester Horton to move to New York for a job with George Carmel, a coat and suit company. Gernreich swiftly developed a profound dislike for the American garment trade's obsession with the word from Paris. 'Everyone with a degree of talent – designer, retailer, editor – was motivated by a level of high taste and unquestioned loyalty to Paris. … After about six months, I began to vomit every time I thought about the imperiousness of it all,' he recalled. 'I produced terrible versions of Dior. I was finally let go.'

The early 1950s were a period of fits and starts for Gernreich, although a legendary meeting with Diana Vreeland at *Harper's Bazaar* in 1951 gave him some encouragement. 'Who are you, young man?' she said. 'You're very gifted.' Some degree of stability was established when he met Walter Bass, with whom Gernreich said he never got along. Nevertheless, their business partnership lasted eight years, partly because Bass enticed Gernreich into signing a draconian seven-year contract. By the time it expired, Gernreich was a star. His first gingham and cotton tweed dresses were snapped up by an influential shop in Los Angeles called Jax. In New York, buyers went into rhapsodies. Gernreich's flair for fresh, youthful, unconstricted sportswear struck a chord with buyers and fashion editors at a time when the influence of Paris was steadily diminishing.

Fashion magazines were emerging as ever-more important style arbiters, a phenomenon that Gernreich recognised earlier than many of his contemporaries and exploited to the full. In March 1952 he created the prototype for the first bra-free swimsuit in wool jersey with a tank top. His first magazine credit was in the February 1953 issue of *Glamour*, featuring a knitted tube dress that was a forerunner of the stretch minis of the late 1980s. Swimsuits really took off for him in 1955 through a deal with Westwood Knitting Mills, for whom he produced wool knitted and elasticated swimsuits. The late 1950s and 1960s were a golden period of creativity for Gernreich, who steadily expanded his business into a veritable empire. In 1956 he produced his first menswear designs, originally waiters'

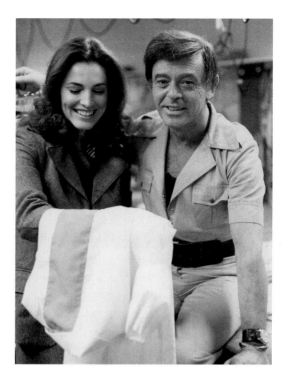

Image 23.2 *Model Rose McWilliams in Gernreich swimsuit. Photo: Bettmann via Getty Images.*

Image 23.3 *Rudi Gernreich, 1972. Photo: Toronto Star Archives/Toronto Star via Getty Images.*

jackets for a Chinese restaurant, recreated as shirt jackets for the beach or home. A women's shoe collection for Ted Saval followed the next year, and stockings were added in 1959. Accessories were important to Gernreich, who believed in the concept of a total look.

The long-anticipated end of his contract with Walter Bass allowed Gernreich to launch his own company, G.R. Designs, in 1960. The youthful energy and bright colours of Gernreich's collections were a harbinger of the youthquake of the 1960s – Gernreich's hemlines were above the knee as early as 1961. From his headquarters at 8460 Santa Monica Boulevard, Gernreich worked fanatically hard, producing thumbnail sketches as a starting point and working them up later with fabric samples and colour swatches. Often, ideas would come to him just before waking or falling asleep, moments that had a profound mystic significance for him. *The New York Times* picked up on Gernreich's soaring profile, dubbing him 'California's most successful export since the orange'.

But Gernreich's fellow designers, particularly on the East Coast, were not so enthusiastic. When Gernreich won the Coty American Fashion Critics Award in June 1963, Norman Norell returned his own Hall of Fame Coty in protest. At the preparations for the Coty Award presentation, even critics who admired him thought a white lingerie satin trouser suit that he planned to include in the show was a little too louche for the times. The Coty jury asked him to withdraw it, a request in which he acquiesced in a rare moment of restraint.

In Europe, the designer who came closest to expressing Gernreich's spirit was Emilio Pucci, based in Italy. Both Pucci and Gernreich had predicted that breasts would be uncovered within a few years. Peggy Moffitt believes competition with Pucci prompted Gernreich to move fast, but he was also encouraged by fashion editors sensing a scoop. Gernreich himself later described the topless swimsuit as the natural extension of his cut-out designs. 'By 1964, I'd gone so far with swimwear cutouts that I decided the body itself – including breasts – could become an integral part of a suit's design.' Orders poured in for the controversial swimsuit, but across the United States store presidents stepped in to prevent the suits being delivered. One store was picketed, another had a bomb threat. Some 3,000 swimsuits were sold, although there is little evidence they were ever worn publicly, except by a club entertainer and a nineteen-year-old Chicago girl, Toni Lee Shelley, who was promptly arrested. The creation of the topless swimsuit made Gernreich a cause célèbre and media favourite for the rest of the career, alternately praised and mocked. All this tended to overshadow his more substantial achievements.

Although *Women's Wear Daily* had been quick to publish a photo of the swimsuit, publisher John Fairchild dismissed Gernreich in his book, *The Fashionable Savages* (1965), saying his clothes were badly constructed. By contrast, another critic, the designer Norman Norell, relented in 1966, acknowledging Gernreich's status as a major name in modern fashion design. It was a period of rich creativity for Gernreich with a series of firsts, both creative and commercial, ranging from the first fashion video (titled 'Basic Black') and the first chain-store link-up (with Montgomery Ward) to the creation of the chiffon T-shirt dress. In October 1966, Gernreich's collection showed two looks: short hemlines and thoroughly Swinging Sixties styles, contrasted with long and dressed up. The designer was turning social commentator: there were no rights or wrongs in fashion any more – nor in society. In a statement published for his resort collection in the following year, he declared: 'For the first time in the history of the world … the young are leading us. There is now a Power Elite of the young.' Once started on the social commentary path, Gernreich just could not stop. By 1968, he was pontificating on the film *Bonnie and Clyde*, castigating the period costume trend it inspired. 'History must be used,' he said. 'Not just restored.'

Gernreich's big theme by then was unisex dressing. 'Today our notions of masculine and feminine are being challenged as never before,' he said. 'The basic masculine-feminine appeal is in people, not clothes. When a garment becomes sufficiently basic, it can be worn unisexually.' Even the skirt was finished, he claimed, drawing a sharp rebuke from *Women's Wear Daily*, which said Gernreich had 'boxed himself into a corner'. The barrage of interest in Gernreich became overwhelming for the designer, who announced in October 1968 that he was taking a year off and disappeared to Morocco and Europe. But he returned from the sabbatical as effervescent as ever, producing a unisex stripped-down look for a special futuristic issue of *Life*, photographed on male and female models with shaved heads and bodies (it was brought to life for Expo 70 in Osaka). By this stage, there was a sense that Gernreich was relying on gimmickry rather than creativity to keep his name in the spotlight, although many of his ideas were forerunners of trends of the 1980s and 1990s. The 1971 spring collection featured models carrying guns and wearing dog tags and combat boots. Gernreich became ever-more obsessed with technology, including spray-on clothes and the concept of transmigration of fabrics to the body. In 1971, he forecast that 'the designer will become less artist, more technician. ... A knowledge of machinery such as computers will be essential.'

Home life for Gernreich was more measured. He lived in Laurel Canyon with his long-term partner, Oreste Pucciani, a professor of French. Interviewed in 1998, Pucciani commented that Gernreich 'lived in an eternal present'. The designer himself once said, 'I felt I had to be experimental at any cost, and that meant always being on the verge of a success or a flop.' His simplest and biggest innovation of the 1970s was probably the thong, a slim strip of fabric that became a bestselling piece of underwear for women by the end of the century. He also produced designs for furniture, rugs and kitchen accessories, plus a fragrance packaged in a chemist's beaker. In his final years, he became obsessed by the potential for gourmet soups and, in a parting gesture, produced the pubikini, photographed by Helmut Newton in 1985 shortly before his death from lung cancer. In the Newton photograph, this sliver of fabric left little to the imagination, revealing a triangle of the model's pubic hairs, which Gernreich had dyed green. To the very end, Gernreich could not resist stirring up mischief.

An exhibition at the Museum of Contemporary Art's Pacific Designer Center in Los Angeles in 2012, titled 'The Total Look: The Creative Collaboration Between Rudi Gernreich, Peggy Moffitt and William Claxton', toured a number of venues in America and reminded a new generation of his impact. A relaunch of the label was announced in late 2018 by European entrepreneur Matthias Kind, with a knitwear collection designed by Los Angeles artist Lisa Anne Auerbach.

Further reading: The best summary of Gernreich's career is Cathy Horyn's 'Naked Ambition' (May 1998), published in *Vanity Fair*. Former Gernreich model and muse Peggy Moffitt collaborated with photographer husband William Claxton on the well-illustrated *The Rudi Gernreich Book* (1991).

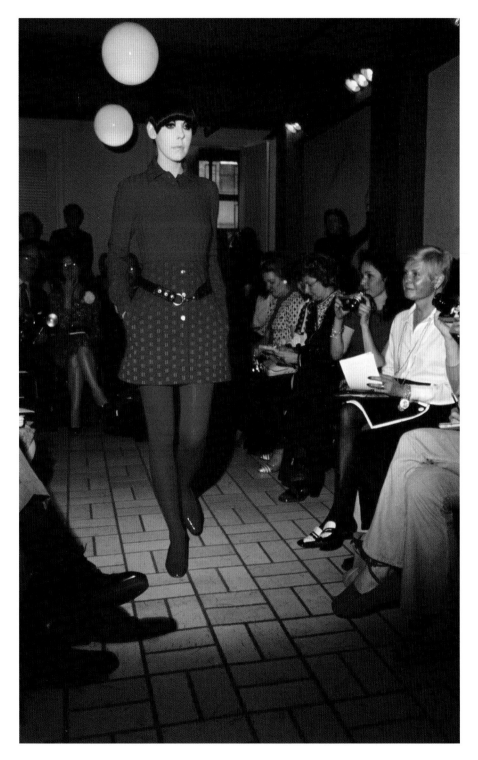

Image 23.4 *Muse Peggy Moffitt, Rudi Gernreich, 1971. Photo: Bettmann via Getty Images.*

24

Yves Saint Laurent (1936–2008)

Saint Laurent perfectly answered the moods and needs of his time.

Yves Saint Laurent was, in the words of the man closest to him, born with a nervous breakdown. Even so, he was also probably the most influential fashion designer of the second half of the twentieth century. He synthesised the ingenious modernity of Coco Chanel and the sensuous lyricism of Christian Dior, his mentor and first employer. The addition, as François Baudot noted in his account of twentieth-century fashion, of 'a breath of youth and his extrasensory perception of the needs and wants of his contemporaries … led to the YSL monogram leaving its stamp on a whole era'.

Saint Laurent reinvented Paris fashion for the young, giving the women of the baby-boomer generation a new wardrobe stocked with easy, youthful clothes that – in their energy, flirtatious assertiveness and borrowings from the 'active' male wardrobe – prefigured the social and political emancipation women were just learning to crave. He was among the first couturiers to understand that, instead of standing by while his ideas were copied and disseminated to a wider market by others, he could produce his own ready-to-wear 'diffusion' or 'boutique' line (iconically named Rive Gauche), making those clothes more easily accessible to younger, less wealthy women. He was the first couturier to truly understand the importance of accessories in creating a look. Often the clothes were really quite simple; it was the accessory 'garnish' that added the bravura and romance.

Hypersensitive, self-centred, narcissistic and emotionally fragile, Yves Saint Laurent was also highly cultivated, literate, diffident and charming with a mischievous sense of humour. When he posed nude in the 1970s for the picture to advertise a YSL men's scent, he told the photographer, Jean-Loup Sieff: 'I want to create a scandal.' The resulting portrait is unforgettable. Backlit and shadowy, wearing only his spectacles, the designer looks directly into the lens, simultaneously confident in his slender, almost adolescent beauty yet projecting an eroticism that's wistful and tentative. In any other period a designer might very well have been ridiculed for such vanity but this was the hippie moment of the Age of Aquarius, Flower Power, Woodstock, peace and love. He had his scandal, and overnight became a gay icon. There were other scandals along the way: the trouser suit that rattled the composure of a thousand maitre d's, the first headline-grabbing transparent blouse, and (a decade later) the steamy mouth-to-mouth onstage embrace with which he thanked Rudolf Nureyev for launching another fragrance, Kouros, before the packed Opéra Comique.

He attracted a gilded circle of protectors, defenders and friends upon whose loyalty he made great demands. In his later years, however, there was scant amusement. Mischief turned to melancholy and his shyness became reclusiveness. Rare sightings on the catwalk revealed an overweight, shambling figure with dyed auburn hair, a pasty complexion and a dazed expression. Even the coterie of rich, hedonistic friends and artistic collaborators fell away as he retreated into an introverted isolation. 'He is simply not interested in other people,' said Pierre Bergé, his closest friend, former lover and business partner (and the man who made the natal nervous breakdown diagnosis).

Rich, famous, multiply honoured by his country and the community of his peers, he succumbed to the despair and pain that had dogged him all his life. He was a man who wore his anguish on his sleeve. He accepted it, indulged it even, as collateral to his genius. In his office he kept a framed quotation from Marcel Proust, whose *A La Recherche du Temps Perdu* he read and reread throughout his life: 'The magnificent and lamentable family of the nervous is the salt of the earth. It's they and no one else who founded religions and created masterpieces.'

Yves Saint Laurent's only real training was a brief period understudying Dior, the master of a formal, ultra-feminine glamour. Yet his only equal in innovation was Chanel who, in 1967 when she was eighty-four, declared him her 'only inheritor'. Like Chanel in the 1920s and 1930s, Saint Laurent perfectly answered the mood and needs of his time. Both responded intuitively to overwhelming impulses towards political and social emancipation for women, giving women the clothes in which to grasp equality. It became easy to forget, given the decades of Saint Laurent's decline into a threadbare and solipsistic reworking of his own best ideas, how dramatic and beautiful those epoch-defining collections were. The Mondrian (1965) with its bright blocks of colour, the Pop-Art (1966), inspired by Andy Warhol, the African (1967), the Safari (1968), the Marlene Dietrich-inspired collection of 1969 when he introduced both the mini and the tuxedo, the Moroccan (1970), the Opera/Ballets Russes (1976) with its opulently clad peasants and gypsies ('My most beautiful collection', said Saint Laurent), the Velasquez (1977), the Chinoiserie (1977), the Picasso (1979), the Collection Shakespeare (1980) dedicated to literature and poetry, Aragon, Cocteau and Apollinaire, the Matisse Collection (1981) and the Cubist (1988) – all these stand out as milestones in fashion history.

Christian Lacroix, a designer of the generation that grew up in Saint Laurent's shadow, told Saint Laurent's biographer, Alice Rawsthorn: 'There have been other great designers this century but none with the same range. Chanel, Schiaparelli, Balenciaga and Dior all did extraordinary things. But they worked within a particular style. Yves Saint Laurent is much more versatile, like a combination of all of them. I sometimes think he's got the form of Chanel with the opulence of Dior and the wit of Schiaparelli.'

Yves Henri Donat Mathieu Saint Laurent was born in 1936 in Oran, Algeria, into a wealthy and prominent family. He grew up knowing himself a misfit in the close, conservative and Catholic 'colon' community. 'No doubt,' he told *Le Figaro* in 1991, 'because I was homosexual.' It was a terrible secret, a preference to be expressed only in furtive encounters with Arab street boys. The gentle, fragile and timid youngster was doted upon by his mother and sisters, whose dolls he dressed. He excelled academically but he was bullied and beaten by his classmates who sensed that the puny, artistic and unathletic boy was unacceptably different. 'Maybe,' he said much later, 'I didn't have what it took to be a boy.' He had, however, all the vanity and arrogance of the outcast who knows himself to be better than his tormentors. He dreamed of escape, of Paris and – as he wrote in his introduction to the catalogue to the 1983–1984 exhibition at the Metropolitan Museum of Art in New York – of his 'name written in fiery letters on the Champs Elysées'.

Theatre and costume design were his first passion (and he was later to prove a brilliant designer for Roland Petit's ballets, for theatre and film) but at seventeen he seized the first opportunity to present itself when he entered a competition for young fashion designers run by *Paris Match* magazine and

Image 24.2 *Yves Saint Laurent on the catwalk, autumn/winter 1991. Niall McInerney, Photographer.* © *Bloomsbury Publishing Plc.*

the International Wool Secretariat. In Paris with his mother to receive third prize, he met Michel de Brunhoff, the influential editor of French *Vogue*, who advised him to finish school and then enrol on a design course at the Chambre Syndicale de la Couture Parisienne. The course, which he started in the autumn of 1954, quickly bored him and, having won that year's IWS competition, he was despatched by de Brunhoff to show his sketch book to Christian Dior, who employed him immediately. When the originator of the New Look died from a heart attack in 1957, he had already made it clear that he considered Yves his natural successor.

His first collection after Dior's unexpected death, in January 1958, which introduced the Trapeze Line, was a success. Ernestine Carter, *The Sunday Times* fashion editor, later noted that it was to become the classic and enduring maternity dress shape. So central was Dior's image to French couture and the lucrative concept of 'Paris Fashion' that the next day's newspaper placards announced: 'Saint Laurent has saved France.' He was just twenty-one. A quarter-century later he wrote, 'Luckily there is a destructive kind of suffering I've never known, the one that comes from lack of recognition.'

Perhaps that initial reaction caused the owner of Dior, textile magnate Marcel Boussac, to give his stripling designer too much freedom. Instead of moving the collection forward by client-comforting increments each season, Saint Laurent went for a new look with every succeeding collection. When his second collection dropped skirts to calf length (ten years too soon, as Carter noted) the French press turned against him. When, in a hasty over-correction, he hobbled them above the knee for spring 1959, the response was vitriolic. Then in 1960, searching for a means of 'poetic expression', he elected to pay homage to the Beat culture of the Left Bank with a collection that featured the biker's black leather blouson jackets (albeit trimmed with mink), black cashmere turtlenecks and short bubble skirts flattering only to the young and hipless. The predominantly mature couture clients showed their displeasure. So did Marcel Boussac who had been protecting Saint Laurent from military conscription by pulling political strings. Boussac opted for patriotism and profits before poetry and lifted his protection.

Saint Laurent's brief induction into the army of France, then engaged in a savage struggle against Algerian nationalists, was a turning point in his life. It ensured that he was forced to start his own label since, at Dior, Boussac hurriedly replaced him with Marc Bohan. But it also precipitated his first breakdown, just nineteen days into his army career, and resulted in the treatment that wrecked his health and launched him on a lifetime of drug and alcohol abuse. At the Val-de-Grâce hospital, he was subjected to a primitive regime of dangerously addictive heavy-duty sedatives. He could not eat and, by the time his friend and lover, Pierre Bergé, secured his release two months later, he was utterly debilitated. Bergé, supported by *Women's Wear Daily*, ever Saint Laurent's champion, set about suing the house of Dior and establishing Saint Laurent's own couture house. 'I had never, ever wanted to be a businessman,' said Bergé whose interests lay in the arts and politics, 'but I agreed to do it for him.' He found an American backer, Jesse Mack Robinson, and in February 1962 the first YSL collection was shown in a small villa in Passy to a packed crowd of fashion cognoscenti. It nodded towards the sobriety of Balenciaga, and the reviews were ecstatic; *Life* magazine dubbed it 'the best collection of suits since Chanel'.

The second collection, six months later, established him as the man who was to dominate international fashion for two decades. It gave a glossy spin to youthful styles culled from the street, introducing the tunic over a pencil skirt, the Norman smock and the upmarket version of the working man's pea jacket. In this, Saint Laurent's work paralleled that of the young Chanel who had plagiarised the clothes of French sailors and Scottish ghillies.

Twenty years later, Saint Laurent reflected, 'The things I like best of all that I have done are the ones I borrowed from a man's wardrobe: the blazer, the trouser suit, the trench coat, knickerbockers, shorts, the safari jacket, the T-shirt, the suit, the whole suit idiom, the ambiguity of all that interests me.' The potent sexual content of androgynous dressing was a factor. He adored women as long as they had boyish bodies, but he created clean-lined, rational clothes that flattered the most womanly of figures. Breasts did not actually frighten him but he liked them small, free and pert in a transparent chiffon shirt under a strict tuxedo rather than magnified into cushiony cleavage by archaic corsetry. His way was the way young women of the 1960s and 1970s perceived themselves – slender and lithe with an upfront, natural coquetry. Like them, he hated what he called 'transvestite' or 'Easter Parade' clothing, the elaborate, tortured confections that betrayed the misogyny of many male designers.

In 1983, Saint Laurent became the first living designer to be given a solo exhibition at the Metropolitan Museum of Art. In 2001, he was awarded the rank of Commander of the Légion d'Honneur, and formally retired the following year. Although their romantic lives had taken different paths in later years, Yves Saint Laurent and Pierre Bergé were married just before Saint Laurent died in Paris in June 2008. Up until his own death in 2017, Bergé proved an able guardian of Saint Laurent's image, mounting several major exhibitions of the enormous archive and sponsoring many luxurious publications.

In 1993 the Yves Saint Laurent business was sold to Sanofi. Saint Laurent continued to design the couture collection until 2002, but in 1998 Alber Elbaz was appointed to design the ready-to-wear. A year later, Gucci Group (which was owned by PPR, now known as Kering) bought the brand, with Tom Ford taking creative control. Stefano Pilati took over in 2004, replaced by Hedi Slimane in 2010. He, in turn, was replaced by Anthony Vaccarello in 2016.

Further reading: There are many lifestyle picture books on Saint Laurent's homes and possessions. Alice Rawsthorn's biography, *Yves Saint Laurent* (1998), is excellent while Alicia Drake's *The Beautiful Fall: Fashion, Genius and Glorious Excess in 1970s Paris* (2006) is good background reading. For a critical appraisal, see Marguerite Duras in the 1988 catalogue *Yves Saint Laurent: Images of Design 1958–1988* and her book, *Yves Saint Laurent: Icons of Fashion Design* (2010). Hamish Bowles's *Yves Saint Laurent Style* (2008) is also illuminating. *Yves Saint Laurent* by Farid Chenoune (2010) is the beautifully illustrated catalogue to the retrospective exhibition in Paris. Yves Saint Laurent's early life and work have been the subject of three feature films of mixed quality.

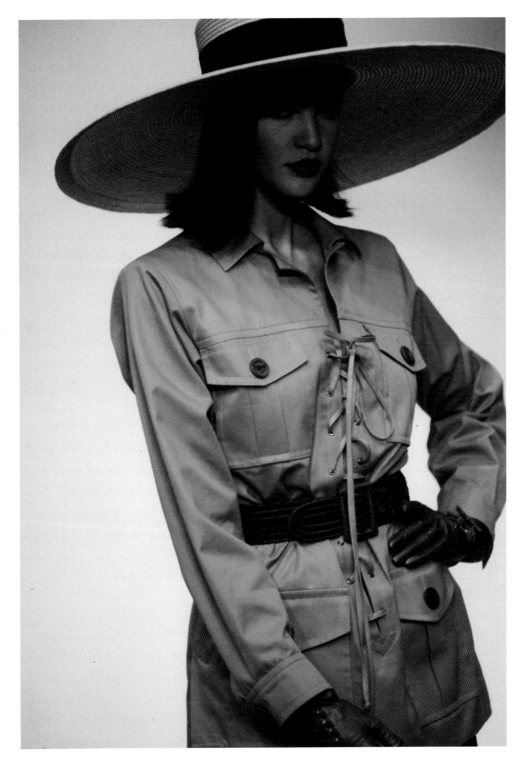

Image 24.3 *Safari jacket, Yves Saint Laurent, spring/summer 1995. Niall McInerney, Photographer.* ©
Bloomsbury Publishing Plc.

Image 24.4 *Moroccan mood, Yves Saint Laurent, spring/summer 1988. Niall McInerney, Photographer.* ©
Bloomsbury Publishing Plc.

back burner while constructing a post-Pill please-myself sexuality that expressed independence, self-determination and a new sense of empowerment.

André Courrèges was not a member of this generation, but he largely understood it and identified with it. He told Brenda Polan in an interview for *The Guardian* in 1979, 'My revolution of 1965 was not a calculated volte-face; it was an instinctive thing, a reaction to a period which was both progressive and aggressive. A designer must be a sociologist; he must look at the lives people lead, the way their houses are built, what their needs and preoccupations are.'

On that occasion, just a decade and a half after the collection that set all Paris on its ears, Polan described Courrèges's salon in some detail:

Today [it] still reflects his identification with the shiny, hard-surfaced clinical world of pushbutton machines and silicon chips. Like the offices and workrooms beyond it, it is all a startling high-gloss white. … Here vast, untinted mirrors reflect shiny white walls, a gleaming white-tiled floor, white leather and chrome furniture and rails of distinctively cut clothes in vibrant-coloured cottons, satins, silks, fine wools and fantasies of feathers and chiffon.

At that time it was easy to make the connection between the decor and the philosophy. The man who had delighted in an invitation to sit in at NASA Mission Control in Cape Canaveral was still locked into the sci-fi vision of a future where man (and woman) walked on the moon and lived in a then only vaguely imagined uncluttered and dust-free domestic world of technological miracles. But there was more to it than that. There was the Balenciaga connection.

André Courrèges was born in Pau, in southern France almost in the shadow of the Pyrenees, in 1923. His father was employed as the major domo in a private chateau and sent his son to a school that specialised in civil engineering – where he gained an understanding of three-dimensional structure that was to become the basis of his innovative garment construction. Growing up during the Second World War in Vichy France, young André trained in Aix-en-Provence as a pilot in the French Air Force but was certain that his interests lay in fashion. The great Cristóbal Balenciaga had been born only miles away in the Basque country on the other side of the border with Spain – and he, Courrèges decided, was the master from whom he would learn. So, as soon as the war ended in 1945, André set out for Paris, aged twenty-two. He studied fashion design at the Chambre Syndicale school and attempted to get a job with his idol. Initially he could not obtain an appointment to plead his case, so he took a job at the Jeanne Lafaurie fashion design house. Eventually, in 1950, he found a way. 'I went to a team of smugglers in Hendaye who carried Balenciaga's patterns and designs between Paris and his offices in Spain,' he told Valerie Guillaume. 'I had a letter passed on to him and I met him. I suggested I should work for him as a junior apprentice. He took me on in the tailoring atelier.'

Courrèges compared his entry into the house of Balenciaga to that of a novice monk preparing for holy orders. He told Georgina Howell in 1989, 'The atelier was pure white, unornamented, and intensely silent. People whispered and walked on tiptoe, and even the clients talked in hushed voices. Once or twice a day the door of Balenciaga's office would open, and you would hear him leave the building to go and pray in the church on the avenue Marceau.'

After five years, Balenciaga sent Courrèges to work in his Eisa couture house in Spain in order to give him 'more freedom and responsibility'. On his return, Courrèges told Valerie Guillaume that he had gone to Balenciaga and told him, 'Nothing grows under a tall tree. I am a little acorn and you are a great oak. I have to leave you to survive.' Balenciaga pretended not to hear. Three years passed and every time Courrèges brought up the subject, Balenciaga would feign deafness. Then came the day when he wandered into Courrèges's atelier and asked, 'Are you leaving? Do you need money? I'll give you some. Do you need help with administration? I'll send you my manager. Do you need clients? I'll send you clients.'

So in 1961, with some financial assistance from the great man, Courrèges set up his own house in partnership with Coqueline Barrière, with whom he had worked at Balenciaga and who was to become his wife in 1966. At first both were still very much under the influence of the master. 'In his atelier I had to think like him. That was no problem for me. Balenciaga taught me about the seventeenth century. The aesthetic simplicity of his clothes and mine was inspired by that period.'

Gradually, however, the couple began to develop their own style – from the feet up. Courrèges had always preferred flat shoes, and they were right for the times, for the mood of women, but they

Image 25.2 *Andre Courrèges with his wife, Coqueline Barrière, 1968. Photo: Hulton Archive via Getty Images.*

dictated an entirely new set of proportions. Coqueline Courrèges told Guillaume, 'Women needed to be able to walk and run again. And I was a dancer myself.' Flat heels, she said, forced the designer to recalculate the proportions of the female body. This created a delicate balance and a hat became essential 'to fill out the silhouette'. The garment had to fall from the shoulders and was accompanied by a mid-calf sock or boot. Courrèges continued, 'The clothes float. You don't feel them. I don't emphasise the waistline because the body is a whole. It is ridiculous to treat the top and bottom parts of the body separately.' In August 1964, *The New York Times* loved his 'controversial pants suits and above-the-knee skirts … they made sense and gave women a bold new perspective about their lives.'

The Courrèges mini, first shown next season in January 1965, took this new perspective a little too far for some. Shown on unusually limber, active, athletic models, these designs included angular mini-dresses cut four inches above the knee and trouser suits in heavyweight fabrics like gabardine. Many of the outfits had cut-out midriffs and bare backs and were worn without a bra. These were accessorised with flat white boots, goggles and helmets inspired by the equipment worn by astronauts. The stark shapes and white and silver colour scheme were immediately labelled 'Space Age'. Initially they met with a stunned silence from the fashion show audience. Backstage in the *cabine* with the models and dressers, the Courrègeses heard no applause. A shocked silence prevailed. As he told it, tears welled in the designer's eyes. 'I received a note. "André," had written the editor of the magazine *L'Officiel de la Couture*, "you were crazy, your collection is too short, with boots in the summer. It won't work. What were you thinking?" '

'I was thinking that I wanted to make women liberated, full of life, modern,' recalled Courrèges. 'I think I achieved all that.' Indeed, just three hours after the show, the fashion photographer Peter Knapp telephoned him to say, 'André, I hear your collection was fantastic; it was genius. The girls from *Vogue* are super-enthusiastic. They're saying you've revolutionised everything.'

Valerie Steele has examined French fashion's lethargy in its response to youth culture and France's yé-yé kids, but she praises Courrèges's 'brilliant couture version of youth fashion'. Speaking to Polan in 1979, Courrèges said, 'I wanted to put women into a total-freedom suit, a ribbed-knit body stocking. In order to introduce an element of fluidity and because few women have perfect bottoms, I topped it with a gabardine hipster mini-skirt and a spaceman visor.' This was to become one of fashion's most enduring images and probably the most copied look in the history of fashion. Dismayed by how ruthlessly and universally his designs were plagiarised, Courrèges did not show to the press again until 1967, although he continued to produce collections shown only to clients. Through the next few seasons, he continued to develop this look, adding bright colours and fresh abstract motifs to the clothes.

In 1966, the Musée des Arts Décoratifs in Paris hosted one of the first exhibitions of early-century-art movements that were to bring about a reassessment of their value. Les Années 25: Art Deco/Bauhaus/Stijl/Art Nouveau marked a turning point, the beginning of a romantic revival that informed

Image 25.3 *Courrèges. Photo: Reg Lancaster via Getty Images.*

Barbara Hulanicki's Biba and the work of Ossie Clark and Zandra Rhodes, shaping much of the retro fashion of the 1970s. It certainly signalled the end of modernism's influence on fashion as perceived by Courrèges. 'An avalanche of folklore, hippie dressing, in short, everything you can get from a rag seller,' he lamented, surveying the Rich Peasant, Russian Steppes, Bedouin, Mongol, Mexican, Indian and general Gypsy looks that crowded each other for tent space on fashion's voyages of the imagination. In 1970 he renamed his couture collection Prototype, his ready-to-wear Hyperbole.

At the end of the decade of disguise, Courrèges's prescience did not desert him. Fashion was once more beginning to march in step with his vision. For some time he had been designing and selling worldwide some of the most desirable clothes for sport – skiwear, tennis, dance/exercise – and he understood that the coming jogging and aerobics trend among women would have a huge influence on the clothes they chose to wear for ordinary life. He told Polan in 1979,

> Now we have reached another turning point and I am starting again to develop the movement I started in 1965. Other designers want to give women the refined style of the 1940s. This does not correspond to their way of living.
>
> So the clothes made for sport must be ennobled and made into part of the rest of life. We must introduce a more relaxed, at-ease style to everyday clothes, even eveningwear. The ennoblement of sporting clothes is achieved not simply by making a tracksuit in silk or wool but by studying the tracksuit and incorporating the elements that make it so comfortably wearable in clothes which are stylish and flattering.

He was correct in this, predicting the upgrading of tracksuit, shell suit, sweatshirt fabric and hi-tech synthetics to daily wear and the importance of Lycra in everything from leotards to business suits.

But his contempt for the fashion system was misplaced. He declared,

> In 15 years women have freed themselves. The retro look is putting them back in prison. Women are no longer decorative coquettes or sheltered wives; they may be coquettes and they may be wives, but they are also workers with full and independent lives. What sort of service is it to them to change the style every year, one year dictating a frilly, layered peasant look, the next big, square shoulders and small waists? There is a decadent spirit of creativity.

And yet women still revel in fashion's wayward changeability. In 1983, the French daily *Libération* wrote, 'Courrèges evokes a modernism so dated one is almost amazed he still exists.' But he did. In 1990 he was still designing and marketing a boutique fashion collection (down to fourteen boutiques from fifty in 1979) worldwide and headed a licensing empire that reportedly grossed an annual $285 million with men's wear, fragrance, home products, champagne and gourmet foods. In the mid-1990s, after several adventures with investors, takeovers and buyouts, André and Coqueline Courrèges regained control of most of their enterprises, selling the brand again in 2011. In 1997 André stepped down to concentrate on painting and sculpture, although he was increasingly incapacitated from Parkinson's disease. He died in 2016.

Further reading: Valerie Guillaume's *Courrèges* (1998), part of the *Fashion Memoir* series, is the most comprehensive account. Valerie Steele's *Paris Fashion: A Cultural History* (1998) is good on historical context.

Image 25.4 *Spring/summer 1968 ready-to-wear, Courrèges. Photo: Bill Ray/Life Magazine/The LIFE Picture Collection via Getty Images.*

26

Valentino Garavani (1932–)

Valentino remained at heart a dressmaker to the rich and famous.

Although in the twenty-first century Italy is a major producer of fashion, a dominant force in the luxury goods industry and second only to Paris in both glamour and the perfection of its product, this pre-eminence is relatively new. Italy may have been one of the cradles of civilisation, giving the world great art and culture, but it does not have a long fashion pedigree in modern times.

Italy's history is as a handful of separate and often warring city-states, each with its own distinct identity; its own aristocracy, landed gentry, professional and merchant class, its university and developed culture – and its own fashionable, opulently dressed elite. This was not, until Risorgimento in the nineteenth century, a single nation with a capital that could claim to be dominant in politics, commerce, the arts and culture. Arguably, although Italy is now a single nation, it still does not have that capital, but rather a series of beautiful, cultured, vital cities, each with a very different character.

After unification, as the new nation industrialised, several efforts, mainly political and nationalistic, were made to capitalise on Italian style and technical skill, but none were successful. Mussolini scolded in 1932, 'Italian fashion … still does not exist. We must create it.' Sofia Gnoli has described how during the Fascist period, a new National Fashion Body regulated the entire system of production, laying the foundation for post-war developments.

After the Second World War, two factors gave the nascent industry a further boost: American investment in the form of the Marshall Plan and the weak lira that attracted American film-makers to Rome and Cinecittà, the well-staffed base of the Italian film industry. An international cast of actresses arrived in the city, and, hard on their Ferragamo heels, came all the players in *la dolce vita* and the louche, nouveau riche jet set. To cater for them, the traditional dressmaking establishments that had survived the war, such as the Fontana sisters, were augmented by a new generation of modern-minded designers, many aristocratic, like Simonetta Colonna di Cesaro and Irene Galitzine. Together they formed Roman haute couture. The rest of

Image 26.1 *Valentino, spring/summer 1992. Niall McInerney, Photographer.* © Bloomsbury Publishing Plc.

the world started to take an interest when Hollywood stars Linda Christian and Tyrone Power married in Rome in 1949. He wore a Caraceni morning suit and she wore a dress by the Fontana sisters.

From this start, Italian fashion was to develop fast in the post-war years, brilliantly promoted as a ready-to-wear industry from 1951 by Giovanni Battista Giorgini, an agent and entrepreneur, who invited the all-powerful American press to a series of shows and fashion exhibitions in and around the Pitti Palace in Florence 'immediately after the great Paris shows'. John Fairchild of *Women's Wear Daily*, who received the first invitation, remembered in 1992, 'The French at that point were struggling to get into the ready-to-wear business as they saw the demand for haute couture fashion melting away before their eyes. What Giorgini did was boldly leapfrog ahead of the French to bring the Italians into ready-to-wear before the French, always slow to move into new ways.'

When Valentino Clemente Ludovico Garavani, a twenty-seven-year-old Paris-trained couturier, returned to Italy in 1959 to set up his own studio, he instinctively located himself in Rome among the couturiers. He wanted the clientele that could afford his exacting perfectionism, the handmade craftsmanship, the clothes for a confident life lived publicly. He went on to develop many product lines, including ready-to-wear collections, but he remained at heart a dressmaker to the rich and famous. Their interminable roll call includes Rita Hayworth, Elizabeth Taylor, Jackie Kennedy (who married Aristotle Onassis in Valentino), Princess Grace, Audrey Hepburn, Sophia Loren, Monica Vitti, Claudia Cardinale, Ornella Muti, Gina Lollobrigida, Marisa Berenson, Elsa Peretti, Jessica Lange, Sharon Stone and Julia Roberts (who accepted her 2001 Oscar in Valentino). Long before the phrase 'red-carpet dress' was coined, Valentino was the master of the genre, producing flattering, impact-making gowns that looked good from every angle and were guaranteed not to be difficult to wear.

His favourite colour, a lush Mediterranean summer poppy red, more orange than scarlet, became known among fashion cognoscenti as 'Valentino red', and nothing was better qualified to make a grand entrance on the grandest of occasions. He discovered the colour when, as a student, he took a holiday in Barcelona and went to the opera. 'All the costumes on the stage were red,' he said later. 'All the women in the boxes were mostly dressed in red, and they leant forward like geraniums on balconies, and the seats and drapes were red too. … I realised that after black and white, there was no finer colour.'

It is a colour that sizzles, that draws every eye in the room. Valentino told Susannah Frankel for *Dazed & Confused* in 2000, 'I know women often say, "Ah, if you want an evening gown, go to Valentino." What is the point of going out if nobody notices you? Stay home! Stay home and invite some friends and you can wear what you like. But if you want to go out and be, for one evening, beautiful, with lots of seduction, sexy and everything, you must do the big number, no?'

Valentino Garavani was born into an affluent family – his father owned electrical supplies stores – in 1932 in Voghera, a small town halfway between Turin and Milan in northern Italy, his country's industrial heartland. As a child he loved drawing and at school displayed an interest in fashion, going on to study at the Santa Marta Institute of Fashion Drawing in Milan while learning French at the Berlitz School. In 1950 his parents subsidised a move to Paris, where he enrolled at the school of the Chambre Syndicale de la Couture Parisienne. He won the International Wool Secretariat's design competition, earning a job at the couture house of Jean Dessès. He stayed for five years acquiring Dessès's taste for sweeping drapery and exoticism, clothes inspired by classical Roman and Greek draperies and Egyptian decoration.

For Valentino's 1991 retrospective, ten sketches from this period were made up to open the exhibition. Bernadine Morris of *The New York Times* wrote that they were 'revealed to be the precursors of themes which he would elaborate on later in his career'. They showed, she noted,

> the basic Valentino shape for day and evening as slender, except for a few bouffant dresses of calf or ankle length, as was the style of the early 1950s, before the mini. The surfaces of the slim, long evening dresses are encrusted with jewel embroidery and the narrow shapes are softened by back-flowing chiffon panels or capes. … We can see in this mini-collection the first appearance of Valentino's red, the prominence of graphic black-and-white embroidery suggesting Meissen china and the black-and-white dress in a shape suggesting a Greek vase. Far more important, however, than any of these details is the unmistakeable sense of elegance and authority.

In 1957 Guy Laroche, the chief illustrator at Dessès, left to set up his own couture house, and Valentino went with him. Two years later, with financial backing from his father, Valentino presented his first collection in his own salon in the Via Condotti in Rome. The actress, Elizabeth Taylor, in Rome filming *Cleopatra*, ordered a white dress to wear for the world premiere of *Spartacus* – and the beautiful women of the world began to beat a path to his door. In 1960 Giancarlo Giammetti, a student of architecture,

Image 26.2 *Valentino Garavani on the catwalk, spring/summer 1996. Niall McInerney, Photographer. © Bloomsbury Publishing Plc.*

Image 26.3 *Valentino, autumn/winter 1995. Niall McInerney, Photographer. © Bloomsbury Publishing Plc.*

joined the young company, becoming Valentino's life partner (until 1972) and managing director of the business; he was to run the business side until Valentino stepped down. In the same year, Valentino launched his ready-to-wear collection. He first showed with Giovanni Batista Giorgini's stars at the Pitti Palace in Florence in 1962. At just thirty, he was allocated the last slot on the calendar, obliging buyers to stay another night, delaying their flights home. But they had heard rumours and they stayed.

In the mid-1960s, Valentino abandoned Florence and the Pitti group and, as the closing couturier of the Rome shows, crowned the presentations of the Fontana sisters, Princess Irene Galitzine, Maria Antonelli, Roberto Capucci and Emilio Schuberth. Valentino's evening presentations became glittering social events in their own right, the audience composed of actresses and the wives of politicians, magnates and millionaires, all in evening wear and their best jewels. Perma-tanned and attended by a family of pugs, the couturier had become a member of the class he dressed, entertaining his clients socially in his many homes and on his yacht. His signature style was now established. Consistently elegant, it rarely changed direction suddenly but adhered to classic tenets of good taste while indulging in expensive detail and opulent decoration. These were clothes that looked rich but old-money rich, never vulgar, always glamorous, always grown-up. In 1968 he told *Women's Wear Daily*, 'I believe only in high fashion. I think a couturier must establish his style and stick to it. The mistake of many couturiers is that they try to change their line every collection. I change a little each time, but never too much, so as not to lose my identity.' His dominant themes – the floral and animal prints, the heavy encrustations of beading, the stark contrast of black and white, the fine pleating – were eagerly looked for in every collection.

In her 2008 monograph on the designer, Pamela Golbin wrote:

As Valentino himself so rightly puts it, he is no innovator in the realm of fashion. Viewed within the broader history of haute couture, he is, however, the recognised champion of a unique silhouette, with a stylistic sensibility uniting supreme grace and timeless allure. … Fluid silhouettes, subtle femininity, and refined sensuality are the hallmarks of Valentino's style. This sensibility – distinguished by a lean, graphic contour – is an integral part of his vocabulary, resulting in styles that are the epitome of understated luxury.

In January 1970 Valentino was the first couturier to put his name to the mini's death warrant when he dropped hems to mid-calf. He was making his influence felt commercially, too, opening ready-to-wear stores in New York, Geneva, Lausanne, London and Paris. In 1975 he began to show his ready-to-wear in Paris. Although no French couturier was likely to concede that Italian workmanship could rival that of the *petites mains*, ready-to-wear Italian manufacturing was already superior to French, a phenomenon that was to lead eventually to Italy's preeminent position in high-quality fashion manufacturing. In the late 1970s he took inspiration for his big-skirted ball gowns from the romantic portraits of the eighteenth and nineteenth centuries, revelling in a fairy-tale prettiness not seen since Dior.

The 1980s was Valentino's decade. It was the decade of flaunt-it fashion, dress-for-success, wide-shouldered suits with tight skirts and gold buttons accessorised by aggressive quantities of gold jewellery and stiletto heels. As the 1980s progressed, the clothes acquired a harder edge, a more imposing, vampy feeling. He developed body-sculpting complex pleating, Oriental-inspired embroideries and Art Deco appliqué work as well as his animal prints (including a tribute to his beloved pugs) and his sophisticated colour combinations.

Italy acknowledged Valentino's contribution to its identity as a fashion force with many honours, including, in 1986, its highest decoration, the Cavaliere de Gran Croce (the equivalent of a British knighthood). In 1982, the Metropolitan Museum of Art in New York City, then directed by Diana Vreeland, invited him to show his collection there. In June 1991, the city of Rome celebrated his thirtieth anniversary with a fashion show of 300 outfits and a black-tie dinner for 500.

Valentino retired in 2007, having already sold his company to an investment group some years previously. Alessandra Facchinetti took over as head designer until she was abruptly fired after her spring 2009 collection. Maria Grazia Chiuri and Pier Paolo Piccioli were named as the new creative directors. The duo had previously designed accessories for the label and were well received. In 2016, Chiuri left to become the first female design director at Dior, while Pier Paolo Piccioli continued to design to acclaim at Valentino as a solo act.

Further reading: Pamela Golbin's *Valentino: Themes and Variations* (2008) is an excellent book and touches on many aspects. *Valentino Garavani* (2015) by Drusilla Beyfus in the *Vogue On* series is a more recent account. For comprehensive background, the catalogue, *The Glamour of Italian Fashion Since 1945*, edited by Sonnet Stanifil for the V&A exhibition of 2014, contains important essays by various authors. For an analytical historical survey, read *The Origins of Italian Fashion 1900–45* (2014) by Sofia Gnoli.

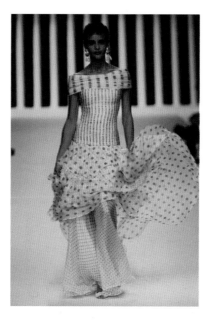

Image 26.4 *Valentino, spring/summer 1992. Niall McInerney, Photographer. © Bloomsbury Publishing Plc.*

collection of eighteenth-century art and furniture at Christie's in 2000, he made it clear that he was resolutely looking to the future. Even a questionable decision to produce a signature capsule collection for mass-market fashion retailer Hennes & Mauritz in 2004 was a defiant statement of youthfulness.

Despite his deep understanding of history, Karl Lagerfeld showed little respect for it. His mantra was 'modern', a word repeated in countless interviews over the decades. Following his appointment as head of design at Chanel in 1982, he simultaneously trashed and cherished the Chanel heritage. The appointment initially shocked the Paris fashion milieu – Lagerfeld was considered a *styliste* rather than a couturier, and he was a German outsider. But his skills, usually (although not always) applied with a lightness of touch and wit, made him synonymous with the modern house of Chanel. 'Only the minute and the future are interesting in fashion – it exists to be destroyed,' he said. 'If everybody did everything with respect, you'd go nowhere.' The Wertheimer family, who control the privately owned label, made it clear that he had a job for life, releasing financial figures only once (in June 2018) to reveal that Chanel is a business with revenues of $10 billion.

Lagerfeld worked at a feverish pace, producing a flood of detailed sketches, a veritable torrent of creativity. A Lagerfeld collection, for whichever label, was marked by clear ideas expressed with confidence and assurance, often with a high degree of wit. His debut for Chanel in 1983 was a triumph, the star piece a *trompe l'oeil* silk crepe dress featuring jewellery-effect embroidery by Lesage, a playful reference to Madame Chanel's delight in jewellery. For inspiration, his first Chanel collection looked back primarily to the 1920s and 1930s rather than to Chanel's post-war comeback. His extravagant use of Chanel's interlocking C motifs was there from the start. While there were always some ready to dismiss Lagerfeld's style as baroque showmanship sharing more in common with Chanel's arch-rival Elsa Schiaparelli, by the end of the 1980s few could seriously challenge Lagerfeld's position at the top of the fashion pyramid, particularly with Yves Saint Laurent close to retirement.

Over the years, Lagerfeld's designs for Chanel drew from all periods of the fashion house's history, often with unexpected juxtapositions, such as denim jeans mixed with a classic soft tweed jacket or a heavy leather biker jacket with a silk tulle ball gown. Lagerfeld's design aesthetic was always brasher than the original Chanel – whether reflected in an intense colour palette for tweeds or in flashy luxury bags and other accessories or in a constant willingness to appropriate street style. But Lagerfeld's oft-strident aesthetic reflected a more strident age. 'I took her code, her language and mixed it all up,' he said in 2004. Humour was one of the most potent weapons in the Lagerfeld armoury. Anna Piaggi, a fashion eccentric of the first order, was drawn to Lagerfeld by his playful eclecticism: the first Lagerfeld-designed dress in her wardrobe was in silk embroidered with sequins with a motif of an Art Deco pop jukebox.

Lagerfeld grew up accustomed to money and luxury and never experienced the financial hardships of many of his contemporaries. He was born Karl Otto Lagerfeld in Hamburg, Germany, the son of a Swedish business magnate who had made a substantial fortune in the condensed milk industry. He claimed a birth date of 1938, although baptismal records suggest he was delivered five years earlier in 1933. His German mother, Elizabeth, was a formative influence on the young designer, a demanding personality who shaped her son to develop a similar iron will and continued to be an important force in his life until her death at the age of eighty-one in 1978. He moved with his mother to Paris in 1953, making his big breakthrough two years later when he won an International Wool Secretariat award for a coat. The young Yves Saint Laurent won the dress award, setting the stage for two careers that marched in parallel through the 1960s, 1970s and beyond. Lagerfeld's path to glory was, however, much slower than Saint Laurent's. The coat award in 1955 enabled Lagerfeld to land his first job at Pierre Balmain, from where he moved to Jean Patou after three years. But he was quickly bored and left within a year in a significant shift from the world of couture to ready-to-wear, freelancing for names ranging from Krizia, Charles Jourdan and Mario Valentino to supermarket chain Monoprix. He was avowedly a *styliste* – the French word for a designer who worked for ready-to-wear labels. That put him, in the eyes of the oft snobbish world of French fashion, at a considerably lower level than the couturier Yves Saint Laurent. Lagerfeld's response was to celebrate his role as *styliste*, deriding the craft of haute couture as old-fashioned and backward looking. The fierce professional rivalry turned deeply personal in the 1970s when Saint Laurent had an affair with Jacques de Bascher, the long-term *amour* of Lagerfeld.

Ever restless, Lagerfeld was briefly disillusioned by the world of fashion design for a period in the early 1960s and moved to Italy in 1964 to study art. Within three years, however, he was back in fashion at the house of Fendi, forming a bond with the Fendi family that has lasted even longer than the Chanel connection. From 1964, he also worked fruitfully with the ready-to-wear house of Chloé under the guidance of founder Gaby Aghion, who taught him how to edit and simplify the flood of designs he was producing. In the 1970s, his work for Chloé established him as one of international fashion's leading designers. The 1972 Deco collection, featuring black-and-white prints and inspired bias-cut dresses, received universal acclaim. For ten years, as chief designer at Chloé, he produced a stream of collections that summed up the fashion spirit of the period, leading to his appointment at Chanel in 1982. He briefly returned to Chloé in 1992, although less successfully.

Lagerfeld's talents extended beyond fashion design into photography and illustration – and no doubt he would have been his own best biographer. Speaking to Roger Tredre in 1994, though, he said he would never write his story for a simple reason – 'I could not write the truth.' Author Alicia Drake was brave enough to exhaustively research Lagerfeld's rivalry with Yves Saint Laurent in the 1970s in her book, *The Beautiful Fall: Fashion, Genius and Glorious Excess in 1970s Paris* (2006). Lagerfeld felt wounded by the book, taking legal action which resulted in its withdrawal in France by publishers Bloomsbury.

Restless and easily bored, Lagerfeld was the German outsider who became the ultimate insider in the gossipy world of Parisian fashion. He was a media dream, accessible and obliging, enthusiastically ready with a pithy quote and a pleasure in stirring up mischief. His wide-ranging interests and exceptional

Image 27.2 *Lagerfeld receives applause, 1990s. Niall McInerney, Photographer. © Bloomsbury Publishing Plc.*

gift for languages made him a one-man publicity machine for whichever label he is representing. He had a sense of theatre (indeed, he has designed costumes for theatre, opera and cinema), invariably arriving fashionably late for appointments, usually in a flurry of energy and impatience, borne with equanimity by his colleagues in the Chanel atelier. His showmanship and extraordinary speed of work were both depicted admirably in the French television documentary, *Signé Chanel*, first screened in 2005. He was admired (and sometimes mocked) as a fashion spectacle in his own right. In the 1950s, Lagerfeld used to drive a cream open-top Mercedes, a present from his father, and wear high heels and carry clutch bags on holiday in Saint-Tropez. Fifty years on, his spectacular diet was partly linked to his desire to squeeze into the slimline tailoring of Hedi Slimane, the young designer at Dior Homme whose work he has championed. He often expressed a cultural affinity with the cultivated aristocrats of eighteenth-century Europe, even half-jesting that in a previous life he was an eighteenth-century gentleman. Since 2012, his treasured cat, Choupette, achieved celebrity in her own right with her own Twitter and Instagram accounts and line of beauty products.

During the first two decades of the twenty-first century, Chanel's presentations became ever-more lavish, with high-spend sets for shows staged in the Grand Palais in Paris or at sumptuous locations around the world. For autumn/winter 2014 ready-to-wear, he mixed up familiar tweed suiting with trackpants and sneakers, all wittily presented in a Chanel 'supermarket' (the shopping baskets were made of Chanel chains). Less successful was the feminist edge to the spring/summer 2015 collection featuring a mock demo for women's rights: while it tapped the mood of the times, left-leaning critics accused Chanel of jumping on a bandwagon. From 2002, Lagerfeld staged an annual Chanel Métiers d'Art show, technically a pre-fall collection, presented in a different location worldwide every year. The event, which usually prompted a media frenzy wherever it popped up, highlighted the craftsmanship of Chanel and the specialist ateliers it worked with, such as Lesage for embroidery, Lognon for pleating, and Lemarié for its signature feathery camellias. The show presented in New York's Metropolitan Museum of Art in December 2018 managed to blend Ancient Egyptian and modern Manhattan street style. In the same month, Chanel showed it was moving with the times by banning the use of exotic skins and furs.

Despite his long career and open engagement with the media, Karl Lagerfeld remained a mystery, the real man behind the fast-talking 'Kaiser' tending to be obscured from view by the media persona. His predilection for dark glasses or the protective carapace of a fan suggested that this was the way he preferred it. Perhaps the truth was not so complicated – his life was his work. Certainly, that appeared to be the reality after the death of his long-time partner Jacques de Bascher in 1989. On the subject of work, Lagerfeld said: 'You have to remember that I do nothing else. That's how I manage. Twenty-four hours a day. I don't go on holiday.'

Lagerfeld's offence at Alicia Drake's exploration of his rivalry with Saint Laurent in the 1970s was clearly deep. Drake sought to delve deep into the Lagerfeld psyche, soliciting comments from a wide variety of sources. She explored his many personal rivalries and his recurring tendency to fall out with even the closest of friends, ranging from Gaby Aghion at Chloé to the model Inès de la Fressange. On his obsession with youth, Drake quoted an anonymous former colleague: 'If you want to understand Karl, you have to understand his fear of death. … He talks about the future non-stop because when he looks at the past he realises that life is behind him and there is only a small portion ahead. This is what makes him work so hard.'

As a designer, he consistently set new standards for productivity and energy, driving fashion forward into the modern age. He also created a template that was followed by Tom Ford at Gucci and a host of designers in the 2010s, showing how fashion and fashion labels can be endlessly revived and made relevant for every new generation.

Further reading: Alicia Drake's *The Beautiful Fall: Lagerfeld, Saint Laurent and Glorious Excess in 1970s Paris* (2006), which was withdrawn from publication in France, provides many interesting insights into Lagerfeld in the 1970s. Lagerfeld was interviewed innumerable times, including by Roger Tredre for *The Observer* newspaper ('Kaiser Karl', 7 August 1994).

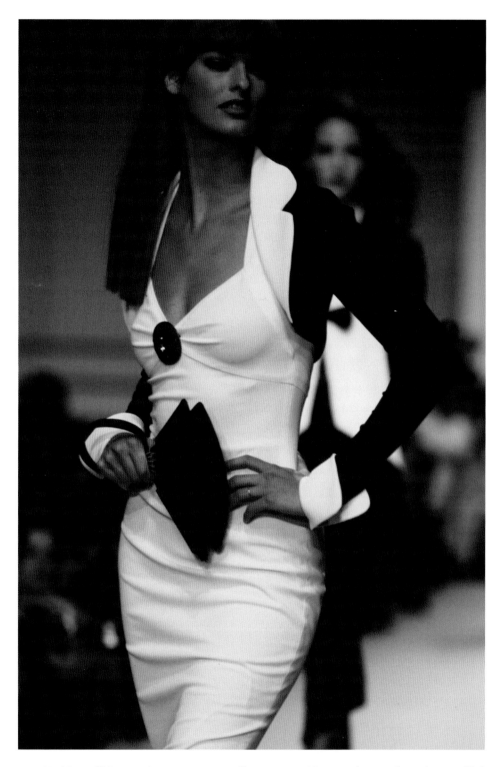

Image 27.3 *Karl Lagerfeld, spring/summer 1992. Niall McInerney, Photographer. © Bloomsbury Publishing Plc.*

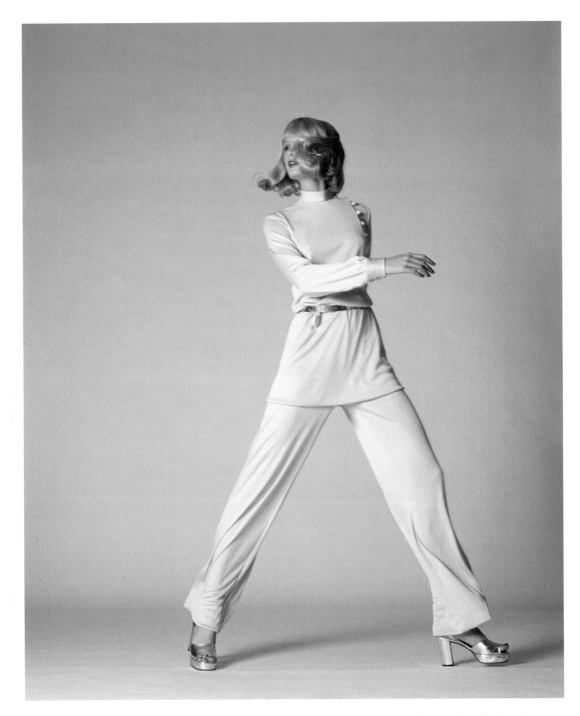

Image 28.1 *Trouser suit in viscose jersey, Halston,* Vogue, *1972. Photo: David Bailey/Condé Nast via Getty Images.*

28

Halston (1932–1990)

The Halston look spoke of understated wealth: cashmere sweaters, silk shirtwaist dresses, simple elegant wool pants.

The fashion lover might say that fashion's minimalists have their moments and then become boring. If James Laver was right and 'clothes are the furniture of the mind made visible', then some claim there's an excess of vacant space in the minds and the imaginations of minimalists. By contrast, the pragmatists who just want a way to dress that looks elegant, sophisticated and as if they don't care too much about keeping up with fashion's changes would say they are never boring. Roy Halston Frowick, known simply as Halston, was the minimalist's minimalist. He was granted high status by contemporary commentators, possibly because of his good looks and personal star quality, a phenomenon not really seen again in a fashion designer until Tom Ford. Patricia Mears, in *Halston* (2001), wrote, 'Halston was a groundbreaking figure. Best known as a modernist who fully advocated the minimalist aesthetic, Halston turned fashion on its ear in the over-accessorised sixties by blending simple, pared-down silhouettes with the most luxurious fabrics.'

Caroline Rennolds Milbank, who categorised him as a 'purist' in *Couture: The Great Fashion Designers*, wrote that he was the right designer for a certain moment.

Halston began making clothes at a time when it was no longer fashionable to appear rich. The new social climate was one in which Park Avenue and Sutton Place matrons consigned their 'important' jewels to vaults rather than lose them to muggers; when cultural impresarios were throwing parties for Black Panthers and waging war on the stuffy, the traditional and the formal. Perhaps it is because his sensibility matured during this period of 'radical chic' that Halston rejected most vestiges of formal dressmaking. Halston makes clothes without zippers or pockets, ruffles or notched lapels, practically without seams.

Roy Halston Frowick was born in 1932 in Des Moines, Iowa, the second son (of four children) of a Norwegian-American accountant with a passion for inventing. Roy developed an interest in sewing from his mother and as an adolescent he began creating hats and embellishing outfits for his mother and sister. Owing to his father's alcoholism and the difficulties he had remaining in employment, the family moved often, first to Illinois then Indiana. Roy graduated from high school in 1950, then attended Indiana University for one semester. After the family moved to Chicago in 1952, he enrolled in a night course at the Chicago Art Institute and worked as a window dresser at the Carson Pirie Scott department store. At this time known as 'Fro', he began a relationship with André Basil, a celebrity hairdresser twenty-five years his senior whose salon was in Chicago's premier hotel, The Ambassador. Basil gave Fro a corner of the salon for a millinery atelier where he would attract the attention of Basil's clients who comprised the cream of Chicago's society as well as the celebrated guests who stayed at the hotel.

In 1956 Basil introduced Fro to Lilly Daché, the queen of New York milliners, and by 1958 he was working for her in her Park Avenue establishment. From this point on he used his middle name, Halston. His ambition quickly outstripped Daché's establishment, and he accepted a post as head milliner at Bergdorf Goodman, America's most exclusive store. When Jacqueline Kennedy attended her husband's Presidential Inauguration in January 1961, she was wearing a coat by Oleg Cassini and a pill-box hat by Halston. The hat was perfectly suited to Mrs Kennedy's rather large head. Unadorned, simple and overwhelmingly youthful, a fitting symbol for a new generation stepping up to power, the hat was one of the most copied items of clothing ever, bought and worn by women across the world.

Generally, Halston's style in millinery was more fanciful than that simple pill-box. Many of his designs bordered on the fantastic; he used mirrors, fringing, jewels and flowers to decorate hoods, bonnets, coifs, and helmets. His innovative scarf hat, a silk square on a frame, was a much-copied design of the 1960s. He was an inventive and technically brilliant milliner with a sense of humour. Diana Vreeland said, 'He was probably the greatest hatmaker in the world. I'd say to him, "H, I had a dream about a hat last night" and I'd go about describing it, and then, by God, he'd give it to me, line by line.'

The chief advantage of working for Bergdorf Goodman, however, was that it opened his eyes to the wider international world of original fashion design. Since the beginning of the century Bergdorf Goodman had boasted a custom design salon where original French designs were copied for clients. As was the now dated way with many American fashion establishments, Bergdorf's still sent its 'designers' to Paris twice a year to the haute couture shows to glean ideas and buy toiles. This was to be Halston's equivalent of the Chambre Syndicale school; his 'sharp eye', wrote Patricia Mears, 'greedily absorbed every detail, every cut of a seam in the creations he saw by Gabrielle "Coco" Chanel, Yves Saint Laurent, Hubert de Givenchy and, his favourite, Cristóbal Balenciaga.'

At Bergdorf Goodman, Halston garnered a following of elegant society women, Broadway actresses, Hollywood stars and influential fashion editors who were to prove ready clients for his ready-to-wear clothing collection when, reluctantly, Bergdorf launched it for him in 1966. Both hats and haute couture were becoming less and less fashionable as the decade passed. Claire McCardell had led the way in marrying original design to mass production techniques. Halston did not aim to reach quite so wide a

Image 28.2 *Halston with Bianca Jagger, 1981. Photo: Rose Hartman via Getty Images.*

Image 28.3 *Halston, 1978. Photo: Denver Post via Getty Images.*

customer base but he understood that a combination of luxury fabrics with cuts simple enough for mass manufacture would be attractive to the kind of women used to couture and now beginning to buy the European 'boutique' collections. Bergdorf Goodman gave him access to the Delman shoe salon to design a complementary range of shoes and a boutique for the collection on the second floor. The first collection, shown with music on dancing young models, consisted of eighteen interchangeable pieces. The presentation aroused media excitement but sales were slow and eighteen months later, Halston left Bergdorf's, setting up his own couture label with modest backing from Mrs Estelle Marsh Watlington of Texas.

By now, Halston was part of a glittering circle of clients and creative friends, including Jackie Kennedy Onassis, Elizabeth Taylor, Rita Hayworth, Marlene Dietrich, Diana Vreeland, Martha Graham, Barbara Walters, Lauren Bacall, Bianca Jagger, Anjelica Huston and Liza Minnelli. In 1972, *Newsweek* magazine designated him 'surely the premier fashion designer of all America'. The simplicity that was his trademark was perceived as clean-limbed, healthy and all-American in contrast to the over-decorated, decadent ethnic peasant looks that were being created by all the European designers. Halston hated fussiness and, in 1973, when invited to participate in a fashion show at Versailles where American designers showcased their work alongside to French designers, he stunned the fashion world by the strict purity of his dresses.

The Halston look spoke of understated wealth: cashmere sweaters, silk shirtwaist dresses, simple elegant wool pants. 'I didn't want to make clothes for kids,' he said. 'I wanted feminine clothes for women between 22 and 55.' Even his evening wear derived its glamour and sex appeal from the fabrics rather than any cleverness of cut. His colour palette was ivory, black, and red, but he understood the principle of accent and emphasis, using fuchsia, electric blue, and deep burgundy. His best known garment was the Ultrasuede shirtwaist dress introduced in 1972. The synthetic mock-suede became a signature fabric, the simple dress a staple of his collections, re-run in many colours and throughout the decade. Its success stemmed from its plainness and the fact that it didn't wrinkle or crease and was machine washable. Deliriously, Halston signed licensing agreements for a range of products in Ultrasuede, including handbags, shoes, boots, belts and bedspreads.

Although Halston showed his clothes on stick-thin models before it was fashionable among designers to do so, he boasted of dressing Miss Average America. In 1978, he told Bernadine Morris of *The New York Times*, 'You have to have something for the woman who is overweight – a loose tunic and pants is good because it elongates the body. You have to have something for the woman with hips – the Princess line works for her. Caftans are fine for the woman whose figure isn't perfect.' That was the year he moved into the Olympic Tower skyscraper next door to St Patrick's cathedral and covered all the walls, including the washrooms, in mirror glass. He could sit at his red lacquer desk and look down on a Manhattan skyline multiply reflected.

In the early 1970s Halston's lover was a Colombian window dresser named Victor Hugo through whom he met Andy Warhol, who became a close friend. In the late 1970s and early 1980s, he enthusiastically embraced the celebrity lifestyle and was frequently featured in the gossip columns, often as a walker for beautiful, sometimes troubled, women. He was one of the faces of the infamous New York nightclub Studio 54. A famous evening in the degenerate history of the club was Halston's birthday party for Bianca Jagger in 1977. During this period, he was also seen partying with his friend Liza Minnelli at gay holiday resort Fire Island. Patricia Mears reports that he took full advantage of the drugs and casual sex that were available at the nightclubs he frequented. Halston had been part of the wild gay party scene since he moved to Chicago in the 1950s. When disco emerged in the 1970s, he frequented the hottest clubs, socialised with celebrities, embraced the most popular drugs, and designed clothes that the celebrities wore to go to the disco and take the drugs. His halter-neck dress of 1974 became a dance-floor staple as did his trademark strapless dresses, one-shouldered sheaths and asymmetrical necklines. All of his designs were simple and unconstructed, usually in solid colours and luxury fabrics. His narrow, elongated silhouettes skimmed over the body and flattered young and old figures alike. Halston's signature sunglasses, worn both day and night, completed the look.

In 1973 Norton Simon purchased all of Halston's companies, his trademark, and his exclusive design services for approximately $12 million. Menswear and perfume were added to the empire two years later: the perfume was known simply as Halston and came in a bean-shaped bottle designed by Elsa Peretti. In 1977 Halston was invited to redesign the uniforms and aircraft interiors and airport spaces for Braniff Airlines. His brief was to create a look that conveyed the urbane sophistication of the late 1970s and early 1980s. He was deemed at that stage in his career to be the designer who best understood a well-bred look. However, his partnership with Norton Simon Industries did not bring the riches Halston had hoped it would. Refusing to allow his name to be put on anything he did not design himself, he found it difficult to meet the level of productivity expected of him. His signature was seen on everything from spectacles to the uniforms worn by Avis car rental employees, but he increasingly felt under pressure to produce even more.

In 1982, amid proliferating licences, Norton Simon Industries asked Halston to design a range for the department store group, JC Penney. He agreed, but it was seen as a step too far downmarket: Bergdorf's and Martha's dropped his collections while formerly faithful friends and clients defected to other designers. Although the Halston III collection for JC Penney was successful, Halston's relationships with his bosses and colleagues deteriorated until finally in 1984 he was locked out of his offices after throwing a ferocious temper tantrum. He was then fired, losing the rights to his own name. In 1988 he was diagnosed with AIDS and sold his New York townhouse and moved to San Francisco where he died in 1990. Of his glittering entourage, only Minnelli stayed true till the end. The label has changed hands several times. In 2012, its latest owner, Hilco, moved its base to Los Angeles and relaunched it as Halston Heritage.

Further reading: Halston (2001), edited by Steven Bluttal with essays by Patricia Mears, is visually telling. *Less Is More: Minimalism in Fashion* (2011) by Harriet Walker places Halston in context.

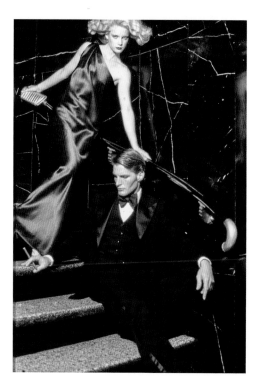

Image 28.4 *Dress, Halston,* Vogue, *1976. Photo: Albert Watson/Condé Nast via Getty Images.*

Image 29.1 *Kenzo, Vogue, 1977. Photo: Arthur Elgort/Condé Nast via Getty Images.*

29

Kenzo (1939–)

In the early 1970s, Kenzo's shows attracted the hysterical crowds; his was the name that defined youthful fashion.

In 1970 Kenzo Takada was the first Japanese fashion designer to show his work in Paris. He was joined very quickly on the catwalks of fashion's capital by his compatriots, Issey Miyake and Kansai Yamamoto. They were three very different designers, and they were all well received. Initially, however, Kenzo, with his bright and cheerful, intensely youthful clothes, was the great success. The world of haute couture had only recently adjusted to the youthquake that was changing the world and shifting its spending power. The chasm that had existed between the couturiers and the manufacturers of ready-to-wear for the masses was narrowing. As London, Milan and New York began to challenge the preeminence of Paris as arbiter and producer of fashion, the couture houses, led by Cardin and Saint Laurent, were creating boutique lines, less expensive versions of their couture, and young designers such as Sonia Rykiel, Emmanuelle Khanh and Karl Lagerfeld at Chloé launched high-fashion lines that were firmly targeted at the ready-to-wear market.

In 1973 the Chambre Syndicale de la Couture Parisienne united with Didier Grumbach's Créateurs et Industriels to form the Federation Française de la Couture, du Prêt-à-Porter des Couturiers and des Créateurs de Mode. This umbrella organisation established the Chambre Syndicale du Prêt-à-Porter des Couturiers et des Créateurs de Mode as a separate and parallel organisation to the Chambre Syndicale de la Couture Parisienne. Significantly, Kenzo was a member from the start of the ready-to-wear group, and he was regarded then and always as a star of French fashion.

When Kenzo had launched his label three years earlier, the hedonistic 1960s were segueing into the more idealistic 1970s, when altruism and a global perspective would dominate youth culture. In the aftermath of 1968 and the Paris riots (which Kenzo witnessed), it was a time of making love, not war, of turning on, tuning in and dropping out. Some experimented with collective living, others took to the hippie trail to discover new, simpler cultures and hoped to find enlightenment or at least

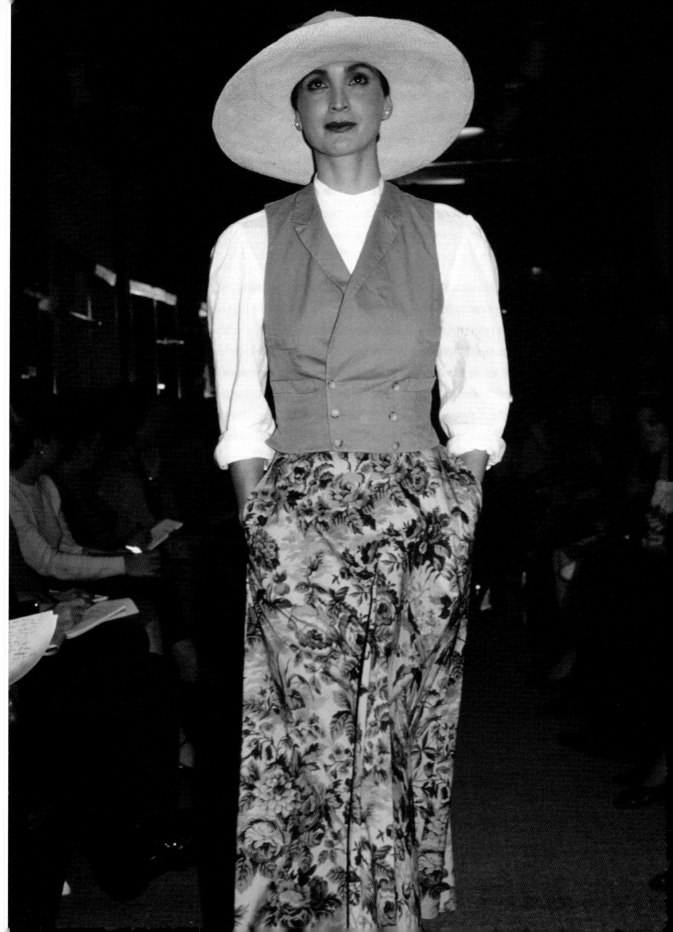

30

Ralph Lauren (1939–)

Ralph Lauren is the great romantic of American fashion, a myth-maker.

In September 2018 Ralph Lauren celebrated his fiftieth anniversary as the king of American fashion with a celebrity-crammed show in New York's Central Park. An extraordinary roll call of the famous paid tribute to his impact on modern America, including Hillary Clinton, Oprah Winfrey, Martha Stewart, Bruce Springsteen, Steven Spielberg, Robert De Niro, Tony Bennett, Jessica Chastain and Kanye West. They joined Lauren's family and fellow designers Calvin Klein, Donna Karan, Diane von Furstenberg, Michael Kors, Tommy Hilfiger and Alexander Wang. All were gathered to witness a parade of Americana filtered through Lauren's unique gaze.

Diane von Furstenberg declared, 'He's as American as Coca-Cola.' Indeed, this show revisited the great Lauren classics, the ones that conjure the prairies and the mountains, the cities and the rural backroads, the railroad and the gold rush, the college campus and the sports field. The clothes were styled for the runway with a perfectly judged mix-and-don't-match insouciance. He showed blanket coats, check shirts and patchwork jackets, denim dungarees and giant-logo'd sweats, biker jackets and pumped-up brightly coloured winter sporting gear, big textured jumpers and skinny Fair Isle sweaters. A khaki army-surplus sweater was teamed with a lushly printed satin full-length skirt; a butch and chunky embroidered leather blouson was shrugged on over a bias-cut velvet evening gown; traditional backwoods rough-wear of plaid or boiled-wool jackets topped urban pinstripes.

Ralph Lauren is the great romantic of American fashion, a myth-maker whose own sensitivity to how clothes and artefacts define an era and its people have allowed him to recreate those eras – if not exactly those people – in his clothing collections, his complete-world home ranges, his elite theme-park stores and most powerfully in his advertising campaigns. He is a designer whose lyrical vision is capable of sweeping along the most minimalist of modernists in its technicoloured embrace. Jane Mulvagh has described how he launched a look that endowed American and European utility and

Image 30.1 *Pioneer woman, Ralph Lauren, spring/summer 1984. Niall McInerney, Photographer.* © *Bloomsbury Publishing Plc.*

sports garments with nostalgic appeal. As he said, 'I paint dreams. These clothes have a heritage, they're not frivolous but things to treasure even when they get old.'

Lauren is as much in thrall to American glamour – as conceived by the Hollywood of Travis Banton and Edith Head – as he is to the class-defining uniforms of America's history. He's equally enamoured of the equestrian, hunting, shooting, fishing, polo-playing garb of old-money east-coast wealth and of the rugged and plain work clothes of the immigrant and pioneer. And he has translated it all into clothes of timeless appeal.

Colin McDowell, in his monograph on the designer, wrote:

> Refreshingly he has separated dress from the tyranny of fashion dictatorship. He has looked specifically at what makes American fashion not only different but unique: sportswear, casual elegance, the luxury of simplicity married to the highest level of workmanship and the very best of fabrics and materials – and he emphasised the timelessness inherent in it. … But the skills of Ralph Lauren are not confined to clothes alone. He has taught us how to create our surroundings, he has educated our taste and he has revolutionised the way we shop.

Lauren was the first to understand what has since been labelled experiential shopping; we may take away a product in a bag but what we are really buying into is the experience offered to us by the constructed ambiance of the shop – whether it be a gentleman's club or a safari tent.

Ralph Lauren was born in 1939, in the Bronx, New York, the fourth and last child of recent immigrants from Russia, Frank and Frieda Lifshitz. Frank was a highly skilled decorator, a specialist in wood grain and marble effects. Ralph was an ordinary little boy who liked to play ball with his brothers and the neighbourhood guys. He did not, as so many other important designers did, make clothes for his sister's dolls. However, according to school friends Lauren's fashion sense was apparent at an early age when he would buy himself expensive suits with the money he earned working at his after-school job. Looking stylish was a priority.

McDowell established two patterns of behaviour in the boy that were to shape the man. He had a fertile fantasy life and totally immersed himself in the role of the moment, playing baseball as his hero, Mickey Mantle; sword-fighting his brothers as the Duke of York 'or some other duke'; and boxing, as Joe Louis, with his brother who was Sugar Ray Robinson. Secondly, he began quite naturally to invest clothes with talismanic qualities, deriving a sense of identity and provenance from his brother's well-worn hand-me-downs. McDowell wrote: 'You don't need a crystal ball to see this as the beginning of a cultural approach that was to be the basis of the Polo Ralph Lauren empire, predicated as it is on the assumption that, while fashion is fickle, "real" clothes are better because they exemplify continuity. How many times has Ralph Lauren said that he responds to old, well-worn clothes and dislikes the concept of fashion because it presupposes newness?'

Ralph's brothers changed their name to Lauren while he was still a teenager, and he followed suit. By the time he finished high school, he realised that his dream of an athletic career was

Image 30.2 *Ralph Lauren with models, spring/summer 1996. Niall McInerney, Photographer.* ©
Bloomsbury Publishing Plc.

unlikely to be realised, so he enrolled at City College in Manhattan to study business management,
dropping out before getting his degree. While waiting to be drafted into the military, he got a
job at Brooks Brothers, a store whose merchandise – all the elements of the classic, upper-crust
gentleman's wardrobe – was identified with a customer base that had gone to prep school and an
East Coast Ivy League university. This was where the so-called preppie look of the early 1980s
was spawned. It enchanted the young Ralph Lauren. 'I thought it was like Mecca,' he said. 'It was
just, "Wow!"'

He was called up into the army reserve and, on being discharged in 1964, took a series of jobs that
led to one with a tie manufacturer named Abe Rivetz, for whom he began designing wide 'kipper'
ties that called for a 'big knot'. Rivetz told him: 'The world's not ready for you, Ralph.' So in 1967, he
borrowed $50,000 and launched his own range of ties, which he sold to Bloomingdale's. 'They cost $20
in an era when men's ties were $5. I made the best stuff in America because I believed that beautiful
things could be made here,' he said. He called his fledgling company Polo, because he wanted a sporty,
classy name, and because he always saw himself as the dashing hero of the chukka. The movie of his
own life was on a continuous loop in Lauren's imagination, the script endlessly tweaked, endlessly
varied, its location shifting regularly. In 2008, he told Lesley White of *The Sunday Times*, 'When I
started with clothes, it wasn't necessarily a fashion message. It was how would I like my kids to grow
up? How do I spend my weekends?'

In 1964 Lauren married Ricky Low-Beer, the blonde nineteen-year-old only child of Viennese Jewish immigrants. A college girl with a classy, educated manner, she was his romantic ideal. They have three children, Andrew, David and Dylan. Despite strong and well-substantiated rumours (detailed at length in Michael Gross's book) of affairs with other women, Lauren has clearly never doubted that his marriage to Ricky would endure, the central relationship of his life.

Polo grew fast. In 1968 the full menswear range was launched, and in the following year the first menswear shop-within-a-shop in Bloomingdale's in Manhattan. In 1971 he launched his first women's wear collection, a line of tailored shirts, and opened the first Polo store in Beverly Hills, California. A year on, he introduced the short-sleeved cotton knit polo shirt with its polo-player logo. It was advertised with the slogan, 'Every team has its color – Polo has 24.' In 1974 Lauren provided the men's clothes for the film *The Great Gatsby*, starring Robert Redford, who became a lifelong friend. He designed the clothes for Woody Allen and Diane Keaton in *Annie Hall* in 1977, starting a trend for androgyny in womenswear – baggy trousers, masculine shirts, waistcoats and ties worn at half-mast. A year later, inspired by his ranch in Colorado, and, of course, by the mythic movies of the Old West, he launched Western wear for men and women, an enduring style within his canon and a riposte to those who accused him of being in thrall to an archaic and irrelevant upper-class Britishness.

Lauren launched his first perfumes, Lauren and Polo for Men, in 1978. The following year, he created the first of his multi-image advertising campaigns in which the pictures were styled as stills from a film. In 1981 his Santa Fe collection, based on traditional Navajo colours, patterns and details, was so beautiful fashion editors wept and so evocative it became the most copied collection of the decade. Simultaneously, the first Polo store in Europe – and the first American designer label store – opened on Bond Street. While women were scrambling to dress as hybrid Native American maidens and covered-wagon pioneer women, men were going preppy. Polo's preppy look was considered the power suit of the early 1980s, the uniform of Tom Wolfe's 'Masters of the Universe' who peopled Wall Street. Lauren sourced many elements in his collections in Britain, especially knitwear and fabrics, and he went to London for his tailoring, commissioning classics like the blue blazer made leaner and younger for his customer. It was supplanted mid-decade by Armani's deconstructed, sleeves-rolled *American Gigolo* look.

In 1982 Lauren launched his home collection, each range within it a complete set dressing for one of his re-imagined worlds. Four years later he opened his flagship store in the Rhinelander mansion on Madison Avenue and the Polo store in Paris. In 1990 he introduced Safari, the fragrance, accessorised by a whole lifestyle package, and as the decade progressed, he developed the Polo Sport ranges for men and women and the Polo Jeans Co for the young. Expanding simultaneously up the market, he introduced the Purple Label men's tailoring collection, personally starring in the advertisements. In 1997 Lauren took his company public while retaining 90 per cent control, and in 1999 he opened the largest Polo store in the world in Chicago with an adjacent Ralph Lauren restaurant, launching the

Ralph by Ralph Lauren collection for sixteen- to twenty-five-year-old women and also acquiring the retailer Club Monaco. In the 2000s Lauren devoted much time to charities and film festivals but found time to launch ranges of fine jewellery and watches.

Ralph Lauren received an honorary knighthood from the British crown in 2018, partly in recognition of his achievement in fashion but also for his charity work in public health, particularly in cancer research. He is so immensely wealthy that he has said he couldn't possible spend it all. He has the ranch in Colorado, homes in Jamaica and on Long Island, an estate in Bedford, New York, as well as his Fifth Avenue Manhattan address and a sublime collection of vintage cars to match.

Further reading: For Lauren's work, see Colin McDowell's monograph, *Ralph Lauren: The Man, the Vision, the Style* (2002). For Lauren's life, see Michael Gross's *Genuine Authentic: The Real Life of Ralph Lauren* (2003). Lauren's own book, *Ralph Lauren* (2017), is visually stunning.

Image 30.3 *Ralph Lauren, autumn/winter 1990. Niall McInerney, Photographer. © Bloomsbury Publishing Plc.*

31

Issey Miyake (1935–)

Miyake himself attributed much of his thinking to the influence of Madeleine Vionnet.

In the introduction to the first book on the work of Issey Miyake, *East Meets West,* published in 1978, Diana Vreeland, then retired from American *Vogue* and heading the Costume Institute at the Metropolitan Museum of Art in New York, wrote, 'His clothes are totally his and his alone. I love you, Issey, and the way you carry on and on and on, from your centuries-old traditions, down through the ages, utilising your total instinct and great integrity to present artistry and beautiful inspirations that are so well applied to the present tense of East and West.'

Miyake's vision is unique. He was the precursor, leader and mentor of a new school of Japanese design, which took the fashion world by storm in the early 1980s. He was not the first Japanese designer to find fame in the West, but he was the first to create something new and revolutionary. He drew deeply on both Oriental and occidental traditions of dress to produce the hybrid style that was to change everyone's perceptions of what clothing could be.

Born Kazunaru Miyake in Hiroshima in 1938, he was cycling to school on 6 August 1945 when the Americans dropped the atom bomb. He lost most of his family, including his mother, who was severely burned and died four years later. She had carried on working as a teacher despite her injuries. Perhaps as a consequence, he has always surrounded himself with strong, clever women. At ten, Miyake developed a bone marrow disease that affects him to this day. 'The Japan I grew up in was a very poor country,' he told Brenda Polan. 'My generation dreamed of going to America. We believed the future lay there.' Post-war Japan was dominated culturally by the occupying American forces. Within that culture the most desirable clothing for men was the classic Ivy League leisure wear worn by off-duty American officers – club ties, button-down shirts, penny loafers and navy blazers. Japanese women of the time craved traditional Parisian chic of the kind featured in the copies of *Vogue* and *Harper's Bazaar* that his sister bought and he read curiously – a desire that Hanae Mori, the first Japanese fashion designer to make a name abroad, sought to satisfy.

When he brought his clothes to New York in 1971 and to Paris in 1973, Miyake never doubted that they would have an international appeal. A lifelong experimenter and collaborator, seeking out

Image 31.1 *Issey Miyake, autumn/winter 1984. Niall McInerney, Photographer. © Bloomsbury Publishing Plc.*

the best and most creative minds to work with, he has always projected confidence in his vision of fashion, a vision that eschews sudden change and looks instead to evolution. He is a clever, gentle, modest man, movie-star handsome and charismatic; consequently, he makes friends and lifelong fans wherever he goes. But a huge part of his magnetism derives from his passionate commitment to his ideas and his willingness to explain, to engage, to proselytise.

Miyake studied art at Tama University in Tokyo, graduating in 1965 with a degree in graphic design. He had begun designing clothing in 1962, and in 1963 he presented his first real collection, entitled A Poem of Cloth and Stone, at the Tokyo Chamber of Commerce and Industry. His stated – and possibly precocious – ambition was to show that clothes could be both utilitarian and visually creative. He said at the time,

> We want to stimulate the imagination through clothing. Though these designs draw their inspiration from contemporary style, it is not really a fashion show. I think the next step will be clothing that looks to the future. There are many long dresses in the show not meant as evening wear, but simply because of the form. I would like this show to mark the birth of visual clothing in Japan.

To develop his skills and his thinking, he enrolled on a course at the Chambre Syndicale de la Couture Parisienne and spent five years in Paris and New York working with established fashion designers. He was less impressed by his time at Laroche and Givenchy than by the youth-focused, mini-loving vitality he found in the weekends he spent in London, visiting the theatre and the galleries, wandering the King's Road, shopping and having his hair cut.

While he was in Paris, the political revolt of May 1968 disturbed everyone, even the denizens of the bourgeois salons of couture. The workers occupied the Renault plant and the students took to the streets, manning the modern-day barricades of burnt-out trams and dustbins and digging up the cobblestones to throw through the clouds of tear gas at the armed and armoured police. London, too, was witness to student rebellion and violence on the streets as youngsters, some left wing, all indignant, marched in support of their American peers being drafted to wage war in Vietnam.

Miyake's friend, the architect Arata Isozaki, wrote in *East Meets West*:

> I am not certain whether or not he had already formed his own critical opinion of haute couture, a staunchly regulated genre of international fashion. However, finding himself in Paris, a city full of suspicion and jealousy, faced by a language barrier which handicapped his liberty, he probably saw no reason to remain where he was, and thus, he took flight. One of the characteristics of the protest movement was impulsive body action; energy was burnt. After that, in the vacuum, the question loomed once again in front of him: 'As a designer, what are clothes?'

His flight from the world of couture took him to New York and the studio of Geoffrey Beene. There his attention was caught by the classless, genderless American uniform of jeans and T-shirt he saw worn by workers, weekending executives and militant students alike. Back in Tokyo in 1970, Miyake

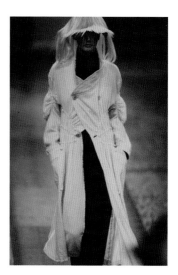

Image 31.2 *Issey Miyake, spring/summer 1994. Niall McInerney, Photographer. © Bloomsbury Publishing Plc.*

Image 31.3 *Issey Miyake, autumn/winter 1994. Niall McInerney, Photographer. © Bloomsbury Publishing Plc.*

set up his design studio and looked back to his own cultural inheritance to examine the possibilities of Japanese work wear, its cheap but laboriously worked textiles, the kimono and the costumes of the samurai of the Edo period, costumes that were elaborately constructed of many simple, rectilinear garments and swathes of fabric. He told Brenda Polan in 1983,

> I thought that the occidental clothing tradition was too tight. I wanted to make things that were free both mentally and physically. I had to free myself from the occidental tradition, of the occidental way, of occidental ideas. But there are still a lot of things to learn from them; it is important to respect that long tradition, the things that Paris couture was really about – even with all its elitism.

For the Japanese, tight clothing was traditionally not at all sexy. 'The Japanese body does not have sculptural beauty and expresses little sex appeal,' wrote the painter, Tadanori Yokoo. 'Sex appeal is a spiritual matter, not a physical one.' Sensuality is found in large volumes of fabric, luxuriously textured, cut in imposing, almost abstract shapes, layered and wrapped. The Japanese use the body as a template for a three-dimensional sculptural shape. At rest, these costumes have a kind of grandeur; in movement, they have a fluid grace. They tease the senses through the imagination. They are subtle, the product of a social system that is constructed to ease relationships on a few overcrowded islands and that is heavily reliant on ritual, formality and restraint.

Miyake had developed a theory he called 'peeling away to the limit', throwing away all the inhibiting ideas about dress imposed by Western cultural imperialism and starting again from the beginning – the bolt of cloth, the hank of yarn. He began his great experiment with *sashiko*, the traditionally patterned, often striped, quilted cotton worn by Japanese peasants. He chose as his collaborator textile designer

Makiko Minagawa, who was interested in mixing various yarns, natural and synthetic, to bring out the 'essence' of a fabric, exploring its potential for movement, texture and tactility as far as possible.

At first, the resulting clothing consisted of pieces of irregularly shaped fabric almost suspended about the body – Miyake was interested in the 'space between' body and clothing – each piece of which could be stripped away. This he developed into layering and wrapping, and his unparalleled feeling for texture, mass and volume became apparent. He himself attributed much of his thinking to the influence of Madeleine Vionnet; she also preferred to suspend the fabric from the body and allow it to follow its own nature, assuming new shapes as the wearer moved. In his collections he would achieve magical effects, creating garments that arrived on the runway as one thing – a jacket, a kimono, a slender skirt – and that would, with the shrug of the shoulder, the swift movement of a wrist, become something else entirely, perhaps a skirt, a pair of shorts, a hooded poncho. His delight in all manner of materials led to experimentation with plastic, bamboo and various kinds of paper to produce masks, hieratic headdresses, pseudo-armour reminiscent of samurai gear, and clothes that evoked thoughts of kites, heraldic banners, origami and modern abstract sculpture.

Speaking to Susannah Frankel of *The Guardian* in 1997, he described his first half-hour show in Tokyo thus:

> There was no music, just a sound system that picked up every little noise. The girl came out in many layers of clothing. She take off her shoes, throws them down. Bang! Bang! She take off garment. Ssh. She drop it on floor. Crash! She take off everything. She has no clothes. End of show. It become big Tokyo scandal. Sponsorship company beg me to stop.

Miyake has a talent for the small scandals that get big headlines. In 1976 he showed his collection in Tokyo on 'Twelve Black Girls', led out by Grace Jones. In the 1980s in Paris he showed his collection on dancers and volunteers of all ages and genders, culminating in the 1995 show starring a group of octogenarians. His collaborations with artists – such as Yasumasa Morimura, Nobuyoshi Araki, Tim Hawkinson and Cai Guo-Qiang among others – and the beauty of his exhibitions are legendary. Simply because they make such extraordinary pictures, the great photographer, Irving Penn, volunteered in 1986 to shoot all of Miyake's collections, something he did with no interference from the designer for a decade. Miyake has claimed that seeing what Penn made of his clothes enabled him to understand his own designs more acutely. He has been given major shows in museums and galleries in Japan, America, France and Britain, but making real clothes for everyone has always been at the heart of his work.

He created Pleats Please in 1993, the year he was made a member of the Légion d'Honneur, France's highest accolade. A-POC (a piece of cloth) was the similarly egalitarian 'cut-and-wear from a tube of fabric' system he developed and launched in 1999. Miyake told Frankel:

> My first dream, and why I decided to open my studio was that I thought to myself, 'If I could one day make clothes like T-shirts and jeans, I would be very excited.' But the more I worked the more I

felt so far away from doing so. I was always doing such heavy things, far away from the people. And then I was thinking, you know, 'Are you stupid? Don't you remember why you started designing in the first place?' And then I thought, 'OK, Pleats Please.' So I started to think how to make it, how to wash it, how to coordinate it, even how to pack it. And I worked on how to keep the price down.

Pleats had long been a theme to which Miyake returned in his main collection, and now he developed a separate collection, chiefly in machine-washable feather-light, uncreasable viscose, of simple, useful, comfortable pieces pleated vertically, horizontally, diagonally, cross-hatched, straight and wriggly that made interesting shapes on the body and often could be worn several ways. As Richard Martin and Harold Koda wrote in their catalogue for the 1994 Orientalism exhibition at New York's Metropolitan Museum of Art, 'Hybrid styles by such designers as Issey Miyake offer the paradigm of dress that cannot be located to a specific place but justly belong to the world.'

Though he handed over the design of the main line to Naoki Takizawa in 1999, Miyake continued to work on Pleats Please, and his style and influence were apparent in the company's products. In 2007, after Takizawa left to launch his own label, a new creative director, Dai Fujiwara, was appointed. Miyake was awarded Japan's Order of Culture in 2010 and honoured with a major retrospective at The National Art Center, Tokyo, in 2016. He is a Commander of the Légion d'Honneur.

Further reading: See Mark Holborn's *Issey Miyake* (1995) and, for background, Claire Wilcox's *Radical Fashion* (2001). Two reviews of Miyake's 2016 retrospective are recommended: by Rafael A. Balboa, 'The Work of Issey Miyake', in *Domus,* and 'Issey Miyake: 45 years at the forefront of fashion' by Tamsin Blanchard in *The Observer.*

Image 31.4 *Issey Miyake, autumn winter 1995. Niall McInerney, Photographer.* © *Bloomsbury Publishing Plc.*

32

Geoffrey Beene (1927–2004)

Beene's experimental, almost transgressive, approach to fabric made him attractive to the manufacturers of the new synthetic fibres.

Like all the great designers who helped to shift fashion on to a new track, Geoffrey Beene challenged accepted criteria. His area of greatest experimentation was fabric. He was an early champion of post-war synthetics, including uncreasable fabrics, the holy grail of women who did not have ladies' maids or unlimited funds for dry-cleaning. A democrat in his approach to the modern lifestyle he assumed his customers led and in his refusal to accept *ancien régime* rules of dress or hierarchies of materials, Beene was a key exponent of American sportswear style, a wearer-focused fashion concept that embraced the utilitarian and practical aspects of clothing and undermined all the conventions about what one could wear when, as well as all the demarcation lines about appropriate fabrics.

Typically, American fashion rejects the distinctions between what should be worn by day and what by night, the kind of 'never wear diamonds before 6 pm' rigidity that used to permit the dowagers who ran high society to spot a *parvenu* at 100 paces. Beene instinctively pursued a youthful customer who cared as little as he did for all those shibboleths. He was, as Jane Mulvagh has observed, a leg man. 'His clothes', she wrote, 'were easy, flirty and showed legs, legs, legs.'

While never compromising on quality of cut, structure or couture-standard technique, he played with mischievous juxtapositions: metallic lamé teamed with grey flannel, cashmere knit and taffeta, blanket-plaid wool and lace. He was one of the earliest American designers to introduce baby doll looks as well as gipsy styles and traditional ethnic fabrics, including simple cottons previously thought downmarket. In the 1980s, when opulence was the order of the day, some of Beene's most enchanting evening designs were the result of taking a conventional daywear style – a shirtwaist dress, say – and growing it to floor-length, then outlining and encrusting the luscious print in sequins and beads. Harold Koda, curator at the Metropolitan Museum of Art's Costume Institute, said, 'It's like someone

Image 32.1 *Geoffrey Beene, spring/summer 1987. Niall McInerney, Photographer. © Bloomsbury Publishing Plc.*

who speaks the English language and through use becomes a poet. His affinity, his exploration of the abstraction of cloth, has allowed him to push its possibilities in ways that are unimaginable.'

Beene, who identified with the Pygmalion myth, said in 1995,

> Clothes should look as if they haven't been born yet; as if a woman were born into them. It's a form of possession, this belonging of one to the other. You mould a woman into what you perceive her as being. What I do is the product of my admiration. I imagine women in an idyllic state. I create a vision of this woman, whether she exists or not. Doesn't every human aim for perfection? For the possibility of it?

At the heart of designer sportswear is the client, an active woman with a busy life and a need for comfortable, useful, easy clothes with pockets.

The history of the style has two strands of antecedents: firstly, Parisian and American couture and conventional men's wear for all occasions, ranging from formal tailoring to leisure wear, and secondly, Seventh Avenue, the commercial, factory-based heart of the American fashion industry that, like all of America's late-nineteenth- and twentieth-century industries, was almost obsessively focused on modernism (the Modern Movement mantra – 'Less is more' – came to apply to Beene's work), on speed, practicality and the constant development and updating that fuelled consumerism. Industrial America has always been about hard-selling the 'latest thing', about whetting consumers' appetites, about an egalitarian emphasis on mass availability. In terms of clothing, the early sportswear designers – Claire McCardell, Vera Maxwell, Tom Brigance, Anne Fogarty, Tina Lesser, Bonnie Cashin, Halston – embraced a kind of version of Italian Futurism, an art movement whose exponents liked to picture the world in constant motion. These were the first designers to envisage women striding out, rather than languidly at rest. Arguably, they saw it not in terms of feminism but in terms of modernity, liberty and the American way. Beene, talking to Brenda Cullerton in 1995, defined beauty as 'a measure of energy'.

'I have never much liked rigid clothes or anything constraining,' Geoffrey Beene told Brenda Polan in an interview in 1984. 'I like freedom. I am an American; I love freedom and the brilliant clothes that are the American working uniform. I love sweatshirts, skirts and loafers, denim, baggy chinos, and I have never in my work deviated from the premise of freedom and effortlessness.' Indeed, in 1968 he famously designed full-length evening dresses based on the American football shirt and sequinned all over.

His experimental, almost transgressive, approach to fabric made him attractive to manufacturers of the new synthetic fibres that became an important part of the development of fashion in the 1950s and 1960s. In the late 1960s he was one of ten international designers commissioned by DuPont to contribute to a promotional project for Qiana, a silky nylon yarn. He chose to have the yarn woven into a satin velour decoupé about which he said, 'Working with this material proved to me that synthetics could be perfected, for it was exactly like a pure silk velour, only it did not crease.' He was disappointed in the long run by the way these fabrics decayed in his archive.

Image 32.2 *Geoffrey Beene, 1990. Niall McInerney, Photographer. © Bloomsbury Publishing Plc.*

Image 32.3 *Geoffrey Beene, spring/summer 1987. Niall McInerney, Photographer. © Bloomsbury Publishing Plc.*

Geoffrey Beene was born Samuel Albert Bozeman Jr in 1927 in rural Haynesville, Louisiana and he was never to lose that warm, melting molasses-over-ice-cream accent. There was also a formality to his diction that may have been dated but that was a joy to the ears of the literate. To call him a Southern gentleman is a cliché – and, anyway, he could be the most irascible and impatient of conversationalists, something of which even his biographer, Brenda Cullerton, complained. He was the erudite grandson of a plantation owner on one side and the town doctor on the other. He first demonstrated his interest in fashion as a boy by redecorating his room and getting his aunts to make up a fabric he bought – tiny orange flowers on a powder blue background – into beach pyjamas using a Simplicity paper pattern. A passion for the way cloth worked with the body was all he took away from three years in the medical school at Tulane University, New Orleans. 'Cadavers were the moment of truth,' he said. He wanted to cut for the body, not into it, and sketched movie-star gowns on the margins of his copy of Gray's Anatomy.

He dropped out, spent three asthmatic, hospitalised weeks in the US Army, was discharged, moved to California to stay with an aunt in the movie business and took a temporary job in the display department of I. Magnin in Los Angeles. 'I didn't leave the South,' he said in 1995. 'I fled. I'm still fleeing.' In 1947 he moved to New York to the Traphagen School of Fashion to study the theory and practice of design, before taking a course at l'Académie Julian in Paris and apprenticing himself to a tailor who had worked for Molyneux. Tailoring was at the heart of his technique, and his love affair with geometry, especially triangles, probably had its origins here. 'My life began there,' he told Cullerton. 'It began the moment people understood what I wanted to do.' In 1951 he returned to the Seventh Avenue garment trade and worked anonymously for several houses before being fired by

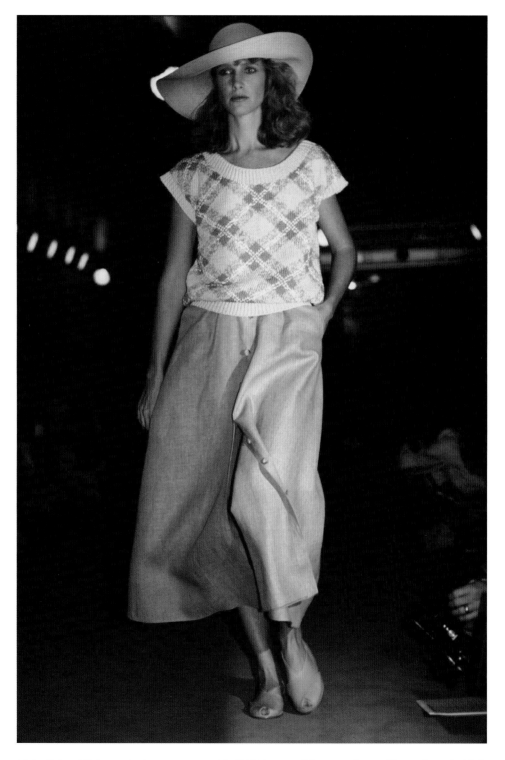

Image 33.1 *Calvin Klein, spring/summer 1991. Niall McInerney, Photographer. © Bloomsbury Publishing Plc.*

33

Calvin Klein (1942–)

*Klein can take credit for refining the American designer sportswear
genre for the body-con generation.*

In the 1980s, when Michael Douglas's febrile film character in *Wall Street*, Gordon Gekko, could declare, 'Greed is good' and have it become the mantra of a generation that was pleased to label itself 'yuppie', three American designers reached out from Seventh Avenue to become the world's biggest fashion brands. Ralph Lauren, Donna Karan and Calvin Klein have quite similar back-stories, but they are very different designers. While Lauren may have dressed *Annie Hall* in 1977, it is Klein who represents the lurch towards androgyny that occurred in the following decade. Nicholas Coleridge, writing in 1988, described a visit to Klein's office. The designer showed him photographs of the model, José Borain, in a man's white shirt, doeskin flannel trousers and a greatcoat. Klein asked him,

> Do you like these pictures? I find these a very sexy way to look. It's like she has thrown on her boyfriend's shirt, man's pants, her friend's trenchcoat. It's a kind of sexiness quite different from hookers' clothes. If I mix tweed with a fabric like silk chamois so you can see the woman's body, and her blouse just rips, that for me is as sexy as anything. A woman in cavalry twill pants and no adornment.

As the monstrous shoulder pads of the time illustrate, the physical ideal for both men and women was gym-pumped, broad-shouldered, narrow-hipped, flat stomached and flaunting boy-sized buttocks. This was the lean and athletic, cool and laid-back all-American achiever Calvin Klein chose to dress. In 1979–1980, Klein launched his 'designer' jeans, the first of their ilk, with six television commercials directed by Richard Avedon and starring Brooke Shields, a fifteen-year-old who had played a child prostitute in Louis Malle's 1978 film, *Pretty Baby*. In the most provocative of the ads Shields asked, 'Want to know what comes between me and my Calvins? Nothing.' The response was predictable, with television stations banning the ads amid welters of publicity. On a TV talk show, basking in the controversy, Klein asserted, 'The tighter they are, the better they sell.'

That goes some way towards defining the paradox at the heart of Calvin Klein's approach to design – and, probably, to life. Rather like Ralph Lauren, that other icon of American style, that other Jewish boy raised in the Bronx, Klein had an instinctive understanding of how to dress a woman or a man to make them look old-money rich, raised in a world of good taste and restrained luxury. He knew the associations of class that silk, glove-soft suede and leather, cashmere tweeds and gabardine bring with them. And he knew the look is a turn-on. He can take credit for refining the American designer sportswear genre for the body-con generation. Yet at the same time he liked to strip down and get dirty with the most vulgar of transgressive imagery. As Michael Gross wrote, 'In Calvin's world, polymorphic perversity is par for the course. Quaint morality is banished.'

With the exception of Gianni Versace a decade later and Tom Ford a decade after that, no other upmarket designer has used sex to sell in quite such an upfront way (and upfront more than describes his ads for men's underpants). Until he finally eschewed drink, drugs, promiscuity and the whole Studio 54 lifestyle in 1986 in favour of embracing the all-American domestic dream with a second marriage to a younger woman, Kelly Rector (they divorced in 2006), even his perfume ads had a pornographic, distinctly homoerotic edge to them. As the first friends in his circle began to die from AIDS, Calvin Klein reinvented himself, becoming Calvin Clean, avatar of middle-class family values. He told *Women's Wear Daily*, 'Love … marriage … commitment. I think it is a feeling that is happening all over the country.' He sold his houses in the gay resorts of Fire Island and Key West and bought an East Side Georgian town house and a vast beach house on Long Island. On the shelf the 1988 scent, Eternity, supplanted 1985's Obsession, while in the ever-iconic ads a family picnic on a beach sidelined a sweaty naked threesome on a shadowy sofa. It's a rare brand that can survive quite such a radical volte-face.

In her business biography, Lisa Marsh wrote in 2003 that Calvin Klein was arguably the most well-known fashion brand in the world. She added, 'It would be safe to say that every man, woman and child in America has owned something that bears the Calvin Klein label at one point or another. To most fashion watchers, professional and pedestrian, the company's brand can be summed up in a few words – modern, clean, sleek, and American.'

Born in the Bronx, New York in 1942, the son of a Jewish grocer, young Calvin taught himself to sketch and sew. His mother was an elegant woman who played an important role in shaping her son's fashion sense by taking him with her when she visited her dressmakers, while his grandmother taught him to use a sewing machine. Klein graduated from New York's Fashion Institute of Technology in 1962 and worked for a series of middle-to-down-market Seventh Avenue manufacturers whose product he loathed. 'Real hooker clothes,' he called them. On his marriage to Jayne Centre, a classmate from his Bronx elementary school, he began to moonlight, creating his own collection on his kitchen table in Queens and having it made up by a Jewish tailor on Coney Island. His current boss found out, threatened to sue him and confiscate the new designs. 'I just broke down and started crying,' he told Coleridge. 'He asked me to leave at that moment and I never worked for anyone again.'

In 1968 his childhood friend Barry Schwartz, having inherited his father's supermarket business, invited Klein to go into business with him. Instead, Schwartz became partner in Klein's own business, lending the designer $10,000 to open a small showroom in the York Hotel on Seventh Avenue, designing and selling youthful, simple coats for women. What happened next has become rag trade legend. The merchandise manager of Bonwit Teller got out of the lift on the wrong floor, glimpsed Klein's coats, liked them and invited him to show them to Mildred Custin, the renowned president of the store. In order to ensure that the clothes did not get creased or soiled, the designer pushed his collection up Seventh Avenue on a clothes rail. Custin placed an order worth $50,000.

Klein always focused on modernity and simplicity. 'I've always had a clear design philosophy and point of view about being modern, sophisticated, sexy, clean and minimal. They all apply to my design aesthetic,' he told *Women's Wear Daily*. He had no respect for the couture tradition, acknowledging Claire McCardell as a significant influence. Of her clothes he said, 'They are the only clothes from the late Forties and Fifties that could still be worn today beautifully.' Through the 1970s, his classic and classy clean-cut look became a working uniform for large parts of a generation of women motivated by the women's movement to forge a path into many industries and professions. His spare sportswear style was most often executed in neutral shades and earth tones, the colours most associated with the semi-desert, bare-bones landscape of Southwestern America and the paintings of Andrew Wyeth – stone, sand, ochre, ubiquitous camel – and Georgia O'Keefe – azure, violet, white, oyster. His daywear classics were tailored in the most expensive flannels, worsteds and tweeds Europe could supply. He

Image 33.2 *Designer Calvin Klein, autumn/winter 1990. Niall McInerney, Photographer. © Bloomsbury Publishing Plc.*

Image 33.3 *Calvin Klein, autumn/winter 1993. Niall McInerney, Photographer. © Bloomsbury Publishing Plc.*

criticised American textile producers for poor quality and lack of innovation. Many jackets were cut like a loose shirt that worked over both skirt and trousers. In 1971 he was a leading exponent of the Big Look, simple loose tops – his smock shape was wildly successful – loose skirts and baggy pants. In 1976 his T-shirt- and chemise-shaped evening dresses made headlines; in 1977 it was metallic effects; in 1978 slinky cotton jersey slip dresses and his all-year-round butter-soft, unstructured suede and leather pieces in pale, show-every-mark colours.

Klein and his first wife, with whom he had a daughter, Marci, were divorced in 1974 and he adopted a hedonistic lifestyle. He was regularly seen at celebrity night spots, such as Studio 54, accompanied by a loose-knit circle of friends, including the designers Halston and Giorgio di Sant' Angelo, artist Andy Warhol and his factory acolytes, and Bianca Jagger. Rumours of drug consumption and sexual excesses abounded, as did rumours that Klein had contracted AIDS. An Italian radio station even erroneously announced his death from the disease. In 1978, twelve-year-old Marci was kidnapped and ransomed for $100,000; Klein paid the ransom and found her alive tied up in a New York tenement. Both his lifestyle and the growing sexualisation of the image conveyed by his advertising fuelled wide speculation about Klein's own sexuality. In their 1994 unauthorised biography, *Obsession*, Steven Gaines and Sharon Churcher alleged that he was a member of a so-called 'Velvet Mafia' of millionaires who swapped lovers. After their marriage in 1986, he and Kelly Rector continued to live in separate apartments.

In 1982 Klein achieved his second great coup with the introduction of Calvin Klein underpants. He launched the snug white briefs in an ad on an enormous billboard in New York's Times Square; the image was an overtly sexual one of a lithe and muscular man wearing nothing but white underwear. Questioned about the homoerotic appeal of the advertising by Karen Stabiner for *The New York Times Magazine*, a spokesperson for Calvin Klein deadpanned, 'We did not try to appeal to gays. We try to appeal, period. If there's an awareness in that community of health and grooming, then they'll respond to the ads.' Klein's billboard has been credited with heralding a new era in imagery of men in advertising. He went on to produce many more of the same, working with contemporary photographers such as Bruce Weber and Herb Ritts.

In 1983 he launched man-style cotton Calvins for women. *Time* magazine called them 'Calvin's New Gender Benders' and *Women's Wear Daily* deemed it 'the hottest look in women's lingerie since the bikini brief'. The boxer shorts had a fly opening. 'It's sexier with the fly,' said Klein. 'These things are carefully thought out.' Adapting to the ethos of the 1980s, he showed he could do classic glamour, opting for a more structured look to his tailoring and crisp details like ruffled lace. On the inauguration of President Ronald Reagan, Klein said, 'We all guessed on Seventh Avenue that glamour would be back and we'd be doing glam evening dresses to show it off because the Reagans are Californian and California is pretty showy. It was a great change from the Carter administration which was very much, you sewed your own dress!' He proved a masterly architect of dramatically streamlined evening wear that owed something to the Adrian and Banton gowns from 1930s movies – all lush satins cut on the bias.

In her business biography, Lisa Marsh wrote,

Many in the industry like to believe the fashion business is all about the design, cut, colour and draping of garments – that it is an artistic endeavour – that the fashion industry is one based more on creativity than on commerce. However, the American designer houses that have reigned supreme … have proven that design is a small part of the business of fashion. These businesses draw breath from things like the marketing and positioning of the company's image, shrewd partnerships with retailers, regular support from the fashion press and, above all, astute business management who can see beyond the hype.

Certainly these things, done so consummately well in America, have resulted in some US brands gaining an undeserved dominance in world markets. But in the case of Calvin Klein, working so successfully to remould American designer sportswear for the 1970s and 1980s, the design input was more than a 'small part'. In 2003, Klein and Schwartz sold the company to Phillips-Van Heusen for $739 million and Francisco Costa took over as creative director, regenerating the brand and restoring its fashion profile. In 2016, he was succeeded in the role by Raf Simons who resigned in December 2018, shortly after the PVH CEO, Emanuel Chirico, expressed disappointment in the returns on the main fashion line. A few months later in March 2019 Chirico closed the fashion collection and its many stores worldwide to concentrate on the far greater profits from the underwear and perfume lines.

Further reading: For the story of a mega brand, read Lisa Marsh's (2003) *The House of Klein: Fashion, Controversy and a Business Obsession.* For the life, read the unauthorised *Obsession* (1994) by Stephen Gaines and Sharon Churcher. *Calvin Klein* (2017), compiled by the designer himself, thoroughly documents his career with visual flair.

Image 33.4 *Calvin Klein, autumn/winter 1993. Niall McInerney, Photographer.* © *Bloomsbury Publishing Plc.*

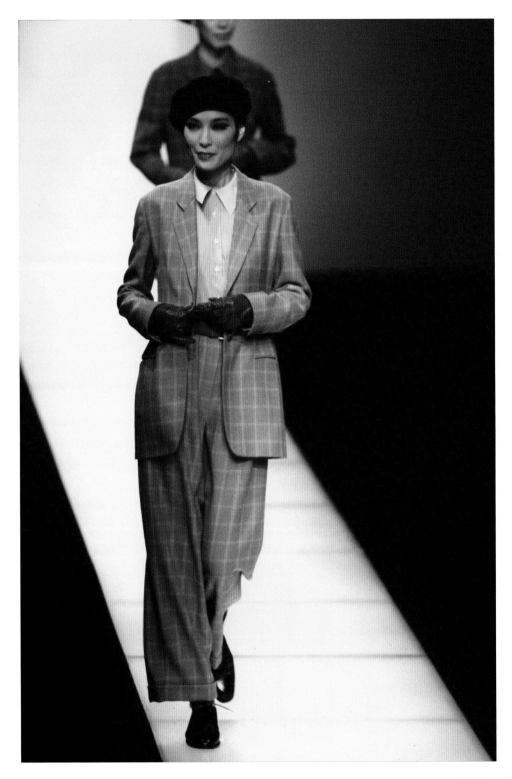

Image 34.1 *Giorgio Armani, autumn/winter 1990. Niall McInerney, Photographer. © Bloomsbury Publishing Plc.*

34

Giorgio Armani (1934–)

*Armani's soft, tactile fabrics and the easy, almost liquid cut make the
wearer feel sensuous, relaxed, at ease.*

Giorgio Armani S.p.A is one of the most profitable companies in Italy – *the* most profitable in some years. In 2016 it was worth 2.9 billion euros. In some years, Giorgio Armani personally is the country's biggest taxpayer. 'Not because I am the richest,' he said with a mischievous twinkle in his eye. 'I am just the most honest.' He was talking to Brenda Polan for *The Financial Times* and knew they would like the numbers. Over the past two decades there have been many approaches to the ageing but robust Armani from conglomerates interested in a share in his success but, while flirting just a little bit with them, he remains in control of the company he founded in 1975.

Fashion is, of course, big business in Italy but, within it, business acumen, the kind that puts the flagship companies of other industries like car manufacturing and pasta production in the shade, is not that common. And Armani maintains its pre-eminence despite the fact that other fashion labels have pre-empted the big headlines. In 2017 Armani closed two of his many labels, Armani Collezioni and Armani Jeans, but continued to grow other divisions of his company, particularly his luxury hotels collaboration with Emaar Properties. While there is doubtless an ascetic side to his character, he doesn't want to work forever, he told Polan. However, as Armani passed his eighty-fifth birthday still in the driving seat, he showed no sign of sliding out from behind the wheel. This is reassuring for the millions of women and men who have adopted Armani's cool, streamlined, modern-minded style as their own. Armani is committed to subtle change, to what he calls 'a soft evolution', at the heart of which is a consistent and rational view of the needs of a contemporary wardrobe. This utilitarian approach is far from bland; while tending towards a grown-up, urban minimalism, the Armani style is imbued with a refined sensuousness, expressed in the restrained luxury of the fabrics, in the sophisticated fluidity of the cut and in the perfection of details and accessories.

The late Gianni Versace, generally perceived as Armani's polar opposite in terms of taste, famously sniffed that a designer whose favourite colour was beige could hardly be expected to know much about sex appeal (this in response to a suggestion from Armani that Versace's own designs might be considered vulgar). But Armani's clothes *are* sexy. It is to do not with direct display but with the way the soft, tactile fabrics and the easy, almost liquid cut make the wearer feel, feelings that are then reflected in the deportment: sensuous, relaxed, at ease.

The man himself appears to be anything but those things. John Fairchild of *Women's Wear Daily* called him 'the monk of fashion' and he does have a reputation for a chilly reserve. His biographer, Renata Molho, described the child and the man thus,

> He was an observer, timid, introverted, and keenly aware of everything going on around him. He was also restless, never contented, always looking for something, whether a rare checkered shirt or a special texture in his relationships with others. These qualities are … fundamental to his complex character; he is immensely adaptable, yet he seems incapable of real satisfaction with what he achieves. He always thinks there must be something more.

He is, above all, intensely pragmatic. He told Brenda Polan, 'I never had a desire as a young man to design fashion. A series of coincidences led me on to a fashion path. Perhaps this starting point is something that already makes me different; I considered this a job like any other. I was never spoilt by the fashion atmosphere, by its preciousness. I never had the attitude that "I am a creative talent; therefore this is what you have to wear." It was a job, a profession. I came from a department store, not an atelier. When I realised – and it was very much as a result of my contact with customers – there was room for me to do something different, that I could devise a different way of dressing, I realised this was going to be my life.'

His refusal to lay claim to any great creative destiny reminds you how very different the north Italian temperament is to the southern. Historically, Lombardy is the home of bankers, merchant princes and industrialists. Armani was born in 1934 in Piacenza, to the south of Milan, one of three children of Maria and Ugo, an industrial manager who was imprisoned after the Second World War for his membership of the Fascist Party, a retribution that left its scars on his family. Giorgio enrolled to study medicine at the University of Milan but left in his third year to do his military service as a paramedic. However, on leaving the army he realised medicine was not for him. In 1957 he took a job in the advertising department of the La Rinascente store and was soon promoted to assistant buyer. He said, 'I was responsible for making sure that the clothes they were buying for the stores were getting the right response from the public.'

In the mid-1960s he was recruited to work for Nino Cerruti who had inherited his family textile company at twenty and had expanded into clothing. Armani's job, after a month's training in the factory, was to design the men's wear collection, Hitman. Instinctively, he chose lighter fabrics than were common in tailoring as well as cooler colours. He discarded layers of internal structure, reduced shoulder pads, moved buttons and pockets and took the stiff formality out of the man's suit, replacing it with something loose, relaxed, youthful. His collection was sensationally successful.

In 1966 Armani met Sergio Galeotti, the ebullient Tuscan who was to become his partner in life as well as business (he died tragically young in 1985). In 1970 the two set up an independent design consultancy working for important labels in Italy, France and Spain. In 1975, just as Gigi Monti of Basile orchestrated the move of the fledgling Italian high-fashion ready-to-wear from provincial Florence to Milan, the flourishing industrial hub, they launched the Armani label with a collection for men and women for spring/summer 1976. The women's wear show featured Armani's first men's wear-inspired jacket for women.

'It was the time when French and English designers were beginning to come to Italy for their production,' he told Polan. Fashion was becoming a global industry, and Armani perceived that he could aspire to an international market.

> To make a mark I would have to do something different. That would not be so easy. And it was a time when fashion was all about flower power, very baroque and decorated. So I made a choice. Women were beginning to be more emancipated and liberated in their way of thinking; I had been used to designing men's wear so I decided to bring into women's wear that sort of practical, rational way of dressing that really did not exist for women, although in America a lot of women embraced that style.

A point of reference was American actress Katharine Hepburn. 'Obviously,' he continues, with a humorous shrug of the shoulders, 'it was necessary to sacrifice any desire to be "creative" but that is what I saw was needed.'

His whole approach was in fact creatively fresh, a leap of imagination that was to capture the hearts of women seeking a way to look in the executive workplace. In 2007 he told biographer Renata Molho that when he started out, he aspired to emulate Chanel and Yves Saint Laurent. 'They modernised fashion, bringing it in line with the way people wanted to live nowadays. They allowed people to live differently through their clothing. They didn't create apparel, they created a different society.' Armani's great breakthrough, in which he still takes pride (while making it clear that he resents being acknowledged for that alone), was his deconstruction of the women's jacket. He stripped out the interfacing and the heavy-duty padding, eliminated the body-sculpting darts and co-opted worsteds and tweeds from men's wear. And, although he cuts a great skirt, more often than not he teamed his easy youthful jacket with the best trousers women had ever worn.

Armani and Galeotti built on their success to create a pyramid of labels that allow access to the Armani cachet at most levels of the market. 'No, no, there was no strategy,' he told Polan.

> I am not a creative genius and I am not a marketing genius. I am not a miracle on the fashion scene. It became clear to me, after the establishment of the Giorgio Armani label, that there was

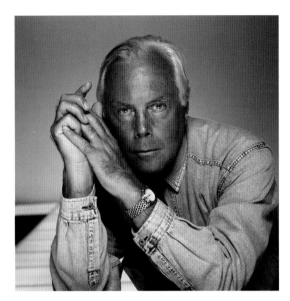

Image 34.2 *Giorgio Armani, 1991. Photo: Terry O'Neill/Iconic Images via Getty Images.*

Image 34.3 *Emporio Armani, spring/summer 1999. Niall McInerney, Photographer. © Bloomsbury Publishing Plc.*

another market out there interested in this style that was younger and had not as much money so, since I was not studying fashion creation on a yacht, I recognised this and created Armani Jeans. But where to sell it? That's how Emporio came about. Then I realised that the young wanted more than just a pair of jeans and a jacket – and that was because I would be in the shop in via Durini [in Milan] and they would come to me and give me advice. So it became a collection and the whole idea changed.

There are Armani labels at every level of the designer market including a couture collection, Privé, which he shows in Paris (a memorable collection, for spring/summer 2019, was inspired by the red lacquer of Art Deco and the work of film director Bernardo Bertolucci). Then there is a junior range, underwear, swimwear, skiwear, golf clothes, spectacles, scarves, ties, shoes, accessories, watches and fragrance. The brand has stores at every level all over the world. Armani said:

I could have become much richer much quicker if I had decided to take advantage of my name by licensing. The decision not to has meant that every line is successful and there is no confusion, no overlapping. The identity is clear and controlled. We financed ourselves every step of the way; I have never had half a lira debt in my life. I don't think this Cinderella story could happen now; I am happy it happened to me but the system has changed. Nowadays there are the big groups which decide who is going to be successful; the press, the industry, finance, it all works together to promote a certain designer. That is the limit of fashion today and the embarrassment.

He deplored the triumph of manufactured image over honest product. 'For someone my age, it is an embarrassment; anyone starting out does not know any different. But I have always liked to fight; I have always fought against the system in a certain sense. If a certain system exists, even if it is in my interest to belong, I have never wanted to be part of it. Yes, I have always been a loner. Obviously, I have had a lot of support from the press but I have never really been part of an explosion of a huge celebration of my fashion and my style. If I have had problems, it has been with the media. Perhaps these subtle changes in my style are not shocking enough. The press like to be shocked; they like to find something that gives them a shock every season. They like revolution, big explosions, not evolution. They just say: Armani is Armani and,' he mimed spitting on his hands and swiping them together in a gesture of dismissiveness, 'wipe their hands. That's not good for me.'

What, he said, he dislikes about the fashion media's hunger for abrupt change is the way it ignores the customer. 'What they all forget,' he said, 'is that we really only have one purpose: to make women and men look better. And anyway, after an explosion, there's nothing left, only ashes. But then there's another explosion, and more ashes.'

This view overlooks the prolonged 'explosion' of the late 1970s and most of the 1980s, which was all about Armani – when everyone, from sleekly ambitious executives of both sexes to brand-obsessed football fans, aspired to the label. In the 1980s the grown-up Armani look was what women finally making their way in the workplace needed. Interviewed by Brenda Polan in 1983 for *The Guardian*, Armani said,

> My clothes are for women who have money. They are not for a teenager who expects novelty; she could not afford them and the quality would be wasted on her since she does not wish to keep anything long. Too much of fashion is aimed at her so that mature women start to think that, since that is all there is, they must wear that too. I hate most of all the idea of women trying to look like children, trying to be a baby doll. So women like to look younger, that is natural but the general trend is for women to try to look like children and that is unnatural.

Armani felt underappreciated in the early twenty-first century, although the major retrospective of his work mounted by the Guggenheim in New York in 2000 and shown in Bilbao, Berlin, London and Rome reminded people of his importance. His business steadily expanded worldwide, while he continued to design for opera, theatre and film – and for sports teams; he dressed the Italian Olympic squad in 2012 and has provided the wardrobe for Chelsea FC since 2007. 'My work is my life, that's for sure,' he said in 2017.

Further reading: A biography by Renata Molho, *Being Armani: A Biography* (*2007*), tells most of the story. The catalogue, *Giorgio Armani*, from the Guggenheim exhibition of 2000, is brilliantly illustrated with a good text. Most up-to-date is the lavishly illustrated autobiographical *Giorgio Armani* (2016).

Part Five

1980s

Image 34.4 *Giorgio Armani, spring/summer 1998. Niall McInerney, Photographer. © Bloomsbury Publishing Plc.*

Introduction

If the 1980s was the decade of excess, when greed was good and glamour was very much the order of the day – in Ronald Reagan's White House and the London of Diana, Princess of Wales – then fashion had the designers to dress it. This was the time of high-camp *Dynasty* dressing, Joan Collins in Bruce Oldfield, Nancy Reagan in Oscar de la Renta, Princess Diana in the Emanuels. It was also the decade of the first of the great reinventions: Karl Lagerfeld took Coco Chanel's legacy, shook it up hard and put it back together mischievously exaggerated and in slightly the wrong order – but often looking more beautiful and covetable than the original.

By the start of the 1980s, Paris had regained much of the initiative in world fashion but it was no longer possible for one national industry to be dominant. The countries, many in the developing world, thought of as manufacturing resources where cheap labour could be exploited to the greater profit of first-world labels, had noticed the vast injustices inherent in the system. One way to fight back was to add value to their products and design was seen as one way to do this. Young potential designers from emerging economies flocked to the design schools of Britain and the United States and new courses flourished in Asian countries. Many fashion students never went home and still contribute to what is a truly international industry from bases in Europe, America and Australia. Others, particularly the Japanese designers, encouraged and enabled thriving domestic fashion cultures upon which labels with global reach have been built. Behind the Iron Curtain of eastern Europe, women still craved fashion and small cadres of designers worked (mostly derivatively) to dress ruling elites.

In the West, the women's movement was gaining momentum and high-earning women in all kinds of professions were becoming consumers of fashion. They did not all want to consume the same kind of fashion. The decade's archetype was doubtless the high-flying achiever 'dressed for success'. She was suited and stilettoed, broad-shouldered, tight-skirted, plunge-necklined, decked in gold buttons, buckles, bangles and chains and cast as the predatory villainess in several contemporary movies (directed by men). In Paris, Thierry Mugler, Claude Montana, *Azzedine Alaia* and, when in the mood, *Jean Paul Gaultier* did the parody version, a cartoon vamp with lip-gloss and attitude. In Italy, Giorgio Armani and the young *Gianni Versace*, and in America Halston, Geoffrey Beene, Calvin Klein, *Donna Karan* and sometimes Ralph Lauren did the well-bred, old-money, seriously grown-up version. In Britain, designers like *Paul Smith*, Sheridan Barnett and Margaret Howell kept pace with menswear-influenced classics featuring, as Smith always put it, 'a twist'.

But there were many alternative ways to dress. In Paris, Kenzo, Issey Miyake and Kansai Yamamoto were still thrilling the fashion crowd with their vibrant, clever textiles and games with structure and volume. Karl Lagerfeld's Chloé was about prettiness and wit, and Pierre Cardin was still voyaging to future landscapes. London was experiencing a creative renaissance with a large number of exciting young designers including *Vivienne Westwood*, Jean Muir, Zandra Rhodes, Katharine Hamnett, BodyMap, Betty Jackson, Wendy Dagworthy, Jasper Conran and *John Galliano*. They had varied styles ranging from Big Look to body-con, androgynous to lyrically romantic, frayed and deconstructed to glittery glam-rock.

The Antwerp Six – Dirk Bikkembergs, Walter Van Beirendonck, Dries Van Noten, Dirk van Saene, Ann Demeulemeester and Marina Yee – presented their collections in London in 1985, adding to the prevailing atmosphere of innovation. In Italy *Gianni Versace* found his signature style, an upfront eroticism that offended feminists and delighted many others. The new kids on the block were *Domenico Dolce* and *Stefano Gabbana* who also purveyed a historicist corseted and clichéd sex appeal – but so beautifully executed that even a feminist felt her treacherous pulse quicken.

Almost as a counterbalance to all the exhibitionistic sensuality heating up the catwalks, the most remarkable moment of the 1980s came at the beginning when the Japanese designers, *Rei Kawakubo* of Comme des Garçons and *Yohji Yamamoto* first showed in Paris. In 1981 both separately sent out an army of grim-faced models, hair shorn, faces painted white or with smeared make-up, wearing clothes that were to change fashion forever. Initially dismissed by some press as 'Hiroshima chic', it was an approach to dress that made high heels and cartoon glamour look dated. Both designers eschewed occidental ideas of female beauty in favour of a more cerebral concept that used the human body as an armature for extraordinary shapes sculpted in fabric. Their collections provoked all fashion's observers and many of its practitioners to reassess their subject.

35

Rei Kawakubo (1942–)

Kawakubo frequently deconstructs – literally and conceptually – and questions the clichés and familiar elements of Western and Oriental clothing and makes us think.

Of the Japanese designers who made a worldwide impact in the 1970s and 1980s, Rei Kawakubo has perhaps strayed furthest from the pure, strict vision of the first collections she brought to Paris in 1981. It is possible that nothing so sensational had happened in fashion in Paris since Christian Dior had unveiled his New Look. The press, in shock, did running mental readjustments on their senses of proportion, propriety and aesthetics. In 1947 they had re-embraced their inner fertility goddess; in 1981 they were forced to reassess the provenance of female sensuality and sexual attraction. Traditional Western fashion has generally (but not exclusively) situated them in the body. Rei Kawakubo insisted they were, in fact, located in the brain. She told Nicholas Coleridge in 1988, 'The goal for all women should be to make her own living and to support herself, to be self-sufficient. That is the philosophy of her clothes. They are working for modern women, women who do not need to assure their happiness by looking sexy to men, by emphasising their figures, but who attract them with their minds.' This dream of anonymous self-sufficiency had been her beacon since childhood, said Kawakubo.

Small and self-effacingly modest, Kawakubo is intensely work-focused, perhaps even slightly masochistic in her passion for doing things the hard way. 'It's boring if things are accomplished too easily, right?' she insisted to Leonard Koren in 1984. 'When I work, I think about the excitement of achievement after hard effort and pain.' In terms of her approach, Deyan Sudjic identifies her as a modernist (she admires Le Corbusier) but Harold Koda pointed out in his text for the 1987 FIT exhibition, *Three Women*, that Japan's thousand-year-old philosophy of aesthetics encompasses irregularity, imperfection and asymmetry as reminders of the fragility and transience of beauty. And Kawakubo was a student of philosophy. It is possible to identify postmodernism in her approach, too, in that she frequently deconstructs – literally and conceptually – and questions the clichés and familiar elements of Western and Oriental clothing and makes us think. Not that she has any didactic

Image 35.1 *Comme des Garçons, autumn/winter 1985. Niall McInerney, Photographer. © Bloomsbury Publishing Plc.*

purpose; she is on an exploration of her own that is to do with the relationship of clothes to the body and the body to clothes, of how sexuality is expressed or not in clothes, and how something entirely new may be made within the challenging limits of what it is possible to make and wear.

Unlike the other designers who changed both fashion in Japan and the world's perception of Japanese fashion, Rei Kawakubo had no formal training. Born in Tokyo in 1942, the daughter of a professor at Keio University, a respected private institution, she started school in a defeated, occupied country and was part of the flowering of talent prompted by the post-war economic boom and the gradually widened horizons that came with it. She studied both Japanese and Western art at her father's university and, on graduating in 1964, went to work in the advertising department of Asahi Kasei, a major chemical company that was Japan's biggest producer of acrylic fibres. In producing promotional material for print and television advertising intended to give acrylic a fashionable image, Kawakubo became a stylist, one of Japan's first. Three years later, alienated by the paternalism traditional within Japanese companies, she became the first freelance stylist. However, gradually she became aware that styling would not satisfy her urge to stretch her imagination for very long. She had invented the Comme des Garçons label (because she liked the way it sounded) for the clothes she designed and made for the advertisements she styled, and by 1973 she had established a company and began to make clothes for sale. 'It wasn't a major decision,' she said. 'Working as a stylist, my responsibility was very small compared with that of the art director and the photographer. I became frustrated with what I was doing and wanted to do more.' She does not regret her lack of formal training. 'If you can afford to take the time to train your eye and develop a sense of aesthetics in a natural way, it has a lot to recommend it.'

If Comme des Garçons had a certain ring to it, it also seemed appropriate for the simplicity of the clothes she was making, clothes that took a masculine wardrobe as a distant starting point. Interviewed by Geraldine Ranson of *The Sunday Telegraph* in 1983, she said, 'Most men don't like women who are capable of working hard. They do not like strong independent women with their feet on the ground.' She did not expect men outside the fashion industry to understand her clothes. 'It's not cute or soft and it doesn't fit a man's image of a woman.' But then, as she had told Mary Russell of *Vogue* in 1982, 'I do not find clothes that reveal the body sexy.'

In 1975 Kawakubo showed her first women's wear collection in Tokyo and began her collaboration with the architect Takao Kawasaki to develop a very particular identity for her shops. She also produced the first of a series of catalogues that enabled her to disseminate images of her clothes styled as she wished them to be seen. 'I try to reflect my approach not just in the clothes, but in the accessories, the shows, the shops, even in my office. You have to see it as a total impression and not just look at the exposed seams and black.'

In 1978 she launched Homme, her men's wear collection; it was followed by Tricot and Robe de Chambre in 1981 and Noir in 1987. The biggest step came in 1981 when, in order to gain recognition

Image 35.2 *Rei Kawakubo, 1998. Photo: Rose Hartman/Getty Images.*

internationally, she took her collection to show at the Intercontinental Hotel Paris – to mixed reviews, some bewildered, some dismissive. However, both she and Yohji Yamamoto (the pair had been lovers) were invited to present a catwalk show the following season, the first time the Chambre Syndicale has ever extended such an invitation to foreign designers. Kawakubo showed an asymmetric monochrome collection that included trousers with sweater cuffs at the ankles topped with hybrid tunic/shawls, voluminous overcoats buttoned left to right *comme des garçons* and boiled-wool knits with the neck hole cut into the chest or the shoulder so that, on the body, the garments made gauche but intriguingly eccentric, abstract shapes. There was no music, just a noise like a train clanging over points, and the models moved sedately and joylessly, their make-up dark, hungry-looking and out-of-synch with the features of their impassive faces.

These clothes were at first sight puritanically austere and intellectual. Fashion was going through a stale patch, repeating itself, and the only hope for rejuvenation appeared to be young London. However, those of us who were there on that evening will never forget the shock and the delight. Shock because no one had made clothes like this before; and delight because although they appeared to espouse a deliberately ugly anti-aesthetic, they were strangely compelling and they demanded that one did more than react with the senses; they insisted one think about them. In 1983, she gravely told Geraldine Ranson that her taste for working exclusively in black and white had remained unchanged for ten years or so. In 1984 Leonard Koren described her as having the purest, most uncompromising and strongest avant-garde vision of all the designers to come to prominence in this period.

During those early days of a palette of various shades of black, she wryly acknowledged the inherent weakness of her method. 'I realised clothes have to be worn and sold to a certain number of people. That's the difference between being a painter or sculptor and a clothing designer. It is, in a sense, a very commercial field. Unfortunately, my collections tend to be very concentrated and focused on very few ideas and this is a commercial problem. I try to get more variety. But I can't; it's not my way.'

Fortunately, it has become her way. Each collection is indeed focused but Kawakubo is an instinctive innovator, constantly challenging her own ingenuity. Having worked through her initial preoccupation with the structure of clothes, she turned her attention to surface and colour. From the 1990s onwards, however, you are much more likely to find hand-painted crinoline ball gowns than dark, torn shrouds in her collections. The creation of her collections depends very much on a series of collaborations with key creatives. She has famously said that with every collection, 'I start from zero.' Hiroshi Matsushita of the Orimono Kenkyu Sha textile company was an early contributor, developing fabrics in response to Kawakubo's questions, suggestions, thoughts and moods. Deyan Sudjic wrote in 1989, 'Matsushita … devised the rayon criss-crossed with elastic that allowed Kawakubo to make the garments in the women's collection of 1984 bubble and boil as though they were melting. And it was Matsushita who formulated the bonded cotton rayon and polyurethane fabric Kawakubo used for her asymmetric dresses of 1986.'

Her method of work is often more about whim and mischief than any straining after pre-imagined effects. She told Leonard Koren, 'The machines that make fabric are more and more making uniform, flawless textures. I like it when something is off, not perfect. Hand weaving is the best way to achieve this. Since this isn't always possible, we loosen a screw of the machines here and there so they can't do exactly what they're supposed to do.'

The fabric is a continuous journey of experiment because, as Matsushita told Sudjic, 'She never likes to do anything twice, so to meet her requirements the mills have had to come up with techniques that have not been tried before; they have had to invent new fabrics. Lately the words she uses [as her starting point] have been softer, a little sweeter. Maybe she has mellowed; it's reflected in the language and in the fabrics.'

With the fabric in place, Kawakubo then works with her large team of pattern-cutters. She told Sudjic, 'Some designers produce detailed sketches and have a pattern made that is based directly on them. I begin with a much more abstract drawing and the pattern-makers need to be able to interpret what I am trying to do. They help me to design.'

In 1996 she showed a spring/summer 1997 collection that perplexed even her most die-hard admirers. Known to Kawakubo as 'Dress Becomes Body Becomes Dress' and to everyone else as the collection of the humps, it distorted skinny, body-hugging clothes in bright spring colours with a series of protuberances that appeared to be attached like some alien limpet-like succubus to random spots around the body, occasionally growing elongated and tyre-like to embrace the waist or hips.

There were also waxed brown-paper puffball skirts and fantastically rosette-pleated tops and jackets on Prince-of-Wales check and pretty, girlish gingham. An uncomfortable crowd shuffled out muttering about the Quasimodo collection: what do you call the particular political incorrectness that appears to mock deformity? The collection sold, the clothes were great talking pieces and then great collector's pieces, and Kawakubo continued to experiment, her reputation undamaged.

In 1995, she said, 'I don't think my clothes have changed enormously over the years, though I hope I always change in the sense of making progress. In the past perhaps I was more obvious about exposing construction techniques. I used patterns that were very complex; I found that a passion. Now I am more interested in the general mood of a collection.' Observers and collaborators reflect that they think she has 'mellowed' over the years. Her marriage to Adrian Joffe, a South African born architect who is managing director of her company, may have something to do with that. Together, in 2004, they launched Dover Street Market, a fresh concept in retail noted for eclecticism and innovation; it features in all 'best stores of the world' guides. There are now several branches in major cities.

If the mood of those earlier collections was sombre and aggressive in its confrontation of the fashion world's expectations, the mood of her mature years is much more light-hearted with a strong bias towards Western shapes. But they are shapes transformed by Kawakubo's unique sense of architecture, her intellectual distancing from her medium and (the factor it was so easy to miss at the beginning) a playful sensuality that lies in tactility and abstract form, a garment's movement on the body whether it flows or, stiff and static, merely changes in silhouette as the wearer turns and moves.

Like Issey Miyake, Kawakubo's influence lies as much in the practical support she has given younger designers such as Junya Watanabe and Kei Ninomiya as in the worldwide impact of her approach to dress. In 2017 she was honoured with a retrospective exhibition at the Metropolitan Museum in New York, *Rei Kawakubo/Comme des Garçons: Art of the In-Between*. At the time she told Andrew Bolton, the curator,

> For more than forty years I have been making clothes. I have never thought about fashion. In other words, I have almost no interest in it. What I've only ever been interested in is clothes that one has never seen before, that they are completely new, and how and in what way they can be expressed. Is that called fashion? I don't know the answer.

Further reading: Deyan Sudjic's monograph, *Rei Kawakubo and Comme des Garçons* (1990), is a must-read. The book of the exhibition, *Rei Kawakubo/Comme des Garçons: Art of the In-Between* (2017), is lavishly illustrated and has a revealing conversation between Kawakubo and curator Andrew Bolton.

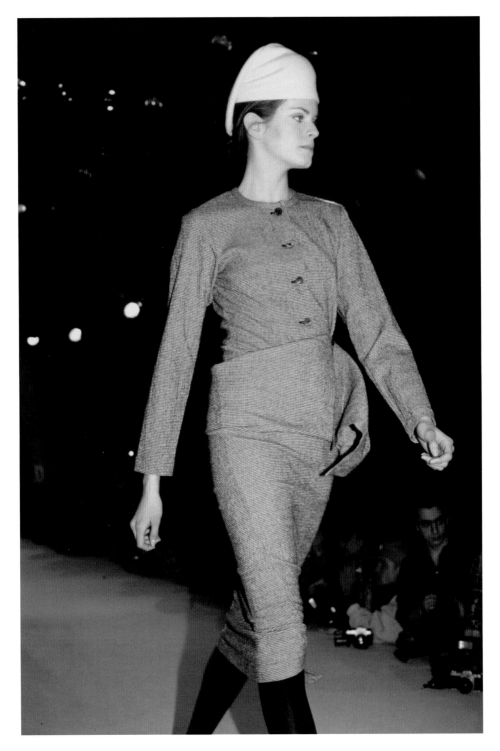

Image 35.3 *Comme des Garçons, autumn/winter 1986. Niall McInerney, Photographer. © Bloomsbury Publishing Plc.*

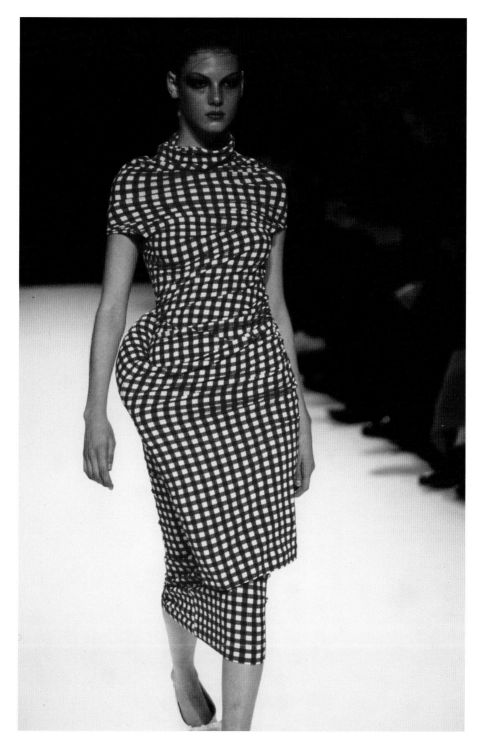

Image 35.4 *Comme des Garçons, spring/summer 1997. Niall McInerney, Photographer. © Bloomsbury Publishing Plc.*

36

Yohji Yamamoto (1943–)

There is often something uneasily disjointed about Yamamoto's sombrely dramatic clothes.

Yohji Yamamoto's aim is to synthesise the traditional understated Japanese aesthetic – with its emphasis on simplicity and purity of response – and what he perceives as the more 'human', body-oriented Western tradition. Less disciplined than Issey Miyake, he casts his net wider in his search for a vocabulary of shapes and textures to express the strange amalgam of intellectualism and sensuality that is uniquely his. As you witness a Yamamoto show you are uneasily aware that a mental adjustment is required, that it is, in fact, irresistible. These clothes are not there to display the body; the body is there to display the structure, the harmonies and sometimes harshly discordant unorthodoxies of the clothes. 'For me,' said Yamamoto, 'the body is nothing. The body is change. Every moment it gets older so you cannot count on it. You cannot control time. I can't believe in the human body. I do not think the human body is beautiful.'

The traditional Japanese approach to dress, as demonstrated in the many layered kimonos that make up a formal ceremonial outfit, is not about the body; it is about the shape the clothes assume on it – hierarchic, imposing in the case of men, dignified, modest, adorned in the case of women – and also the colour and surface texture. The latter is historically a matter of weave, pattern and embroidery. The body is treated like a sculptor's armature, the metal skeleton that the artist will clothe in clay. In fact, the sculpture analogy is a good one; not only does Yamamoto tend to think of himself functioning within the ranks of artists but his design handwriting is sculptural, plastic, his clothes very much things of curves, planes and tactile volume, of fragments of geometric shapes. Like Miyake, who had been showing successfully in Paris for a decade when Yamamoto and Rei Kawakubo first showed there, he is preoccupied with the texture of fabrics and the potential of large, abstract, asymmetric shapes to display it. With Kawakubo, Yamamoto started a look that was consistent to a large degree with the work being produced at that time by the avant-garde designers of Britain and that became known, just as derogatively, as 'Baglady Chic'. His method is a more intellectually purposeful postmodernism than that employed by Vivienne Westwood and John

Image 36.1 *Yohji Yamamoto, autumn/winter 1983. Niall McInerney, Photographer. © Bloomsbury Publishing Plc.*

Galliano, but there's a connection. While he is drawn again and again to the strict tailored curves of the *fin de siècle* – often topping his ingeniously cut and gathered-up long skirts and long narrow jackets with the vast lampshade-like tulle and organza hats of the period – they are more of an insistent backbeat than the melody. He is, as François Baudot pointed out in his book in the *Fashion Memoir* series, 'exceptionally responsive to contemporary trends – in the same way that couturiers of preceding generations responded to cubism, say, or the Ballets Russes or Pop Art'. Baudot identified Arte Povera, work pulled together from detritus – rags, wood shavings, mud, coal – as a major influence on Yamamoto's approach. Baudot wrote that Yamamoto

> tried to break away from a fossilised conception of what clothes were. He did this by disrupting the codes by which clothes made their appeal; by rethinking the glamorous signals sent out by their external appearance; by redefining their relationship with the male or female body; and, ultimately – to near universal incomprehension – by radically reinterpreting the respective contributions of beauty and ugliness, past and future, memory and modernity.

When Geraldine Ranson of *The Sunday Telegraph* visited Tokyo in 1982, she remarked that on Yamamoto's labels was printed the statement, 'There is nothing so boring as a neat and tidy look.' In 2002, in *Talking To Myself* with Carla Sozzani, Yamamoto wrote, 'I think perfection is ugly. Somewhere in the things humans make, I want to see scars, failure, disorder, distortion.' Indeed, while they may be evocatively beautiful, there is often something uneasily disjointed about his sombrely dramatic clothes, something reminiscent of some moody forgotten dream you once woke from, vaguely disturbed. For that reason, they are loved by adherents of the Goth subcultural style.

Born in Tokyo in 1943, Yohji Yamamoto was brought up by his mother, Fumi, who was widowed by the Second World War and worked for sixteen hours a day as a dressmaker to pay for her son's education. He initially took a law degree at Keio University (where Rei Kawakubo was studying at the same time) but decided to work with his mother in her dressmaking business. She had dreamed of an important career in the law for him, but agreed on the condition he trained for the job with her at the famous Bunka School. He still remembers his discomfort at being the only boy in his class and the oldest student by far. He graduated in 1969, winning a competition for a trip to Paris – where he managed to survive for eight months on no money, observing, learning, haunting the Left Bank boutiques. He returned to Tokyo and, in 1971, started his own business, the Y's Company Ltd. He did not show on a catwalk until 1977, when he already had a strong following. In Japan, the women who wore his black clothes were already known as 'crows'. 'The samurai spirit is black,' said Yamamoto. 'The samurai must be able to throw his body into nothingness, the colour and image of which is black.' In 1981, he and his colleague and former lover, Rei Kawakubo of Comme des Garçons, set the fashion world alight when they showed in Paris. Many commentators loathed what they called 'Post-Hiroshima Style' but many others loved the challenge it offered to conventional ways of thinking about fashion. In *Libération*, under the headline, 'French fashion has found its masters: the Japanese,' Michel Cresson wrote, 'The outfits he offers in 1982 for us to wear in the next twenty years are infinitely more feasible than those proposed by Courrèges and Cardin in around 1960 for the year 2000, which today look as old-hat as a Soviet sci-fi film.'

Yamamoto told Nicholas Coleridge in 1984,

> There was a moment when the Paris prêt-a-porter looked set to die. It had run out of ideas. Thierry Mugler and Claude Montana, what they were doing was almost couture; it was so restricted. Then we went to Paris and it happened, the spirit of our clothes was free. *Marie-Claire* were the first to understand, yes, they had the first understanding. … In fashion I think there is always a feeling of anti-something. In magazines they think anti, anti, anti. They like a certain look for a time, then they are anti it; not indifferent but anti. In 1981, they were anti western clothes, so they needed and accepted us, and tried to understand my concept of sexuality. I don't feel sexuality at all in the normal meaning. A fantasy of mine is a woman, forty or fifty years old. She is very skinny with grey hair and smoking a cigarette. She is neither a woman nor a man but she is very attractive. She is sexy for me. She is walking away from me and as I walk after her she calls out, 'No, Yohji, do not follow.'

Patricia Mears wrote of Yamamoto and Kawakubo in her essay in *Japan Fashion Now* (2010) that their work had 'a seismic, course-altering impact on women's clothing during the late twentieth century. … They have rightfully been credited with instigating profound aesthetic changes that have since permeated all levels of fashion, such as deconstruction and the dominance of the colour black.'

Image 36.2 *Designer Yohji Yamamoto, autumn/winter 1995. Niall McInerney, Photographer. © Bloomsbury Publishing Plc.*

Image 36.3 *Yohji Yamamoto, spring/summer 2000. Niall McInerney, Photographer. © Bloomsbury Publishing Plc.*

In 1984, in the first of the many new collections he developed over the years, Yamamoto deconstructed and reconstructed men's clothing, creating a new classicism – severe white shirts, puny-shouldered dark suits with three-button jackets with narrow lapels and slender trousers. Embraced rapidly by the artistic intelligentsia, the look powerfully influenced menswear for a decade. More than most designers, Yamamoto is interested in the contribution the wearer makes. 'Whether a season's fashion is interesting or not does not depend on the designers who created it, but on those who see it and buy it.' His men's clothes as much as his women's have always attracted a particularly interesting wearer who responds to the boldness of his intention and the subtlety of its execution, to the seriousness of his approach to design – which many of them share – and to the lightness, mischief and wit that can always be found at the heart of the collection. He told Baudot in 1997,

> Making a garment means thinking about people. I am always eager to meet people and talk to them. It's what I like more than anything else. What are they doing? What are they thinking? How do they lead their lives? And then I can set to work. I start with the fabric, the actual material, the 'feel' of it, I then move on to the form. Possibly what counts most for me is the feel. And then when I start working on the material, I think my way into the form it ought to assume.

His long-running collaboration with Adidas, the Y-3 line launched in 2003, was one of the first and most successful between a cutting-edge designer and a mass-market brand. It was carefully chosen of course. The trainer was modern, fit for purpose from a purist's point of view and an iconic item of clothing in the mainstream and across a range of subcultures. Best of all, its origins lie in western campus sports, making it something that Yamamoto, an outsider to all those things, could have a lot of fun with. Of all the Japanese designers he is perhaps the most in denial about the influence his own culture has had on his work – even though some of his most beautiful clothes are largely sourced from what appear to be cannibalised kimonos. 'I happen to have been born in Japan. But I've never labelled myself in that way,' he has said. In the 1980s, he was always rather impatient with the fashion press's somewhat bewildered initial tendency to lump Japanese designers together into a school or movement and its assumption that this must be the way all Japanese women were dressing. He said, 'People talk about the Japanese as if they're all together in some kind of designers' mafia. In Japan, maybe they're popular somewhere at the edge of things. But it's got nothing to do with ordinary people.'

If it sounds elitist, it was meant to. Yamamoto started off more the fine artist than the fashion designer. His clothes were difficult to understand, loaded, like a difficult poem or painting, with references and symbols, often disguised or distorted, and layers of meanings. His collections still include garments of great strangeness and of a sort of theatrical ugliness that makes unusual demands on the understanding of the observer. His attitude has inevitably undergone some changes. In 1984 he told Leonard Koren,

Since I began this fashion-making job, I have been thinking, 'What is fashion for me?' For about ten years I couldn't believe in it because fashion is always changing. The people who follow it are superficial. The most important thing is, 'What's new?' But in the last two or three years I've found something in it. In fashion, one can find new kinds of expression about human beings – things that pure art like painting, sculpture and cinema can't express. Only fashion can. I can't explain exactly why it is, but the problem of what people are wearing and the influence over people of fashion is awesome. I think there's a new way to create so I think there's a future for me.

So it has proved. In shedding some of his seriousness, Yamamoto learned to love fashion and over the years a new joyfulness has been evident in his work. He enjoys the way women enjoy his clothes, recognising that the spirit of self-conscious playfulness they bring to them is that extra human element that makes them work, that extra element that neither a picture not a sculpture nor even a movie contains.

Further reading: François Baudot's *Yohji Yamamoto: Fashion Memoir* (1997), is useful for a quick overview, supplemented by Yuniya Kawamura's *The Japanese Revolution in Paris Fashion* (2004). Edited by Louise Mitchell, *The Cutting Edge: Fashion from Japan* (2005) is also of value. *Japan Fashion Now* (2010), edited by Valerie Steele, is a thoughtful analysis.

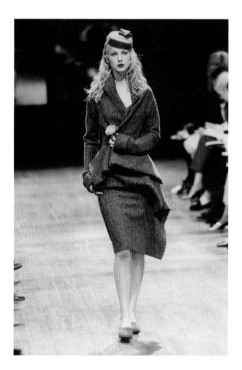

Image 36.4 *Yohji Yamamoto, autumn/winter 1998. Niall McInerney, Photographer. © Bloomsbury Publishing Plc.*

37

Vivienne Westwood (1941–)

Clothes are a language Westwood uses to deconstruct cliché and convention.

In terms of creativity and the ability to place fashion at the heart of a vital popular culture, Vivienne Westwood is one of the very greatest designers of the twentieth century. Her method is not so very different from that of many designers, particularly other British designers trained in an art-school tradition and, interestingly, a generation of Japanese designers who used this occidental approach to invent an original Oriental fashion. However, the conscious, didactic way she demonstrates it is unique. In 1991, when she was working through ideas related to both Christian Dior's New Look and early eighteenth-century clothing, she told Brenda Polan, writing for *The Independent on Sunday*,

> Clothing has always reconstructed and modified the structure of the body and it still does today. What seems to surprise and upset people is reconstructions that don't accord with what they consider to be the norm, the present accepted idea of beauty. If you design a dress with a *sellier*, the padding that gives it a rounded form has become a subversive act. Perhaps I mean it to be a subversive act. Perhaps I want to question people's prejudices about what is beautiful, what makes a lady beautiful. Through fashion, I try to re-evoke the past and reflect on it.

Westwood trained as a teacher and there is still a good deal of the pedagogue about her: ideas and analysis excite her. Clothes are a language she uses to deconstruct cliché and convention. She confronts prejudices and questions them – not always totally coherently but with courage and purpose. The subjects of her explorations of dress and its emotional and rational subtext have always been clearly signposted in the names and themes of her collections which, when watched on a catwalk, stimulate the intellect as well as the senses – including the sense of humour. While she revels in the joy, the sheer fun of the fashion she makes, she is serious and very political in the way she uses it as an investigative tool. She is much preoccupied with the culture and its decline, believing that the French are the inheritors and keepers of a true intellectual tradition. In 2007, in a conversation with Brenda Polan

Image 37.1 *Vivienne Westwood, autumn/winter 1981. Niall McInerney, Photographer. © Bloomsbury Publishing Plc.*

at London's ICA as part of a conference titled *The Death of Taste*, she answered a question on her response to current culture and its relationship to her concept of civilisation:

> The best thing about my job, and the worst thing, is that it is non-stop and you never, never can stop. Some of my best thoughts occur at night, just because I am reading and I am hatching ideas. Everybody must have that experience where the ideas are sort of there and then you develop them and you think you mustn't forget that, and sometimes you even get up and write it down. And then I must just say, because it's an incredible, fantastic tip to give to people, I always write thirty quotations, a few of them in French when I can … I'll write thirty quotations, poetry and all kinds of things. For example, Rousseau – if you read some it's so concentrated, you can just go over that quotation and you can find answers for all sorts of things that are in your mind at that particular time.

As Susannah Frankel remarked in *The Guardian* in 1997, 'At any given time Westwood has at least two, maybe three ideas, or even sentences on the go concurrently, uttered in hushed Derbyshire tones, that career and collide until they either explode into meaning, often minutes and even hours later, or at times peter out entirely, leaving anyone who's interested to fill in the gaps.' Among fashion journalists and academics, there are very many who, out of admiration for the woman and her spirit as well as her work, are happy to do that.

Vivienne Isabel Swire was born in Glossop, Derbyshire in 1941, the first of three children. Her father came from a long line of shoemakers and her mother worked as a weaver in one of the town's cotton mills. She always liked fashion and remembers her mother pointing out a neighbour's New Look outfit in 1947. It was a look she would emulate in her teenage years when she made her own clothes. She remembers customising her grammar school uniform into a pencil skirt. 'It was a new thing, putting that on was such a symbol of sexuality,' she told Claire Wilcox in 2003. In the late 1950s, the family moved to Harrow on the outskirts of London and, at sixteen, Vivienne started a foundation course at Harrow School of Art. She left after one term and began to support herself selling jewellery from a stall in the Portobello Road market. She abandoned this for work in a factory that would enable her to save up for teacher-training college. She was working as a primary school teacher in 1962 when she met her first husband, Derek Westwood, at a dance but the marriage collapsed some time after the birth of their son Ben. In 1965 she met Malcolm McLaren, the father of Joe, her second son, born in 1967. McLaren was to change the course of her life.

A typically rebellious child of the sex, drugs and rock 'n' roll 1960s, McLaren was influenced by the Situationists and Guy Debord's book, *La Société du Spectacle*, a collection of perverse aphorisms that was later to give a language to Punk. He loved clothes but felt that, in the current boutique culture of London, there was nothing for him. He would style Vivienne with traditional garments juxtaposed in subversive ways and encouraged her to razor-cut and bleach her hair. They opened their first shop, Let It Rock, which launched Punk, on the King's Road in 1971. By 1975, the shop had been renamed Sex, the interior sprayed with pornographic graffiti, hung with rubber curtains and stocked with sex and fetish wear. Westwood thrilled to the sense of trespass the clothes aroused. 'All the clothes I wore people would regard as shocking, I wore them because I just thought that I looked like a princess from another planet.'

In 1976 McLaren, now manager of the Sex Pistols, renamed 430 King's Road yet again, this time Seditionaries – Clothes for Heroes, and redesigned its interior to include shots of an upside-down Piccadilly Circus and a ruined Dresden. Spotlights poked through roughly hacked holes in the ceiling and there was a live, caged rat in the table. The Seditionaries collection summed up Westwood and McLaren's work, encompassing the ripped garments of 1950s pin-up pictures; the leather, chains and badges of the bikers; the straps, safety pins and buckles of the fetishists. As Westwood said, 'You couldn't imagine the Punk Rock thing without the clothing.' Deliberately confrontational, the look was first excoriated, then absorbed into mainstream fashion as a style element with a frisson of danger.

By the early 1980s McLaren was focused on music and Westwood began to see herself as a fashion designer. In need of change, they chose to examine history. The shop became World's End, the interior a lurching pirate galleon with small windows, a low ceiling and a sloped decking floor. The fascia had a drooping slate gable and a large clock displaying thirteen hours, the hands travelling rapidly back in time. The autumn/winter 1981 Pirate collection, shown at Olympia to cannon fire and rap music by McLaren, evoked the golden age of piracy, an age of highwaymen, dandies and buccaneers. It was immediately acclaimed and copied all around the world. For the next season they showed Savage, a collection that combined Native American patterns with leather frock coats, Foreign Legion hats

Image 37.2 *Vivienne Westwood, 1990s. Niall McInerney, Photographer.* © *Bloomsbury Publishing Plc.*

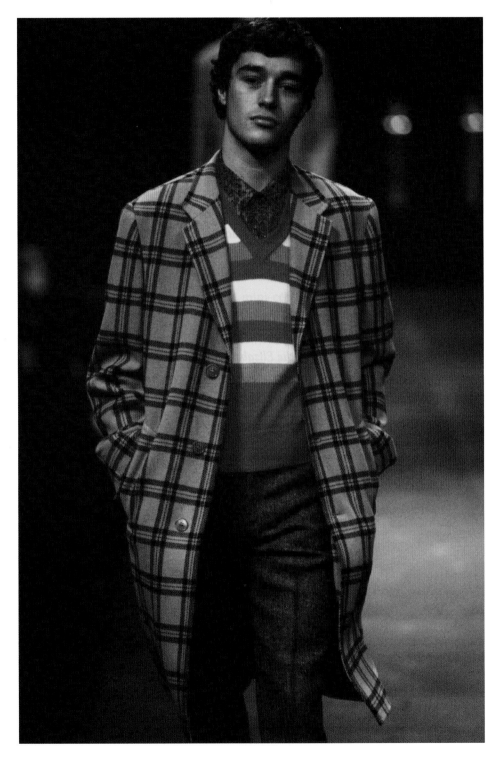

Image 38.1 *Paul Smith, autumn/winter 1996. Niall McInerney, Photographer. © Bloomsbury Publishing Plc.*

38

Paul Smith (1946–)

Smith turned a quirky idea of Britishness into a global language of fashion.

Since the 1980s, Paul Smith has been an outstanding force in British fashion, best known for a quirky, humorous design sensibility applied to classic British tailoring. For years he played down his abilities as a designer, but by the early 1990s Smith emerged as the complete package – a designer, retailer and businessman all rolled into one. A pioneering Western designer in Japan, Smith outsold Armani and Chanel there in the late 1980s – in 2019, he still had 165 stores in the country.

In creative terms, Sir Paul Smith (he was knighted in 2000) has been overlooked, perhaps because of his lack of formal fashion training. His consistent challenge to notions of good taste has made him an important postmodern influence in men's fashion, spilling over into womenswear too (he launched a women's collection in 1994). Smith loves the traditions of Savile Row-style tailoring, but he also loves kitsch and off-the-wall eccentricity. 'What is good taste? What is bad taste?' he said in 1990. 'They are both so near. It's just lovely to shove these in a food-mixer and throw them around.' In a later comment, he said: 'The wrong thing with the wrong thing is the speciality of the house.' American novelist William Gibson, taking as his point of reference a nineteenth-century London clothes market, summed up his style neatly: 'It is as though he possesses some inner equivalent of the Houndsditch Clothes Exchange – not a museum, but a vast, endlessly recombinant jumble sale in which all the artefacts of his nation and culture constantly engage in a mutual exchange of code.'

Gibson highlights Smith's fascination with the found object. Whether in London or Tokyo (undoubtedly his favourite city outside Britain), Smith is perpetually looking out for things that might be reinterpreted in the arena of fashion or simply sold in one of his shops for fun. Countless products, ranging from postage stamps to piles of fruit, are turned into T-shirt photo prints, reflecting a love of photography and the surreal inherited from his father. A childlike imagination is at work: a pair of fake eyeballs, for example, is turned into cufflinks and buttons. In the 1980s, veteran British designer Sir Hardy Amies was one of many who found his shops a treasure trove of ideas and entertainment.

Smith was, and is, a unique figure in British fashion. Although British designers since the 1980s have proved among the most thrillingly imaginative in the world, filling the design studios of major fashion houses in Italy, France and America, they have shown little ability to build and sustain their own businesses. Before Smith, it was left to an American, Ralph Lauren, to translate classic British style for a modern international market. In the menswear market, some British names, such as Sir Hardy Amies, remained traditional in outlook, while others, including Aquascutum, Daks-Simpson, Jaeger and Gieves & Hawkes, made half-hearted efforts to move forward, rarely causing more than a ripple on the international scene. Only Burberry, through the services of a far-sighted American chief executive, Rosemarie Bravo, made progress in the late 1990s and the early Noughties. Paul Smith might be compared to Vivienne Westwood, another great British designer who has played around with classic style. But where Westwood was an aggressively subversive force, Smith's approach was playful and more accessible. He turned a quirky idea of Britishness into a global language of fashion. 'My thing has always been about maximising Britishness,' he has said. As he put it himself in an interview in 1981, he produces 'classics with a twist' – a term that has since been used so often it has become a cliché.

Smith has no time for conceptual fashion, saying 'I don't like … stupid ideas that can't be worn.' He is also proudly anti-big business, challenging the corporate style of the modern designer fashion business and the sameness of designer stores the world over. His influence as a retailer is likely to grow, rather than diminish, through the 2020s, in particular his championing of individuality in stores, ranging from the big pink Insta-hit store in Los Angeles to the intimate space in London's Coal Drops Yard. A portrait of the designer by James Lloyd in London's National Portrait Gallery sums up his character well: energetic, irreverent, level-headed and perhaps a good deal tougher than his easy-going public persona might suggest. Interviewed by Roger Tredre in 1990, Smith was modest about his design skills: 'A few years ago, I would have said that I was just a getter-togetherer of fashion. But more recently I would say that I am a designer because I do have ideas that start with a blank sheet of paper.'

Paul Brierley Smith was born in Beeston, Nottingham, in 1946. He left school without qualifications at the age of fifteen, whereupon his father, Harold, instructed him to work in a clothing warehouse, where he was little more than a gofer. It was the early 1960s, when fashion was on the verge of a youth-led explosion. Smith began putting together displays in the warehouse and creating his own fashion shoots. His ambition at this point was to become a professional cyclist, but a major accident at the age of seventeen changed all that. Smith spent six months in hospital and emerged with a different outlook on life. He started hanging out with art students in pubs and ingesting the art and fashion of the time. For a few years, he energetically embraced the late 1960s counterculture, dressing the part to the disgust of one elderly man who stopped him in the street to admonish him: 'I fought in the war for you and you dress like a bloody girl.' He joined forces with a student womenswear designer named Janet, taking charge of the menswear department of her shop in 1966 and learning the rudiments of retail. Smith opened his first shop, Vêtement Pour Homme, in 1970, selling such designers as Kenzo and Margaret Howell and initially a few locally made shirts and jackets. The shop evolved at a slow pace, developing steadily, if unspectacularly, throughout the decade. Smith's personal style had shifted towards a more dressed-up look, including bespoke suits, cashmere sweaters and made-to-measure boots with Cuban heels.

The Paul Smith label was not formally launched until 1976 in Paris. New lightweight fabrics were expanding the options for men's tailoring. Giorgio Armani was making softer suits in Italy. Smith took some of these lessons but did not push them nearly as far, preferring to make his impact by playing with suits in different ways. A pinstripe suit was paired with a navy blue spot shirt and white plimsolls. A Prince of Wales check or a chalkstripe might turn up in unconventional colourways, with brightly coloured linings. From the beginning, he had support in his experiments from his lifelong partner Pauline Denyer (they married in 2000), who studied at the Royal College of Art and therefore had a technical training that Smith had never enjoyed. She designed the early collections, he later admitted. In their early twenties, they visited the couture shows in Paris, attending Chanel, Cardin, Balmain and Yves Saint Laurent. Smith's approach to design was more in line with this tradition than the unconstructed shapes that swept through fashion in the early 1980s, inspired by Japanese designers such as Rei Kawakubo and Yohji Yamamoto. 'At that time, a lot of our art colleges lost the ability to create clothes in a traditional way,' recalled Smith. 'A lot of exciting things were happening, of course … but I really wish that this foundation had continued. Unconstructed suits hurt my eyes.'

Image 38.2 *Designer Paul Smith. Niall McInerney, Photographer. © Bloomsbury Publishing Plc.*

Image 38.3 *Paul Smith, autumn/winter 2000. Niall McInerney, Photographer. © Bloomsbury Publishing Plc.*

Smith's influence extended far beyond his own label. For many years, he was discreetly working as a menswear consultant for Marks & Spencer, Britain's biggest clothing retailer, ploughing the money he earned back into his own business. Likewise, a thriving wholesale business enabled him to maintain momentum whenever his own shops were quiet. A key move was the freehold purchase and opening of a shop at 44 Floral Street in London's Covent Garden in 1979. It was the first fashion store to open on the street. He bought the unit next door shortly afterwards and resolved to keep its old wooden-panelled fittings, developing the Paul Smith retail style, an eccentric mix of old and new. The shop evolved to become one of the most important stores in modern British fashion history, a place of pilgrimage for modern menswear enthusiasts, not least for its artistic and witty shop windows. Smith's retail experience, learned the hard way, was invaluable as he developed his business. 'You have to be 90 per cent businessman and 10 per cent designer,' he said.

The 1980s were a golden decade for Smith. While the made-to-measure tailors of Savile Row struggled to survive, British tailoring was assured of a place on the modern map of fashion thanks to Smith, with a number of smaller designers, such as Richard James, also developing in his wake. The Paul Smith label caught the wave of a newly prosperous Britain. Every go-ahead young creative type in 1980s London had a Paul Smith suit, along with a pair of boxer shorts and a Filofax personal organiser, which were both sold and promoted by Smith. Well ahead of many European designers, Smith spotted the golden potential of Japan, signing a license with C. Itoh in 1984 and travelling back and forth twice a year ever since. This commitment reaped rewards and prompted other designers to follow his lead. Regular *tenjikai* (exhibitions of new collections) are staged in Tokyo, where Smith has a celebrity status of extraordinary dimensions. He was more cautious about the emergence of China as an important new market in the early years of the twenty-first century, opening a first store in Shanghai in 2004.

Elsewhere, the retail development of Paul Smith continued apace, with a first store opened in New York on Fifth Avenue in 1987, a store in Paris in 1993, and a new London shop on Sloane Avenue in 1997. Perhaps his most unusual shop was Westbourne House, a large Victorian residence in Notting Hill, redesigned by Sophie Hicks. In six rooms over three floors, the complete Paul Smith collection was sold, together with a bespoke tailoring service. Smith's womenswear, launched in 1994 and produced in Italy, has had a lesser impact than his menswear, drawing on his menswear collection for much of its inspiration and look. Smith has often stood aside from the mainstream of the designer industry in Britain, avoiding the British Fashion Awards, which he once criticised as 'self-congratulatory'. He became frustrated with the failure of British industry to produce the management to nurture new designers although he worked hard behind the scenes in an advisory capacity to try and drum up some momentum. The designer also spoke out regularly against the uniformity of modern fashion designers. In speeches around the world, he argued the case for a new spirit of individuality in fashion. A great shop, he said, should be like an Aladdin's cave 'where you'll see something hideous next to something wonderful, something low-priced next to something high-priced.'

Smith ardently believes everyone can have a go at design. In that sense, he may point the way forward for the future of design, with a do-it-yourself mood sweeping through modern popular culture supported by new technology that allows the consumer to have an input too. In recent years, he has collaborated with a huge variety of businesses, ranging from Land Rover to John Lobb to Leica. As an outspoken individualist, Smith represents a note of hope for independently owned fashion design businesses. Now in his seventies, he continues to work, guiding his business through a downturn in 2017. Smith himself is reluctant to over-philosophise about his contribution to fashion. 'I ended up designing clothes that I wanted to wear myself and felt good in,' he said. 'Well made, good quality, simple cut, interesting fabrics, easy-to-wear. No-bullshit clothing.'

Further reading: Paul Smith effectively explored his approach to design in *You Can Find Inspiration in Everything (and If You Can't, Look Again)* (2001). *Hello, My Name is Paul Smith* (2013) is the catalogue of the exhibition at London's Design Museum. Paul Smith's entertaining talks are full of insights about his approach to design: his address to the Oxford Union (2018) is available on youtube.com.

Image 38.4 *Paul Smith, autumn/winter 1995. Niall McInerney, Photographer. © Bloomsbury Publishing Plc.*

39

Azzedine Alaïa (c. 1935–2017)

Alaïa developed a cut that tenderly emphasised and enhanced all the female erogenous zones.

Life for fashion editors trying to pin down a handful of consistent trends to guide their readers became pretty tough in the early 1980s. The round of catwalk shows felt like chaos, but it was possible to identify three main strands. In the first and most exciting category were the experimental/intellectual designers, the Japanese in Paris, the young Britons such as Vivienne Westwood, BodyMap, Katharine Hamnett, Betty Jackson, and the Antwerp group that included Anne Demeulemeester, Martin Margiela and Dries Van Noten. Then there were the modernist minimalists headed by Giorgio Armani, Calvin Klein and Zoran. Holding the centre ground were the fantasists or romantics, represented by the restrained, soft romanticism of Yves Saint Laurent, Karl Lagerfeld and the early Gianni Versace. Some designers in this centre ground took a more aggressive route inspired in part by comic-strip artists, showing a vision of womanhood that merged Barbie with the heroine from an erotic pulp sci-fi comic. In this set, the most eclectic imagination belonged to Jean Paul Gaultier, while Thierry Mugler and Claude Montana created their own takes on pop-culture sirens, at their most extreme showing moulded plastic breast plates with tip-tilted 1950s breasts, ultra-cinched torsos, bondage details and the highest of stilettos.

But the ultimate dress-me-as-a-vamp hero of the time was Azzedine Alaïa, a diminutive Tunisian dubbed by *Women's Wear Daily* the 'King of Cling' and by British journalist Georgina Howell 'the Titan of Tight'. Brenda Polan was taken to meet him in his cramped and crowded studio in the Latin Quarter of Paris in 1982. Introductions were performed by the London retailer Joseph Ettedgui, who had introduced Kenzo to Britain and was about to do the same for Alaïa. It became the only interview Polan had ever conducted sitting on a (closed) lavatory while the interviewee stood in the doorway. At that point the small man dressed all in black – black Nehru jacket, black cotton trousers, black velvet slippers – was suddenly, and to his own surprise, the hottest name in Paris. There were no press clippings for some basic research so bread-and-butter questions had to be asked. In response to one of the first, he was evasive but charming. 'How old? Does it matter? I am as old as the pharaohs.'

Image 39.1 *Alaïa, autumn/winter 1986. Niall McInerney, Photographer. © Bloomsbury Publishing Plc.*

'second-skin dressing'), all America wanted it and beat a path to his modest door. Perhaps most notably in that first collection, Alaïa invented a new garment, the body. A streamlined silhouette was central to his look, so he adapted the dancer's leotard for everyday wear with skirt or trousers. The fashion body, unlike the dancer's version, closed at the crotch, secured by poppers or small buttons. In 1985, Donna Karan was to popularise the body, basing her first own-label collection around it.

Reflecting in 1983, journalist Marina Sturdza of the *Toronto Star* explained that

> his address has been a loosely kept secret of the Paris cognoscenti for at least a decade. That's why it's a giggle to see the beau monde of fashion, press and buyers alike, rank and position regardless, protocol be dammed, crammed by the dozen into a meagre space intended to accommodate a very few at best; craning and jostling to catch even a glimpse of Alaïa's models as they sporadically flash by.

What they had all come to see were some of the sexiest clothes ever to grace an inadequate excuse for a catwalk. Apart from the zips, Alaïa always chose a clean and simple line with little in the way of decorative detail or fuss. He preferred dark or neutral colours – the expensive palette of the very rich: black, navy, brown, beige, greige, taupe and soft pastels. His genius lay in the intricate cut and the way it displayed the body, revelling in pneumatic womanly curves. He worked directly on the body, repeatedly draping, fitting and cutting. One inspiration was Madeleine Vionnet's multi-seaming techniques and bias cuts; another was Charles James's engineer's obsession with a carapace-like structure.

What was new was the freedom of movement that came with Alaïa's alliance of stretch fabric and intricate structure. Feather-light and unconstraining, these clothes permitted a woman to move in a way that was modern and stride-out easy and, because she felt so sexy in them, terribly seductive. The husbands and lovers of Alaïa's customers were among his biggest fans and good friends.

He dominated Parisian ready-to-wear for a few seasons, opening boutiques in Paris, New York and Los Angeles, and influencing the mass market everywhere. His fame could not help but attract many more private clients, including Tina Turner and Madonna, and as a consequence his attention became brutally divided. In addition, his perfectionism meant an endless reworking of the clothes for his ready-to-wear collections, which were shown later and later. Initially, a journalist would have to stay on a couple of extra days in Paris to see his show, then it was a week, but when it became a month, press and buyers became exasperated. In October 1986 *Women's Wear Daily* (*WWD*) chose to interpret Alaïa's dilatoriness and lack of professionalism as disdain for the hand that fed him – the major store groups in the United States – and ran an editorial saying his day was done. He riposted, 'I'll rub them out in a second – even the biggest customers. I'm not afraid of anyone, even the President of the United States.' But *WWD* had not just power on its side; it had the right of it. Azzedine Alaïa, influential as he was, did not move on when fashion moved on and, at the heart of the problem, he couldn't deliver the clothes into the stores when he said he would.

In 1992 he stopped producing ready-to-wear collections and refocused on couture. But when, in 2000, a 1980s revival resulted in Alaïa tribute outfits on several catwalks, Patrizio Bertelli of Prada bought his company to add to a portfolio of designer labels that already included Helmut Lang and Jil Sander. The acquisition was not a success. In 2007 Prada sold the company back to Alaïa and he refinanced it with backing from Richemont, the luxury group that owns Cartier, Chloé and Dunhill. In 2008 Alaïa was named Chevalier de la Légion d'Honneur.

With Richemont's support, Alaïa established an archive and gallery in his headquarters in the Marais. He died in Paris in 2017. The following year, the Design Museum in London staged a beautifully conceived exhibition, Azzedine Alaïa: The Couturier, which he had helped to curate before his death. Music star Lady Gaga said: 'There was no one who did what he did. No one knew a woman's body like him.'

Further reading: *Alaïa* (2018), an updated edition of a monograph, is an authoritative overview with an introduction by Carla Sozzani and Christoph von Weyhe. François Baudot's *Alaïa* (1996), in the *Fashion Memoir* series, is a good overview, while Francesca Alfano Miglietti's *Fashion Statements: Interviews with Fashion Designers* (2006) takes us a little closer.

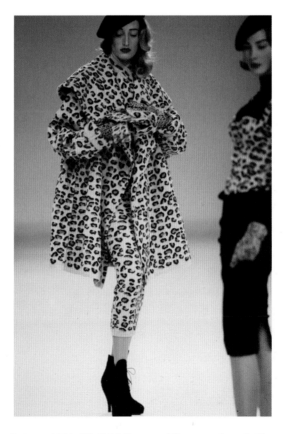

Image 39.4 *Alaïa, autumn/winter 1991. Niall McInerney, Photographer. © Bloomsbury Publishing Plc.*

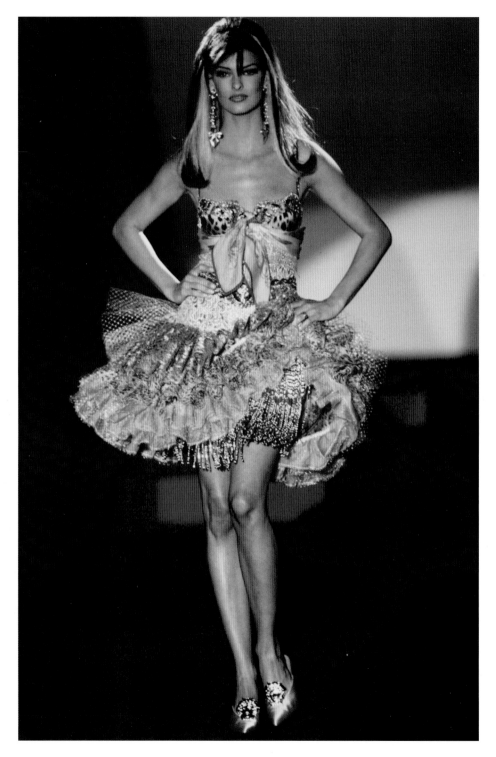

Image 40.1 *Versace, spring/summer 1992. Niall McInerney, Photographer. © Bloomsbury Publishing Plc.*

40

Gianni Versace (1946–1997)

Versace was one of the most skilled designers in the history of fashion because he learned the intricacies of structure before he learned to sketch.

From the 1950s onwards, Italian fashion, wherever it was made, was primarily showcased in two cities, Rome and Florence. But as the 1960s gave way to the 1970s, a group of ready-to-wear designers grew dissatisfied with the shows based at and around the Palazzo Pitti in Florence. Many of them were based in the industrial north and considered the edgy commercial city of Milan with its international airport more appropriate than provincial, hard-to-get-to, tourist-trap Florence. In the initial break-away group, organised by Gigi Monti and Beppe Modenese, were Mariuccia Mandelli of Krizia and her husband Aldo Pinto, Rosita and Tai Missoni and Walter Albini. Newcomers Nino Cerruti, Giorgio Armani, Gianfranco Ferré and Gianni Versace quickly joined them.

Born in 1946 into an impoverished, devout and hard-working family in Reggio di Calabria, Gianni Versace studied dressmaking at his mother's knee. At university, he studied architecture (as did several of Italy's greatest fashion designers) but in 1972 he opted for fashion, moving to Milan to work for various design houses including Complice, Genny and Callaghan. In 1978 he showed his first women's wear collection under his own name at the Palazzo della Permanente Art Museum of Milan, following it, that autumn, with his first men's wear collection. His work was acclaimed from the first showing and, from the earliest days, in the Italian way, his company was his family. His older brother, Santo, ran the business side while his sister, Donatella, ten years his junior, learned from him as he had learned from their mother, becoming his assistant and eventually his successor. In 1982, Versace met his partner, Antonio D'Amico, a model who also worked as a designer for the company, their relationship enduring until the designer's death.

Known colloquially as the couturier to courtesans, the king of high-class hooker style, even 'the first post-Freudian designer', Versace designed as effectively for theatre and opera as for rock stage, club scene and grand, grand occasion. He almost singlehandedly created the supermodels of the 1990s, who once walked down his runway five abreast, arm-in-arm, their own legendary status reflected back to enhance the glamour of their creator. He also changed the direction of fashion, pushing it towards a high-octane eroticism that earned him a fervent following among the demi-monde of rock stars and expensive groupies and the equally fervent disapproval of some fashion commentators. Judy Rumbold, writing in *The Guardian* about the autumn/winter 1991 show, sounded weary,

> It was the usual benign smutfest, featuring trademark vertiginous heels, high hair and prohibitively priced tartwear for the rich and famous. The finale, however, was a little bit different. Accompanied by something loud and earnest by George Michael, Versace sent several thousand pounds' worth of liberally oiled Euroflesh – Naomi Campbell, Cindy Crawford, Christy Turlington and Linda Evangelista – down the catwalk wearing babydoll mini-dresses in pink, orange and lime. But they weren't just showing off the clothes; here was modelling way beyond the call of duty. ... Clearly this wasn't just about frocks. This was showmanship, theatre, but most importantly for Versace, the oldest swinger in Milan, it was near as damn it rock'n'roll.

While other designers had occasionally dressed the stars of Hollywood, Cinecittà and the music industry, Versace actively sought the connection, not only importing references to the rock scene and its flamboyant, excess-driven, decadent lifestyle, but doing hard-nosed contra-deals whereby the celebrities wore the clothes he gave them and turned up to his parties and shop openings in return for the clothes and, in many cases, a generous fee. Rebecca Arnold wrote in 2001,

> For his customers, flaunted wealth snubbed its nose at good taste. His advertising was equally extravagant, parading an array of supermodels in various stages of undress, caught in a sun-drenched world of Italian villas, furnished with the designer's home-style range of silk cushions, throws and fine china, all embellished with the splendours of classical and Renaissance motifs. His gilt Medusa head logo had gained status during the 1980s, made famous by the rock stars and celebrities who wore the clothes, blurring the lines between the fashion and entertainment industries still further, as each gained credibility from the association. His work provided a fantasy version of decadent excess, which spread from his hugely successful (and widely pirated) designer denim line to the couture range he developed.

In 1993, Versace opened what was then, at £11 million, the most expensively shop-fitted store in the history of London, a many-floored Old Bond Street emporium that housed all the collections from denim to couture. The shop itself was breathtakingly expressive of Versace-Baroque: it featured Siena marble in ten different colours and gold leaf by the kilo, with craftsmen by the score and a team of fresco-painters from La Scala flown in and specially accommodated. The morning after the £15,000 opening party (which Versace attended clad in one of his swimming-pool-blue scarf-print silk shirts and tight black jeans), Brenda Polan reported in *The Daily Mail*, 'While the rock stars and well-kept girlfriends fingered the clothes, the commercial establishment and society rent-a-guest crew, as well as the press, gawped uneasily at the rococo décor. Behind me, a voice redolent of Eton and the City murmured, "It's the prettiest laundrette in London."'

Rumours of Mafia connections dogged him, perhaps unsurprisingly given his origins in Reggio Calabria as well as the extraordinary speed with which his label was established, his enormous wealth and opulent lifestyle, and some of the characters he was seen to hang out with. After his shocking murder, on the steps of his Miami beach mansion in 1997, the rumour circulated that it was a Mafia execution. However, in the end, the police concluded that this was all nonsense – the murder was the work of a lone psychotic obsessive, Andrew Cunanan.

Reflecting a decade after his death, Cathy Horyn wrote in *The New York Times* in July 2007, 'A lot has been lost in the decade since Versace's death in Miami Beach – a great talent, most visibly. Try to imagine your wardrobe without the jolt of a print, the vitality of a stiletto, the glamorous bric-a-brac of chains and doodads. This was Versace's doing. His influence melted and spread far beyond the sexual heat of his runway.'

The origin of that sexual heat was not hard to find. Versace was an open and amusing conversationalist, a man of enormous charm, generous with his time. He told Brenda Polan, interviewing him for *The Guardian* in 1981,

> When I was a small boy and my mother would take us to church we had to pass the street of the prostitutes and my mother would say, 'Cover your eyes. Do not look at these women. Never look at them.' But, of course, I would look and to me they were so beautiful, so glamorous. They were forbidden. They were attractive. So, of course, they stay in mind. Until now.

Gianni Versace was one of the most skilled designers in the history of fashion because he learned the intricacies of structure before he learned to sketch. Even more than Azzedine Alaïa, he could cut and

Image 40.2 *Designer Gianni Versace, spring/summer 1993. Niall McInerney, Photographer. © Bloomsbury Publishing Plc.*

Image 40.3 *Versace, autumn/winter 1994. Niall McInerney, Photographer. © Bloomsbury Publishing Plc.*

stitch garments from many pieces so that they would reshape the body while remaining light and comfortable. He could construct skimpy dresses that blatantly revealed more than they concealed yet stayed in place – like the safety-pin dress fledgling actress Elizabeth Hurley wore to the premiere of *Four Weddings and a Funeral* in 1994. His work with glove-soft leather has never really been equalled and his development of both gilded fabrics and his unique patented metal 'chain-mail', Oroton, allowed him to sculpt garments that satisfied both a fetishist's fantasy and an art lover's pleasure in the most beautiful of baroque decoration. The cerulean blue satin sheath decorated with glass beads and gold studs in curlicues that Diana, Princess of Wales, wore to be photographed by Patrick Demarchelier cleverly expressed her latter-day personality: part lady, part saint, part vamp. Garments that embodied within them such conflicting references came easily to him. He was steeped in art history, in Minoan ceramics, Graeco-Roman imagery (his private collection was museum quality) from statues and coins, and in the lush and florid decorative style of the seventeenth and eighteenth centuries and the gilded Art Deco. He understood equally well street style and popular culture – particularly rock culture – and the subcultures of sexual deviance with their props of leather and metal, rubber and shiny PVC, straps and studs, buckles and shackles, corsetry, cross-lacing and safety pins.

Richard Martin, who curated the Metropolitan Museum of Art's 1997 exhibition just after the designer's death, situated him within a history of fashion that, before it adopted bourgeois values of property and propriety, focused on sensuality. He was the epoch-defining designer of the late 1980s and early 1990s because he restored to high fashion a sense of erotic purpose. Martin wrote, 'Gianni Versace reorganised the etiquette of apparel. He did not aspire to decorum. Rather, he accorded fashion with desire, substituting the lust of fashion and body concupiscence for the cause of correct behaviour and social calibration.'

Many twentieth-century designers – from Yves Saint Laurent to Jean Paul Gaultier, from Vivienne Westwood to John Galliano – have found vibrant references from street culture and oppositional or marginalised subcultures. But Gianni Versace fixated on, and celebrated, characters only sketchily referenced by the others – the prostitute and the rent boy. Versace was not alone in his preoccupation with the fallen woman, the Magdalen. She was a heroine of Federico Fellini and Luchino Visconti, great Italian film directors of Versace's formative years, the years during which an impoverished Italy reconstructed itself. 'No one,' wrote Martin,

> had taken the prostitute into fashion as Versace did. In a feat worthy of literature, Versace seized the streetwalker's bravado and conspicuous wardrobe, along with her blatant, brandished sexuality, and introduced them into high fashion. But Versace did not ... simply convey the prostitute to the salon and the runway. He did what fashion can do when it finds inspiration on the street. He represented her as glamour, accepting the extreme flirtatiousness of her short skirts, the seduction of shiny cloth and cognate materials, and understanding the motive of sex, but rendering each hyperbolic and expressive, not merely a portrayal of what had existed in the wardrobe of the street. ... In making his deliberate

choice to exalt the streetwalker, Versace risked the opprobrium of the bourgeoisie. As a designer and as a human being, Versace never sought the middle road or the middle class. Rather, he forged a unity between the independent of spirit and will, the rich, the young and the intrepid.

Although some of the homoerotic images to issue from Versace's private darkroom were often discomfortingly parodic, his insistence on showcasing the male as sexual commodity has been seen by some commentators as liberating for both genders. The supermodels on Versace's catwalk so often referenced drag queens 'doing' Marilyn Monroe, Brigitte Bardot, Tina Turner or Madonna, posing interesting questions about femininity and identity. Versace was, in fact, in step with a generation of young women who claimed to be post-feminists and in control of their provocative and sometimes sluttish sexuality. Rebecca Arnold wrote, 'Fashion had been growing more playful in its appropriation of references to gay culture since the 1980s. As fashion shows became more grandiose, more theatrical, they drew upon the tenets of camp, revelling in the freedom to exaggerate and dramatise femininity in a manner that was self-conscious in its postmodernity. The role of fashion as entertainment, reinforced by Versace with his flamboyant shows … had brought overstatement and parody to the industry.' And to the culture.

After Versace's death in 1997, his sister Donatella took over as creative director; he bequeathed his share of the company to her daughter, Allegra. The recession of 2008 was difficult for the company but it survived and diversified. In 2018, Versace was bought by new American luxury group Capri Holdings, which also includes Michael Kors, for $2.1 billion.

Further reading: The best, most analytical book is Richard Martin's *Gianni Versace* (1997), which accompanied the exhibition at the Metropolitan Museum of Art, New York. For an account of the label's history, Deborah Ball's *House of Versace: The Untold Story of Genius, Media and Survival* (2010) is informative.

Image 40.4 *Versace, spring/summer 1990. Niall McInerney, Photographer. © Bloomsbury Publishing Plc.*

41

Jean Paul Gaultier (1952–)

Gaultier's experiments with sportswear, stretch fabrics and underwear used as outerwear influenced all levels of the fashion market.

The long-lasting image of Jean Paul Gaultier as the *enfant terrible* of French fashion took many years to lay to rest. But the great iconoclast of modern French fashion in time became part of the establishment he once shunned, championing the joy of couture and spending seven years as creative director at the house of Hermès, a byword in understated luxury.

This is not to disparage Gaultier's achievements, for many great arch provocateurs before him have, over time, become accepted by the mainstream – a sign of their influence. Gaultier's openness about sex and homosexuality was considered shocking to many in the 1980s but was part of mainstream popular culture by the Noughties. His championing of diversity and blurred gender lines appears prophetic from the viewpoint of the early 2020s. And when Hermès appointed him creative director in 2003, the company recognised that behind the many playful and provocative designs was a rigorous technician with great tailoring skills.

At heart, Gaultier has also remained indisputably French and Parisian, despite his love of London street style and international travels. He was a dominant force in designer fashion through the 1980s; the tickets for his shows were the most coveted in Paris. But his critics said he was a designer for fashion victims, who pinched most of his ideas by wandering round Camden Market in London. His clothes made all the headlines but were considered unwearable – skirts for men, conical bras for women. Pastiche fashion, the critics said.

But by the early 1990s, his status as a pioneering designer who mixed up styles and embraced cross-cultural diversity was being recognised. Likewise, his experiments with sportswear, stretch fabrics and underwear used as outerwear were influencing all levels of the fashion market. To Gaultier's delight, there was also a new appreciation of the talents he had picked up in his early days in the design studios of Paris: his exquisite tailored jackets, the delicacy of his colour sense and the immaculate finish of his

Image 41.1 *Jean Paul Gaultier, 1990s. Niall McInerney, Photographer. © Bloomsbury Publishing Plc.*

clothes. Gaultier has mellowed in his later years, although his collection of autumn/winter 2008, which attracted much negative comment for its surfeit of exotic animal skins, showed that he has not lost the ability to be controversial. He has probably taken more risks, both creatively and personally, than any other designer in history – and sometimes paid the price. Arguably his greatest career mistake was to become a television presenter on the British TV show *Eurotrash*, a satirical romp through the wilder extremes of contemporary European popular culture. Although the show was an undoubted hit and authentically reflected Gaultier's eclectic creative inspirations, it almost certainly deprived him of the opportunity to take up the reins at Christian Dior. LVMH boss Bernard Arnault was not amused.

The greatest Gaultier shows have been cavalcades, carnivals of the imagination, inspired by an extraordinary host of references, blending couture and street fashion with abandon, often presented on models who defy conventional interpretations of beauty. Inspiration has ranged from Jewish rabbis, the Dadaists and Mongolian Inuits to tattoos, sadomasochism and flea markets. At the heart of so many of his shows, however, is an enduring affection for Paris, particularly the Paris of the interwar years. Popping up at the end of the show is the man himself, one of the most instantly recognisable figures in world fashion, usually in his trademark striped sailor T-shirt, always with an impish grin.

Jean Paul Gaultier was born in 1952 in the suburbs of Paris to hard-working parents, Paul, a bookkeeper, and Solange, a secretary. Marie Garrabe, his grandmother, was the biggest influence on his childhood, allowing the young Gaultier considerable freedom on his weekly visits. In modern-day terminology, she might be described as an alternative therapist, operating from her own home, which was decorated with old-style furnishings. His other childhood influence was television, particularly a documentary about the Folies-Bergère, where the feathers and glitz excited him and were the beginning of his creative and sexual awakening as a gay man. Feigning sickness, he bunked off school to pursue his interest in fashion, looking at newspapers and magazines and drawing obsessively. In his formative years in the 1960s, his interest was in the world of haute couture rather than the new generation of ready-to-wear *créateurs*, although anything the teenage Gaultier learned was self-taught, gleaned from magazines. Gaultier's first dresses were for his mother, an achievement that encouraged him to compile sheaves of drawings to send to would-be employers. At Christian Dior, Marc Bohan showed no interest, but Pierre Cardin offered the eighteen-year-old Gaultier work in 1970. Although he only lasted eight months before becoming a victim of a redundancy round, it was an important period. Cardin served as the perfect mentor for Gaultier for he had an open mind and was developing his innovative L'Espace Pierre Cardin, a theatre and exhibition venue. 'He told me that everything is possible,' Gaultier recalled years later.

Gaultier then worked briefly at Jacques Esterel and at the Cincept style agency before landing a job at the house of Patou under design director Michel Goma and, later, Angelo Tarlazzi. At Patou, though, he became disillusioned by the straitjacketed formalities of the world of haute couture, which he had previously held in such high esteem. Much of the rest of his career was spent reacting against the restrictions of couture, inspired by visits to London, where he felt energised by the city's creative (and sexual) energy, particularly in the post-Punk period. By 1974, Gaultier was back at Pierre Cardin

Image 41.2 *Designer Jean Paul Gaultier. Niall McInerney, Photographer. © Bloomsbury Publishing Plc.*

in a curious position at Cardin-Philippines, part of the designer's fast-growing international empire. Such an experience opened Gaultier's eyes to new cultures and influences, encouraging him to look widely for inspiration in the years that followed. Returning to Paris within a year, he made contact with an old school friend, Donald Potard, who introduced him to the fledgling jeweller Francis Menuge, who became his lover. Another important influence was the exotic model Anna Pawlowski. Scraping together funds, the friends produced the first Jean Paul Gaultier collection in October 1976, including a studded leather jacket paired with a tutu – a sign that Gaultier was an unconventional kind of designer.

The early Gaultier collections were characterised by a flood of contrasting designs and ideas, created in circumstances of financial desperation. An initial two-year contract in 1979 with Japan's Kashiyama, thanks to the support of Kashiyama creative director Dominique Emschweiller, set Gaultier on a more professional footing. Simultaneously (and not coincidentally), the press began to take fulsome notice of Gaultier, even if much of the interest was founded on his ability to entertain – he was an oddity, a cult, a cause célèbre. He was 'Paris's Court Jester', according to *WWD* in 1984. In a prolonged interview with biographer Colin McDowell, Gaultier denied that his intention was to destroy the past. 'I use and respect tradition, but try to find new elements which will make it younger.' His goal was to question notions of good taste, but founded on the solid base of the tailoring skills he had acquired in the milieu of haute couture.

Gaultier was also keen to break down what he saw as artificial barriers between menswear and womenswear. Why shouldn't men wear skirts? His introduction of men's skirts in 1985 and constant repetition of the theme was no gimmick but was based on a fundamental belief that clothes should not be gender specific. 'Masculinity is not connected to the clothes you're wearing – it's in the mind,' he said.

The late 1980s saw Gaultier's business expand rapidly, backed by Gibo in Italy and Kashiyama in Japan. The Gaultier aesthetic was well represented in his Paris store in rue Vivienne, blending ancient-look mosaics with his innovative clothes, and in stores in Milan, London and Brussels. Gaultier's openness about his sexuality and mix-it-up approach to design brought him into the heart of rapidly evolving popular culture, working with photographer Jean-Baptiste Mondino on advertising campaigns and videos, choreographer Régine Chopinot, film directors Peter Greenaway and Pedro Almodovar. The early 1990s were even better for Gaultier, who forged on with growing confidence, despite the personal blow of the death of his partner, Francis Menuge, from AIDS in 1990. A commission to design a wardrobe for Madonna's Blonde Ambition tour in 1990 led to the creation of his most celebrated piece, a corset including a conical bra, which Gaultier later chose as the bottle shape for his Jean Paul Gaultier fragrance. Launched in 1993 and packaged in a tin can, it has since been renamed Jean Paul Gaultier Classique and has become one of the most successful of all designer fragrances. The selling power of the name is undiminished: he launched a new fragrance, Scandal, with Puig in 2017.

Gaultier has constantly challenged mainstream thinking and stirred up controversy, ranging from nuns as strippers in 1991 to a magnificent collection shown on black models in 1997 at a time when the French government was clamping down on immigration. His fashion shows have often been spectacles, lavishly mounted in a variety of different locations, paving the way for the imaginative shows staged by designers such as Alexander McQueen and Viktor & Rolf in the Noughties. Gaultier's arrival under his own name in the haute couture arena was a long time in coming, despite the infusion of new talent that gave couture renewed vigour in the 1990s. His first collection, in January 1996, was shown to no music in a pastiche of the old couture style, but the collection, called the Couture Man, was entirely for men. A women's collection followed a year later.

Gaultier was treated with reverence in French fashion circles into the Noughties, although by then many of the barriers he had broken through were no longer considered barriers. His work, it could be argued, was done. Hermès bought a 35 per cent stake in his business in 1999, providing him with a solid foundation for the years ahead. But the pressures of maintaining a couture operation, always a loss-making part of the business, forced Gaultier to make job cuts in 2004. 'We've run up the stairs two at a time,' said Donald Potard, his long-term business partner and president of the house. 'Now we need to catch our breath to continue operating all of our activities.' At Hermès, where he was appointed creative director of womenswear in May 2003, he showed that he could adapt to another house's style. Pascale Mussard, artistic director, said: 'People ask what Gaultier has brought to Hermès but it's not arrogant to consider what Hermès brought to Gaultier. You could say we help each other see with each other's eyes.'

For Gaultier, the distance between himself and Hermès was not so great. When he worked at the couture house of Patou, he used to wear riding boots and was teased by the vendeuses ('they asked me where was my "orse'"). In interviews he recalled the comment of the photographer Helmut Newton that Hermès is 'the most important sex shop in the world,' highlighting the leather, whips and stirrups. His biographer, Colin McDowell, points out that Jean Paul Gaultier 'hides his seriousness behind a facetious facade.' In so doing, he sums up the playful postmodern spirit of contemporary popular culture and has inspired young designers and other artists in the 1990s and beyond (including Martin Margiela and Nicolas Ghesquière) to dispense with convention and pursue their inner dreams. Academic Barbara Vinken sees him as inheriting the mantle of Elsa Schiaparelli – 'a kind of surrealism against the grain, which consciously makes a fool of itself.' But another, more straightforward Vinken observation may be more appropriate: 'Gaultier has plundered the attic of fashion, and offers his customers his most daring and cheeky finds.'

His enduring status was highlighted by the success of an exhibition first staged in 2011 at the Montreal Museum of Fine Arts, The Fashion World of Jean Paul Gaultier: From the Sidewalk to the Catwalk. It went on to tour twelve cities worldwide and attract more than two million visitors. At his spring/summer 2013 show, he announced the closure of his ready-to-wear line, preferring to concentrate on couture, which he now recognised as his true love. He had become disillusioned by the dominance of the big luxury groups in the designer fashion system, decrying the obsession with money and marketing and (a particular gripe) the buying of influence by paying celebrities to wear brands.

What shines through in all of Gaultier's work and career is his lifelong love of fashion. 'I am not interested in business,' he said in the early 1990s. 'I didn't do fashion to be rich and famous. I don't want to hand everything over to assistants and become a businessman.' Many years later, in 2016, the passion still shone through: 'In my designs, I reinvent myself again and again. It's what keeps me young.'

Further reading: The Fashion World of Jean Paul Gaultier: From the Sidewalk to the Catwalk (2011) is the catalogue to the exhibition of the same name and essential reading. *Jean Paul Gaultier* (2000) by Colin McDowell is a good analysis. Gaultier himself had fun with a comic book-style autobiography, *A Nous Deux La Mode* (1990), which is only available in French. The designer was also interviewed by Roger Tredre for *The Independent* ('A One-man Revolt Against the Cliché', August 2 1990).

Image 41.3 *Jean Paul Gaultier, 1990s. Niall McInerney, Photographer.* © *Bloomsbury Publishing Plc.*

42

Dolce & Gabbana (Domenico Dolce 1958–, Stefano Gabbana 1962–)

The success of their partnership has rested on the attraction of opposites.

The most successful design partnership in fashion history, Domenico Dolce and Stefano Gabbana, burst onto the fashion scene in the mid-1980s through a mixture of talent, perspiration, inspired marketing and luck. They were the last Italian designers of the twentieth century to make a real mark, creating extravagant fashion collections that played with themes and periods with happy abandon. Their success was founded on sharp tailoring combined with street style and a flair for bringing to life the Italy of their and their customers' dreams.

The fashion press called them maximalist mix masters, making the comparison with DJs who mix music to create a kaleidoscope of sounds. Domenico Dolce and Stefano Gabbana were rarely hesitant in their creative vision, churning out ideas in abundance and ransacking the decades (in particular the 1930s to the 1980s). Interviewed by *Harper's Bazaar* in 2015, Gabbana said: 'Dolce & Gabbana is like black or white – anything in the middle is difficult.' In their magpie approach to fashion design, they summed up the free spirit of modern fashion. Among their hits: pinstripe mannish tailoring for women, underwear worn as outerwear, curvaceous dresses, spectacularly colourful coats and, invariably, lashings of leopard print. Despite an occasional misstep, they have a talent for tuning in to the mood of the times. As Gabbana put it, 'Fashion has to be in step with the times. Today more than ever, conceptual just doesn't pay back and is destined to fail.'

In their later years their collections have displayed a taste that teeters into kitsch – and their enthusiasm for stirring up controversy via social media finally hit a brick wall in late 2018 in China with

Image 42.1 *Dolce & Gabbana, spring/summer 1993. Niall McInerney, Photographer. © Bloomsbury Publishing Plc.*

an ill-judged promotional video dubbed xenophobic. Leaving aside that furore, the Dolce & Gabbana signature has often encapsulated the best of Italian fashion. Journalist Sarah Mower, who edited their celebratory twentieth anniversary book, said they represented 'a kind of psychic map of Italy'. The success of their partnership has rested on the attraction of opposites, as they have acknowledged in interview after interview; Dolce is the craftsman while Gabbana has his finger on the pulse of popular culture. As Gabbana put it: 'We start from two really different points. He starts from the left, I start from the right. And we meet in the middle.'

Domenico Dolce, the older of the two, was born in Sicily in the village of Polizzi Generosa in 1958. His father was a tailor specialising in suits for local gentry's weddings, while his mother owned a general haberdashery store. Legend has it that Dolce's crib was set up in his father's workroom. Dolce grew up playing with fabrics; at seven he made a pair of trousers. At an exceptionally early age, the pattern was set for his life. Stefano Gabbana was born four years later in 1962 in Milan. There was no fashion in his family background: his father was a printer from Venice. An exceptionally good-looking young man, Gabbana moved to Milan to study graphic design in the early 1980s, a period when the city's fashion industry was flourishing as never before. The designer that caught the eye of Gabbana most strongly was Elio Fiorucci, Italy's ebullient king of kitsch style.

Gabbana met Dolce on the phone initially when the latter answered a job enquiry call in the office where he was working. Dolce had moved to Milan from Sicily to study design and quickly landed a job as an assistant at a local fashion house. Taking Gabbana under his wing, he taught him to sketch and understand the design process before Gabbana was obliged to spend eighteen months on military service. By late 1982, Gabbana was back in town and the two were sharing an apartment. Their focus on work was relentless (Gabbana thinks he was probably thirty before they took their first holiday). But they also partied hard, out until the early hours at Amnesia and other hot clubs of the time, enjoying the sheer decadence of the fashion industry.

Dolce & Gabbana staged their first show in October 1985 as part of a group showing for three young designer labels at the back end of the Milan show season. Despite their disregard for the power dressing that was dominant in fashion at the time, their complicated geometric cuts received encouraging press coverage. But their manufacturer took fright and promptly pulled out. The duo appeared to be out of business before they had even started. Dolce's family came to the rescue, producing a second collection for the two young designers. It was named Real Women, not least because they could not afford models and had to enlist friends to model the clothes. The collection was full of fabrics used in unconventional ways, including a coat made out of sweatshirting and a dress in a rubberised wool. The beginnings of a buzz began to ripple through the Milanese fashion scene. By the third collection, for spring/summer 1987, store buyers were showing interest, even if the versatile clothes, which could be worn in two or more different ways, were not easy to explain to customers. Was it a skirt or a dress?

Image 42.2 *Designers Domenico Dolce and Stefano Gabbana, spring/summer 1994. Niall McInerney, Photographer. © Bloomsbury Publishing Plc.*

In fact, it was both. Dolce & Gabbana were also drawing on the innovative brilliance of Italy's textile manufacturers, working with such new fabrics as stretch silk and a transparent organza jersey.

Up until their fourth collection, Dolce had resisted drawing on his Sicilian roots for inspiration. 'I'd come to Milan because I wanted to break from the past,' he explained. 'I dreamed modern! I resisted going back there.' Gabbana, by contrast, had no such qualms. For a photo shoot, he persuaded a non-fashion photographer, Fernando Scianna, to join them in Sicily with the model Marpessa to produce moody black-and-white images that had an authentic aura of Sicily. Black and white paid homage to the Italian cinema of the 1940s, when neo-realist directors such as Roberto Rossellini produced gritty movies set in the Deep South. Another key influence was Visconti, whose film *Il Gattopardo* was the inspiration behind the designers' spring/summer 1988 collection. All this was laced with erotic elements, as academic Barbara Vinken has noted: 'There is a touch of Sicilian passion, in the manner of Sophia Loren: an affirmative, even aggressive feminine eroticism, adult and dominant.'

Curiously, British and American store buyers were quicker to appreciate Dolce & Gabbana than the Italians. From Rossellini to Sophia Loren to Anna Magnani, all the great icons of twentieth-century Italian popular culture were referenced by the two designers. Their models, ranging from

Further reading: Dolce & Gabbana published books to mark both their tenth and twentieth anniversaries. The latter, *20 Years Dolce & Gabbana* (2005), includes a well-written text by Sarah Mower that exhaustively documents their collections. *Vogue on Dolce & Gabbana* (2017), written by Luke Leitch, is a succinct summary.

Image 42.3 *Dolce & Gabbana, spring/summer 1996. Niall McInerney, Photographer. © Bloomsbury Publishing Plc.*

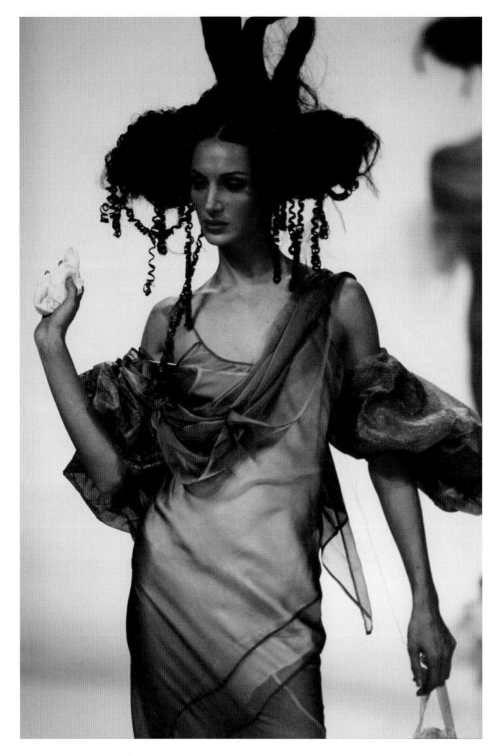

Image 43.1 *John Galliano, spring/summer 1993. Niall McInerney, Photographer. © Bloomsbury Publishing Plc.*

43

John Galliano (1960–)

The fashion show was, for Galliano, a theatre where the imagination should roam.

British designer John Galliano is one of the most significant of a steady stream of talents who have emerged from London's Central Saint Martins School of Art & Design (now known simply as Central Saint Martins) since the 1980s. He was the first British designer of the modern era to head a Parisian haute couture house. He consistently took fashion shows to new heights of theatricality, most notably for the house of Christian Dior, where his shows were of unequalled extravagance, displaying fantastical imagination. Galliano brought back romance to fashion in 1997 when he became chief designer at Dior, fifty years on from the launch of Dior's New Look. After a spectacular fall from grace in 2011, he re-emerged in late 2014 as creative director of Maison Margiela.

To his critics, his clothes both before and during his years at Dior veered close to costume, bearing little relation to the modern-day world (and often with no connection to the showroom range sold to buyers). But the fashion show was, for him, a theatre, where the imagination should roam. His meticulously themed collections, often inspired by complex fictional tales with a heroine at the centre, unashamedly pursued flights of fancy. Over the years, he produced many complex, difficult-to-wear, unforgiving clothes that delighted fashion editors although less so store buyers and customers. But, thanks to his talent and an effectively exploited ability to charm, he rode a surf of goodwill – and in the process created some of the most beautiful clothes of the late twentieth and early twenty-first centuries. His willingness to experiment inspired a generation of young designers. Even as a college student, he had an obsessive curiosity, a desire to push ideas to their limits. Early in his career, for example, he devised his own form of cutting in the round so that sleeves followed the shapes of the arm and jackets turned into curvy sculptures. Later, he cut fabric on the bias, so that it clung to the body. 'It's a sensuous way of cutting, very fast and fluid, with a great respect for women's bodies,' he told Roger Tredre in 1990. 'It's like oily water running through your fingers.'

All his achievements appeared to turn to dust in February 2011 when a drunk Galliano was captured on video shouting anti-Semitic insults at fellow drinkers in a Paris café. He was fired from both Dior and his own brand John Galliano within twenty-four hours. It took him years to work his way back, professing his shame and connecting earnestly with the Jewish community, supported by Rabbi Barry Marcus of the Central Synagogue in London. His downfall also provoked much media discussion about the pressures placed on modern fashion designers. Asked in 2015 whether he would have left Dior had he not been sacked, he said: 'I think I would be dead.'

Juan Carlos Antonio Galliano was born in Gibraltar in 1960 to a Spanish mother and Gibraltarian father, moving to London as a child. He joined Saint Martins before its merger with Central when it was still known as St Martin's School of Art. Among the lecturers was the fashion writer Colin McDowell, who later became his biographer. Galliano researched his collections intensively, spending hours in the library of the Victoria & Albert Museum building up a meticulous picture of an imaginary heroine who would be the true muse of each collection. Multilayered stories were created that fed directly into the design process. The theatricality of Galliano's approach to fashion might be traced to his student days: he worked as a dresser at London's National Theatre and frequented a nightclub called Taboo where his friends included Leigh Bowery, the flamboyant Australian costume designer and living artwork, and Stephen Jones, the milliner and a long-term collaborator.

Galliano's initial rise was meteoric. The 1984 graduation collection, Les Incroyables, inspired by the costumes of the French Revolution period, was famously bought by London designer store Browns, and the young designer was inundated with interview requests by fashion editors. Commenting on that first collection, a college contemporary of Galliano said: 'It was streets ahead of everyone else. I felt physically sick. It was so good I felt I might as well give up designing because I would never get anywhere near that.' Galliano immediately launched his own label and became the darling of London Fashion Week: within three years, he was British Designer of the Year. However, the bare facts of this rapid rise conceal a story of struggle, partly financial to secure backing and resources for each new collection, and partly personal as the strains of the fashion world's expectations wore down the designer. He was always a highly strung and intense individual, sometimes literally trembling with nerves before a new collection was shown.

In the mid-1980s, Galliano became one of a group of young designers, including Alistair Blair and Richard James, backed by the Danish businessman Peder Bertelsen. He staged his first show in Paris in 1990, albeit without the support of Bertelsen, who had withdrawn from the fashion fray. Next, he found backing from Fayçal Amor, the businessman behind the Plein Sud label, although this partnership again faltered as the orders failed to materialise and the costs of Galliano's extravagant shows soared. Despite an exalted media profile, Galliano was dropped by Amor and was at a low point in a promising career, apparently doomed to follow the path of many young British designers before and since: lauded too early, pressurised to the limit and obliged to abandon dreams of a signature collection and join the backroom design studio of a major foreign label. However, he had a powerful fairy godmother in the form of Anna Wintour, editor of American *Vogue*, who lobbied on his behalf in early 1994. 'She flew me to America and introduced me to the right people,' recalled Galliano. A backer was identified in the form of John

Bult of American investment house PaineWebber. Within three weeks of Bult's stepping in, Galliano had produced a small but perfectly formed collection of seventeen high-glamour outfits shown in the Parisian townhouse of Portuguese millionairess Sao Schlumberger. 'The marketing director said, "Look John, you need to edit your collection, produce it in so many colours and so many fabrics, and you need to be really choosy about who you sell to," recalled Galliano. 'I really learnt a lot from that little collection.'

Friends and long-term collaborators rallied around, including the British designer, Steven Robinson, who was by Galliano's side continuously until his tragically early death in 2007. Another key supporter was Lady Harlech, born Amanda Grieve, who acted as both stylist and muse for Galliano for many years before being edged out (specifically by Robinson) and lured away to work with Karl Lagerfeld at Chanel. They sensed that women were tired of dressing down, of the grungy looks that had dominated fashion through the early 1990s. Working day and night, they came up with a sharply focused collection inspired by the fitted tailoring of the 1950s and with a preponderance of outfits for the evening and cocktail hours. The fashion world went into a collective swoon. Back in Paris, he produced a second collection of fit-and-curve daywear and Oriental-inspired evening wear, which had journalists and buyers grasping for superlatives. In just two collections, he had brushed aside deconstruction and encouraged women to dress up and dream again.

In 1995, Galliano landed a major breakthrough when he was appointed head designer at Givenchy by Bernard Arnault, chairman of LVMH, the luxury goods conglomerate. Not since the days of

Image 43.2 *John Galliano at Dior, spring/summer 1997. Niall McInerney, Photographer. © Bloomsbury Publishing Plc.*

Charles Frederick Worth had a British name pulled off such a coup in the capital of fashion. He completed one couture and two ready-to-wear collections before moving on to the ultimate prize – artistic director at Christian Dior, the fashion house also owned by LVMH. Simultaneously, he continued to develop his own signature label with a spectacular show in October 1996 staged as a circus in an empty wine warehouse. His first couture collection for Dior was presented in January 1997, an auspicious year for the house of Dior, marking the fiftieth anniversary of the New Look. Galliano had immersed himself in the Dior archive in rue Jean Goujon, much as he had done in the Victoria & Albert Museum as a student in the early 1980s. For once, he fell in love with a real personality from the past, Mitzah Bricard, a muse to British couturier Edward Molyneux in the 1930s and later to Dior himself. Part homage to Dior, part assertion of Galliano's own romantic spirit, the collection was staged at the Opera Salon of the Grand Hotel in Paris and was hailed as a dazzling triumph. Among a plethora of ecstatic press comment, *The International Herald Tribune* summed it up: 'Surely Galliano's sixteen-year career has been a dress rehearsal for this sublime moment?' Galliano's finest homage to Dior himself, however, came eight years later in 2005 (the autumn/winter collection) with a series of ten tableaux inspired by the couturier's work, including the Bar suit, which was frequently reinterpreted by Galliano.

The backing and security of LVMH also gave Galliano the opportunity to sort out his personal life, where all-night partying and hedonism had been the order of the day. *Gods and Kings*, a controversial book by American journalist Dana Thomas published in 2015, confirms that, despite some spells of calm, Galliano never did sort himself out: he was always teetering on the edge. Galliano also alienated many with an increasing arrogance. Thomas points out that he had the world at his feet – and a salary to match. Others of his generation, including the brilliantly talented John Flett, a former friend and Central Saint Martins fellow graduate, who became addicted to heroin and died in 1991, were not so fortunate.

In an earlier and rather more affectionate 1997 biography, Colin McDowell highlighted Galliano's love of historicism and the allure of Orientalism. From a twenty-first-century perspective, those interests have the whiff of excessive cultural appropriation. In his defence, Galliano's delight in a rich resource of references was whipped up in very Galliano-esque confections, usually decontextualised, as historian Farid Chenoune has pointed out. While as a student he had used the library as his source of inspiration, as a designer he travelled regularly ('the most powerful source of ideas', he said). He has always loved the process of researching a collection, saying research feeds his mind – wherever it might take him. 'Creativity has no nationality, so I don't want to leave any stone unturned. I love understanding and seeing different cultures.' Galliano is a fierce defender of the role of fashion. 'Fashion is escapist, not elitist, and I think now more than ever it has a role to play,' he said in 2008. 'Dior dared women to dream, to bring back romance, femininity, and seduction. He brought joy back onto the streets. I think this is my role.'

Galliano's work is often laced with unsettling elements and references (although rarely pushed as far as Alexander McQueen, who graduated from Saint Martins after Galliano). Referencing his student days at the club Taboo, he has explored sexual fantasy, most notably through his autumn/winter 2001 couture collection for Dior, which was unofficially dubbed 'Freud or Fetish'. In a thought-provoking comment, he argued that Dior was 'the first true fetishist designer. He had an Oedipus complex, he was in awe of his mother and his New Look was full of fetish symbolism'. Appreciative of the glories of French cultural heritage, Galliano managed to adapt to Parisian style at Dior without losing his British sense of irreverence, displaying continuity in his creative evolution from that memorable French Revolution college graduation collection.

After his sacking from Dior in 2011, Galliano spent time in rehabilitation at a clinic in Arizona. In 2013 media reports emerged that he was working in a low-key kind of way at Oscar de la Renta's studio in New York. Galliano returned fully to the limelight in October 2014 by taking up the role of creative director at Maison Margiela. Here, he has continued to innovate, merging the deconstructionist house style with his own more theatrical instincts. His approach is based on the idea of *décortiqué*, the thorough deconstruction of something to its core. His spring/summer 2019 show for Maison Margiela was a well-received genderless blend of menswear and womenswear for 'digital nomads', while the inventive tailoring in the autumn/winter 2019 collection was another hit, suggesting that Galliano's years as an influential designer are far from over.

Further reading: Galliano: Spectacular Fashion (2019) by Kerry Taylor is a thorough summary of his career. John Galliano's impact at Dior is eulogised in *Dior: 60 Years of Style* (2007) by Farid Chenoune. A decade earlier, Colin McDowell wrote an insightful monograph, *Galliano* (1997). Galliano has been profiled exhaustively since the very beginning of his career and was interviewed on several occasions by Roger Tredre in the early 1990s. See in particular 'The Grind Behind the Glamour' (1990) and 'Galliano Meets His Maker' (1992). *Gods and Kings: The Rise of Alexander McQueen and John Galliano* (2015) by Dana Thomas provides a frank and often unflattering take on his life and career.

Image 43.3 *Dior show, 1990s. Niall McInerney, Photographer.* © *Bloomsbury Publishing Plc.*

44

Donna Karan (1948–)

Karan put working women in clothes – mostly black – that were easy, chic, carefree.

In 1996, when Donna Karan took her company to the stock market, *New York* magazine put her on its cover. The picture showed a youthful, doe-eyed woman with glossy long dark hair looking straight to camera, her hands before her mouth in a praying posture. The copy beneath read, 'Donna Karan, Corporate Goddess. The most successful woman on Seventh Avenue has gone New Age, and now she's going public. Will Wall Street love Donna as much as her customers do?' Inside, journalist Rebecca Mead concluded, rightly, that Wall Street doubtless would. Donna Karan is the third and youngest of what fashion observers came to think of as the great triumvirate dominating American fashion in the 1980s and 1990s, the threesome – Lauren, Klein and Karan – who made the rest of the world take American fashion seriously for the first time.

Backed by marketing, advertising and public relations techniques at which Americans excel, these three designers became global brands at an astonishing speed, each quickly establishing an identity that not only set them apart in terms of all-American modernity but neatly set them apart from each other. If Lauren appealed to the romantically aspirational, the dreamer and fantasist, and Klein to a classic, understated, minimalist, country-mansion moneyed chic, Karan was sharply focused on young, ambitious working women, those moving up corporate and professional ladders, paying their own bills, making their own rules. She put them in clothes – mostly black – that were easy, chic, carefree. While Lauren's twenty-page runs of movie-still style advertisements recorded reimagined mythic times and communities, Karan's best known version from 1992 shows the inauguration of a woman president (model Rosemary McGrotha), all pinstripe suit and pearls. The slogan, 'In Women We Trust', was Karan's mantra and one reason the women of the press loved her. However hard they tried, she implied and women believed, male designers could never get inside women's skins in the way she could. 'I am a woman,' Karan told Brenda Polan for *The Mail on Sunday* in 1994. 'I'm a female designer, a working wife and mother. I understand the lives of other women and the last thing any

Image 44.1 *Launch collection, Donna Karan, autumn/winter 1985. Niall McInerney, Photographer.* © *Bloomsbury Publishing Plc.*

trick she employed of tying a sweater around the waist so that it draped concealingly around the hips, creating an illusion that all the perceived bulk in that area was knitwear.

The collection with which Karan launched her own label – 'a little niche business for me and my friends' – in 1985 was based around the body, a leotard with poppers closing it at the crotch, and various wrap pieces that were layered on top of it. The body stayed put and did not wrinkle or ruck up or come untucked as ordinary shirts and jumpers did. It looked trim and tidy all day. In the 1940s, Claire McCardell had been one of the first to incorporate the leotard into everyday fashion. Later Azzedine Alaïa would use them as an integral part of his mega-streamlined, second-skin approach to dressing. However, no one has ever had quite the impact as Karan did when she made the body the central theme of her first collection under her own label. Her rationale was closer to McCardell's than Alaïa's – not eroticism but convenience – although the wrap skirt showed a lot of leg.

The clothes were photographed in ads showing various working-woman scenarios, disembarking from a plane, catching up on office work at home. Karan told Catherine Milinaire and Carol Troy in 1978 for their book, *Cheap Chic*,

> I believe that a woman's professional clothes have to come from the inside out. The clothes are never going to make the woman. … But I guarantee you that if a woman's together, she's going to know enough about herself to look outta sight. … And when you have an assurance about yourself, honey, you can walk into any room and command anything. But you've got to work at it. It doesn't come easily.

In 1982 Karan married for a second time. Stephan Weiss, who died in 2003, was a sculptor who joined Karan in her company. The Donna Karan collection was pure luxury, using expensive materials and high-quality manufacturing techniques, so in 1989 they launched DKNY (Donna Karan New York), a younger, less pricey line. For this, Karan said, she

> wanted a name bigger than me, one that expressed my passion for the world. New York, to me, is the visualisation of the entire universe. Paris is Paris, it's not the world. Italy is Italy. New York is the world. It is the bridge. It's the spot that expresses the world. I wanted to say that I was a conscious designer of the people of the world, inspired by Chinatown, uptown, downtown, all the aspects, Central Park, people living in the street, all of it, the beauty, the electricity, the sickness, music, dance, theatre, art; it's all here. Both companies, Donna Karan and DKNY, which evolved later – and which came out of my need for a pair of jeans, jeans that would fit a woman's body – are about everyone, all of us, the larger family.

The hugely successful DKNY collection was followed by a jeans collection, men's wear, children's clothes and scent – Weiss sculpted the sensuous templates for the perfume bottles. 'Stephan was a genius,' Karan told Ingrid Sischy in 2004. 'I couldn't have done it without Stephan. … He understood the art of doing business.' Her fan base is wide and impressive, including Isabella Rossellini, Anouk Aimé, Demi Moore, Jeremy Irons, Bruce Willis, Hillary Clinton, Barbra Streisand, Liza Minnelli, Candice Bergen, the last four of whom wore her 1993 cold-shoulder gown. 'The ball of the shoulder,' said Karan, 'is the only part of a woman's body that does not age. A woman never gains weight at her shoulder point.'

In 2002, Karan sold her company to LVMH, the European luxury conglomerate. However, its heart remained in America, a country where women aspire to look neither hard-edged and threatening in the boardroom nor vulgarly seductive in the bedroom. The urban American woman, an achiever in her chosen field, wants to look grown-up, intelligent, confident and in control of her own sensuality. It's a balance that Karan is uniquely skilled at maintaining. So some observers were not surprised that, when she left the company in 2015, LVMH phased out Donna Karan International, and appointed Dao-Yi Chow and Maxwell Osbourne to design at DKNY. In 2016 it sold all the company's brands to the G-III Apparel Group (manufacturer of Calvin Klein and Tommy Hilfiger clothes), which signed an exclusive deal with Macy's to market DKNY.

Karan has retained her lifestyle brand Urban Zen, started in 2007 as a commercial companion piece to her charitable foundation of the same name. 'We were selling soulful, global handcrafted products to support the Foundation,' she wrote in her autobiography, *My Journey*. The clothes that she designed with Mark Kroeker were

> the kind of pieces I've always wanted: high-end styles that transcended fashion and were all about comfort. We designed a capsule collection of easy tops, palazzo pants, a jumpsuit, a few cashmere pieces and some scarves. There was no retail strategy behind them, only the desire to make clothes I personally wanted. It was incredibly freeing to design for myself again and not to have to cater to an established customer's expectations or the industry's rigid schedule.

Further reading: *My Journey* (2015) by Donna Karan tells her own story. Ingrid Sischy's *The Journey of a Woman: 20 Years of Donna Karan* (2004) contains all the major advertising imagery and an extended interview with the designer. For context, Valerie Steele's *Women of Fashion* (1991) is excellent.

Part Six

1990s

Image 44.3 *Donna Karan, autumn/winter 1988. Niall McInerney, Photographer. © Bloomsbury Publishing Plc.*

Introduction

The 1990s saw a decisive rejection of the power dressing of the previous decade. Fashion became minimal and decidedly low key in the early years of the 1990s. Grey was the preferred colour, and slimline silhouettes with narrow shoulders dominated the fashion catwalks. Names such as Germany's Jil Sander and Austria's Helmut Lang focused on evolution rather than revolution, advancing step by step. Both were arch-minimalists, Lang achieving a cult following and playing by his own rules (to pick two marketing innovations among many: he showed his autumn/winter 1998 online and advertised his brand on New York taxis).

For a while, this led to a new emphasis on casual style (American casualwear retailer Gap was a hip choice in the early years of the decade). There was also a deviation into grunge, a dress-down look inspired by rock bands and teenagers from Seattle, picked up by young designer *Marc Jacobs*. A more conceptual response was the deconstructionism of Belgium's *Martin Margiela*, creating new shapes by rethinking garments in their component parts.

The sense of moderation could not last. Dolce & Gabbana, in their very irreverent way, Gianni Versace (until his death in 1997) and *Tom Ford* at Gucci led a return to glamour. Ford's success encouraged the business trend for hot young designers to be parachuted in to revive venerable old fashion houses. The globalisation of fashion advanced apace through the decade, creating untold wealth for luxury brands but also prompting fears about the homogenisation of world culture.

The fashion show became ever-more spectacular, driven by big budget spending and the rise of the supermodels. Names such as Linda Evangelista, Christy Turlington, Naomi Campbell and Cindy Crawford had their every move (and hair colour) documented and discussed. From the mid-1990s, the press scrum descended on fashion weeks in ever-greater numbers, while many countries, from Brazil to Australia, sought to find a place on the international fashion map through their own fashion weeks. On an uneven playing field, though, Western designers remained dominant – the Europeans and Americans had decades of history and all the marketing cards stacked in their favour.

The boundaries between high and low culture were being pulled down throughout the 1990s. Designers stole from the street as much as the street stole from designers. Cross-cultural references were piled high. Whereas designers working in previous decades of the twentieth century had tended to reference one earlier decade, the 1990s saw *every* decade of the century plundered and remixed.

Retro fever swept through fashion, worn best by the supermodels, although by the end of the decade they in turn were replaced as cover girls by Hollywood celebrities once again.

Always ready to challenge the status quo was the intellectual *Miuccia Prada*, who became influential for her deliberate championing of 'bad taste', including 1970s furnishings prints. *Marc Jacobs* was the ultimate magpie designer, a creative maelstrom of talent. Furiously talented British designer John Galliano led the way for a revival of haute couture in a modern idiom. Another Brit, *Alexander McQueen*, combined beauty and savagery in his exhilarating shows. Besides the mould-breaking and constantly innovative *Martin Margiela*, British designers, including conceptualist Hussein Chalayan, created the most buzz in the final years of the twentieth century, often emerging from the hothouse of London's Central Saint Martins School of Art & Design.

45

Miuccia Prada (1949–)

Prada is a risk-taker, constantly pushing the boundaries of taste.

When Miuccia Prada, who had a PhD in political science but no fashion or design experience, took over the family business in 1978, she did so with gritted teeth. But this Italian intellectual went on to become the most consistently influential international designer through both the 1990s and Noughties. Perhaps her status as an outsider gave her a broader vision of fashion design, understanding how it fits into the wider creative firmament and beyond to the world of politics and current events. Even today, she stays relatively aloof from the fashion game, with a much-cited penchant for walking in the mountains in her spare time, wearing the dirndl skirts of her youth.

As the journalist Alessandra Galloni pointed out in 2007, Miuccia Prada has spent most of her career apologising for what she does, her collections expressing her own ambivalence towards her involvement in fashion. By the time she had reached her mid-fifties, she had formulated a strong case for fashion, convincing herself (as much as anyone else) of its importance and relevance in society. 'It's true women often don't want to admit it. And yet fashion enthralls everyone. … Some say it's about seduction, but I think that's limiting. What you wear is how you present yourself to the world, especially today, when human contacts are so quick. Fashion is instant language.' She is a risk-taker, constantly pushing the boundaries of taste, including her own, excited by the challenge of moving fashion forward. Each of her collections, said Ingrid Sischy, editor of *Interview* magazine, is 'some kind of throwing down the gauntlet to established ways of thinking.' An outstanding example of this was her autumn/winter 2008 collection in which she explored lace, treating its reinvention as an intellectual challenge. Her starting point was to avoid the colour white. Lace, for her, was an opportunity to explore ambiguity, to posit a series of interpretations, although in the final analysis she expressed herself still uncertain. 'I still don't understand why I like lace,' she said. 'But it is such an accompaniment of women, through childhood, marriage and being a widow.'

Image 45.1 *Prada, autumn/winter 1997. Niall McInerney, Photographer. © Bloomsbury Publishing Plc.*

The very speed of change in fashion both frightens and enthrals Prada. 'In the end, I like the changes,' she said in an interview in 2004.

> In fashion, once you've got something, you're already thinking about what's next. ... Every day I'm thinking about change, it's a constant anxiety and probably a reflection of society's anxiety in general. The big deal about fashion is really very recent, this hysterical pursuit of newness. It may be a good thing, or a bad thing, but it's really defining this moment.

Suzy Menkes, fashion editor of *The International Herald Tribune*, made the contrast with many of Prada's contemporaries in fashion: 'While designers mostly live in a fashion bubble, she has an urgent connection to what is happening in the world. ... No other creator has the same ability to distil the essence of what is modern, sampling the cultural heritage, anchoring shifting society and making it all seem relevant.' Paradoxically, Miuccia the intellectual has recently sought to theorise less about fashion, voicing a plea in interviews that the clothes should simply be allowed to speak for themselves. While enjoying the pressures of the modern fashion system and its commercial imperatives, she has also gone through periods of depression over its constant demands. 'Now the world is so complicated and loud, unless you scream no one listens,' she said in 2006 with a hint of resignation. Her youthful enthusiasm for communism has clearly influenced her approach to design: challenging bourgeois notions of good taste, opting for the unconventional time after time, creating seemingly ugly colour combinations and looks that both bemuse and enchant. Ironically, the price tags on her accessories and clothes put them out of reach of all but the wealthy – a paradox that has certainly not escaped her attention.

Like many great designers, she was a double act from the beginning, having met her husband Patrizio Bertelli shortly after she took over at Prada. A passionate, combative personality, Bertelli was a supplier to Prada through his company, I Pellettieri d'Italia, based in Arezzo. He is generally considered the business brains behind the growth of Prada, although his wife has emphasised his creative contribution, too. 'If I hadn't met him, I probably would have given up – or at least not been able to do what I have done,' she said. In the late 1990s, Prada developed into a group of designer labels, overextending itself through ambitious acquisitions that delivered poor returns. The financial fallout, which took many years to sort through, hampered the growth of Prada but did not stop Miuccia from producing a stream of outstanding collections that delighted and baffled fashion buyers and editors in equal measure.

Grandfather Mario Prada founded Fratelli Prada, an Italian leather goods business, in 1913. Miuccia was born Maria Bianchi in 1949 to Luigi Bianchi and Luisa Prada and had an isolated childhood for reasons that are still unclear but that culminated in her being adopted by her mother's sister in adulthood. By the time she reached university in the late 1960s, the student wave of political activism was at its height. Miuccia, with a PhD in political science in her sights, was captivated by the energy of the period, signing up to the Communist Party and becoming fully engaged in the fight against capitalism. She has played down this period in interviews: 'I was young in the Sixties, when

Italian society was first becoming obsessed with consumerism, but my big dreams were of justice, equality and moral regeneration. I was a Communist but being left wing was fashionable then. I was no different from thousands of middle-class kids.'

However, she had another side to her intense personality – that of the bohemian with a creative streak, dressing in Yves Saint Laurent for a student march, studying mime at Milan's Teatro Piccolo. All this changed in 1978 when she took over Prada, which had been run by her mother following her grandfather's decision to step aside after the Second World War. Progressing to the family business was a tough move, she recalled. 'You know, I had to have a lot of courage to do fashion,' Prada recalled, 'because in theory it was the least feminist work possible. And at that time, in the late Seventies, that was very complicated for me. Of course, I liked it a lot but I also wanted to do something more useful.'

Miuccia Prada's impact was not immediate. For seven years, she learned the nuts and bolts of her new trade, developing experience and confidence with the support of Patrizio. She did not sketch, preferring to work at a conceptual level, and then building a collection from there. The breakthrough came in 1985, when Prada sidestepped the family heritage in leather and produced a collection of heavy-duty nylon bags that became must-haves for fashion editors the world over –with their readers in hot pursuit just a step behind. The handbag was reborn as a key fashion accessory, while nylon was rediscovered as a fashionable material. The nylon bags rapidly turned the Prada label into a fashion powerhouse, although it was another four years before Miuccia launched ready-to-wear in 1988. Her first collections received a mixed response, but by the end of the decade were setting the tone for a new spirit of minimalism, following on from a decade characterised by excess and extravagance. 'The reason Prada works is because it whispers, it doesn't shout,' she has said. 'If you want to be recognised wearing my clothes, you can be. And if you don't, you don't have to be.'

Image 45.2 *Miuccia Prada at a show, mid-1990s. Niall McInerney, Photographer. © Bloomsbury Publishing Plc.*

But sometimes Prada could shout – regularly, her collections oozed a sense of a designer challenging her own instincts, attempting to work against her own notions of good taste, as if embarked on an intellectual exercise for personal stimulus. 'It's very easy to know what I like and it's very easy to do what I like. But I tend to have, let's say, good taste,' she said. 'This is very boring for me. So, basically, I have to work with what I think is bad and wrong. In my company they're always worried about that, everyone is always complaining.' Prada says she is rarely interested in a look. She works on a concept, often referencing the past, but resolute about making it contemporary. For her spring/summer 2009 collection, she drew criticism for sending the models down the runway in python-skin platform heels (some of them fell over). The clothes themselves –'cave-woman couture', she called them – were still more provocative, deconstructed, mixed up, crinkled and rumpled. It was an exercise in sophisticated seduction that puzzled and excited her audience in equal measure.

With her interest in other creative forms, Miuccia set up the Prada Foundation in 1993 to showcase leading contemporary artists. Outside her office window, she installed a playground slide that descended three levels; this playful touch was in fact an artwork by Carsten Höller. She also worked with leading architects on her stores, including Rem Koolhaas for New York and Herzog & de Meuron for Tokyo. An installation, titled *Waist Down*, which toured Asia, America and Europe in 2005 and 2006, highlighted both her seriousness and playfulness with its focus on skirts designed by Miuccia, including her popular circle skirts. In 2008, she commissioned a short animation, *Trembled Blossoms*, to mark the spring collection, a lush landscape of flowers and nymphs with suggestions of Art Nouveau, Liberty and Aubrey Beardsley. Other projects have included temporary architecture-specific wallpapers, environments and interactive media for the Prada Epicenters in New York, Beverly Hills and Tokyo in a series of collaborations.

The fashion business grew simultaneously. A second label, Miu Miu (her nickname), was launched in 1992, bringing the Prada vision to a wider audience. Prada Sport followed in 1994. In the late 1990s, Prada Group joined in the enthusiasm of the time for acquisition, snapping up an extraordinary portfolio of labels, including three of the most admired designers of the era – Austria's Helmut Lang, Germany's Jil Sander and France's Azzedine Alaïa. This marriage of talents proved disastrous: Sander resigned twice as the business that bore her name struggled to break even, while investment was unsuccessfully lavished on turning Helmut Lang into a superstar. Prada Group hinted at a stock market flotation on a number of occasions in an effort to put its finances back in order, only to cancel time and time again. When the global economic crisis erupted in late 2008, Miuccia Prada was left lamely musing that maybe her business was not the kind of business that was best suited to the financial markets. The more high-profile scrutiny of the markets would certainly not be to her tastes. Prada herself avoids the celebrity circuit. 'I am a very private person and don't like the high-profile nature of the fashion business. It's dangerous to have such a large public image and I'm not as interested as some designers in becoming famous because it would take away the realities of my life.'

She has adapted more enthusiastically than many of her contemporaries to the speeding up of the fashion system in the early twenty-first century. This trend was driven by the fast fashion of mass-market companies such as Spanish retail brand Zara. As a young woman, Miuccia Prada was content to develop an idea that could be relevant for six months. By 2008, however, she commented that an idea might satisfy her for two days. The turnover of ideas has become ferocious, she acknowledged. 'My goal now is to change our stores every two months – that's what I would like.' Through the 2010s, she continued to make Prada an ever-relevant force on the catwalk. Highlights included the bold electric colours and stripes of spring/summer 2011; the collection of her greatest hits for autumn/winter 2013 inspired by the cinema and specifically film noir; and the layered, mixed-up beauty of the autumn/winter 2016 collection replete with cryptic allusions, details and hints of a response to troubled political times. In 2019, Prada under the direction of Miuccia appeared as relevant as it had ever been to the creative debate that constantly runs through the best of designer fashion.

An eloquent interviewee, Miuccia Prada has made comments over the years that reflect the insecurities that many people working within the fashion industry share as to the true status of their chosen profession. Her brilliance has been to turn this insecurity to powerful use through a series of inspirational collections, driving forward fashion to its current status as a key component of modern popular culture. In 2016, she said that commercial considerations were becoming less important for her. 'I am a fashion designer and I do a commercial job, but at the same time we want to be creative and we always want to push limits. … I really want to focus on what I like, what I care about.'

Further reading: Miuccia Prada speaks brilliantly about her own work, so interviews with her are frequently illuminating. An essential read is 'Miuccia Prada & Raf Simons', her conversation with Simons in *System* magazine issue 8 (autumn/winter 2016). Vanessa Friedman's interview for *Ten* (autumn 2000) is interesting.

Image 45.3 *Prada, spring/summer 1998. Niall McInerney, Photographer.* © Bloomsbury Publishing Plc.

46

Martin Margiela (1959–)

Margiela sensed what was coming, what was in the air. He was looking seasons ahead.

The emergence of the Belgian designers in the late 1980s was one of the more unexpected twists in fashion history. A country with no great reputation for fashion produced not simply one but a veritable profusion of design talent, spawning a movement that continues to throw up surprises into the twenty-first century. Top of the list from the original wave was Martin Margiela, who showed new ways of wearing familiar clothes, drawing on inspiration from flea markets and introducing a new kind of fashion that was swiftly labelled deconstructionist, with a stripped-down functionalist aesthetic.

Although not one of the so-called Antwerp Six, who first showed their work collectively at London Fashion Week in the mid-1980s, Margiela is regularly categorised together with his fellow Belgian near-contemporaries (the most influential of the other six was Ann Demeulemeester, and the most commercially successful was Dries Van Noten). The Belgians all imbibed the earnest hard-working fashion aesthetic of their college, Antwerp's Royal Academy of Fine Art, developing outstanding technical skills coupled with a high seriousness in their approach to fashion design. Antwerp, at the heart of Flanders, was also the centre of a broader cultural boom, reflecting the rising confidence and dominance of the Dutch-speaking north of Belgium.

Margiela's high seriousness was approved in France, where the conceptual approach to fashion design has always been respected. An exhibition staged in Rotterdam in 1997 featured a collaboration between the designer and a microbiologist. Margiela chose one outfit from the eighteen collections he had made to date, recreated in white, then sprayed with mould and yeast and allowed to grow. Another snapshot of Margiela's approach: in spring 1998, he produced a collection full of flat garments inspired by the shape of plastic supermarket shopping bags. The seams were cut so that the clothes could lie flat, demonstrated in the show by men in white coats carrying around the clothes on hangers. A season later, he showed T-shirt dresses on ten life-size wooden puppets, with the folds heat-bonded to polythene vinyl. All this was a fashion conceptualist's heaven. Likewise, the stores, often in obscure

Image 46.1 *Maison Martin Margiela, spring/summer 1999. Niall McInerney, Photographer.* © Bloomsbury *Publishing Plc.*

locations with no name above the door, became cult locations. A recurring feature of the shops was a line of thrift store sofas and chairs, covered by one continuous white slipcover. Footprints on the white carpeting were stamped with one of Margiela's signature Tabi boots dipped in black ink. The previous life of the store location was respected; thus, in Taipei, where Margiela opened in a former fast-food restaurant, the burger bar's original fixtures were retained and simply painted white.

Martin Margiela was born in 1959 and grew up in Genk in the Limburg region of Flanders. After studying in Antwerp in the late 1970s (some years before Demeulemeester, Van Noten and Dirk Bikkembergs), he initially found work designing raincoats for a Belgian firm and then briefly worked in Italy. But Margiela's heart was set on the higher planes of creativity and for him there was only one place to learn – Jean Paul Gaultier, the great iconoclast of Parisian fashion, who was at the peak of his influence in the mid-1980s. Margiela applied several times for work at Gaultier's studio; sheer persistence eventually got him through the door. Margiela left Gaultier after three years to set up his own business with friend Jenny Meirens, who had run a boutique in Antwerp. The business was financed on a shoestring through well-paid commercial work for Italian manufacturers. For all the uncompromising aesthetic of his own label, Margiela was from the beginning a highly versatile designer, as was made clear a decade later in 1998 with his appointment as womenswear designer at the house of Hermès.

Margiela's early collections instantly intrigued buyers from Europe's more avant-garde stores, although few placed orders. His first collection featured the exceptionally narrow shoulder – Margiela called it the 'cigarette shoulder' – which was a statement of defiance at a time when 1980s power dressing ruled. In October 1989, he caused a sensation by showing his collection on a rubble-strewn wasteland in the twentieth arrondissement of Paris. The models stumbled down a makeshift catwalk with eyes painted white, wearing plastic dresses, papier mâché tops, jackets with the sleeves ripped off, skirts apparently made from lining materials and oversized men's trousers. It was an experimental tour de force, making the mainstream shows of the Paris season seem blandly conventional. Geert Bruloot, owner of Louis, an Antwerp store, was an early supporter and friend: 'It was a shock, but it was also a revelation. Margiela sensed what was coming, what was in the air. He was looking seasons ahead, taking the most everyday kind of clothes and showing new ways of wearing them.' Other designers, such as Helmut Lang and Jean Colonna, were also presenting a challenge to the major fashion houses, following the challenge that Japanese designers such as Rei Kawakubo and Yohji Yamamoto had presented several years earlier. The deconstructionist designer believed in showing precisely what he was doing, with hemlines unfinished, stitches visible and even the tailor's markings retained. Fashion, he believed, was not an art – it was a craft, 'a technical know-how' for the wearer to explore and enjoy.

Drawing inspiration from flea markets or street style, Margiela would turn sometimes ordinary clothes into fashion by mixing and changing the shapes and fabrics. In the process, he challenged conventional ideas of what fashion could be, showing new ways of wearing familiar items. He also took little notice of the pressures of the modern fashion system to come up with new ideas every six

Image 46.2 *Maison Martin Margiela, spring/summer 1996. Niall McInerney, Photographer.* © *Bloomsbury Publishing Plc.*

months, preferring to refine and develop concepts over several seasons, revisiting garments again and again. His autumn/winter 1993 collection displayed the breadth of his influences and his willingness to acknowledge his sources, including a dress made from four black flea-market dresses sewn together and a nineteenth-century priest's coat that the designer liked so much he did not tamper with the original design. In 2001, academic Rebecca Arnold argued that Margiela's approach 'undermined the notion of designer as unique, individual creator, by conceding that each design is the product of fashion's history'. She saw Margiela sharing the same spirit as Japanese designer Rei Kawakubo, recognising imperfection as 'a route to authenticity … in contrast to fashion's traditional role as the purveyor of ephemeral, perfect fantasies'.

By the early 1990s, the designer had already achieved an exceptional status, paradoxically fuelled by his reluctance to meet the fashion media, let alone give interviews. Innate shyness was certainly one reason for this. However, he also preferred people to look at his clothes rather than him. A statement from Maison Margiela said: 'The withdrawal of a designer's profile creates a space that the garments may fill.' Back in March 1993 he briefly relented and invited a handful of journalists (including Roger Tredre) to his atelier on the boulevard Saint-Denis. Wearing his trademark navy blue peaked cap with black jeans and a black T-shirt, he explained why he was so media shy: 'I wanted to express myself through the clothes, and consolidate in that way.' The veil of secrecy was reimposed shortly afterwards, with interviews conducted by fax or email with the team rather than with Margiela the individual. The first Margiela label, a scrap of muslin inscribed with no name, no words, was in itself a statement questioning the modern designer system. From 1997, Margiela introduced a series of labels differentiated only by numbers.

Margiela often preferred to present his clothes on real people rather than models. In an interview with *The Independent* newspaper in 1999, he and his team commented: 'It remains … important for us that someone finds their way of dressing as opposed to a way of dressing as prescribed by anyone else or an overriding trend'. All of the house's collections were identified with a number system, from 0 to 23. Number 1 was (and still is) the women's wear collection; number 14 is men's wear.

Margiela's arrival at Hermès in 1998 shocked both insiders and outsiders at the venerable French house. Hermès boss Jean-Louis Dumas had become aware of Margiela's work through his daughter, an actress, who had modelled for the designer. Dumas invited him to lunch at his home in early 1997 and considered him 'a good rider for a good horse', using equine terminology in keeping with the house's tradition. His first show was a low-key kind of triumph, the Margiela iconoclasm tempered by his new role. The versatility of the clothing was a key note, including a coat that could be turned into a cape and seamless sweaters that could be worn inside out. Writer Rebecca Mead, in a profile for *The New Yorker*, called them 'quietly subversive. Stripped of all ostentation, they were to be valued from the inside, even if the wearer risked drabness'. In 2003 Margiela was succeeded at Hermès by his one-time mentor, Jean Paul Gaultier.

Margiela's long-time uncompromising approach did not translate into overnight business success. Development was slow and often difficult. His first store did not open until the year 2000, in Tokyo. Most of his stores were in hard-to-find locations with fascia that were only intelligible to the insider. Financial pressures recurred, hindering the development of the house. By 2002, the company found a sympathetic investor and kindred spirit in Renzo Rosso, owner of Diesel, Italy's innovative denim brand. Rosso became a majority shareholder and replaced Jenny Meirens as president, helping to bankroll retail openings in key fashion cities, including London and New York. But Margiela and Meirens continued to run the business and make the creative decisions. 'I love this man', Rosso said, promising a hands-off approach. 'This is not an acquisition. I'm not buying a fashion company like other groups have done. I'm investing in Margiela so two friends can work together to grow a very special brand'.

The deal was a pivotal moment for Margiela's business. After a low-key start to the new relationship, a period marked by heavy investment in shops and production, sales shot up in 2007 by 50 per cent to 60 million euros, driven by the designer's popularity in Japan. Margiela moved into new territory, launching both a fragrance and jewellery. A shop was opened on Via Spiga, Milan's celebrated fashion street. A new wave of professionalism swept through the business side of the company. That Maison Margiela changed dramatically in character was not in doubt. Margiela had become part of a larger experiment by Renzo Rosso to create an alternative kind of luxury fashion group. For a short while, all seemed promising, but in truth Margiela had had enough of the fashion system. In 2008, he resigned, quitting the world of fashion. His departure was so discreet that it was not publicly revealed until December 2009.

In late 2018, responding to a special prize at the Belgian Fashion Awards, he explained his decision to retire. The year 2008 was, he said, 'the very year I felt that I could not cope any more with the worldwide increasing pressure and the overgrowing demands of trade. I also regretted the overdose of information carried by social media, destroying the "thrill of wait" and cancelling every effect of surprise, so fundamental for me.' He concluded on a more positive note, observing 'a growing interest for creativity in fashion by some upcoming designers'. And Maison Margiela has endured, driven creatively by John Galliano since 2014.

Margiela's lasting influence as a designer can be observed everywhere, including the denim sector, where the recycling and deconstruction of styles are well-established. A new generation of young designers has also drawn inspiration from his work. In the twenty-first century, when the issues around sustainability have become ever-more pressing, Margiela may come to be seen as a true pioneer of a new way forward for fashion.

Further reading: Academic Rebecca Arnold makes interesting observations in *Fashion, Desire and Anxiety* (2001). Margiela was well profiled in 'The Crazy Professor' (1998) by Rebecca Mead for *The New Yorker*. *WWD* has reported his career thoroughly, not least through the writing of Paris editor Miles Socha, such as 'Art versus Commerce: Can Margiela Expand Without Selling Out?' (2 May 2008).

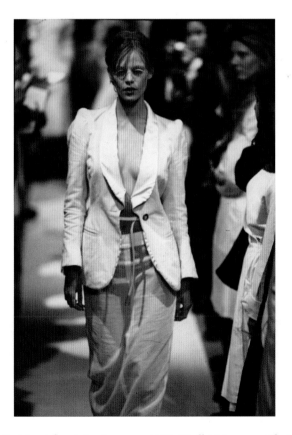

Image 46.3 *Maison Martin Margiela, spring/summer 1993. Niall McInerney, Photographer.* © *Bloomsbury Publishing Plc.*

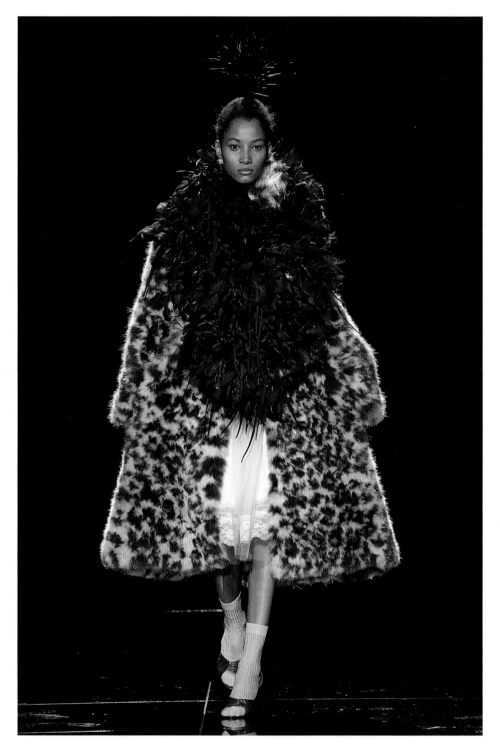

Image 47.1 *Marc Jacobs, autumn/winter 2019. Photo: Victor VIRGILE/Gamma-Rapho via Getty Images.*

47

Marc Jacobs (1963–)

Jacobs was for many years the designer of his generation most copied by the international chain stores.

If you wanted to feel the pulse of modern fashion in the first decade of the twenty-first century, then Marc Jacobs was invariably the best designer to check out. No other designer so consistently influenced the broader clothing market in the decade, a period when fashion was moving with oft bewildering speed from one extreme to another. To his critics, the American designer's collections were dominated by too many pastiches of previous periods, particularly the 1970s, a decade to which he has returned time and time again. To his fans, including most fashion editors and many fashion industry professionals, he was the endlessly inventive New Yorker who had injected a fresh street-inspired spirit into designer fashion. Anna Wintour, editor of American *Vogue* and a long-time admirer, highlighted his knack for 'making the conservative seem cool … and making the cool seem conservative'.

In a fashion world more competitive than ever before, Marc Jacobs is one of a very small group of designers to have survived the buffetings of building a label from scratch, although his label lost momentum in the second half of the 2010s. The patronage and investment of Bernard Arnault, chairman of LVMH, the world's largest luxury conglomerate, has been critical. While his celebrated grunge collection of 1993 established him as a designer with a street touch, the primary note of much of his work in the 2000s was a sense of elegance. Consider his collection of autumn/ winter 2007, a homage to the Yves Saint Laurent of the 1970s, thoroughly grown-up and (like all of his clothes) eminently wearable. Marc Jacobs may not have created any striking new design innovations or silhouettes, but he enthusiastically responded to the rapid turnover of trends in the fast fashion era and was for many years the designer of his generation most copied by the international chain stores.

Although considered by many of his supporters to be the ultimate downtown designer, in truth Marc Jacobs is uptown by origin, growing up in his grandmother's apartment on the Upper West

Side of Manhattan. Perhaps it is the fusion of uptown sophistication mixed with downtown youthful energy and street vibe that best explains his attraction to a wide cross-section of customers.

The full story of Jacobs's childhood is shrouded in some mystery, but the bare facts are that his father, who worked at the William Morris talent agency, died when he was only seven; his mother remarried several times and spent time in various hospitals. The young Jacobs was brought up by his grandmother rather than his mother. Materially, he was comfortably off, although one can only guess at the psychological impact of losing a parent so young. His grandmother took him to New York department store Bergdorf Goodman and encouraged him in his interest in fashion. 'One big thing she taught me was that quality was more important than quantity,' Jacobs recalled many years later. Jacobs grew up fast, realising at an early age that he was gay, checking out copies of *Playgirl* magazine, but has spoken of his insecurity as a young man. At the age of just fifteen, his uncle, who was president of the same agency where Jacobs's father had worked, arranged work experience for him in the company's mailroom. One of the agents, covering music, secured him guest-list entry to gigs: 'I loved anything garagey rough – the Speedies, the Screams or Gang of Four,' he recalled decades later in an interview with *Rolling Stone.* 'I would get turned on by a band's look first, and once I did, I found I actually liked the music.' This love of music has remained a constant through his career.

He enrolled in the High School of Art and Design and worked at the fashionable New York boutique Charivari, encouraged by buyer Barbara Weiser who took him (aged just twenty) with her on a tour to Japan. The story goes that the designer Perry Ellis walked into Charivari one day, whereupon Jacobs asked him for career advice. Go to Parsons, said Ellis, referring to New York's Parsons School of Design, the preeminent fashion design college in America. At Parsons, Jacobs made an exceptional impact, creating a student collection in 1984 of sweaters handmade by his grandmother and inspired by the British artist, Bridget Riley. They won him two prestigious Gold Thimble Awards. Among the guests at the awards event was Robert Duffy, a young and ambitious businessman, who swiftly became Jacobs's long-term business partner, sticking with him and guiding him through a decade of see-saw swings in fortune. Duffy, who worked for Reuben Thomas, a Seventh Avenue dress company, persuaded his boss to launch a new collection, named Sketchbook, designed by Jacobs. The first collection, for spring 1985, included spectacularly large hand-knitted sweaters with bright pink smiley faces. From the very beginning, Jacobs was a designer who believed in an upbeat smiley message for a young generation.

Jacobs's career trajectory in the late 1980s went through a series of twists and turns. Dropped by Reuben Thomas, he worked briefly with Canadian clothing magnate Jack Atkins, followed by a company called Epoch-3 and then Kashiyama-USA. His breakthrough came in 1988 when he was appointed vice-president of design at Perry Ellis (the designer had died in 1986), with his business partner Robert Duffy as president. This was a remarkable achievement for a designer who was only twenty-five, sparking a storm of media interest and gossip on Seventh Avenue. For five years, Jacobs's

Image 47.2 *Marc Jacobs with Linda Evangelista, autumn/ winter 1995. Niall McInerney, Photographer. © Bloomsbury Publishing Plc.*

Image 47.3 *Marc Jacobs, autumn/winter 1995. Niall McInerney, Photographer. © Bloomsbury Publishing Plc.*

creative progress at Perry Ellis was scrutinised, analysed and discussed in merciless detail. Already, the Jacobs signature – youthful, playful, ironic, accessible – was apparent. His steady creative evolution reached a peak with his spring/summer 1993 collection, the so-called grunge collection, inspired by the street and music scene in Seattle, Washington, and the music of Sonic Youth. Ironically, that scene was defiantly anti-fashion, favouring vintage store clothes and combining styles and influences in a deliberately haphazard manner. Jacobs's catwalk take on this Seattle style caused a maelstrom of media excitement, not all of it complimentary. It was an important moment for high fashion, prompting a reassessment of what designer fashion could mean. Although many designers before Jacobs, most notably Jean Paul Gaultier, had ransacked the energy of the street and music scene, few did so with the assurance of Jacobs. Looking back more than a decade later, he said: 'It was my vision and interpretation of street clothes, with the imperfection that I've always loved. It was also a reflection of the attitude of young people towards fashion.'

However, the response from the designer's bosses at Perry Ellis, who had shown courage in approving his appointment in the first place, was unremittingly negative. They considered the grunge collection a step too far, believing it trampled on the Perry Ellis signature and would spell commercial disaster. Jacobs and Duffy were summarily fired. It was a shock, but Jacobs bounced back within three seasons, showing on a shoestring budget in a downtown loft, with star models lending support and the entire New York industry begging for a ticket. Jacobs moved on to another plane in 1997, when Bernard Arnault, chairman of LVMH, signed him as creative director to develop ready-to-wear for Louis Vuitton, the jewel in the crown of his luxury group. The challenge for Jacobs was to develop a signature style for Vuitton, which was known almost exclusively as a luxury luggage and accessories brand. 'My designs are more eclectic, romantic and quite small-scale,' he acknowledged to *WWD*.

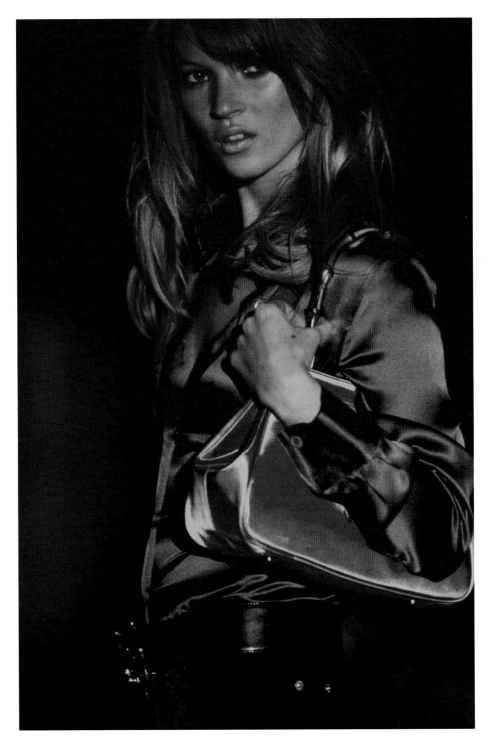

Image 48.1 *Model Kate Moss, Gucci, autumn/winter 1995. Niall McInerney, Photographer. © Bloomsbury Publishing Plc.*

48

Tom Ford (1962–)

He has an obsessive, perfectionist eye. No detail of the Gucci brand renaissance escaped his eye.

American designer Tom Ford made his name as a dynamic force in fashion in the 1990s, responsible for a spectacular makeover of the historic Italian fashion house of Gucci. More than that, he was, in the words of John Demsey, president of Estée Lauder, 'the combustion that drove the entire Nineties'. While Karl Lagerfeld dominated the 1980s, Ford was the star of the 1990s, becoming as much a celebrity as the many famous names he dressed. A natural inheritor of the mantle of Halston, Ford had an immaculate personal sense of style, combined with an ability to articulate his vision in interviews that made him a hot favourite with fashion editors. He was – and still is – also preternaturally handsome. As Graydon Carter, editor-in-chief of *Vanity Fair*, put it: 'Virtually all women who meet him want to have sex with him.' And a good number of men, too.

By the late 2010s, Tom Ford had turned his own-name brand, first launched in 2004 with eyewear and fragrances, into a money-spinning multi-product empire. Ford always had an all-embracing vision of fashion, driving the mood during the 1990s when fashion became an ever-more influential form of popular culture. 'For me fashion doesn't stop at clothes,' said Ford. 'Fashion is everything. Art, music, furniture design, hair, makeup … all those things go together to make a moment in time.' Ford also smashed any lingering hang-ups about sexuality and sex in the modern world. Anna Wintour, editor of American *Vogue*, noted his work was 'always charged with some kind of erotic frisson'. He was open about his homosexuality, living with the fashion writer Richard Buckley. He explored sexuality fully in his work for Gucci and expropriated imagery from the world of pornography for some controversial advertising campaigns: he always claimed people looked best naked rather than clothed. 'Sex,' he said, with all the confidence in the world, 'is something that I think about all the time.' Did his more controversial advertising images objectify women? Ford batted the question aside, saying he objectified men just as much: 'I'm an equal opportunity objectifier.'

Despite his influence and status, there was a view that Ford himself had limited design talents and played more the role of impresario or stylist for his hard-working design studio. It was a charge he deeply resented. 'It just drives me crazy,' he said in an interview for the book *Tom Ford*, published after he left Gucci. 'I don't pose around in a white lab coat with bolts of fabric on the floor like Yves did. But I've been working in this business for twenty years. I know how to cut a dress; I can climb on the table and cut it with scissors and pin it down.' He was proud to be a commercial designer, saying he never wanted to be anything else. His job, he said, was to make women beautiful. 'I feel fashion more than I think it,' he said. 'My first instinct is gut.'

He also has an obsessive, perfectionist eye. No detail of the Gucci brand renaissance escaped his eye. Nothing was too mundane for his attention. *Vogue*'s Anna Wintour dubbed him the 'Flaubert of fashion', after the detail-obsessed French novelist of the nineteenth century. Ford created the 1990s template for a young designer to be brought in to revive an old brand. Karl Lagerfeld had led the way at Chanel in the 1980s, but Ford perfected the concept, setting a trend that led to Marc Jacobs at Louis Vuitton, John Galliano at Dior, and many more. However, in retrospect, it is clear that he overreached himself in his later years at Gucci. After Gucci Group's acquisition of Yves Saint Laurent in 1999, he appointed himself creative director of YSL. He drew a wave of criticism in France for his irreverent approach to the YSL legacy. In 2001, he sent out models in a men's wear show wearing YSL horn-rimmed glasses. 'They were a nod to Saint Laurent, but I did not want to be too literal,' Ford said. Saint Laurent snubbed the show and made his displeasure even clearer by attending the Dior menswear show on the following day. After leaving Gucci Group, Ford acknowledged that YSL was unfinished business. 'It just hasn't hit its stride yet. ... I wanted to conquer Saint Laurent.'

Tom Ford was born in San Marcos, Texas, in 1962, and grew up in Santa Fe, New Mexico. His grandmother was a flamboyant influence on his early years, teaching Ford the importance of good dress sense. By the age of twelve, he had his first pair of Gucci loafers. Already, his perfectionist temperament had emerged: he developed an exceptional visual eye, rearranging the furniture at home and eager to dress his family and friends to meet his own exacting standards. But fashion was not his initial calling. At eighteen, Ford arrived in New York to study art history at New York University. It was the back end of the 1970s, a decade that was a major inspiration for Ford at Gucci. Nightclub Studio 54 was a favourite haunt for the young man, who got to know Andy Warhol and his entourage. With his dazzling good looks, Ford made money as a leading male model and built an impressive circle of contacts in the fashion world. He dropped out of New York University to switch to Parsons School of Art, enrolling on the environmental design course. He transferred to the Paris branch of Parsons at the age of twenty, a move that had a profound impact. 'I cried the first time I walked around in Paris. Everything was so beautiful I just couldn't believe it. ... I felt instantly comfortable.'

His first job in fashion design was at Cathy Hardwick, who hired Ford because he was attractive rather than for any apparent brilliance in his portfolio. His natural flair for fashion rapidly developed,

Image 48.2 *Tom Ford on the catwalk at Gucci, 1990s. Niall McInerney, Photographer. © Bloomsbury Publishing Plc.*

Image 48.3 *Gucci, spring/summer 1996. Niall McInerney, Photographer. © Bloomsbury Publishing Plc.*

for he was poached in 1988 by Marc Jacobs and then moved to Perry Ellis as design director, a remarkable role for a man who was still only twenty-six. In 1989, Gucci, a historic but ailing label, hired Dawn Mello, an American retail executive who had transformed the fortunes of New York department store Bergdorf Goodman, to run the business. Although Mello stayed at Gucci little more than a year, it was she who made the key appointment of Ford to design womenswear, recommended by his long-time boyfriend, Richard Buckley (they married in 2014 and have one son). When Mello returned to New York and Bergdorf Goodman, Ford's role at Gucci became more prominent. By 1992, he was design director, but he clashed with Maurizio Gucci, who thought Ford was rather too fashion focused for a label with a history of classic style. Domenico De Sole, then director of Gucci's American operation, stepped in to save Ford. In the early 1990s, the company had to design a team approach, and Maurizio Gucci was usually involved to Ford's intense irritation. There were times when Ford was ready to return to America and start up his own label, but he hung on. 'I had this incredible drive,' he reflected later. 'I was going to be a successful fashion designer if it killed me.'

In 1994, Gucci was bought by Investcorp, an investment firm, and Ford was finally made creative director. A year later, the fashion world was shocked by the murder of Maurizio Gucci, gunned down in a contract killing organised by his ex-wife. Ironically, the year in which Maurizio Gucci died was also the year the brand exploded back into life. With Ford at the creative helm and Domenico De Sole established as chief executive, a partnership was created that turned Gucci into the most successful fashion label of the decade. No expense was spared in creating the Ford vision. Photographer Mario Testino and stylist Carine Roitfeld, later editor of French *Vogue*, were collaborators with Ford in creating the slick, sexy, modern Gucci style. His autumn/winter 1995 collection, shown in the spring of that year, was a high-octane tribute to the late 1970s, with blue velvet hipsters and satin shirts. It was judged a tour de force. Ford's moment had come.

By the autumn/winter 1996 collection, Ford's vision for Gucci was complete, with its revival of late 1970s' glamour combined with touches of history from the Gucci archive and an overriding dose of Italian modernism. The elements included pinstripe tailoring for women, red velvet tuxedos, white jersey gowns with peepholes and gold fastenings, dark eyes and a look of androgyny that recalled the work of photographer Helmut Newton. Sleek, sexy, modern, as Ford put it, claiming he had brought back 'a certain sexual glamour which we probably hadn't seen since the late Seventies, because of the way that AIDS altered fashion.' Separately, Ford was intensely involved in the business development of Gucci, and ailing licenses around the world were bought back or closed. Gucci stores were designed in collaboration with Bill Sofield, who created an alluring mix of clean lines and rich materials that summed up the new Gucci image. The Asian financial crisis of 1998 was only a blip in the label's forward momentum. Ford took creative risks, including a collection for spring/summer 1999 inspired by the singer and actress Cher, but press and buyers alike lapped it up. Under Ford and De Sole, Gucci Group became a business worth in excess of $4 billion and boasted a stable of names that included Yves Saint Laurent as well as young British designers Stella McCartney and Alexander McQueen.

Gucci Group, together with Bernard Arnault's LVMH, led the way in the true globalisation of luxury and pioneered the broadening of its customer base. As rising income levels around the world brought designer style within the reach of millions more people, designer labels were booming. They were now mass luxury brands, even if many of their customers reserved their spending for the fragrances and accessories rather than the clothes. Even the 9/11 terrorist attack on New York in 2001 appeared to have little effect on business: on the day of the attacks, the New York store of YSL received forty-two calls from women wanting the peasant blouse, Ford meticulously noted. The growth of the luxury sector led to a period of consolidation as leading luxury businesses sought to buy up brands with global potential. As part of this process, Gucci was itself the object of a titanic struggle for control between Bernard Arnault's LVMH and François Pinault's Pinault-Printemps-Redoute (PPR), ending in the law courts in Amsterdam. PPR won out in 2000, to Ford's approval. Four years later, however, PPR's efforts to exert greater managerial control over Gucci Group led to Ford's downfall.

The departure of both Ford and De Sole in 2004 was abrupt. Although the full details of the fallout are still unclear to this day, PPR executives clearly thought the spotlight of attention was too firmly focused on the personality of Ford himself. The designer was devastated by the outcome. 'I was depressed. I wallowed in self-pity,' he admitted in an interview. The self-pity did not last long: he launched his own Tom Ford label in 2004 with eyewear and fragrances, expanding into men's wear through a single Tom Ford store at 845 Madison Avenue in New York. In 2008, the concept was rolled out worldwide through linkups with leading designer retailers, with women's wear added in 2010. The Tom Ford label is driven by sharp super-deluxe tailoring and has a West Coast sense of glamour about it. The business is still expanding, with the recent addition of new skincare and cosmetics lines. Remarkably, through all this post-Gucci reinvention, Ford also found time to develop a long-nurtured career as a film director, directing *A Single Man*, based on a Christopher Isherwood novel, which was nominated for an Academy Award, and *Noctural Animals* (2016), which won a prize at the Venice Film Festival. Both films were well received, critics commenting on the brilliance of Ford's visual eye.

Ford has mellowed in recent years, living between Los Angeles, Santa Fe and London, content as a father and husband, even speaking approvingly of Alessandro Michele's work at Gucci. For charisma alone, Ford could arguably claim a place among the world's great designers. 'This job is a total ego thing in a way,' he acknowledged, the living embodiment of the designer as style dictator. 'To be a designer and say, "This is the way people should dress, this is the way their homes should look, this is the way the world should be."'

Further reading: Tom Ford produced an outstanding summary of his own career in a collaboration with writer Brigid Foley: *Tom Ford* (2004) features an extended interview with the designer and strong visual coverage of the highlights of his years at Gucci.

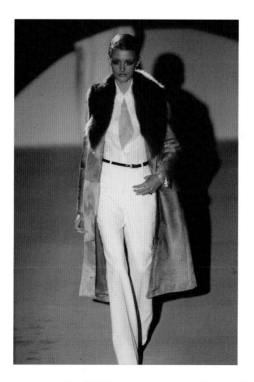

Image 48.4 *Gucci, autumn/winter 1996. Niall McInerney, Photographer. © Bloomsbury Publishing Plc.*

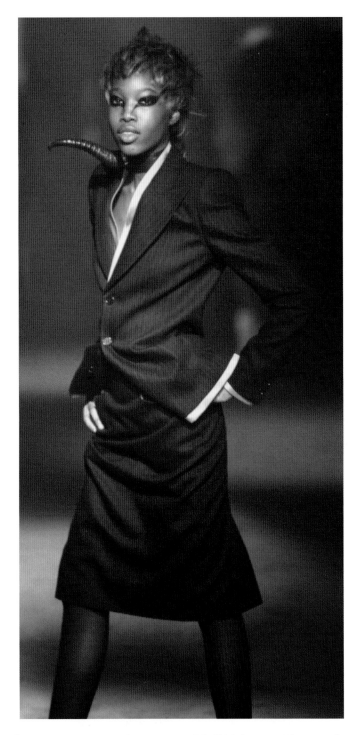

Image 49.1 *Alexander McQueen, autumn/winter 1997. Niall McInerney, Photographer. © Bloomsbury Publishing Plc.*

49

Alexander McQueen (1969–2010)

McQueen's work was shot through with autobiographical influences.

British fashion has produced countless young designers full of loudmouthed attitude and shock-tactics clothes. Many of them have sparkled briefly, like fireworks, only to fall swiftly to earth. However, Alexander McQueen, who could always out-swear his contemporaries and enjoyed creating a furore on and off the catwalk, proved an exceptional talent on the international stage before his death by suicide in 2010, aged forty, on the eve of his mother's funeral.

His success did not seem so likely back in 1996 when the young designer upset the Parisian fashion establishment after landing the job of head designer at Givenchy. McQueen swiftly alienated the French by making no attempt to speak French, deriding the still-revered Hubert de Givenchy as 'irrelevant', and producing a shockingly ill-judged first collection that even he admitted was 'crap'. In retrospect, the Givenchy experience, which lasted for four years, represented a huge learning curve for the designer.

By late 2000 – shortly before leaving Givenchy to the relief of both parties – McQueen secured his long-term future by selling 51 per cent of his own label to Gucci Group. In creative terms, the designer was also reinvigorated, producing inspired collections season after season presented through some of the most memorable fashion shows of the Noughties. At the heart of his collections was superbly constructed tailoring, cut with confidence and elan, skills which were applied to playing with the shape of the body. His best work had a certain toughness about it – he described his clothes as 'armour' – worn by women who want to look powerful. As he put it: 'It kind of fends people off. You have to have a lot of balls to talk to a woman wearing my clothes.'

McQueen's work was also shot through with autobiographical influences, a characteristic acknowledged by the designer many times. To take just one specific event from his own life: as an eight-year-old he witnessed one of his sisters being beaten up by her husband, a traumatic event that he said had a profound impact on his attitude to women and to his design. He joked that he was the fashion industry's therapist. Certainly, fashion shows with a disturbing undercurrent were a feature of his career, ranging from collections based on Hitchcock heroines, the cult film *Picnic at Hanging Rock*, the William Golding novel *Lord of the Flies* and asylums. 'My own living nightmares' was how he has described his presentations. Death and decay were McQueen preoccupations, summed up by a dress made from decaying flowers that featured in his autumn/winter 2007 collection. 'I just use things that people want to hide in their head,' he said in 2002. 'Things about war, religion, sex, things that we all think about but don't bring to the forefront. But I do, and force them to watch it.'

But while darkness was often dominant, romance was an equally integral feature of the McQueen vision of the world, as his long-term stylist and friend Katy England noted. 'We all carry both the dark and the light with us,' he said in 2008. 'I don't see why it shouldn't be reflected in my work.' He often saw beauty in the apparently ugly, with an aesthetic sense that chimed with contemporary British artists such as Jake and Dinos Chapman or Damien Hirst. 'I find beauty in the grotesque, like most artists,' he said in 2007. 'I have to force people to look at things.' This philosophy was explored brilliantly after his death in *Savage Beauty*, a sell-out exhibition staged in 2011 at the Metropolitan Museum of Art in New York and in 2015 at London's Victoria & Albert Museum. Designer Sarah Burton, who took over creative direction after McQueen's death, softened the savagery but retained the beauty (and obsessive technical excellence), designing royal bride Kate Middleton's wedding dress in 2011 and ensuring the long-term future of the Alexander McQueen label.

Lee Alexander McQueen, born in 1969, was the youngest of the six children of an East London cab driver, an unlikely background that media reports turned into the fairy-tale story of an East End rough lad made good. The designer, who rightly grew to hate the stereotyping, did not serve his own cause well by joking that he was 'a big-mouth East London yob'. The real story of McQueen's rise was more prosaic, founded on a childhood obsession with drawing fashion (he claims to have begun as early as three) and a capacity for working hard. His mother, a part-time genealogist, encouraged him to apply for work in Savile Row in 1986 after he had left school with just two qualifications, both in art. Savile Row was no longer the force it had once been in men's tailoring, but McQueen was fortunate to land his first job at Anderson & Sheppard, perhaps the most demanding and perfectionist of the remaining tailors on the Row. After two years learning how to cut and make trousers, he moved to Gieves & Hawkes, where he focused on jackets. It was an extraordinary learning experience that gave him a technical expertise well beyond any of his contemporaries – and all before he had turned twenty.

After Savile Row, McQueen worked briefly at Bermans & Nathans, the theatrical costumiers, and for the designer Koji Tatsuno. He then landed a job with Romeo Gigli by buying a one-way plane ticket to Milan and presenting his portfolio. A year on, when Gigli's business was under pressure, McQueen returned to London and undertook a postgraduate fashion degree at Central Saint Martins College of Art & Design. His degree collection was bought by the eccentric talent-spotter Isabella Blow (1958–2007), then a fashion editor at *Vogue*, who promptly made it her mission to bring the name Alexander McQueen (Lee had been dropped) to the attention of the wider world. McQueen's early collections drew mixed reviews, including accusations of misogyny, which the designer fiercely rejected, blaming fashion editors' misinterpretations. An early collection, titled Highland Rape (from 1995, reprised and developed in his autumn/winter 2006 collection), was not intended as a tasteless reference to the act of rape, but was a reference to the English slaughter of the Scottish clans in the eighteenth century. The models wore ripped and shredded clothes mostly pieced together by McQueen himself from fabric shop remnants. A later show for Givenchy using fibreglass mannequins was not a rejection of real women but an exploration of a blank canvas as a more objective means of viewing a new collection. McQueen's early creation of bumsters (trousers cut so low that the cleft of the buttocks was revealed) also did not endear him to some of his female critics, although it was intended as an experiment in lengthening the torso – and was a harbinger of a low-rise jeans trend in the broader fashion market.

Working and living out of a studio in Hoxton, East London, McQueen built his label steadily although finances were always tight, as they were (and still are) for most young British designers. In 1996, the opportunity to take the helm at Givenchy, despite the fact that he had designed no more than eight collections under his own name, was too good to be missed. Givenchy, owned by the LVMH conglomerate, chose McQueen as a second young British designer in succession, following in the steps of John Galliano, provoking the suggestion among the Parisian fashion set that the venerable house of Givenchy had been turned into a nursery for new talent. Speaking in 2000, McQueen commented: 'Maybe I was too young to take on Givenchy. But nobody in my position would have done any different. I had to accept it.' Years later, he was philosophical about the experience, acknowledging that he learned a lot from the atelier. His mistake, he said, was to try to be someone he wasn't. 'When

Image 49.2 *McQueen with stylist Katy England, Givenchy spring/summer 2000. Niall McInerney, Photographer.* © *Bloomsbury Publishing Plc.*

I was in Paris I tried to mould in with this concept of couture and this hierarchy, but it's just not me. I can't play that game. I think it looks stupid when designers play these bourgeois characters. At the end of the day, I'm left with the real me. What you see is what you get.'

The acquisition of a majority stake in his own label by Gucci Group in 2000 did not mean the end of the pressure for McQueen. In 2004, when Gucci Group creative director Tom Ford and chief executive Domenico De Sole left the business they had dominated, McQueen found himself answering to a new chief executive, Robert Polet, who declared that all the smaller labels in the Gucci Group should break even within three years or expect to be sold. McQueen, who had sensibly nurtured his own label all through the Givenchy years (displaying an impressive business acumen, unusual for a British designer), tripled sales within three years and achieved the Polet target by 2007 through a variety of new projects, including the McQ secondary line, menswear, accessories and footwear. A skull-print scarf was a particular hit, selling phenomenally and prompting a flood of street fashion copies. In 2009, McQueen also created a capsule collection for Target, a mainstream American retailer.

McQueen briefly found personal equilibrium, becoming a Buddhist and marrying his partner George Forsyth in 2000, but the relationship did not last. The designer appeared to have mellowed. In 2006, he said: 'The more I mature, the less confrontational I become. I've softened a bit in my old age.' The death by suicide of his long-time supporter Isabella Blow in 2007 also spurred him on. 'I found a new love for [designing] because she loved it and she found me because of what I was good at. … It was a wake-up call.' McQueen subsequently went on a pilgrimage to India and the results fed into his next collection. However, for his employees, he remained a difficult, demanding, complex, tempestuous boss who brought his own inner demons to all relationships, both professional and personal, as much as to his work.

His fashion shows were artistic events, sharpened through McQueen's interest in historical references, shot through with spectacle, mystery, violence, tenderness and beauty. For his memorable spring/summer 1999 collection, the model Shalom Harlow played the role of a dying swan while being spray-painted by robots. His spring/summer 2001 collection, titled Voss, was staged in a large mirrored box, on which audience and models could watch their own reflections. The provocative show ended with the naked appearance of fetish writer Michelle Olley wearing a fetishist's mask and covered in moths. Fashion historian Caroline Evans wrote, 'In the staging of this show, McQueen oscillated between beauty and horror, turning conventional ideas of beauty upside down.'

Working with leading London stylist Katy England and film and special effects teams, McQueen produced spellbinding shows that tended to blow through his budgets but left even veteran show attendees speechless. For his autumn/winter 2006 collection, staged in March 2006, he concluded with an apparently glass pyramid at the heart of which appeared a curl of white smoke that unfurled to reveal the shape of the model Kate Moss in a white ruffled dress. The vision, created through a hologram, danced and blurred and vanished – a moment of magic. His spring/summer 2010 show, Plato's Atlantis, was another marvel, dominated by spectacular digital prints and a futuristic energy, the event streamed on photographer Nick Knight's showstudio.com, with models walking between two giant motion-controlled cameras that rolled back and forth. Music star Lady Gaga also served up her latest single as part of the soundtrack, causing millions of her fans worldwide to turn to showstudio.com, crashing the site.

During his last years, McQueen increasingly retreated from the fashion circuit, rarely staying long at parties, preferring his own company or that of a close-knit circle of friends. His suicide by hanging at his flat in Mayfair on February 11 2010 followed the recent death of his beloved mother. In an interview with British *Harper's Bazaar* in 2007, he acknowledged his preference for outsider status. 'I came to terms with not fitting in a long time ago. I never really fitted in. I don't want to fit in. And now people are buying into that.' He remained to the end an obsessive about his work, determined to make an enduring mark: 'I'm interested in designing for posterity. … There are only a handful of designers that influence other designers, and I have to keep one step ahead of the game. As a designer, you've always got to push yourself forward; you've always got to keep up with the trends or make your own trends. That's what I do.'

Further reading: Alexander McQueen's life and career is thoroughly covered in *Gods and Kings: The Rise and Fall of Alexander McQueen and John Galliano* (2015) by Dana Thomas, a well-researched book that nevertheless upset many in the fashion world with its personal details. *McQueen* (2018), a documentary film with a respectful and touching perspective, was directed by Peter Ettedgui and Ian Bonhôte. Interviews include 'The New Kingdom of Alexander McQueen' by Nick Compton for *i-D* (August 2002) and 'Killer McQueen' by Harriet Quick for *Vogue* (UK, October 2002). *Fashion at the Edge: Spectacle, Modernity and Deathliness* (2003), by Caroline Evans, makes many interesting observations about his work.

Image 49.3 *Alexander McQueen, spring/summer 2009. Photo: Guy Marineau/Condé Nast via Getty Images.*

50

Nicolas Ghesquière (1971–)

Balenciaga under Ghesquière produced ready-to-wear rather than couture, but the young designer saw a new middle way for high fashion.

Nicolas Ghesquière was barely noticed when he first arrived at the ailing house of Balenciaga in 1997. Perhaps more by luck than by design, the owners of Balenciaga had discovered a designer with a genuine admiration for the late couturier and sharing his same exacting standards. Ghesquière was also a child of the 1980s, looking resolutely forwards. Over several seasons, he developed a confident signature of his own that referenced the glorious past of Balenciaga but also hurtled it forward into a new century as one of the most influential labels in fashion. Commenting on his autumn/winter 2008 collection, Suzy Menkes, fashion editor of *The International Herald Tribune*, wrote: 'The makeover of Balenciaga is exceptional because of the seamless flow of past and present, often uniting in a single outfit.'

Sadly, it all ended in acrimony, with Ghesquière leaving in 2012 full of bitterness towards his employers. He felt, as he put it to *System* magazine, 'as though I was sucked dry, like they wanted to steal my identity while trying to homogenize things.' Balenciaga promptly launched a lawsuit over his comments, which was settled out of court in 2014. By then it was already old news, with Ghesquière well entrenched in his second major position, at Louis Vuitton.

Ghesquière is every bit the modern designer: full of inspired creative ideas but seeing no inconsistency with the concept of building a brand and driving forward a business. The fusion between creativity and commerce, noted by fashion historian Nancy Troy in her study of early twentieth-century couturiers such as Paul Poiret, is complete. Applauding his spring/summer 2007 collection, fashion editor Cathy Horyn of *The New York Times* wrote: 'If he isn't the most important designer of his generation, it's hard to think who would be. Certainly, Mr Ghesquière is one of a handful of young visionaries trying to look at the future of fashion in a believable way.' Balenciaga under Ghesquière produced ready-to-wear rather than couture, but the young designer saw a new middle way for high fashion, merging craft and couture touches with high-tech materials and street

Image 50.1 *Louis Vuitton, spring/summer 2017. Photo: Estrop via Getty Images.*

inspiration. For ready-to-wear, he worked with Lesage for embroideries and Lemarie for feathered work, both specialist names associated with couture. 'I don't think couture fits our world,' he said in 2007. 'Anyway, I have the luxury of using the couture techniques in my ready-to-wear.'

Unlike Balenciaga, who draped fabric directly, Ghesquière has always preferred to sketch. 'I have my ideas in drawing form on a board, along with the fabric, and then I try to find the shape and silhouette, and work through each idea to build the show collection.' His team then brings the ideas to life. In common with Balenciaga, he had an obsession with precise cut and with perfecting every piece. 'There is no compromise,' he told *WWD*. 'If we have to try twenty times [to perfect] a dress, I try it twenty times.' Discipline and a perfectionist sensibility still drive him forward at Louis Vuitton. The process of editing is also important, he has said. 'Fashion is about selection, editing. You have to be very severe in your selection, so you keep something to yourself – even in the way you present yourself.' This sense of severity has also been tempered with a dose of mischief-making: for his spring/summer 2004 Balenciaga collection, he chose to show no trousers on the runway, puzzling fashion editors by excluding the garment for which he was then most admired.

His influence on the broader fashion market is immense. Ghesquière has a futuristic touch, creating a kind of sci-fi fashion that excites his customers. He is also gloriously unpredictable, making the shows at the crowded Balenciaga showroom in Paris and at much grander venues for Louis Vuitton among every season's hot tickets. When he revived floral prints for his spring/summer 2008 collection, buyers and press alike decreed florals as one of the key trends for that summer. His signature looks of slimline trousers, shrunken jackets and soft handbags have been widely admired and copied. His trousers made young women drool in the early Noughties. James Aguiar of Bergdorf Goodman told *Vogue* in 2001: 'What Ghesquière has done is to give a young girl the thing she wants most: to look cool and hip. And he cuts the sexiest trousers for women.'

Ghesquière is the son of a Belgian golf-course owner and a French mother. Born in Comines in the north of France in 1971, he spent most of his childhood in the provincial French village of Loudun in western France. The young Ghesquière was an enthusiast for sports, including riding, fencing and swimming – he still swims regularly in the Ritz swimming pool in Paris. At the tender age of twelve he said he wanted to be a fashion designer, sketching dresses in his school books and creating dresses from curtains. Internships as a schoolboy at Agnès B and Corinne Cobson gave him a taste of the fashion industry. School over, he assisted at Jean Paul Gaultier for two years, an important period during which Ghesquière said he learned 'an aesthetic of mixing'. He then moved to design knitwear at Pôles, followed by a series of freelance design jobs, including Callaghan in Italy. At Balenciaga, he began by working for the Asian licensee, designing the unpromising categories of uniforms and funeral clothes. By the mid-1990s, the house of Balenciaga was a shadow of its former self: the great perfectionist couturier had closed the business in 1968 and its revival as a serious fashion house was considered unlikely.

Ghesquière was appointed head of design at Balenciaga in 1997 at the age of twenty-five, replacing Josephus Thimister and initially considered a temporary stand-in for Helmut Lang. The move barely raised a ripple of interest in the media. But Lang never signed his contract and Balenciaga owners Groupe Jacques Bogart were impressed by the young man's talent, particularly in delivering a promising small collection for a Japanese licensee. 'When I arrived at Balenciaga, it was full of ghosts – good ghosts and bad ghosts,' Ghesquière has recalled. 'Some people didn't speak to me. … Maybe they thought I would just do something disrespectful, or try to re-do things right away. And, of course, that was not my intention.' His first few collections attracted little buzz in Paris and Ghesquière was hampered by the fact that he had no access to the Balenciaga archives, relying instead on books and Irving Penn's photographs. Even so, by 2001 the word was beginning to circulate that Ghesquière was someone special, and the designer was profiled at length in American *Vogue*. His interest in vintage and in the 'unbeautiful' was noted by *Vogue* writer Sally Singer. From the beginning, Ghesquière had also been exploring new volumes, reacting to years of slim silhouettes. Blousons of linked circles and apron tunics that spiralled in strips around the body were highlights of his first collection. Then came fleece batwing tops with tight cuffs, followed by leggings, referring back to the 1980s. For spring 2001, he decorated jersey cocktail dresses with touches of lace, ruffles and pearls.

Inez van Lamsweerde, the Dutch photographer, pointed out that the designer's starting points

are things that come from a collective memory. There are certain elements you remember from your childhood – something you saw, something you wore – and these can trigger a string of associations. The way a jacket is closed, for instance, can make you recall music. Nicolas takes a cue like that and then strips it down and rebuilds it in a modern way.

Image 50.2 *Nicholas Ghesquière, 2016. Photo: Bertrand Guay/AFP via Getty Images.*

Steadily, the fashion world began to acknowledge that here was a young man who was not only reviving a celebrated fashion house but was a major force in his own right. His flatteringly cut trousers became must-haves for fashion editors, while his ability to mix couture style with a contemporary dress-down sensibility drew the attention of the high street copyists.

Tom Ford's enthusiasm for Ghesquière led to PPR-owned Gucci Group buying Balenciaga in 2001 and, with it, access to the archives. But when Ford and chief executive Domenico De Sole walked out in 2004 and a new chief executive, Robert Polet, was brought in, the omens did not look good for Ghesquière. Balenciaga, despite its heritage, was lumped in with emerging brands such as Alexander McQueen and Stella McCartney. The pressure was on to turn the business into profit. Ghesquière's insistence on maintaining a high-cost atelier in Paris (the clothes were manufactured in Italy) was considered an expensive luxury by the new management team. On top of this, the young designer had a reputation for being uncompromising and troublesome. It was a sign of insecurity, the designer said later. 'I used to be more defensive and less comfortable because I was feeling threatened.'

With the Lariat handbag, Ghesquière created a money-spinner that pleased his new boss. Celebrities and wealthy customers worldwide fell over themselves to place orders for the multi-zipped bag with a braided handle and dangling pulls. In 2003, Ghesquière launched a collection titled Balenciaga Edition, recreating ten or fifteen couture pieces from the archives. His autumn/winter collection for 2006 was a highly praised homage to the great couturier, timed to coincide with a major Balenciaga retrospective at the Musée de la Mode et du Textile in Paris. From the boxy suits to the windowpane checks, the spirit of Balenciaga ran through every piece, but always reworked to make them fresh for a twenty-first-century audience. While Ghesquière's collections had tended to reflect Balenciaga's own preference for round shapes, for spring 2007 the designer opted for a straight silhouette, with pinched, padded and highlighted sleeves. Cathy Horyn of *The New York Times* called it 'an ideological break with the retro futurism of Balenciaga. What we are now seeing is the contemporary future of Nicolas Ghesquière.'

By then his status was ensured. Ghesquière was featured in *Time*'s 100 Most Influential People of 2005. He was made a Chevalier des arts et lettres, an award of merit bestowed by the French government that highlights contributions to French culture. Through all this, he kept a low personal profile. Ghesquière remains cautious about overstating the role of fashion as commentary on the world. 'You have to look at the world and then forget it,' he said in 2007. 'Of course I live in my time and I'm really curious. But, at the same time, I don't think it has a direct impact on my worth.'

Although designer fashion in the twenty-first century has become a big global business, Ghesquière believes there is still the freedom to experiment. 'What is really interesting about being a designer today is that you can occupy those two positions: being a forward thinker and at the same time someone who sells clothes.' In the great economic slowdown of 2009, the fashion world looked to Ghesquière to suggest a new way forward for design. The austerity of his autumn/winter 2008 collection seemed to presage the onset of hard times. His spring/summer 2009 collection featured innovative cocoon shapes and fabric that appeared to melt around the body, prompting further eulogies, even from those who found his designs hard to pin down. As Julie Gilhart, a veteran buyer for Barneys New York, put it: 'He has a knack for showing us things that are not quite in our vernacular yet.'

At Louis Vuitton, Ghesquière made a confident debut for autumn/winter 2014 full of his familiar cropped proportions and futuristic silhouette – 'understated, young, contemporary, relevant' according to a *Vogue* review. That same confidence has been maintained: his spring/summer 2017 collection was staged in the Louvre's Pavillon de l'Horloge and brilliantly fused frock coats from the Louvre's days as a royal palace with modern sportswear. 'I thought anachronism was interesting,' he said afterwards. 'How today can we incorporate pieces considered as costume into an everyday wardrobe?'

The next stop is obvious – and has been so for years. The launch of the house of Nicolas Ghesquière, discussed for most of the 2010s, seems only a matter of time.

Further reading: A thorough summary is 'The story of Nicolas Ghesquière and how Balenciaga became 21st century fashion', in 032c (17 October 2013). His incendiary interview with *System* was published in 2012.

Part Seven

2000s–2010s

Image 50.3 *Balenciaga, autumn/winter 2009 ready-to-wear. Photo: Karl Prouse/Catwalking via Getty Images.*

51

Raf Simons (1968–)

Simons' interest in sub-cultures, honed in the clubs of Antwerp in his youth, has been translated directly into fashion.

In the spring of 1998, Belgian designer Raf Simons had just turned thirty when he showed his autumn/winter 1998 Radioactivity collection in Paris. While the narrow-shouldered skinny tailoring caught the eye, the overall concept of the presentation made just as big an impact. For this collection, his third shown in Paris, the designer was directly inspired by influential German electronic band Kraftwerk and their 1978 album The Man Machine, most literally in a sequence where the models wore red shirts and black ties, their hair slicked back. *Red* shirts, not black: Kraftwerk were referencing Russian Constructivism, not German fascism. As for Simons, he just loved Kraftwerk's music: 'It was nothing to do with fashion, only with music,' he said years later, acknowledging the extent to which broader culture has influenced his work.

That evening in Paris, journalist Roger Tredre, thrilled by what he had seen, slipped backstage as the audience applause still echoed to solicit a quote from the designer. Simons started to speak, then abruptly collapsed in a heap of tears, overwhelmed. The collection proved to be a breakthrough moment in a career that has endured and prospered beyond the imaginings of a young Flemish student obsessed with youth culture who had started out studying furniture design. Nearly a quarter of a century later, Simons has shown himself to be the most creatively exciting and consistently impressive of all the Belgian designers, making his name in men's wear before expanding his talents to women's wear.

The tears have recurred at many of his catwalk shows – as well as in the documentary film by Frédéric Tcheng, *Dior and I*, which movingly sums up his prowess and emotional commitment. Emotion in fashion can be hard to explain to an outsider, easy to dismiss as the hypersensitive outpourings of overly precious individuals. But it is this very intensity, this very emotion – founded on a no-holds-barred commitment to creativity – that turns the best of fashion into more than clothes, in the process telling us something about the world around us.

Image 51.1 *Dior Couture, autumn/winter 2012. Photo: Stephane Cardinale/Corbis via Getty Images.*

Besides the celebrated skinny tailoring, Simons' most enduring contribution to high-end men's wear has been to fuse it with street style as well as to regularly reference the energy and anger of the street. His Riot, Riot, Riot collection of autumn/winter 2001 featured camouflage bombers with printed newspaper quiltings. Oversized hoodies and balaclavas summed up an even more militant spirit of rebellion in the following collection for spring/summer 2002, dramatically titled Woe Unto Those Who Spit on the Fear Generation … The Wind Will Blow It Back. Both collections were shown shortly before the 9/11 attacks in America ushered in a much angrier age. Simons continued to innovate with men's wear thereafter, his collection of autumn/winter 2004 marking a new maturity focusing on shape and form.

Simons prides himself on being an innovator. In the process, he has drawn on a wide array of influences including music, art, interiors, performance, images and words, and consistently pushed himself to take on new challenges. His interest in subcultures, honed in the clubs of Antwerp in his youth, has been translated directly into fashion. As graphic designer Peter Saville put it in 2011: 'Raf is one of the great pioneers of convergence, transporting the art of subcultures into contemporary fashion.'

Besides his own menswear label, he has also reinvigorated three great fashion brands: Jil Sander (2005–2012), Christian Dior (2012–2015) and Calvin Klein (2016–2018, a brief but creatively exceptional stint). Simons, like many designers, hates being pigeon-holed and the variety of his work for these three names, as well as his own men's wear label, demonstrates his versatility and an enthusiasm to surprise and challenge, challenging himself as much as his customers.

He emerged in the mid-1990s, ten years after the first wave of Belgian designers, led by the Antwerp Six and Martin Margiela, had widened the parameters of fashion. Many of them came from the Royal Academy of the Arts in Antwerp and its fashion course, both technically and creatively rigorous and liberating under the tutelage of Linda Loppa and, later, Walter Van Beirendonck, himself one of the Antwerp Six. Simons himself had studied elsewhere – and not even fashion – graduating in Industrial Design and Furniture Design in 1991 from a college in Genk, a town in the eastern Belgian province of Limburg. The fashion names on all the students' lips were Martin Margiela and also Helmut Lang, whom Simons acknowledged as early heroes. Two hours away by train was Antwerp, where Simons used to hang out at the café Witzli-Poetzli with fledgling fashion designers such as Olivier Rizzo, Willy Vanderperre and Veronique Branquinho. Simons was still working on furniture design, but both Loppa and Van Beirendonck saw his potential as a fashion designer and encouraged him. Van Beirendonck gave him an internship in his design studio and took him to the Paris shows. He squeezed into Martin Margiela, the all-white spring/summer 1990 collection, an experience that proved decisive. From then on, fashion replaced furniture in his creative affections.

The move to design Jil Sander in 2002, following the eponymous designer's departure, was a first step into womenswear. Over seven years, he built his reputation afresh, nudging the label towards a softer aesthetic, introducing a new romanticism, embracing colour. His final show at Jil Sander, for

Image 51.2 *Raf Simons at Calvin Klein 205W39NYC, 2018. Photo: Angela Weiss/AFP via Getty Images.*

Image 51.3 *Calvin Klein, spring/summer 2018. Photo: Victor Virgile/Gamma-Rapho via Getty Images.*

autumn/winter 2012, was judged an outstanding success, conceived as a tribute to the modern woman within the context of family life, shown on a runway adorned with plexiglass cubes of flowers.

Raf Simons's ascent to the position of creative director at Christian Dior in 2012 was received with some bewilderment in Paris, where he was – despite the increasing romanticism of his vision for Jil Sander – still perceived in some quarters as an arch minimalist. In the documentary, *Dior et moi*, ruminating weeks before his first couture show at Dior, he addressed the issue directly: '[They] see me as a minimalist. I'm not. I find it surprising. Did I take on a minimalist brand? Yes. Does that mean that I am only about minimalism? Let them judge after the show.'

As a record of an intense and exceptional period in Simons' career, *Dior et moi* is a precious resource. We learn how Simons works: not by sketching himself but through the organised and methodical creation of a series of files for his design team around themes (for that first collection, they included 'bar language', referencing Dior's celebrated bar jackets, and 'modern ball gowns'). We are introduced to his long-term creative partner Pieter Mulier, who has an easy charm that complements Simons' own intensity. We witness his insistence on clothes that are good to wear: 'I want the girls to be comfortable.' And we observe his personal passions: 'There is no day that I am not looking at art – it relaxes me and inspires me.'

He has had a lifelong interest in art. Aged eighteen, he attended the Chambres d'Amis exhibition in Ghent, curated by Jan Hoet, where artists exhibited their works in private homes, the aim being to present contemporary art as accessible and grounded in the real world. In June 2013, he chose the new Larry Gagosian art gallery at Le Bourget to present his spring/summer 2014 menswear collection. At Dior, his first collection marked the start of a long-term collaborative relationship with American artist Sterling Ruby. One of the designer's favourite pieces in that collection was a chine silk dress printed with a spray-paint work by Ruby.

Previously, most designers who had explored collaborations with artists perceived them primarily as an opportunity to add a decorative flourish to a collection. By contrast, Simons developed a more intense two-way approach. In 2014, this reached its logical conclusion with the launch of the Raf Simons/ Sterling Ruby men's wear collection where designer and artist received equal billing, with Ruby directly involved in the making process, painting and dyeing fabric in his studio in Los Angeles. That collection, full of bleaching and hand-painting, proved hugely influential and summed up a decade when the word 'collaboration' was on every designer's mind. Simons displayed how it could best be done.

The relationship with Sterling Ruby was renewed at Calvin Klein, where Raf Simons was appointed chief creative officer in 2016. As with Jil Sander, it was perceived as a surprising move: Simons had complained regularly in interviews about the pace of work. When he quit Dior in late 2015, it appeared that he was following the example of his heroes Helmut Lang and Martin Margiela and backing out of the fashion game. But the allure of Calvin Klein, a designer name with global reach and a broad appeal – including millions who just buy the fragrances and underwear – was immense. And, as he hinted in an interview shortly before his appointment, 'I do think it's interesting if your voice reaches out to the world.'

The Calvin Klein label had been treading water for some years, trading on its heritage as purveyor of all-American simple shapes and clean lines with lashings of youthful sex appeal. Simons took on the challenge of a balancing act that acknowledged the heritage while treating the brand afresh. With his shows, he used Calvin Klein as an exploratory laboratory to examine aspects of the American psyche, often with unsettling references and dark undertones. This approach was given an added relevance with the election of President Donald Trump and the beginning of an exceptionally troubled period in American politics and life. In business terms, Simons was given free rein to reach the broader Calvin Klein customer as much as the fashion pack. Brands and sub-brands were renamed and recalibrated, not necessarily with the catchiest of titles (Calvin Klein 205W39NYC brand took designer nomenclature to new levels of absurdity).

His first collection, for autumn/winter 2017, was presented in a location festooned with flags, fringes and denim, decorated by Sterling Ruby. 'I've always been thinking of America,' Raf said. 'Now is the moment to focus on it. Energy and youth! You have to think about youth now, they are the future.' But the second collection was darker as Simons became obsessed with the late Andy Warhol, introducing the Pop artist's controversial car-crash prints. As with his collaborations with Ruby, Simons sought a full-on engagement with the Warhol estate, agreeing a three-year deal with the Andy Warhol Foundation for the Visual Arts that gave him access to the archive.

Vanessa Friedman, chief fashion critic of *The New York Times*, writing in October 2018, commented:

> When I first heard that one of Raf Simons's Big New Ideas for the transformation of Calvin Klein was Andy Warhol, I rolled my eyes. … Turns out he was more prescient than anyone knew. Just a

year later we are living in a Warhol moment inside a Warhol moment inside a Warhol moment – in a country run by the most Warholian president we have ever had, at a time when Instagram has made everyone an influencer for fifteen minutes.

Simons' spell at Calvin Klein was short-lived. In December 2018, after reports emerged of below-par sales and over-spent budgets, his contract was cut short by mutual agreement. Most media analysis focused on the uncomfortable fit between a designer with little experience of the mass-market world of jeans and underwear (on which the brand's profits were based) and a company that had never worked with a high-end conceptual designer. For fashion editors who had swooned over his collections at Calvin Klein, his departure was another illustration of the ongoing tension between free-spirited creative designers and the commercial demands of the marketplace.

Like many designers in the twenty-first century, Simons has often complained about the pace of work in the modern fashion system, but he has found his own ways of coping. He has also remained excitingly relevant in any debate about modern culture – a designer who wants to participate in that debate and ceaselessly move forward. 'I used to be very fragile about how people would react to my work,' he said shortly before leaving Calvin Klein, 'but I have become more and more at peace with the idea that bad reactions can also be good, because at least it's a dialogue.'

Further reading: An outstanding commentator on Raf Simons as a men's wear designer is academic Nick Rees-Roberts. See 'Raf Simons and Interdisciplinary Fashion from Post-Punk to Neo-Modern' (*Fashion Theory*, Vol. 17 2013. Issue 1). Raf Simons' conversation with Miuccia Prada in issue 8 of *System* is illuminating. Vanessa Friedman's October 2018 feature for *The New York Times*, 'Warhol & I', is full of good insights.

Image 51.4 *Raf Simons, autumn/winter 2004. Photo: Thomas Concordia/WireImage via Getty Images.*

Image 52.1 *Dior Homme, spring/summer 2007. Photo: Pierre Verdy/AFP via Getty Images.*

Slimane has had an equivocal relationship with fashion, but not with the process of creation. As he put it in late 2018: 'Through creation, I have rediscovered what it means to feel unburdened.'

Further reading: For a summary of his design philosophy, read 'Hedi Slimane's First Celine Interview', by Laurence Benaïm for *Le Figaro*, published in English on *businessoffashion.com* in September 2018. 'Hedi Slimane, fashion's sharpest designer' by Carola Long for *The Financial Times* in January 2018 is a good summary. Also recommended: 'Mr Provocative' (April 2013) by Eric Wilson for *The New York Times*, and 'Slimane Speaks' (July 2000) by Miles Socha for *WWD*. *Anthology of a Decade: Hedi Slimane*, published by JRP Ringier in 2011, documents his black-and-white photography during the 2000s.

Image 52.4 *Saint Laurent, spring/summer 2013. Photo: Victor Virgile/Gamma-Rapho via Getty Images.*

Image 53.1 *Céline, spring/summer 2011. Photo: Pierre Verdy/AFP via Getty Images.*

53

Phoebe Philo (1973–)

The effect of Philo's new luxe minimalism was rather like that of Dior's Corolle Line: the women in the audience immediately felt overdressed.

The mature work of Phoebe Philo at Céline places her firmly within the tradition of minimalist designers, many of them dress reformers of high seriousness who, at heart, find fashion's relentless urge towards novelty and waste deeply problematic. While part of a system that is all about a creative response to change, to time's passing, they also aspire to make work that is timeless. Usefulness, utility, purity, simplicity, honesty and austerity are all part of their lexicon. However, as Harriet Walker noted in her book *Less Is More* (2011), twenty-first-century minimalism 'has managed to straddle the seemingly polar opposite tropes of reduction and excess by creating plain, sober garments in the richest, most luxurious fabrics available.'

Phoebe Philo, interviewed by Alexandra Shulman, then editor of British *Vogue*, in 2014, said, 'I work with the most beautiful fabrics in the world, with experts to develop them, and the clothes are very well made. They will stand the test of time. These are investment pieces. As designers we must make things for the world we live in.' She added, 'I find mediocrity hard. I find that whole area difficult as I care very much about what I do.'

Her words echo those of her predecessors who have embraced the virtues of modernity expressed through minimalism. From Poiret through Fortuny to Balenciaga, Givenchy and Armani to the futurists Cardin and Courrèges, the urge to refine and simplify has been one end of the arc of the pendulum that is fashion. Among those who have expressed that urge to a greater or lesser degree are McCardell, Halston, Beene, Klein, Karan, Zoran and Wang (all Americans); Miyake, Kawakubo and Yamamoto (Japanese); Belgian Martin Margiela; German Jil Sander; Brits Jean Muir and Sheridan Barnett; and the Turkish-British experimentalist, Hussein Chalayan.

There are many motives for minimalism, including the search for a Zen-like purity, a cleanliness of being. Many simply address definitions of good design, as did architect Mies van der Rohe when he coined the phrase 'less is more', which became the title of Harriet Walker's book. And many are about giving people, and women in particular, a rational, logical, long-lived wardrobe. This last motive is strongly associated with, if not rooted in, feminism and the lives woman actually lead. It is a theme within Philo's work and owes much to the style of her mother's breakthrough generation of working women and the second wave of the women's movement in the 1970s.

Philo was born in 1973 to British parents, Celia, an art dealer and graphic artist, and Roger, a surveyor, who were working in Paris. The family returned to Britain when she was two and she was brought up in Harrow, a suburb of London. On her fourteenth birthday she asked for a sewing machine in order to remake her own clothes. 'It was always in me,' she told Shulman, 'the love of fashion, of clothes.'

She attended South Harrow Comprehensive School before gaining a coveted place at Central Saint Martin's College of Art & Design, part of University of the Arts London, graduating in 1996. In her penultimate year, following the system at the college under Professor Wendy Dagworthy, she assisted Stella McCartney on her graduate collection. This was famously the student show that set the fashion press aback (and picture editors clearing the front page) by the appearance on its catwalk of Stella's friends, models Naomi Campbell, Yasmin Le Bon and Kate Moss. On her own graduation a year later, Philo became McCartney's design assistant at Chloé, succeeding her in the top job when McCartney left to start her own fashion house in 2001.

Chloé was founded in 1952 by Gaby Aghion as a luxury ready-to-wear business, a relatively new concept at that time. From the beginning its mood was youthful and often romantic. She and her partner, Jacques Lenoir, employed a series of talented young designers who would go on to make names for themselves: Michèle Rosier, Maxime de la Falaise, Graziella Fontana, Tan Giudicelli, Guy Paulin, Carlos Rodriguez and, latterly, Martine Sitbon. In 1966, they appointed as head designer Karl Lagerfeld, who made the Chloé show one of the hottest tickets of the 1970s and early 1980s, an unmissable twice-yearly joy of sensuous but youthful femininity and mischievous wit. Jackie Kennedy, Brigitte Bardot, Maria Callas and Stella McCartney's own mother, Linda, all loved these pretty clothes. Aghion retired in 1985, selling the company to Alfred Dunhill, which was in turn absorbed by the Richemont Group.

Stepping up to the top job in 2001, Philo was very conscious that Chloé had a signature style that needed to be respected. The late 1990s had seen several instances of new head designers ignoring a brand's heritage, its DNA, or parodying it to political effect, and the results had not always inspired confidence – or commercial success. Chloé's president, Ralph Toledano, liked consistency and continuity. He told the press, 'On the one side we all love Stella, but on the other it is important for the house to maintain its identity. With Phoebe, we will continue in the same direction.' McCartney's Chloé had taken a modern, stride-out-suited-and-booted approach to Chloé's youthfulness but McCartney was not so comfortable with the sweet prettiness – or with the need for a luxury goods label to use leather and fur.

Philo, on the other hand, was prepared to work with both and to embrace the label's traditional take on femininity, rooted in Lagerfeld's vision of his customer as a clever, knowing version of Colette's ingénue, Gigi. In 2005, Philo told *Vogue*, 'My relationship with fashion is playful and very expressive of what I am feeling at the time.'

Image 53.2 *Phoebe Philo, 2011. Photo: Francois Guillot/AFP via Getty Images.*

Of Philo's first collection British *Vogue* wrote that the designer had recalled the Chloé of past generations, the floaty, feminine label it had been in the 1960s. 'Philo offered a collection dripping with charm: gorgeous puff-sleeved shirts appeared amid odd pieces of slickly tailored satin; sexy white trouser suits came with doily-work keyhole cutouts running diagonally across both legs; jeans sparkled with embroidery on their back pockets, and sweet cuffed, cream flannel bloomers were teamed with baby blue zip-up leather jackets, with pretty petticoats of scalloped lace in a collection that showed a style all Philo's own.'

Subsequent collections managed to be faithful to the brand's identity while maintaining Philo's own cool-girl manner. For autumn/winter 2002, her second collection was a confident parade of military tailcoats, curvy jackets, chiffon tops and velvet flares that drew huge applause from the fashion editors. For evening, she added silver bugle beads to layered chiffon tops and tunics in patterns inspired by Leon Bakst.

In 2004 Philo married the British gallerist and art dealer, Max Wigram, with whom she now has three children, Maya, Marlowe and Arthur. In 2006 she resigned from Chloé to be able to concentrate on family life. 'I wasn't living my true life,' she told Penny Martin of *The Gentlewoman* in 2010. 'My life with Max consisted of fitting a week's worth of conversations and everything that goes on between a couple into two days: Saturday and Sunday. It felt manufactured and fake.'

Her absence from fashion's front line lasted two years until she accepted the creative directorship of LVMH's Céline on the condition that her studio and design team were London-based. She told *Vogue* editor Shulman, 'I felt that it was time for a more back-to-reality approach to fashion, clothes that are beautiful, are strong and have ideas, with real life driving them.' Céline was the brand that would give her that opportunity.

Céline Vipiana established her eponymous label in 1945 as a luxury business making made-to-measure shoes for children. In 1960, it refocused on women's shoes and in 1967 launched a ready-to-wear collection called 'couture sportswear', a nod to the American fashion genre. The company became part of the LVMH stable in 1996, the year before Vipiana retired. She was replaced by the American designer, Michael Kors, who left Céline in 2004 to focus on his own label. Roberto Menichetti was appointed in 2005 but stayed for just one year, then Ivana Omazic designed the collections until 2008 when Philo was headhunted to direct the brand. Pierre-Yves Roussel, CEO of LVMH's fashion division, said that the company wanted to give her the opportunity to express her vision. With her first collections for the house, that vision was identified as a cool, restrained and grown-up minimalism.

'Céline was very attractive as historically it has not had an iconic designer, so I could start with a clean slate,' she told Harriet Quick in 2010. Sarah Mower, in her *Vogue* review of Philo's first collection for Céline, for autumn/winter 2010, commented, 'Phoebe Philo has always had a great sense of who she is. That centeredness informs her way of designing clothes that reflect fashion as it's really lived, rather than anything arty or conceptual, and it gives her work the vitality so many young women identified with during her wildly successful pre-marriage, pre-family run at Chloé.'

In a pure and limited palette of caramel, beige, white and black, the clothes were essentially simple shapes in the most luxurious of fabrics constructed in precise and complex ways to render them flattering, wearable and comfortable. The effect of Philo's new luxe minimalism was rather like that of Dior's Corolle Line: the women in the audience immediately felt overdressed. They exited longing for that wardrobe. And Philo couldn't have been more right – minimalism's moment had come again. As Sarah Mower wrote, 'The pairing of sharp, whipcord-trimmed skirts, fine leather tees, piqué shirting, over-the-head cross-laced dresses, and modified military jackets was shot through with pragmatism and a crucial underlying appreciation of classic Parisian taste.'

It was a decade since minimalism had been a force in fashion. Its anti-fashion ethos had no place in the celebrity culture of the early Noughties when ostentatious, status-driven display and excessive consumption (particularly of overly decorated expensive handbags) dominated the media. The financial crash of 2008 brought even the most profligate up short: companies and banks collapsed and lives were destroyed. The panicky drive of governments to impose a new austerity gave fashion, as ever, its cue.

Accepting the job at Céline, Philo had felt its identity was hers to make. Indeed, the company had cleared the decks for her to the extent of demanding no quick trip to the archives and allowing a season's hiatus while she prepared her first collection. 'I felt quite clear from the offset about what I wanted to do in terms of fashion – or certainly what I didn't want,' she told Vanessa Friedman of *The Financial Times* in 2010. 'I wanted something that felt honest, that was a mixture of what I wanted to wear and how I wanted to live. I felt it needed to be quite simple and very real.'

As she had at Chloé, Philo presided over an enormous cultural and commercial success at Céline. She is a formidable design talent who has so far proved brilliantly capable of updating the romantic style of Chloé in a mature and intelligent way and then of expressing her own mid-thirties instinct for a rigorous, rational ethic at Céline. In doing so, she has earned a reputation for infallibility in the matter of fashion's zeitgeist.

In *Less Is More*, Harriet Walker wrote, 'Philo's pieces are determinedly pragmatic and wearable – and therefore commercial – but also highly intelligent and aspirational; they represent the modern incarnation of minimalism, which wears both its intellectual and commercial credentials with equal balance. It was the logical next step. … Philo reasserted its roots in high fashion and its intrinsic links to the fortunes and fate of modern women.' Philo told *Vogue* in 2012, 'For me, the ultimate wardrobe is a white shirt, a pair of black trousers, a skirt, maybe three coats. Two jackets, a high heel, a flat shoe and a trainer. A bag. Maybe only one bag. And maybe a scarf.'

Philo was named British Fashion Council British Designer of the Year in 2005 and 2010 as well as CFDA International Designer of the Year in 2011. She was appointed OBE in 2014 and named by *Time* magazine as one of the world's 100 most influential people. She announced her departure from the house in December 2017, with the appointment of Hedi Slimane as her successor received by the fashion press with some disappointment. A comeback at some point seems more than likely.

Further reading: No monograph focuses on Philo, but *Less Is More* (2011) by Harriet Walker examines minimalism in fashion, including Philo's work, in the light of 'the new minimalist revival'. Three articles stand out: Penny Martin's 'Phoebe Philo Designs the Clothes Women Actually Want to Wear', from *The Gentlewoman* Issue 1 (2010); Harriet Quick's 'Philo Facts', from British *Vogue* (2010); and Hamish Bowles's profile, 'The Phoebe Files', in US *Vogue* (2013).

Image 53.3 *Céline, autumn/winter 2013. Photo: Victor Virgile/Gamma-Rapho via Getty Images.*

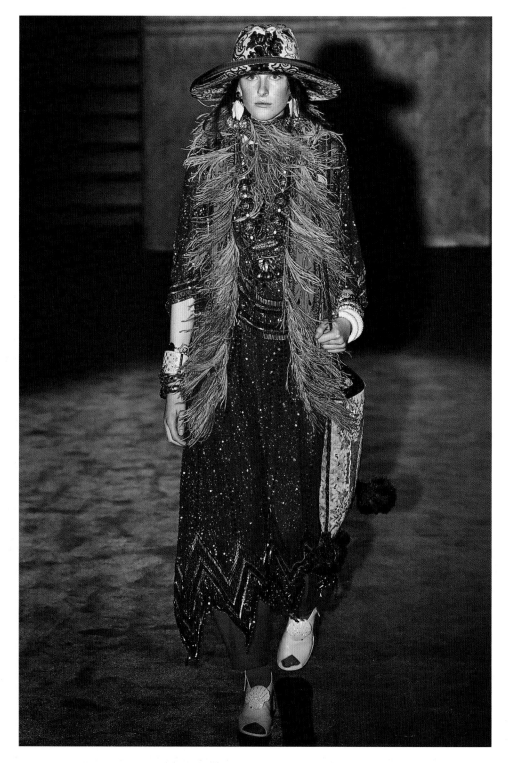

Image 54.1 *Gucci, spring/summer 2019. Photo: Victor Virgile/Gamma-Rapho via Getty Images.*

54

Alessandro Michele (1972–)

*Michele loves the internet and its vast richness of images as much as he
does the art gallery and the street.*

When in 2015 Francois-Henri Pinault, CEO of the luxury group Kering, fired the CEO and design director of Gucci, the highly profitable but lately lustre-lacking flagship brand, his replacement CEO, Marco Bizzarri, was tasked with appointing a new design director – fast. His choice, announced speedily to an industry happily laying bets on each and all of fashion's star mercenaries, was Alessandro Michele. The response was uniformly, 'Who?'

'The softest decision for me,' Bizzarri told Imran Amed of *The Business of Fashion*, 'would have been to get a big name. But do I want to make a decision that people are expecting, or do I want to make a decision that I feel is the right one?'

Michele was the insider, anonymously working away as leather goods designer and then associate to Frida Giannini, the design director, at Gucci for twelve years. Bizzarri had set aside half an hour for coffee and a chat at Michele's Rome apartment in order to familiarise himself with the workings of the design studio. Instead, they talked for four hours – and the future design direction of the house was shaped. It was to be Michele's vision, his romantic eclecticism, his totally modern sense of rich diversity that is both current and reaches back into history to plunder references and motifs, of gender-fluidity and of the pointlessness of the ever-changing treadmill that is the fashion system. 'I do not do fashion,' he has said many times. 'I design clothes that should be good enough to keep and treasure over many seasons. I design a way to live.'

Just a week before the men's wear show for autumn/winter 2015, Bizzarri challenged Michele to put a whole new collection on the runway in Milan. He managed it. There have been few fashion sensations quite like it. Tim Blanks, reporting for *Vogue*, was enthralled but puzzled by the new Gucci, which he described as 'nonconformist, romantic, intellectual. … Right proper existential. Was it enough?'

Journalists were still wondering by the time of the women's wear show, but they were starting to get what he was about. 'There's a significant amount of good will for Michele,' wrote Nicole Phelps in

Vogue, 'and it's clear from Instagram that he wrapped a lot of the audience in his poetic embrace – from the looks of it, they'll be wrapping themselves in his fur with embroidered crystal birds on the back. But to make his vision stick, he'll need to give it a lot more substance going forward.'

By the menswear show for spring/summer 2016, hints of increased sales at Gucci were starting to restore confidence in the brand. Tim Blanks wrote: 'Welcome to the New Punk. Alessandro Michele has brought a radically different culture to Gucci. … If it isn't exactly new, the magpie sensibility of Michele's Gucci – scouring time, place, and gender for scraps – has a Marmite impact. (Marmite, for the uninitiated, is a yeast-based food paste that its UK marketers confidently advertised with the slogan, "Love it or hate it.") That, in itself, is Punk. So is Michele's ardent faith in the power of youth. Tattooing, piercing, decorating themselves in a new kind of geography of the body – Michele takes all of these as youthful tokens of a new shamanism.'

If it was by no means really new, it was undoubtedly an intoxicated maximalism whose time had come. The passion for vintage pieces was now more than twenty years old. It is a style of dressing long espoused by the young, charity-shop resourceful, skilled in repurposing second-hand finds, in decorative self-styling, delighting in provocative fashion rule-breaking and perfect for narcissistic today-I-am-wearing selfies on Instagram. It is Michele's wide erudition and willingness to absorb all aspects of modern culture that has made him particularly receptive to 'the New Punk'. He loves the internet and its vast richness of images as much as he does the art gallery and the street – and he contributes to it with what one journalist called 'the merry bedlam of his imagination'. Visually, in terms of the self-images available to all people, the internet is a realm without borders, categories, classes, racial or gendered exclusions. There, one constructs one's identity in freedom. For many it may be a spurious freedom; the real world may be hard and intolerant. But Michele understands the extent to which the internet generation lives both in its imagination and online.

Alessandro Michele was born in Rome in 1972. His mother was assistant to an Italian executive in Rome's film industry and his father was a technician for Alitalia and a spare-time sculptor. Outings with his father were, he has said, not to soccer matches but to museums and art galleries. But even a stroll along the street with a parent well informed in the history of architecture could enchant; from Roman empire through medieval times to the Renaissance (his favourite period), through the Baroque and Rococo to the neoclassical revivalism of the Risorgimento, the modernism of the Futurists and the pompous monumentalism of the Fascist period. All the rich architectural juxtapositions of Rome fuelled his postmodern sensibility. His design headquarters are in a sixteenth-century Roman palazzo built to plans drawn by Raphael – a building restored by his predecessor, Frida Giannini. It is opulently furnished with an antiquarian's mad-hoard collection of carpets, furniture and objets d'art from many parts of the world and many eras of history. He told Frank Bruni, 'The past is something alive, that talks with you every day. If we put that seed in the present, something can grow.'

Image 54.2 *Alessandro Michele with Lana del Rey and Jared Leto at The Costume Institute Gala, 2018. Photo: Frazer Harrison/FilmMagic via Getty Images.*

Significantly, Michele's earliest fashion memories are from an earlier period of story-telling, dressing-up-box romantic excess – the 1970s. He adored his mother's twin, his 'super-stylish' aunt Giuliana who worked as a film editor in television and enjoyed the transformative power and the sheer fun of clothes. He told Jonathan Wingfield of *System*, 'She'd spend all her money on Chanel, furs, dresses and platform shoes. I was in love with her and I guess she introduced me to the idea that you could transform yourself through clothes; before we went out together, she's always ask me, "Lallo, would you prefer if I wore the blue or the red shoes?"'

Michele himself started to use appearance to construct a subversive identity at a very young age. 'My mother had a lot of problems with me. When I was about thirteen, I dyed my hair super-blond and tried to pierce my own ears because I was in love with the Sex Pistols and Sid Vicious. … I have to say my first fashion inspiration came more through music than 1980s fashion gods like Giorgio Armani. At the time but also now, music seems a more authentic way of expressing yourself through clothes than pure fashion.'

He studied at the Accademia di Costume e di Moda in Rome, learning how to design both theatrical costume and fashion. This dual discipline is an important clue to Michele's archaeological approach to dress; the correct costume is a major factor in conjuring a period, its moods and preoccupations, in theatre, opera and cinema. The previous great romantics of fashion – Poiret, Fortuny, Dior, Saint Laurent, Westwood, Versace, Lauren, Dolce & Gabbana, Galliano – were historicist in different ways. All examined archaic dress in detail, deconstructing it and remaking it with a modern sensibility but they tended to find their inspiration in one period, country or culture per collection. Or if more than one, then there was an internal consistency to the actual clothes. Michele is the great magpie or, as Frank Bruni of *The New York Times* put it, 'eccentric, eclectic, inclusive'. On meeting him, Bruni described the designer's appearance thus: 'He's a fop. He's a lumberjack. He's a hipster. He's also a Christmas tree, ornamented to a fare-thee-well. He loves jewels, typically wears multiple bracelets and has bulbous rings – one shaped like a fox, another like a wolf – on all of his fingers except for his thumbs. … He's messy and mesmerising.'

On graduating, Michele was hired first by the Italian knitwear brand, Les Copains, then as a senior accessories designer at Fendi, working with Karl Lagerfeld, another man who cherished a good archive. In 2004 he was poached away to Gucci by Tom Ford and moved to the design office in London – based there because Gucci was a Florentine company and Ford did not want to live in a tourist city with no airport, however pretty. However, within months both Ford and CEO Domenico De Sole had left the company and in 2005 Frida Giannini was appointed to lead the design team – and take it back to Italy. In 2008, Michele was appointed leather goods design director, promoted by 2011 to an associate director role. As head of leather goods, he was responsible for Gucci's money-spinners, the handbags, although his work had to remain in step with Giannini's vision. She was very much the inheritor of Tom Ford's 1990s Gucci miracle, which was all about glossy, high-octane sex appeal. Giannini had remained true to that concept, but its time was past.

The latter years, Michele has said, were a period of creative stagnation. Bored and unfulfilled, he was about to leave the company when that fateful meeting with Bizzarri took place. 'Gucci had become soulless,' he reflected. Both Bizzarri and Pinault were impressed by the freshness and completeness of Michele's vision, and the confidence with which he committed to it. Pinault said: 'He is one of those guys who, despite the size of the brand, despite the power of the brand, says, "This is my personal creative universe, and I will work with that and the icons and symbols of the brand to create something new." And he was right.'

'My vision was quite complicated in terms of aesthetic,' Michele told Wingfield, 'and the way it could be put together. I explained that while I see myself as Italian, I also feel like a contaminated Italian because I lived in London and it had changed by perception of things.' Initially, much of the reaction to Michele's first collections was about his blurring of gender distinctions. He believes that the current culture sees people as existing somewhere and anywhere they choose on a scale of masculine/feminine, so he designs his clothes to be worn by anyone – as long as they have a Punk/Baroque point of view. He uses the same fabrics, styles and accessories for both women's and men's ranges and sends out men in his women's shows and women in his men's. But he is not trying to be in any way provocative. 'I thought it was such a normal thing. It is what is happening in the world. This is not a time when fashion can stay inside the box.'

He himself is more interested in a garment's history, the associations it has and the memories it may summon. But he's not making fancy dress, so instead he opts for a mash-up of styles, clashing fabrics, colours, prints, textures and motifs, ancient and modern. He told Wingfield, 'It is more a matter of expressing romanticism or what it meant to be unique in contemporary society, or simply the idea of freedom. I think the power of my work is that I had the courage to bring this kind of diversity together and create a kind of chemical reaction. I feel that by taking fragments that are apparently dead and putting them together in new ways, you create something modern and beautiful.'

Michele was the British Fashion Council International Designer of the Year in 2015 and 2016, and CFDA International Designer of the Year in 2016.

Further reading: Two major articles are of particular interest: 'We smile, we say hello to everybody, we enjoy ourselves' (2016) by Jonathan Wingfield in *System*, and 'Alessandro Michele, Fashion's Modern Mastermind' (2018) by Frank Bruni in *The New York Times*.

Image 54.3 *Gucci, autumn/winter 2019. Photo: Pietro D'Aprano via Getty Images.*

Image 55.1 *Balenciaga, autumn/winter 2016. Photo: Victor Virgile/Gamma-Rapho via Getty Images.*

55

Demna Gvasalia (1981–)

Gvasalia always wants to innovate in a twenty-first-century spirit.

Vetements is a fashion collective that sells oversized hoodies for $1,200 upwards. This kind of pricing has made the brand, founded in 2014 and based in Zurich, Switzerland, a target for mainstream media ridicule. Not that any of it bothers Demna Gvasalia, the radical leading design spirit behind Vetements. He delights in taking a familiar piece of clothing – a hoodie, a T-shirt, a pair of jeans – and making it utterly covetable, the *must* garment of the moment, sprinkling magic design dust over the most basic of vêtements – the French word for clothes (although the fashion brand has no circumflex accent). He loves the trainer as much as any piece in the fashion lexicon, creating a trend in the late 2010s for big 'dad' sneakers and designing the bestselling wide-soled Balenciaga Triple S trainer. Gvasalia knows his fashion history but don't expect him to pay homage to it. 'I don't think elegance is relevant,' he shrugs.

Gvasalia's success at Vetements was quickly recognised by the broader luxury industry with his appointment at Balenciaga in 2015, taking up the mantle of Nicolas Ghesquière. In his new role, he immersed himself in the legendary couturier's working methods and designs, in particular developing volume through garments such as outsized bomber jackets, referencing the voluminous couture coats of the 1950s. And if Gvasalia's playful way with T-shirts and hoodies at Vetements initially overshadowed his technical skills as a tailor, his most recent collections for Balenciaga have certainly rectified that perception.

Speaking in 2019 to *WWD*, Gvasalia noted that Balenciaga 'worked on volumes first and foremost, not decoration. What I found at Balenciaga was kind of a gift for me. … Balenciaga's approach to volume was so perfectly suitable for me with my personal taste for volume.' He links this explicitly to being dressed in large-size hand-me-downs when he was a child. As a designer, oversize has become what he calls his 'design territory'.

Since 2015, Gvasalia has thus split his time between an independent cutting-edge collective in the form of Vetements and a luxury juggernaut in Balenciaga, and it is the very difference between the two experiences that appeals to the designer. Vetements, as he sees it, is 'always very much like "it's ugly, that's why we like it."' At Balenciaga, by contrast, 'ugliness doesn't exist at all'.

In an interview with Alexander Fury, Gvasalia muse Lotta Volkova noted, 'The way we work at Vetements is kind of a sign of our time. I think it represents a whole remix of cultures, a remix of references. You're constantly bombarded by information, social media. It's why young people feel so related to it.' Gvasalia told Suleman Anaya at *023c*, 'We start the season defining what *kind* of garments we like. Is it skirts? Is it pants? Is it jackets? Is it a pea coats? Is it a bomber jacket?'

Gvasalia always wants to innovate in a twenty-first-century spirit. The spring/summer 2017 show for Vetements was symptomatic of his approach. Vetements had been invited to show on the first evening of haute couture week in Paris. With no atelier to draw on, Gvasalia and Lotta Volkova came up with a radical solution: a collaboration to surpass all other collaborations, joining forces with no less than seventeen long-established brands, ranging from fellow luxury labels such as Manolo Blahnik and Brioni to heritage names such as Levi's and Dr Martens. Staged during opening hours at department store Galeries Lafayette, the show was conceived as a modern response to the very essence of couture – showing off the expertise of ateliers, the difference being that in this case the ateliers were specialist brands to which Vetements had outsourced the expertise.

Vetements brought street style and street clothes crashing into the world of high fashion. While Gvasalia was not the first to do so (the parallels with Raf Simons are striking), he did it with a new level of commitment and an often electrifying brio. In interviews, Gvasalia has sometimes preferred to dwell on the similarities, rather than the differences, between old and new. Speaking in early 2018, he said: 'Whether it's a Vetements hoodie or a couture dress, it's still about the person putting it on and thinking: "I am happy with this, I am happy with how I look."'

Demna Gvasalia and his brother Guram (his long-term business partner) were born in Sukhumi, Georgia, in 1981 and 1986 respectively, in the north-western region of Abkhazia, then part of the Soviet Union. Coming from a close-knit family, he has recalled the impact of his half-French Jewish grandmother, who wore lace maxi skirts and jewellery painted with nail varnish.

Georgia was in turmoil during these years, achieving a troubled independence in 1991 only for Abkhazia to explode again in conflict a year later. Thus, when Gvasalia was twelve, his hometown of Sukhumi was a war zone. In the spring/summer 2019 collection for Vetements, Gvasalia directly referenced the traumas of this period, showing printed targets on tees with bullet holes and gimp masks that represented, he said, how he felt. The show was staged in concrete vaults of the Paris Périphérique, drawing deliberate parallels with the migrant crisis (the venue was near migrant aid camps). A Vetements app redirected users to a Wikipedia page about the ethnic cleansing of Georgians in Abkhazia.

The threat of ongoing separatist violence in Abkhazia persuaded the family to flee the region in search of a more stable existence, a long, hard process that concluded with the family settling in Düsseldorf, Germany. 'Taking risks is something I got used to as a kid and that is in the DNA of

Vetements,' he said years later. 'In fashion now, you need to take risks to survive.' Gvasalia had initially studied economics, concluding quickly that the subject would make him 'the most unhappy person in the world'. His breakthrough was to squeeze onto the MA fashion course at the Royal Academy of Arts in Antwerp, achieved despite poor preparation and a flimsy knowledge of the Belgian designers from the famed college. Tutors Linda Loppa and Walter Van Beirendonck spotted the young Georgian's innate intelligence and creative energy, which flourished in Antwerp's busy studios.

Gvasalia's design path could not have been more perfect to prepare him for a major position in the industry. From Antwerp, he joined Maison Margiela, working on womenswear at the company during the last months before Margiela himself retired and as part of the studio-driven realignment that followed. Years later, he said: 'My real studies, where I learned about clothes, was working at Margiela, especially in this kind of transitional period after Martin left; when the company was trying to modernise its DNA and find ways to continue its history. For me it was like an MA in fashion.'

Gvasalia has always been upfront about the influence of Margiela, even dedicating his autumn/winter 2018 Vetements collection, *The Elephant in the Room*, to the designer. The collection included a take on Margiela's shoe design, the split-toed Tabi. He has called Margiela's approach 'investigative fashion', founded on the idea of taking apart a garment to understand how it was constructed, then constructing it anew. 'You really needed to understand the construction of the garment and to kind-of be in love with it in order to make something out of it.'

From Margiela, Gvasalia moved to Louis Vuitton, where he was once again well placed, working with the effervescent Marc Jacobs for two collections and then the perfectionist Nicolas Ghesquière for a further two. Margiela, Jacobs, Ghesquière: three giants of twenty-first-century fashion, three designers with radically diverse ways of working, teaching the hungry Gvasalia that there are many ways to make fashion. 'I was really lucky to work with all the people I worked with,' he acknowledged. 'I learned an immense amount and different ways of doing things.'

He was thirty-three when he founded Vetements, already confident and with a remarkable knowledge of fashion. From the very start, the brand had a distinctive niche, based on what academic Synne Skjulstad has described as 'a combination of unexpected moves, humour, irony, and contradictory intellectual anti-conceptualism … permeating both the collection and public profile'. Skjulstad has also highlighted Gvasalia's self-assurance in the world of the internet – he does most of his research online. The influence of the internet is evident in both the brand's design and communication practices: taking a break from fashion shows, Vetements even presented the entire spring/summer 2018 collection on Instagram.

The input of his brother Guram, who became CEO, was an important part of the early success of the brand. Buyers were asked to trust the unconventional Vetements way of doing business – staging shows when they wished, selling what they wanted when they wanted, taking lessons from the regular 'drops' of influential street brands such as Supreme. Guram is critical of the excesses of the fashion

Image 55.2 *Demna Gvasalia, 2017. Photo: Dimitrios Kambouris via Getty Images*

Image 55.3 *Vetements couture, autumn/winter 2018. Photo: Kristy Sparow via Getty Images*

system, in particular overproduction with too much so-called 'deadstock' ending up in outlet stores. At Vetements, he told *The Financial Times* in 2017, 'We control how much merchandise we sell to each store to make sure they don't overbuy'. By doing so, the company also restricts access to its product, intensifying the exclusivity and desirability of every Vetements piece.

Gvasalia's influences have been diverse, ransacking both high and low cultures, questioning whether a division between the two is of any relevance in the modern age, citing artist Marcel Duchamp as an inspiration for his appropriations. Unlike probably every other designer in this book, he is comfortable to describe his clothes as 'product'. He has made his own versions of IKEA's blue Frakta bags and deluxe versions of Crocs foam clogs. He perceives garments 'as a tool of communication' and has willingly dipped into politics and campaigning, supporting America's left-leaning would-be Democrat nominee Bernie Sanders in his autumn/winter 2017 show and campaigning for the World Food Programme two seasons later. His upbringing in Germany has been referenced through a very literal take on *polizei* jackets and hoodies adorned with the word 'Weltschmerz', which can be approximately translated as 'world-weariness'. A long-term friend is Russian designer Gosha Rubchinskiy, who modelled in an early Vetements show. Writing in *Vogue* Japan, fashion editor Suzy Menkes noted: 'The impact of plain and simple clothes, with a powerful, underlying message, has turned Vetements … from an unknown fashion collective into a brand that seems to define the social upheavals across the world.'

By 2018, media gossip suggested that the Vetements bubble was on the verge of bursting. Gvasalia hit back vigorously with a press release in March 2018: 'To the disappointment of all the haters, we would like to declare that Vetements is in the strongest creative and financial state it has ever been.' Four months later, he delivered his tenth Vetements collection, one of his most inventive to date, dedicated to Georgia. And then, in September 2018, he followed up with an exceptional spring/summer 2019 collection for Balenciaga that sought to reinvent tailoring for a new generation. He called it 'neo-tailoring' – ultra-lightweight jackets and fabrics with no shoulder pads, intended to feel like wearing a jogging suit, as the designer put it. 'It's something new in tailoring that is actually comfortable,' he said. 'You don't need to wear a shirt because the shirt has been transformed into a jacket.' For Balenciaga for autumn/winter 2019, he paid homage to the modern Paris street with a collection that ranged from brilliantly accomplished tailoring through to bags for water bottles presented as luxury products.

Gvasalia has emerged as a star designer who is thoroughly attuned to the mindset of young luxury consumers and the frenetic world of social media. He is set to be an influential player in designer fashion through the 2020s.

Further reading: Demna Gvasalia's approach to design is explored thoroughly in 'Monoprix at 40 Rue de Sevres' by Anja Aronowsky Cronberg in the edition of the journal *Vestoj* titled 'On Authenticity' (2017). An interview with *WWD* (February 2019) is full of insights on his design philosophy.

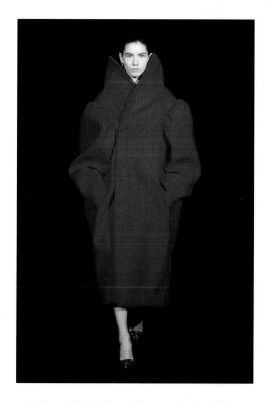

Image 55.4 *Balenciaga, autumn/winter 2019. Photo: Estrop via Getty Images.*

Bibliography

Aboud, A., ed. (2013), *Hello, My Name Is Paul Smith: Fashion and Other Stories*, New York: Rizzoli.

Anaya, S. (2015), 'Demna Gvasalia on Vetements, Balenciaga and The System', *032c*, Issue 29, Winter.

Armani, G. (2016), *Giorgio Armani*, Milan: Rizzoli.

Arnold, R. (2001), *Fashion, Desire and Anxiety*, London: I.B. Tauris.

Arnold, R. (2009), *The American Look: Fashion, Sportswear and the Image of Women in 1930s and 1940s New York*, London: I.B. Tauris.

Ash, J. and E. Wilson, eds. (1992), *Chic Thrills: A Fashion Reader*, London: Pandora.

Assouline, P. (2018), *Alaïa: Livre de Collection*, Paris: Assouline.

Baines, B. B. (1981), *Fashion Revivals: From the Elizabethan Age to the Present Day*, London: Batsford.

Balboa, R. A. (2016), 'The Work of Issey Miyake', *Domus*, 3 May.

Ball, D. (2011), *House of Versace: The Untold Story of Genius, Murder and Survival*, New York: Random House.

Ballard, B. (1960), *In My Fashion*, New York: David McKay.

Banks, J. (2018), *Norell: Master of American Fashion*, New York: Rizzoli.

Barber, L. (1998), 'The Frock Prince', *The Observer*, 29 November.

Barille, E. (1997), *Lanvin*, Paris: Editions Assouline.

Barnes, R. (1994), *Mods!* London: Plexus.

Baudot, F. (1996), *Alaïa*, Fashion Memoir series, London: Thames & Hudson.

Baudot, F. (1997), *Yohji Yamamoto*, Fashion Memoir series, London: Thames & Hudson.

Baudot, F. (1999), *Fashion: The Twentieth Century*, London: Thames & Hudson.

Beaton, C. (1989), *The Glass of Fashion*, London: Cassell.

Beene, G., J. Wolcott, M. Luther and P. A. Parmal (2005), *Beene by Beene*, New York: Vendome Press.

Benaïm, L. (1997), *Issey Miyake*, London: Thames & Hudson.

Benaïm, L. (2015), *Dior: The New Look Revolution*, New York: Rizzoli.

Benaïm, L. (2018), 'Hedi Slimane's First Celine Interview', *Le Figaro/Business of Fashion*, 25 September.

Bender, M. (1967), *The Beautiful People*, New York: Coward-McCann.

Bergé, P. (1997), *Yves Saint Laurent*, Fashion Memoir series, London: Thames & Hudson.

Bergé, P., F. Muller and H. Bowles (2008), *Yves Saint Laurent: Style*, New York: Abrams.

Bertin, C. (1956), *Paris A La Mode*, trans. M. Deans, London: Victor Gollancz.

Beyfus, D. (2015), *Vogue on Valentino Garavani*, London: Quadrille.

Blanchard, T. (2016), 'Issey Miyake: 45 Years at the Forefront of Fashion', *The Observer*, 10 April.

Blasberg, D. (2005), Gaultier interview, *Ten*, Winter.

Blum, D. E. (2003), *Shocking! The Art and Fashion of Schiaparelli*, New Haven, CT: Yale University Press.

Bluttal, S. and P. Mears (2001), *Halston*, London: Phaidon.

Bolton, A. (2017), *Rei Kawakubo/Comme des Garçons: Art of the In-Between*, New York: The Metropolitan Museum of Art Publications.

Bond, D. (1992), *Glamour in Fashion*, London: Guinness Publishing.

Boucher, F. (1996), *A History of Costume in the West*, London: Thames & Hudson.

Bovier, L. (2011), *Hedi Slimane: Anthology of a Decade*, Zürich: JRP Ringier.

Bowles, H. (2011), *Balenciaga and Spain: Spanish Master*, New York: Rizzoli.

Bowles, H. (2013), 'The Phoebe Files', *Vogue* (US), March.

Breward, C. (1994), *The Culture of Fashion: A New History of Fashionable Dress*, Manchester: Manchester University Press.

Breward, C. (2003), *Fashion*, Oxford: Oxford University Press.

Breward, C., C. Becky and C. Cox, eds. (2002), *The Englishness of English Dress*, Oxford: Berg.

Breward, C., E. Ehrman and C. Evans (2004), *The London Look: Fashion from Street to Catwalk*, London: Yale University Press.

Breward, C., G. Gilbert and J. Lister (2006), *Swinging Sixties Fashion in London and Beyond 1955–1970*, London: V&A Publications.

Brubach, H. (1992), 'The Religion of Woman', *The New Yorker*, 6 July.

Brubach, H. (1999), *A Dedicated Follower of Fashion*, London: Phaidon Press.

Bruni, F. (2018), 'Alessandro Michele, Fashion's Modern Mastermind', *The New York Times*, 15 October.

Buxbaum, G., ed. (2005), *Icons of Fashion: The 20th Century*, Munich: Prestel.

Byatt, A. S. (2016), *Peacock & Vine: On William Morris and Mariano Fortuny*, New York: Knopf.

Carter, E. (1977), *The Changing World of Fashion*, New York: Putnam's.

Carter, E. (1980), *Magic Names of Fashion*, London: Weidenfeld and Nicolson.

Cartner-Morley, J. (2000), 'Drama Kings', *The Guardian*, 23 September.

Cawthorne, N. (1996), *The New Look: The Dior Revolution*, London: Hamlyn.

Celant, G., ed. (1994), *The Italian Metamorphosis 1943–1968*, New York: Guggenheim Museum Publications.

Celant, G., I. Sischy, et al. (2000), *Armani*, New York: Guggenheim Museum Publications.

Charles-Roux, E. (1976), *Chanel*, London: Jonathan Cape.

Charles-Roux, E. (1981), *Chanel and Her World*, London: Weidenfeld and Nicolson.

Chase, E. W. and I. Chase (1954), *Always in Vogue*, London: Victor Gollancz.

Chenoune, F. (1993), *A History of Men's Fashion*, Paris: Flammarion.

Chenoune, F. (1996), *Jean Paul Gaultier*, Paris: Editions Assouline.

Chenoune, F. (2007), *Dior: 60 Years of Style*, London: Thames & Hudson.

Chenoune, F. (2010), *Yves Saint Laurent*, New York: Abrams.

Clarke, L. (ed.) Polan, B. (2007), 'The Measure, Vivienne Westwood in Conversation', *The Death of Taste*, London: University of the Arts London.

Colegrave, S. and C. Sullivan, eds. (2001), *Punk: A Life Apart*, London: Cassell.

Coleman, E. A. (1989), *The Opulent Era: Fashions of Worth, Doucet, Pingat*, London: Thames & Hudson.

Coleridge, N. (1988), *The Fashion Conspiracy*, London: Heinemann.

Collins, A. F. (1994), 'Haute Coco', *Vanity Fair*, June.

Compton, N. (2002), 'The New Kingdom of Alexander McQueen', *iD*, August.

Cosgrave, B. (2007), *Made For Each Other: Fashion and the Academy Awards*, London: Bloomsbury.

Cox, C. (2004), *Stiletto*, London: Mitchell Beazley.

Craik, J. (2005), *Uniforms Exposed: From Conformity to Transgression*, Oxford: Berg.

Cronberg, A. A. (2017), 'Monoprix at 40 Rue de Sevres', *Vestoj*, Issue 8.

Cullen, O. and C. K. Burks (2019), *Christian Dior*, London: V&A Publications.

Cullerton, B. (1995), *Geoffrey Beene*, New York: Abrams.

Cunningham, P. A. (2003), *Reforming Women's Fashion, 1850–1920*, Kent: Kent State University Press.

Daria, I. (1990), *The Fashion Cycle*, New York: Simon & Schuster.

De Combray, R. (1982), *Armani*, Milan: Franco Maria Ricci Editore.

De la Haye, A. (1996), *The Cutting Edge: 50 Years of British Fashion*, London: V&A Publications.

De la Haye, A. and C. Dingwall, eds. (1996), *Surfers, Soulies, Skinheads and Skaters: Subcultural Style from the Forties to the Nineties*, London: V&A Publications.

De la Haye, A. and V. Mendes (2014), *The House of Worth: Portrait of a Fashion Archive*, London: V&A Publications.

De la Haye, A. and S. Tobin (1994), *Chanel: The Couturière at Work*, London: V&A Publications.

De la Haye, A. and E. Wilson, eds. (1999), *Defining Dress: Dress as Object, Meaning and Identity*, Manchester: Manchester University Press.

De la Hoz, C. (2016), *Audrey and Givenchy: A Fashion Love Affair*, Philadelphia, PA: Running Press.

De Looz, P. E. (2013), 'The Story of Nicolas Ghesquière and How Balenciaga Became 21st Century Fashion', *032c*, October 17.

De Marly, D. (1980), *Worth, Father of Haute Couture*, New York: Homes Meier.

De Marly, D. (1990), *History of Haute Couture, 1850–1950*, London: B.T. Batsford.

De Nicolay-Mazery, C., and H. de Givenchy (2010), *Cristóbal Balenciaga, Philippe Venet, Hubert de Givenchy: Grand Traditions of French Couture*, Paris: Flammarion.

De Osma, G. (1984), *Fortuny*, London: Aurum Press.

De Réthy, E. and J.-L. Perreau (1999), *Christian Dior: The Early Years 1947–1957*, London: Thames & Hudson.

Dermonex, J. (1991), *Madeleine Vionnet*, trans. A. Audubert, London: Thames & Hudson.

Derrick, R. (2003), *People in Vogue: A Century of Portraits*, London: Little, Brown.

Descott, A.-M. (1978), 'Seeking Your Fortuny', *Sunday Times Magazine*, 23 July.

Deslandres, Y. (1987), *Poiret*, London: Thames & Hudson.

Di Trocchio, P. (2014), 'Madame Grès: Couturier at Work', *Fashion Theory*, 18 (4): 465–471.

Dior, C. ([1957] 2007), *Dior by Dior*, trans. A. Fraser, London: V&A Publications.

Dior, C. ([1954] 2008), *The Little Dictionary of Fashion: A Guide to Dress Sense for Every Woman,* London: V&A Publications.

Dior, C., R. Donnedieu de Varbres, B. Arnault and J.-L. Dufresne (2005), *Christian Dior: Man of the Century*, Granville: Musée Christian Dior.

Dior et Moi (2014), [Film] Dir. Frédéric Tcheng, France: CIM Productions.

Dolce, D. and S. Gabbana (1996), *10 Years of Dolce & Gabbana*, New York: Abbeville Press.

D'Orazio, S. (2007), *Gianni and Donatella*, Hamburg: teNeues.

Drake, A. (2006), *The Beautiful Fall: Fashion, Genius and Glorious Excess in 1970s Paris*, London: Bloomsbury.

Dufresne, J.-L. (2006), *Christian Dior et Le Monde*, Granville: Musée Christian Dior.

Dufresne, J.-L. (2007), *Dior: 60 Annees Hautes en Couleurs*, Granville: Musée Christian Dior.

Duras, M. (1988), *Yves Saint Laurent: Images of Design 1958-1988*, New York: Alfred Knopf.

Duras, M. (2010), *Yves Saint Laurent: Icons of Fashion Design*, Munich: Schirmer/Mosel.

Eastoe, J. and S. Gristwood (2008), *Fabulous Frocks*, London: Pavilion.

Edelman, A. H. (1997), *The Little Black Dress*, London: Aurum.

Elting, L. (1999), 'Revealing the Accomplishments of Madame Paquin, the Very Queen of Dressmakers', MA diss., Courtauld Institute of Art, London.

English, B. (2007), *A Cultural History of Fashion in the 20th Century: From the Catwalk to the Sidewalk*, Oxford: Berg.

English, B. (2011), *Japanese Fashion Designers: The Work and Influence of Issey Miyake, Yohji Yamamoto and Rei Kawakubo*, Oxford: Berg.

Esquevin, C. (2008), *Adrian: Silver Screen to Custom Label*, New York: Monacelli Press.

Etherington-Smith, M. (1983), *Patou*, London: Hutchinson.

Evans, C. (2003), *Fashion at the Edge: Spectacle, Modernity, and Deathliness*, New Haven, CT: Yale University Press.

Evans, C. (2013), *The Mechanical Smile: Modernism and the First Fashion Shows in France*, New Haven, CT: Yale University Press.

Evans, C. and M. Thornton (1989), *Women and Fashion: A New Look*, London: Quartet Books.

Ewing, E. and A. Mackrell (1992), *History of 20th Century Fashion*, London: Batsford.

Fairchild, J. (1965), *The Fashionable Savages*, New York: Doubleday.

Fairchild, J. (1989), *Chic Savages*, New York: Simon & Schuster.

Ferragamo, S. (1957), *Shoemaker of Dreams*, London: Harrap.

Ferragamo, W. and S. Kung (2008), *Salvatore Ferragamo: Evolving Legend 1928-2008*, Milan: Skira.

Flanner, J. (1940), 'Pioneer', *The New Yorker*, 13 January.

Flaviano, O. (2019), *Yves Saint Laurent Haute Couture Catwalk 1962-2001*, London: Thames & Hudson.

Foley, B. (2001), 'Who's Number One?', *WWD special edition*, July.

Foley, B. (2004), *Marc Jacobs*, New York: Editions Assouline.

Foley, B. (2018), *Ralph Lauren: 50 Years of Fashion: Reported by WWD*, New York: Rizzoli.

Ford, T. (2004), *Tom Ford*, London: Thames & Hudson.

Frankel, S. (2001), *Visionaries,* London: V&A Publications.

Frankel, S. (2004), 'The Feeling Is Miuccia', *The Independent*, 21 February.

Fraser, K. (1981), 'Feminine Fashions', *The New Yorker*, 13 July.

Fraser, K. (1984), *The Fashionable Mind: Reflections on Fashion 1970–1982*, New York: Random House.

Fraser-Cavassoni, N. (2017), *Vogue on Calvin Klein*, London: Quadrille.

Friedman, V. (2008), 'Prada', *Ten*, Autumn.

Friedman, V. (2018), 'Warhol & I', *The New York Times*, 24 October.

Frowick, L. (2014), *Halston: Inventing American Fashion*, New York: Rizzoli.

Gaines, S. (1991), *Halston: The Untold Story*, New York: Putnam.

Gaines, S. and S. Churcher (1994), *Obsession: The Lives & Times of Calvin Klein*, New York: Birch Lane Press.

Gale, C. and J. Kaur (2004), *Fashion and Textiles: An Overview*, Oxford: Berg.

Galloni, A. (2007), 'The Designer Defends Prada', *The Wall Street Journal*, January 25.

Garavani, V. (2014), *Valentino: At the Emperor's Table*, New York: Assouline.

Garelick, R. K. (2014), *Mademoiselle: Coco Chanel and the Pulse of History*, New York: Random House.

Gaultier, J. P. (1990), *A Nous Deux la Mode*, Paris: Flammarion.

Gerber Klein, M. (2018), *Charles James: Portrait of an Unreasonable Man: Fame, Fashion, Art*, New York: Rizzoli.

Gnoli, S. (2014), *The Origins of Italian Fashion: 1900-1945*, London: V&A Publications.

Golbin, P., ed. (2006), *Balenciaga Paris*, London: Thames & Hudson.

Golbin, P. (2008), *Valentino: Themes and Variations*, New York: Rizzoli.

Golbin, P., ed. (2009), *Madeleine Vionnet: Puriste de la Mode*, Paris: Les Arts Décoratifs.

Gorman, P. (2001), *The Look: Adventures in Pop and Rock Fashion*, London: Sanctuary.

Green, J. (1998), *All Dressed Up: The Sixties and the Counterculture*, London: Pimlico.

Grigoriadis, V. (2008), 'The Deep Shallowness of Marc Jacobs', *Rolling Stone*, December.

Gross, M. (1995), *Model: The Ugly Business of Beautiful Women*, New York: William Morrow.

Gross, M. (2003), *Genuine Authentic: The Real Life of Ralph Lauren*, New York: Harper Collins.

Gross, E. and F. Rottman (1999), *Halston: An American Original*, London: Harper Collins.

Grossiord, S., ed. (2015), *Jeanne Lanvin*, Paris: Paris Museums.

Guillaume, V. (1998), *Courrèges*, Fashion Memoir series, London: Thames & Hudson.

Hall, S. and T. Jefferson, eds. ([1976] 1996), *Resistance Through Rituals: Youth Sub-Cultures in Post-War Britain*, London: Routledge.

Hastreiter, K. (2008), *Geoffrey Beene: Fashion Rebel*, Paris: Assouline.

Hawes, E. (1938), *Fashion Is Spinach*, New York: Random House.

Heathcote, P. (1960), 'The House of Dior', *The Guardian*, 1 August.

Hebdige, D. ([1979] 1993), *Subculture: The Meaning of Style*, London: Routledge.

Heller, Z. (1997), 'Jacobs' Ladder', *The New Yorker*, 22 September.

Hesse, J.-P. (2010), *Pierre Cardin: 60 Years of Innovation*, New York: Assouline.

Hesse, J.-P. (2017), *Pierre Cardin*, New York: Assouline.

Holborn, M. (1995), *Issey Miyake*, Cologne: Taschen.

Hollander, A. (1978), *Seeing Through Clothes*, Berkeley: University of California Press.

Hollander, A. (1994), *Sex and Suits*, New York: Alfred Knopf.

Hopkins, H. (1963), *The New Look: A Social History of the Forties and Fifties in Britain*, London: Secker & Warburg.

Horyn, C. (1998), 'Naked Ambition', *Vanity Fair*, May.

Horyn, C. (2007), 'Q&A: Nicolas Ghesquière', *The New York Times,* 29 June.

Howell, G. (1990), *Sultans of Style*, London: Ebury Press.

Howell, G. (1991), *In Vogue*, London: Random Century.

Howell, G. (1998), *Diana: Her Life in Fashion*, London: Pavilion.

Jacobs, L. (1999), *Beauty and the Beene: A Modern Legend*, New York: Abrams.

Janbon, C. (1999), 'Callot Soeurs', MA diss., Courtauld Institute of Art, London.

Join-Dieterle, C., S. Train and M.-J. Lepicard (1991), *Givenchy: 40 Years of Creation*, Paris: Paris Musées/Palais Galliera.

Jones, T., ed. (2001), *Smile I-D: Fashion and Style. The Best from 20 Years of I-D.* Cologne: Taschen.

Jones, T. (2012a), *Rei Kawakubo*, Cologne: Taschen.

Jones, T. (2012b), *Yohji Yamamoto*, Cologne: Taschen.

Jones, T. (2012c), *Vivienne Westwood*, Cologne: Taschen.

Jorgensen, J. and D. L. Scoggins (2015), *Creating the Illusion: A Fashionable History of Hollywood Costume Designers*, Philadelphia, PA: Running Press.

Karan, D. (2015), *My Journey*, New York: Ballantine Books.

Karimzadeh, M. (2006), 'Can You Handle It?', *WWD The Magazine*, Fall.

Kawamura, Y. (2004), *The Japanese Revolution in Paris Fashion*, Oxford: Berg.

Keogh, P. C. (1999), *Audrey Style*, New York, Harper Collins Publishers.

Kirke, B. (1998), *Madeleine Vionnet*, San Francisco: Chronicle Books.

Klein, C. (2017), *Calvin Klein*, New York: Rizzoli.

Koda, H. (1987), *Three Women: Madeleine Vionnet, Claire McCardell, Rei Kawakubo*, New York: Fashion Institute of Technology.

Koda, H. (2001), *Extreme Beauty: The Body Transformed*, New York: Metropolitan Museum of Art Publications.

Koda, H. (2003), *Goddess: The Classical Mode*, New York: Metropolitan Museum of Art Publications.

Koda, H. (2008), *Rei Kawakubo: ReFusing Fashion*, Detroit: Museum of Contemporary Art Detroit.

Koda H. and A. Bolton (2005), *Chanel*, New York: Metropolitan Museum of Art Publications.

Koda H. and A. Bolton (2007), *Poiret*, New York: Metropolitan Museum of Art Publications.

Koda, H., J. Giler Reeder and R. Rucci (2014), *Charles James: Beyond Fashion*, New York: Metropolitan Museum of Art Publications.

Koike, K. (2016), *Issey Miyake*, Cologne: Taschen.

Koren, L. (1984), *New Fashion Japan*, Tokyo: Kodansha International.

Krell, G. (1997), *Vivienne Westwood*, Fashion Memoir series, London: Thames & Hudson.

Kurutz, S. (2018), 'How Marc Jacobs Fell Out of Fashion', *The New York Times*, 2 June.

Längle, E. (2005), *Pierre Cardin: Fifty Years of Fashion and Design*, New York: Vendome Press.

Lauren, R. (2017), *Ralph Lauren*, New York: Rizzoli.

Laver, J. (1969), *A Concise History of Costume*, London: Thames & Hudson.

Lee, S. T., ed. (1975), *American Fashion: The Life and Lines of Adrian, Mainbocher, McCardell, Norell, and Trigère*, New York: Fashion Institute of Technology.

Leitch, L. (2017), *Vogue on Dolce & Gabbana*, London: Quadrille.

Lister, J. (2019), *Mary Quant,* London: V&A Publications.

Lobenthal, J. (1990), *Radical Rags: Fashions of the Sixties*, New York: Abbeville Press.

Long, C. (2018), 'Hedi Slimane, Fashion's Sharpest Designer', *The Financial Times*, 21 January.

Long, T. A. (2015), *Charles James: Designer in Detail*, London: V&A Publications.

Lonsdale, S. (2000), *Japanese Style*, London: Carlton Books.

Loyaute, B. (2006), *Pierre Cardin Evolution*, Paris: Flammarion.

Mackrell, A. (1990), *Paul Poiret*, London: Batsford.

Mackrell, A. (1992), *Coco Chanel*, London: Batsford.

Madsen, A. (1990), *Coco Chanel*, London: Bloomsbury.

Marras, A. (2010), *Kenzo*, New York: Rizzoli.

Marsh, L. (2003), *The House of Klein: Fashion, Controversy and a Business Obsession*, New York: Wiley.

Martin, P. (2010), 'Phoebe Philo Designs the Clothes Women Actually Want to Wear', *The Gentlewoman*, Issue 1.

Martin, R. (1987), *Fashion and Surrealism*, New York: Rizzoli.

Martin, R. (1997a), *Gianni Versace*, New York: Metropolitan Museum of Art Publications/Abrams.

Martin, R. (1997b), *Versace*, Fashion Memoir series, London: Thames & Hudson.

Martin, R. (1998a), *American Ingenuity: Sportswear 1930s–1970s*, New York: Metropolitan Museum of Art Publications.

Martin, R. (1998b), *Charles James*, Fashion Memoir series, London: Thames & Hudson.

Martin, R. and H. Koda (1989), *The Historical Mode: Fashion and Art in the 1980s*, New York: Rizzoli.

Martin, R. and H. Koda (1990), *Giorgio Armani: Images of Man*, New York: Rizzoli.

Martin, R. and H. Koda (1994a), *Madame Grès*, New York: Metropolitan Museum of Arts Publications.

Martin, R. and H. Koda (1994b), *Orientalism: Visions of the East in Western Dress*, New York: Metropolitan Museum of Art Publications.

Martin R. and H. Koda (1996), *Haute Couture*, New York: Metropolitan Museum of Art Publications.

Massey A. (2000), *Hollywood Beyond the Screen*, Oxford: Berg.

Masui, K. and C. Masui (2019), *Kenzo Takada*, New York: ACC Art Books.

McCardell, C. (1956), *What Shall I Wear?* New York: Simon & Schuster.

McConathy, D. (1975), 'Mainbocher', in S. T. Lee (ed.), *American Fashion: The Life and Lines of Adrian, Mainbocher, McCardell, Norell, and Trigère*, New York: Fashion Institute of Technology.

McDermott, C. (1987), *Streetstyle: British Design in the Eighties*, London: Design Council.

McDermott, C. (1999) *Vivienne Westwood*, London: Carlton Books.

McDowell, C. (1987), *McDowell's Directory of Twentieth Century Fashion*, 2nd edn, London: Frederick Muller.

McDowell, C. (1989), *Shoes: Fashion and Fantasy*, London: Thames & Hudson.

McDowell, C. (1997a), *Forties Fashion and the New Look*, London: Bloomsbury.

McDowell, C. (1997b), *John Galliano*, London: Weidenfeld & Nicolson.

McDowell, C. (1997c), *The Man of Fashion: Peacock Males and Perfect Gentlemen*, London: Thames & Hudson.

McDowell, C. (2000), *Jean Paul Gaultier*, London: Cassell & Co.

McDowell, C. (2002), *Ralph Lauren: The Man, the Vision, the Style*, New York: Rizzoli.

McDowell, C. (2003), *Fashion Today*, London: Phaidon.

McQueen (2018), [Film] Dir. Ian Bonhôte and Peter Ettedgui, London: Misfits Entertainment.

McRobbie, A., ed. (1989), *Zootsuits & Second-Hand Dresses: An Anthology of Fashion & Music*, London: Macmillan.

McRobbie, A. (1994), *Postmodernism and Popular Culture*, London: Routledge.

Mead, R. (1998), 'The Crazy Professor', *The New Yorker*, 30 March.

Mears, P. (2007), *Madame Grès: Sphinx of Fashion*, New York: Fashion Institute of Technology.

Mellor, D. A., and L. Gervereau, eds. (1997), *The Sixties: Britain and France, 1960-1973 The Utopian Years*, London: Philip Wilson.

Mendes, V. (1990), *Pierre Cardin: Past, Present, Future*, London: 3Nishen Publishing.

Menkes, S. (2006), 'The Mistress of Us All', *The International Herald Tribune*, 27 February.

Menkes, S. (2008), 'Balenciaga – Austerity Chic', *The International Herald Tribune*, 26 February.

Menkes, S. (2011), *The Fashion Universe of Jean Paul Gaultier: From the Street to the Stars*, New York: Abrams.

Merceron, D. L. (2007), *Lanvin*, New York: Rizzoli.

Miglietti. F. A. (2006), *Fashion Statements: Interviews with Fashion Designers*, Milan: Skira.

Milbank, C. R. (1985), *Couture: The Great Fashion Designers*, London: Thames & Hudson.

Milbank, C. R. (1989), *New York Fashion: The Evolution of American Style*, New York: Abrams.

Milinaire, C. and C. Troy (1978), *Cheap Chic*, New York: Crown Publishers.

Miller, A., P. Tarr and N. Dalva (2005), *Geoffrey Beene: A Design Tribute*, New York: 2wice Arts Foundation.

Miller, L. E. (1993), *Balenciaga*, London: Batsford.

Miller, L. E. (2007), *Balenciaga,* London: V&A Publications.

Miller, L. E. (2017), *Balenciaga: Shaping Fashion*, London: V&A Publications.

Mitchell, L., B. English and A. Fukai (2005), *The Cutting Edge: Fashion from Japan*, Sydney: Powerhouse Publishing.

Mitsuda, A. (2010), *Yohji Yamamoto: My Dear Bomb, A Biography*, Antwerp: Ludion Editions.

Moffitt, P. and W. Claxton (1991), *The Rudi Gernreich Book*, New York: Rizzoli.

Mohrt, F. (1998), *The Givenchy Style*, Paris: Assouline.

Molho, R. and A. Shugaar (2007), *Being Armani: A Biography*, Milan: Baldini Castoldi Dalai.

Molloy, J. T. (1980), *Women: Dress for Success*, New York: Foulsham.

Morais, R. (1991), *Pierre Cardin: The Man Who Became a Label*, London: Bantam Press.

Morand, P. (2008), *The Allure of Chanel*, trans. E. Cameron, London: Pushkin Press.

Morris, B. (1975), 'Norell', in S. T. Lee (ed.), *American Fashion: The Life and Lines of Adrian, Mainbocher, McCardell, Norell, and Trigère*, New York: Fashion Institute of Technology.

Morris, B. (1978), 'Halston's Special Way with Tradition', *New York Times*, 20 December.

Morton, C. (2008), 'John Galliano's Year of Magic', *Harper's Bazaar* (UK), April.

Mower, S. (2005), *20 Years Dolce & Gabbana*, Milan: Dolce & Gabbana S.r.l.

Mulvagh, J. (1988), *Vogue: History of Twentieth Century Fashion*, London: Viking.

Mulvagh, J. (2011), *Vivienne Westwood: An Unfashionable Life*, London: Harper Collins.

Nava, M. (1992), *Changing Cultures, Feminism, Youth and Consumerism*, London: Sage.

Norman, P. (1990), *The Age of Parody: Dispatches from the Eighties*, London: Hamish Hamilton.

Ormen, C. (2017), *All about Yves*, trans. A. Reece, London: Laurence King.

Palmer, A. (2009), *Dior: A New Look, a New Enterprise*, London: V&A Publications.

Palmer, A. (2019), *Christian Dior: History and Modernity*, Munich: Hirmer.

Parkins, I. (2012), *Poiret, Dior and Schiaparelli: Fashion, Femininity and Modernity*, London: Berg.

Pasi, M. (1987), *Versace Teatro*, trans. W. Weaver, Milan: Franco Maria Ricci.

Pasols, P.-G. (2005), *Louis Vuitton: The Birth of Modern Luxury*, trans. L. Ammon, New York: Abrams.

Penn, I. (1998), *Irving Penn Regards the Work of Issey Miyake*, London: Jonathan Cape.

Piacenti, K. A., S. Ricci and G. Vergani (1985), *Salvatore Ferragamo*, Florence: Palazzo Strozzi.

Piaggi, A. (1980), *Lagerfeld's Sketchbook*, New York: Weidenfeld & Nicolson.

Piaggi, A. (1982), *Armani*, Milan: Franco Maria Ricci.

Pochna, M.-F., and J. Galliano (2008), *Christian Dior: The Biography*, New York: Duckworth.

Poiret, P. (1931), *My First Fifty Years*, trans. S. H. Guest, London: Victor Gollancz.

Polan, B. (1979), 'A New Look from the Man Behind the Mini', *The Guardian*, 15 August.

Polan, B. (1982), 'Mary Comes Back into Fashion', *The Guardian*, 4 March.

Polan, B., ed. (1983), *The Fashion Year 1983*, London: Zomba.

Polan, B., ed. (1984), *Fashion 84*, New York: St Martins Press.

Polan, B (2000), 'Armani', How to Spend It Magazine, *The Financial Times* (London).

Polhemus, T. (1994), *Street Style: From Sidewalk to Catwalk*, London: Thames & Hudson.

Polle, E. (2013), *Jean Patou: A Fashionable Life*, trans. A. Keens, Paris: Flammarion.

Potvin, J. (2013), *Giorgio Armani: Empire of the Senses*, Farnham: Ashgate.

Probert, C. (1981), *Shoes in Vogue since 1910*, London: Thames & Hudson.

Quant, M. (1965), *Quant by Quant*, London: Cassell.

Quick, H. (2002), 'Killer McQueen', *Vogue* (UK), October.

Quick, H. (2006), 'Saint Nicolas', *Vogue* (UK), August.

Quick, H. (2010), 'Philo Facts', *Vogue* (UK), April.

Rawsthorn, A. (1998), *Yves Saint Laurent*, London: Harper Collins.

Rees-Roberts, N. (2015), 'Raf Simons and Interdisciplinary Fashion from Post-Punk to Neo-Modern', *Fashion Theory*, 19 (1): 9–41.

Ricci, S. (2006), *Walking Dreams: Salvatore Ferragamo 1890-1960*, Mexico City: Editorial RM.

Ricci, S., ed. (2008), *Salvatore Ferragamo: Evolving Legend 1928–2008*, Milan: Skira.

Ricci, S. and C. Risaliti (2012), *Salvatore Ferragamo: Inspiration and Vision*, Milan: Skira.

Ricci, S. and C. Sisi (2018), *1927 The Return to Italy: Salvatore Ferragamo and the Twentieth Century Visual Culture*, Milan: Skira.

Richards, M. (2000), *Chanel Key Collections*, London: Hamlyn.

Riello, G. and P. McNeil, eds. (2006), *Shoes: A History from Sandals to Sneakers*, Oxford: Berg.

Riley, R. (1975), 'Adrian', in S. T. Lee (ed.), *American Fashion: The Life and Lines of Adrian, Mainbocher, McCardell, Norell, and Trigère*, New York: Fashion Institute of Technology.

Rossi, W. A. (1977), *The Sex Life of the Foot and Shoe*, London: Routledge & Kegan Paul.

Rowbotham, S. (2001), *Promise of a Dream: Remembering the Sixties*, London: Verso.

Saillard, O., ed. (2014), *Madame Grès: Sculptural Fashion*, Lichtervelde: Cannibal/Hannibal.

Saillard, O. (2016), *Dior: Christian Dior 1947-1957*, trans. B. Mellor, New York: Assouline.

Saillard, O. and A. Zazzo, eds. (2012), *Paris Haute Couture*, Paris: Flammarion.

Saillard, O., A. Alaïa, and B. Delanoe (2013), *Alaïa: Palais Galliera du 28 septembre 2013 au 26 janvier 2014*, Paris: Paris Musées.

Sailiard, O., D. Veillon and P. Bergé (2017), *Yves Saint Laurent: The Scandal Collection 1971*, New York: Abrams.

Sainderichin, G. (1998), *Kenzo*, Fashion Memoir series, London: Thames & Hudson.

Saint Laurent, Y., Vreeland, D., et al. (1983), *Yves Saint Laurent*, New York: Metropolitan Museum of Art Publications.

Salazar, L. (2011), *Yohji Yamamoto*, London: V&A Publications.

Samek, S. (2013), 'Uniformly Feminine: The "Working Chic" of Mainbocher', *Dress*, 20 (1): 33–44.

Sato, K. (1998), *Issey Miyake: Making Things*, Paris: Fondation Cartier/Scalo.

Savage, J. (1991), *England's Dreaming: Sex Pistols and Punk Rock*, London: Faber and Faber.

Schiaparelli, E. (1954), *Shocking Life*, New York, E.P. Dutton.

Schiaparelli Berenson, M. (2014), *Elsa Schiaparelli's Private Album*, London: Double-Barrelled Books.

Schoumann, H. (2002), *Chloé*, New York: Assouline.

Secrest, M. (2014), *Elsa Schiaparelli: A Biography*, London: Penguin.

Shimizu, S. (2016), *Creativity Is Born: Issey Miyake and Reality Lab*, Tokyo: PIE International.

Singer S. (2001), 'Bonjour Jeunesse', *Vogue* (US), March.

Sir Paul Smith | Full Address and Q&A | Oxford Union (2018), [YouTube], Available online: https://www.you tube.com/watch?v=Q_uTkBYOvIs.

Sirop, D. (1989), *Paquin*, Paris: Editions Adam Biro.

Sischy, I. (1998), *Donna Karan New York*, New York: Vendome Universe of Fashion.

Sischy, I. (2004), *The Journey of a Woman: 20 Years of Donna Karan*, New York: Assouline.

Sischy, I. (2013), 'Galliano in the Wilderness', *Vanity Fair*, July.

Slinkard, P. (2016), *Making Mainbocher: The First American Couturier*, Chicago, IL: Chicago Historical Society.

Smith, P. (2001), *You Can Find Inspiration in Everything (And If You Can't, Look Again)*, London: Violette Editions.

Socha, M. (2000), 'Slimane Speaks', *WWD*, 5 July.

Socha, M. (2008), 'Art versus Commerce: Can Margiela Expand Without Selling Out?', *WWD*, 2 May.

Sozzani, F. (1999), *Dolce & Gabbana*, London: Thames & Hudson.

Sparke, P. (1987), *Japanese Design*, London: Swallow Publishing.

Stanifil, S. (2014), *The Glamour of Italian Fashion Since 1945*, London: V&A Publications.

Steele, V. (1991), *Women of Fashion*, New York: Rizzoli.

Steele, V. (1996), *Fetish: Fashion, Sex and Power*, Oxford: Oxford University Press.

Steele, V. (1997), *Fifty Years of Fashion: New Look to Now*, New Haven, CT: Yale University Press.

Steele, V. (1998a), *Paris Fashion: A Cultural History*, New York: Oxford University Press.

Steele, V. (1998b), *Shoes: A Lexicon of Style*, London: Scriptum Editions.

Steele, V. (2010), *Japan Fashion Now*, New Haven, CT: Yale University Press.

Steele, V. and J. Park (2008), *Gothic: Dark Glamour*, New Haven, CT: Yale University Press.

Stegemeyer, A. (1996), *Who's Who in Fashion*, New York: Fairchild Publications.

Stevens, J. (1987), 'Introduction,' in N. Coleridge and S. Quinn (eds.), *The Sixties in Queen*, London: Ebury Press.

Stewart, M. L. (2005), 'Copying and Copyrighting Haute Couture: Democratizing Fashion, 1900–1930s', *French Historical Studies*, 28 (1): 103–130.

Sudjic, D. (1990), *Rei Kawakubo and Comme des Garçons*, New York: Rizzoli.

Taylor, K. (2019), *Galliano: Spectacular Fashion*, London: Bloomsbury.

Teboul, D. (2002), *Yves Saint Laurent, 5 Avenue Marceau, 75116 Paris France*, New York: Abrams.

Thomas, D. (2007), *Deluxe: How Luxury Lost Its Lustre*, London: Allen Lane.

Thomas, D. (2015), *Gods and Kings: The Rise and Fall of Alexander McQueen and John Galliano*, London: Allen Lane.

Tonchi, S. and M. L. Frisa (2016), *Versace*, New York: Rizzoli.

Trasko, M. (1989), *Heavenly Soles: Extraordinary Twentieth Century Shoes*, New York: Abbeville Press.

Tredre, R. (1990a), 'A One-Man Revolt against the Cliche', *The Independent*, 2 August.

Tredre, R. (1990b), 'The Grind Behind the Glamour', *The Independent*, 18 October.

Tredre, R. (1990c), 'The World According to Paul Smith', *He Lines*.

Tredre, R. (1992), 'Galliano Meets His Maker', *The Independent*, 13 August.

Tredre, R. (1993), 'Who Is that Guy Everyone's Talking About?', *The Independent*, 10 April.

Tredre, R. (1994), 'Kaiser Karl', *The Observer*, 7 August.

Tredre, R. (1995), 'King of Couture', *The Observer*, 23 July.

Tredre, R. (2001), 'YSL Menswear', *WGSN.com*, 1 February.

Troy, N. J. (2003), *Couture Culture: A Study in Modern Art and Culture*, Boston, MA: MIT Press.

Tsurimoto, S., ed. (1983), *Issey Miyake: Bodyworks*, Tokyo: Shogakukan.

Vergani, G. (1992), *La Sala Bianca: The Birth of Italian Fashion*, Milan: Electra.

Vermorel, F. (1996), *Fashion and Perversity: A Life of Vivienne Westwood and the Sixties Laid Bare*, London: Bloomsbury.

Vinken, B. (2005), *Fashion Zeitgeist*, trans. M. Hewson, Oxford, New York: Berg.

Vreeland, D. (1997), *D.V.*, New York: Da Capo.

Vreeland, D. and A. Isozaki (1978), *Issey Miyake: East Meets West*, Tokyo: Heibonsha.

Walford, J. (2007), *The Seductive Shoe: Four Centuries of Fashion Footwear*, London: Thames & Hudson.

Walker, M. (2006), *Balenciaga and His Legacy*, New Haven, CT: Yale University Press.

Walker, H. (2011), *Less Is More: Minimalism in Fashion*, London: Merrell.

Wallach J. (1998), *Chanel: Her Style and Her Life*, New York: Doubleday.

Watson, L. (1999), *Vogue: Twentieth Century Fashion*, London: Carlton.

Welters, L. and A. Lillethun (2007), *The Fashion Reader*, Oxford: Berg.

Westwood, V. and I. Kelly (2014), *Vivienne Westwood*, London: Picador.

White, N. (2000), *Reconstructing Italian Fashion*. Oxford: Berg.

White, P. (1973), *Poiret*, London: Studio Vista.

White, P. (1986), *Elsa Schiaparelli: Empress of Paris Fashion*, London: Aurum Press.

Wilcox, C., ed. (2001), *Radical Fashion*, London: V&A Publications.

Wilcox, C. (2003), *Vivienne Westwood*, London: V&A Publications.

Wilcox, C., ed. (2007), *The Golden Age of Couture: Paris and London 1947-1957*, London: V&A Publications.

Wilcox, C., V. Mendes and C. Buss (2002), *The Art and Craft of Gianni Versace,* London: V&A Publications.

Williams, B. (1945), *Fashion Is Our Business*, Philadelphia, PA: J.B. Lippincott.

Wilson, E. (1985), *Adorned in Dreams*, London: Virago.

Wilson, E. (2013), 'Mr. Provocative', *The New York Times*, 17 April.

Wingfield, J. (2012), 'What Works Best Is Just Going Back to Work', *System*, Issue 1.

Wingfield, J. (2016a), 'We Smile, We Say Hello, We Enjoy Ourselves', *System*, Issue 7.

Wingfield, J. (2016b), 'There's Something Wrong About this Idea of Big Brands', *System*, Issue 8.

Wood, G. (2007), *The Surreal Body,* London: V&A Publications.

WWD Staff (2019), 'Demna Gvasalia on Appropriation, "Ugly" Sneakers and the Curse of Pre-Collections', *WWD*, 26 February.

Yamamoto, Y. and C. Sozzani (2002), *Talking to Myself,* Milan: Carla Sozzani Editore/Tokyo: Yohji Yamamoto Inc.

Yamamoto, Y. and W. Wenders (2014), *Yohji Yamamoto*, New York: Rizzoli.

Yohannan, K. and N. Nolf (1998), *Claire McCardell: Redefining Modernism*, New York: Abrams.

Zahm, O. (2008), 'Nicolas Ghesquière', *Purple Fashion Magazine*, spring/summer.